PRESENTED TO

_____

Name

_____

Date / Occasion

Personal Note

_____

_____

_____

_____

_____

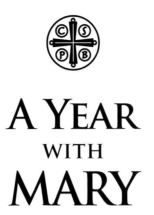

A YEAR
WITH
MARY

A YEAR
WITH
MARY

DAILY MEDITATIONS
ON THE
MOTHER OF GOD

PAUL THIGPEN

SAINT
BENEDICT
PRESS

CHARLOTTE, NORTH CAROLINA

AUTHOR'S DEDICATION

For Leisa
*Wife, mother, grandmother,
and Proverbs 31 woman par excellence*

PUBLISHER'S DEDICATION

For Jackie Gallagher
*A true daughter of Mary, without whose exemplary devotion
to faith and family Saint Benedict Press simply would not exist*

SAINT
BENEDICT
PRESS

Charlotte, North Carolina
2015

Introduction

Books about the Blessed Virgin abound. Yet after nine centuries, the words of St. Bernard of Clairvaux still ring true: "Of Mary, there is never enough!" She's a mystery that faithful Christians seek to understand more fully, an ocean "full of grace" still awaiting deeper exploration.

In fact, as an adult convert to the Catholic faith, I found the mother of Jesus to be more than a mystery; she was a perplexity—or perhaps I should say that traditional Catholic devotion to her puzzled me. Coming from a Christian tradition that was rightly zealous, and jealous, for the honor of her Son, and suspicious of anything that seemed to eclipse his glory, I entered the Church with questions about how best to understand her and, more importantly, how to relate to her.

Even before my conversion, I had felt the irresistible attraction of her moral and spiritual beauty. She was, as the saints of old described her, the mirror of her Son's righteousness. Hers was the soft radiance of a moon that modestly reflected the blazing brilliance of the Sun, who had himself conquered my heart long before.

Yet even then, she held out to me the promise of a relationship much more proximate, more affectionate, more intimate. After all, she had carried in her womb the incarnate God, my Brother. No wonder the achingly sweet strains of Schubert's *Ave Maria* always moved me so deeply: Somewhere in my depths, I knew it was the lullaby of a loving mother I had never known, yet longed to meet.

Who was this woman on whom the Son of God himself had laid the incomparable burden, the inexpressible dignity, of becoming his human mother? Had we somehow made her his rival? If she was so important, why did the Scripture seem to say so little about her? (As it turned out, the Scripture had much more to say about her than I had ever dreamed.)

To answer these and many other questions, I set out to explore that ocean of grace. My map was provided, not only by Scripture, but by the profound insights of numerous saints and other spiritual writers from across the centuries. My compass was the exquisite poetry of their Marian devotion.

PAUL THIGPEN

That high adventure began before my conversion, contributed significantly to it, and has lasted more than twenty-five years, as I have grown in the faith of the Church. I now know that my exploration will last a lifetime, and beyond. In many ways, this book is one of the fruits of that journey.

In this volume you'll hear from saints and theologians, popes and poets, lay and religious, monks and mystics, Fathers and Doctors of the Church. They hail from lands all around the globe, speaking to us in a hundred tongues from every age of the Church's long story. Perhaps modesty should have forbidden it, but I've even dared to offer a few prayers of my own—so intense was my desire to join the chorus of praise to the Queen now enthroned at the King's right hand in glory.

Through this collection of meditations, I invite you to discover more fully "the riches of his glorious inheritance in the saints" (Eph 1:18)—and most especially in the saint of saints, the Mother of God. You'll find excerpts from biblical passages, theological essays, papal documents, liturgical sources, historical anecdotes, popular devotions, stories, prayers, poems, and hymns. The intent here is not to be comprehensive—that would be impossible—but rather eclectic, and representative of the fabulous treasury of Marian literature.

For truly, of Mary, there is never enough.

Paul Thigpen
March 25, 2015
The Feast of the Annunciation of the Blessed Virgin Mary

How to Use this Book

If this book is to achieve its purpose, you must read through the texts slowly, attentively, and prayerfully, with an open mind and heart. It's best, if you can, to set aside a regular time daily for this and other spiritual reading, and the volume is designed so you can take up one meditation each day for an entire year.

The reflections aren't tied to particular days of the year, so you can start anywhere, and skip around if you like. There are, however, some topical clusters of readings regarding, for example, Mary in Scripture, Mary's virtues, her titles, her sorrows, the other events of her life, and the Rosary. So you might find some advantage in reading them in the order presented.

Before you read each day, I urge you to offer a quick prayer to the Holy Spirit to enlighten you by his grace. Then ask Our Lady to help you, too, so you can understand and apply what you're reading.

Each meditation has a brief introduction. After the reading, you're asked to consider in God's presence what the author is saying. These questions are intended to spur you to ponder, not just what the text means, but *what it means for you personally.*

Finally, each day has a brief closing prayer related to the reading. Most of these prayers are from saints and other spiritual writers, but some are original, and some are simply traditional Catholic prayers. You may of course choose to pray in your own words instead.

An entire year of profound and powerful thoughts about Our Lady is in your hands. If you read and reflect on them carefully, I guarantee that you will have a whole new relationship with her, and with her Son, when the year is done. Prayerfully reading these meditations has certainly transformed me.

As you begin reading, make your own this prayer of St. John Eudes:

You angels of Jesus and his saints, pray for me, that our loving Savior may give me new grace and new love for him, to devote this year and my whole life, purely and solely, to the service of his glory and love. Amen.

PAUL THIGPEN

A Note on the Texts

With a few exceptions noted in the Acknowledgements, these readings are gathered and adapted from public domain sources, mostly in older English translations. If this book were intended as a scholarly tome, the texts would be strictly translated—and as a result, they would require extensive, and intrusive, explanatory notes. Many words in the original translations are unfamiliar to most readers today ("lictors," "abnegation," "disordinate," "turpitude"). Others have changed their meanings. (A hundred years ago, for example, "confusion" typically meant "ruin" or "shame," not "misunderstanding" or "perplexity.")

My goal, however, was instead to provide short and simple readings about Mary, profound in their insights yet easily accessible to contemporary readers. So I've adapted the texts rather freely to achieve that goal. I've modernized the language, and where earlier standards of style called for long, complex sentences and interminable paragraphs, I've broken them up into shorter, more manageable pieces.

In some places I've added clarifying words, such as a brief identifier for a biblical or historical character mentioned. In other places, I've condensed the text to fit the space available. In every case, nevertheless, I trust the original meaning has been illuminated rather than obscured.

Quotations from Scripture are from the Revised Standard Version (2nd Catholic Edition) unless the writer's argument depends on a significantly different translation, such as the Septuagint or the Vulgate. Scriptural references (such as "see Jn 3:16") are indirect quotations and may not reflect the exact wording of any particular biblical translation.

A note on the authors chosen for inclusion here: My intention was to feature as many writers as possible. But any compilation of this sort, with 365 substantial readings rather than brief quotes, must depend heavily on several teachers whose Marian writings are extensive and widely recognized as classic texts on the subject. Among these are St. Louis de Montfort, St. Bernard of Clairvaux, St. John of Damascus, Blessed John Henry Newman and, most especially, St. Alphonsus Liguori.

St. Alphonsus' work *The Glories of Mary* is uniquely comprehensive, not just in the scope and detail of its Marian subject matter, but also in its citations of numerous saints, theologians, and other spiritual writers. So the preponderance of quotes selected from that particular text was perhaps inevitable. On the one hand, the author offers a number of provocative original insights. On the other, when his insights are drawn from the common spiritual tradition, he makes them all the more convincing by showing how many of the Church's spiritual giants concur on a matter. In quoting St. Alphonsus, then, we necessarily quote many other saints and spiritual writers.

After some deliberation, and for several reasons, I decided not to include selections taken directly from alleged private revelations. Such texts can prove extremely problematic, both in historical provenance and in proper interpretation. I should note, however, that St. Alphonsus in particular is fond of citing the visions of St. Bridget of Sweden, St. Gertude the Great, and a few others.

A final note about the way many of our selected writers have approached their meditations on Mary. Only a little is said about the events of her life in the Gospels; we have no biography of Jesus' mother. So we shouldn't be surprised to find that much of what has been written about her involves either "theological deduction," as we might call it, or a kind of "sanctified speculation."

What I mean to say is this: A great deal of what we know about Our Lady (such as her status as "Mother of God") has been logically deduced from the data, so to speak, of Divine Revelation. (Our understanding of the Blessed Trinity would be another such deduction.) Meanwhile, the imaginative recreation of scenes from her life, based in part on common human experience, has often yielded profound insights by speculating about what could, or should, or almost certainly *must*, have happened.

I trust you will discover in these pages that both approaches to Marian reflection have proven fertile ground for a deeper, richer understanding of Our Lady that leads us to love and serve her more eagerly.

A Year with Mary

The Daily Readings

Of Mary, there is never enough!

St. Louis-Marie Grignion de Montfort was one of the Church's greatest promoters of devotion to Our Lady. To those who would suggest that Mary should not have a prominent role in Christian faith and practice, he responds that we can never say enough about her.

Every day from one end of the earth to the other, in the highest heights of the heavens and in the profoundest depths of the abysses, everything preaches, everything publishes, the admirable Mary! The nine choirs of angels, men of all ages, sexes, conditions and religions, the good and the bad —even the demons themselves, willingly or unwillingly—are compelled by the force of truth to call her "blessed."

St. Bonaventure tells us that all the angels in heaven cry out incessantly to her: "Holy, holy, holy, Mother of God and Virgin"; and that they offer to her, millions and millions of times a day, the angelical salutation, *Ave Maria*, prostrating themselves before her, and begging of her in her graciousness to honor them with some of her commands. Even St. Michael, as St. Augustine says, although the prince of the heavenly court, is the most zealous in honoring her and causing her to be honored.

The whole earth is full of her glory, especially among Christians, by whom she is taken as the protector of many kingdoms, provinces, dioceses, and cities. Many cathedrals are consecrated to God under her name. There is not a church without an altar in her honor, not a country nor a canton where there are not some miraculous images of her.

After that, we must cry out with the saints: "*De Maria numquam satis*"—"Of Mary, there is never enough!"

—St. Louis de Montfort, *True Devotion to Mary*

IN GOD'S PRESENCE, CONSIDER . . .

Is devotion to Jesus' mother a part of my devotion to Jesus? Have I considered how her unique role in the world's salvation deserves my gratitude and praise?

CLOSING PRAYER

From a prayer of St. Alphonsus Liguori: *I love you, Mary, my Mother, and I wish I could speak with a thousand tongues, so that all might know your greatness, your holiness, your mercy, and the love with which you love all those who love you.*

Mary takes us to Jesus

St. Louis de Montfort assures us that devotion to Mary is not a distraction from devotion to Jesus. Nor does he consider his mother a rival whose honor somehow detracts from his own.

If we're establishing sound devotion to our Blessed Lady, it's only in order to establish devotion to our Lord more perfectly, by providing a smooth but certain way of reaching Jesus Christ. If devotion to Our Lady distracted us from our Lord, we'd have to reject it as an illusion of the Devil. But this is far from being the case. This devotion is necessary, simply and solely because it's a way of reaching Jesus perfectly, loving him tenderly, and serving him faithfully.

Here I turn to you for a moment, dear Jesus, to complain lovingly to your divine Majesty that the majority of Christians, and even some of the most learned among them, fail to recognize the necessary bond that unites you and your Blessed Mother. Lord, you are always with Mary, and Mary is always with you. She can never be without you, because then she would cease to be what she is.

Dear Jesus, would it please you if we were to make no effort to give pleasure to your mother because we're afraid of offending you? Does devotion to your holy mother hinder devotion to you? Does Mary keep for herself any honor we pay her?

Is she a rival of yours? Is she a stranger having no kinship with you? Does pleasing her imply displeasing you? Does giving ourselves to her constitute a deprivation for you? Is love for her a lessening of our love for you?

Keep me from this way of thinking and acting, and let me share your feelings of gratitude, esteem, respect, and love for your holy mother. I can then love and glorify you all the more, because I'll be imitating and following you more closely.

—St. Louis de Montfort, *True Devotion to Mary*

IN GOD'S PRESENCE, CONSIDER . . .

Do any of my family members or friends claim that devotion to Mary dishonors Jesus? How might these insights help me make a reasonable reply to that claim?

CLOSING PRAYER

Lord Jesus, thank you for giving us your Blessed Mother to be our mother. Holy Mary, thank you for always leading us to your divine Son.

Prayer to Mary is good and right

St. Alphonsus Liguori, one of the great Marian theologians, notes that it's an article of the Catholic faith that we can and should call on Mary and the other saints to pray for us. And it's only reasonable to do so.

It's not only lawful but beneficial to invoke and pray to the saints—and more especially to the queen of saints, the most holy and ever-blessed Virgin Mary—so that they may obtain for us God's grace. This is an article of faith. It has been defined by ecumenical councils, against heretics who condemned it as injurious to Jesus Christ, who is our only Mediator. But if the prophet Jeremiah after his death prayed for Jerusalem (see 2 Mc 15:14); if the elders in the Book of Revelation presented the prayers of the saints to God (see Rv 6:8); if St. Peter promises his disciples that after his death he will be mindful of them (see 2 Pt 1:15); if holy Stephen prays for his persecutors (see Acts 7:59); if St. Paul prays for his companions (see Acts 27:24; Eph 2:16; Phil 1:4; Col 1:3)—in short, if the saints can pray for us, why can't we ask the saints to intercede for us? St. Paul recommends himself to the prayers of his disciples: "Brethren, pray for us" (1 Th 5:25). St. James exhorts us to pray one for another: "Pray one for another, that you may be healed" (Jas 5:16). So we can do the same.

No one denies that Jesus Christ is our only mediator of justice, and that he by his merits has obtained our reconciliation with God. But, on the other hand, it is impious to assert that God is not pleased to grant graces at the intercession of his saints, and more especially of Mary his mother, whom Jesus desires so much to see loved and honored by all.

Who can pretend that the honor bestowed on a mother doesn't redound to the honor of the son? For this reason St. Bernard says, "We must not imagine that we obscure the glory of the Son by the great praise we lavish on the mother; for the more she is honored, the greater is the glory of her Son."

—St. Alphonsus Liguori, *The Glories of Mary*

IN GOD'S PRESENCE, CONSIDER . . .

Has anyone ever tried to convince me not to ask Mary or the other saints to pray for me? How might St. Alphonsus' insights help me respond convincingly?

CLOSING PRAYER

From the "Litany of the Saints": *All you holy, righteous, and chosen ones of God, pray for us!*

Mary's hymn of praise to God

The longest quote from Jesus' mother was recorded in St. Luke's Gospel: a hymn of praise to God, inspired by her encounter with her kinswoman St. Elizabeth.

My soul magnifies the Lord,
    and my spirit rejoices in God my Savior,
    for he has regarded the low estate of his handmaiden.
For behold, henceforth all generations will call me blessed;
    for he who is mighty has done great things for me,
    and holy is his name.
And his mercy is on those who fear him
    from generation to generation.
He has shown strength with his arm,
    he has scattered the proud in the imagination of their hearts,
    he has put down the mighty from their thrones,
    and exalted those of low degree;
    he has filled the hungry with good things,
    and the rich he has sent empty away.
He has helped his servant Israel,
    in remembrance of his mercy,
    as he spoke to our fathers,
    to Abraham and to his posterity for ever.

—The Blessed Virgin Mary, *Luke 1:46–55*

IN GOD'S PRESENCE, CONSIDER . . .

When I consider myself honestly, which category in Our Lady's hymn am I more likely to fit: those who are proud, mighty, rich? Or those who fear God, those who are lowly, those who are hungry?

CLOSING PRAYER

Blessed Mother of my Lord, help me to humble myself before God so that he can lift me up again in mercy. Teach me by your example to hunger for righteousness, so that I can be filled.

"All generations will call me blessed!"

St. Alphonsus invites us to be among those whom Mary prophesied would call her blessed down through the generations.

How many who were once proud have become humble by devotion to Mary! How many who were ruled by passion have become restrained! How many in the midst of darkness have found light! How many who were in despair have found confidence! How many who were lost have found salvation by the same powerful means! All this, Mary clearly foretold in the house of Elizabeth, in her own sublime canticle: "Behold, henceforth all generations will call me blessed!" (Lk 1:48). And St. Bernard, interpreting her words, says, "All generations call you blessed, because you have given life and glory to all nations; for in you sinners find pardon, and the righteous find perseverance in the grace of God."

For this reason, the devout monk Lanspergius has our Lord address the world in this way: "Men, poor children of Adam, who live surrounded by so many enemies and in the midst of so many trials! Endeavor to honor my Mother and yours in a special way. For I've given Mary to the world, so that she may be your model, and so that from her you may learn to lead good lives. I've given her also to be a refuge to which you can flee in all your afflictions and trials. I've made this daughter of mine in such a way that no one need fear or have the least reluctance to turn to her. For this purpose I've created her of such a kind and compassionate disposition that she doesn't know how to despise anyone who takes refuge with her, nor can she deny her favor to anyone who seeks it. The mantle of her mercy is open to all, and she allows no one to leave her feet without consoling him."

May the immense goodness of our God be ever praised and blessed for having given us such a great, such a tender, such a loving mother and advocate!

—St. Alphonsus Liguori, *The Glories of Mary*

IN GOD'S PRESENCE, CONSIDER . . .

Am I among those who call Mary blessed? Is it my frequent habit to take time to praise her for her role in my salvation, and to ask for her assistance in living a holy life?

CLOSING PRAYER

With St. Elizabeth, I greet you, my Lady: *"Blessed are you among women, and blessed is the fruit of your womb!" (Lk 1:42).*

Mary foreshadowed by Noah's dove and the rainbow

The Fathers of the Church began a long tradition of discovering in the Old Testament figures and events that foreshadow Mary. Here, St. Alphonsus tells how earlier theologians saw Noah's dove as her symbol.

Mary was foreshadowed by the dove that returned to Noah in the ark with an olive branch in its beak as a pledge of the peace that God granted to men (see Gn 8:11). With this in mind, St. Bonaventure addresses our Blessed Lady this way: "You are that most faithful dove." "Mary," he adds, "was the heavenly dove that brought to a lost world the olive branch, the sign of mercy, since she in the first place gave us Jesus Christ, who is the Source of mercy, and then, by his merits, obtained all graces for us."

Again, the rainbow described by St. John in the Book of Revelation, which encircled the throne of God, was an express figure of Mary: "And round the throne was a rainbow" (Rv 4:3). St. Bernardine of Siena says that "it was of this rainbow that God spoke when he promised Noah that he would place it in the clouds as a sign of peace, so that upon looking at it, he might remember the eternal peace that he had promised in his covenant with man: 'I set my bow in the cloud, and it shall be a sign of the covenant between me and the earth . . . I will look upon it, and remember the everlasting covenant'" (Gn 9:13, 16).

"Mary," says the saint, "is this bow of eternal peace. For just as God, when he sees it, remembers the peace promised to the earth, so does he, at the prayers of Mary, forgive the crimes of sinners, and confirm his peace with them."

—St. Alphonsus Liguori, *The Glories of Mary*

IN GOD'S PRESENCE, CONSIDER . . .

How do the parallels between the figures and events of the Old Testament and those of the New Testament help to enrich our understanding of the faith? What other Old Testament figures and events foreshadowed Mary?

CLOSING PRAYER

From a prayer of St. Tarasius: *Mary, in you is the curse of Adam done away, and the debt of Eve is paid. You are the ark of Noah, and rainbow of reconciliation with God in a new generation.*

Mary is more spacious than Noah's ark

Though Noah's ark foreshadowed Mary, St. Alphonsus notes, she's even more accommodating than that huge ship!

Mary has been called an ark more spacious than that of Noah. For only two animals of every kind were brought into the ark of Noah. But under the mantle of Mary, the righteous and sinners all find their place.

This was one day revealed to St. Gertrude in a vision. She saw a multitude of wild beasts, such as lions and leopards, who took refuge under the mantle of Mary. Not only did she not drive them away, but with her gentle hands she caressed them, so that they might not flee away.

The animals that entered Noah's ark remained animals. But sinners who are received under the mantle of Mary don't remain sinners. She is certain to change their hearts and to render them dear to God.

The Blessed Virgin herself said to St. Bridget: "However much a man may have sinned, if he returns to me with a genuine intention of repentance, I'm ready at once to receive him. I don't pay attention to the sins with which he's burdened, but only to the good disposition in which he comes. And then I don't refuse to anoint and heal his wounds, for I am called, and truly am, the Mother of Mercy."

Mother of Mercy, I will then say to you, in the words of St. Bernard, "Remember that it has never been heard of in any age, that any sinner who turned to you was rejected by you." I am a miserable sinner, but I turn to you and trust in you.

—St. Alphonsus Liguori, *The Glories of Mary*

IN GOD'S PRESENCE, CONSIDER . . .

Given the pattern of sins in my life, which beast entering the ark might best represent me? Am I asking Mary to help me be transformed more fully into God's image instead?

CLOSING PRAYER

From a prayer of St. Alphonsus: *In you, O Mother of God, I have unbounded confidence. From you I hope for grace to be sorry for my sins as I should, and from you I hope for strength never again to fall into them.*

The Old Testament foreshadowed Mary

St. John of Damascus provides multiple examples of the Old Testament foreshadowing of Mary.

Inexhaustible goodness of God! Boundless goodness! He who called what did not exist into existence, and filled heaven and earth, whose throne is heaven, and whose footstool is the earth—he has made the womb of his own servant a spacious dwelling place, and in it the mystery of mysteries is accomplished. Being God, he becomes Man, and is marvelously brought forth without injury to his mother's virginity. He is lifted up as a baby in earthly arms—the One who is the brightness of eternal glory, the form of the Father's substance, by the word of whose mouth all created things exist. Truly divine wonder!

Holy mother and Virgin, what is this great mystery accomplished in you? Blessed are you among women, and blessed is the fruit of your womb. You are blessed from generation to generation, you who alone are worthy of being blessed. Behold, all generations will call you blessed, just as you have said. You are the royal throne that angels surround, seeing upon it their true King and Lord. You are a spiritual Eden, holier and more divine than the Eden of old. For that Eden was the dwelling of the mortal Adam, while the Lord himself came from heaven to dwell in you.

Noah's ark foreshadowed you, for you held the seed of the new world. You brought forth Christ, the salvation of the world, who destroyed sin and its angry waves. The burning bush foreshadowed you, and the tablets of the Law, and the Ark of the Covenant. Just as Jacob saw the ladder bringing together heaven and earth, so you are placed between us, and have become the ladder of God's communion with us, of him who took upon himself our weakness, uniting us to himself, and enabling us to see God.

—St. John of Damascus, *First Homily on the Dormition*

IN GOD'S PRESENCE, CONSIDER . . .

How might Mary be foreshadowed by Eden, Noah's ark, Moses' burning bush, the stone tablets of the Ten Commandments, and Jacob's ladder? What is it about each of these that offers a parallel to her role in our salvation?

CLOSING PRAYER

From a prayer of St. Tarasius: *O purest one! You are the book of Moses, the lawgiver, on which the New Covenant is written with the finger of God. You are Aaron's rod that budded. You are like David's daughter, all glorious within, wrought about with diverse colors.*

Rebecca is an image of Mary

In her preparation of food for her husband Isaac, St. Alphonsus notes, Rebecca foreshadowed Mary's desire to render sinners dear to her Lord.

The Old Testament patriarch Isaac desired to eat some wild game. So he promised his blessing to his son Esau if he would procure this food for him. However, Rebecca was anxious for her other son, Jacob, to receive the blessing. So she called him and said, "Go to the flock, and fetch me two good kids, that I may prepare from them savory food for your father, such as he loves" (Gn 27:9).

St. Antoninus says: "Rebecca was a figure of Mary, who commands the angels to bring her sinners (symbolized by the kids), so that she may prepare them in such a way (by obtaining for them sorrow and intention to repent) that she can render them dear and acceptable to her Lord." Here we may well apply to our Blessed Lady the words of the Abbot Franco: "O truly wise woman, who knew how to dress these kids so well that they are not only equal to real venison in flavor, but often superior to it!"

The Blessed Virgin herself revealed to St. Bridget that "there is no sinner in the world, however much he may be at enmity with God, who doesn't return to him and recover his grace, if he turns to her and asks her assistance." The same saint one day heard Jesus Christ address his mother, saying that "she would be ready to obtain the grace of God for Lucifer himself, if only he humbled himself so far as to seek her aid." We know that proud spirit will of course never humble himself so far as to implore the protection of Mary. But if such a thing were possible, Mary would be sufficiently compassionate, and her prayers would have sufficient power to obtain both forgiveness and salvation for him from God. But what can never happen with regard to the Devil has been proved in the case of sinners who turn to this compassionate mother.

—St. Alphonsus Liguori, *The Glories of Mary*

IN GOD'S PRESENCE, CONSIDER . . .

How might Mary "dress" me so that I can become more "palatable" to the Lord? What "spices" (virtues) do I need that I'm now lacking?

CLOSING PRAYER

Blessed Lady, beloved of God, fragrant with "all chief spices" of the holy virtues (Sg 4:14), draw me close after you, and let us run together (see Sg 1:4), so that I may imitate your holiness, and the fragrance of your virtues may become mine as well.

Mary: the vine, the cedar, the Ark

St. Alphonsus notes several additional images of Mary from the Old Testament.

Mary is said to be "terrible" to the powers of hell, "as an army in battle array" (Sg 6:10). She is called terrifying because she knows well how to array her power, her mercy, and her prayers, to the defeat of her enemies, and for the benefit of her servants, who in their temptations turn to her most powerful aid.

"As the vine, I have brought forth a pleasant odor" (Ecclus 24:23). These words the Holy Spirit has Mary speak in the book of Ecclesiasticus. "We are told," says St. Bernard in commenting on this passage, that "all venomous reptiles fly from flowering vines": for as poisonous reptiles fly from flowering vines, so do demons fly from those fortunate souls in whom they perceive the perfume of devotion to Mary.

She also calls herself, in the same book, a cedar: "I was exalted like a cedar" (Ecclus 24:17). Cardinal Hugo of St. Cher remarks on this text that this comparison is made for two reasons. First, Mary was untainted by sin, just as the cedar is incorruptible. Second, "like the cedar, which by its fragrance keeps away moths, so also does Mary by her sanctity drive away the demons."

Among the ancient Hebrews, victories were gained by means of the Ark of the Covenant. In this way Moses conquered his enemies, as we learn from the Book of Numbers. "And when the Ark was lifted up, Moses said: 'Arise, O Lord, and let your enemies be scattered'" (Num 10:35).

It is well known that this Ark was a foreshadowing of Mary. For as manna was in the Ark, so is Jesus (of whom manna was a foreshadowing) in Mary; and by means of this Ark we gain the victory over our enemies on earth and in hell. "In this way," St. Bernardine of Siena well observes, "when Mary, the Ark of the New Covenant, was raised to the dignity of Queen of Heaven, the power of hell over men was weakened and dissolved."

—St. Alphonsus Liguori, *The Glories of Mary*

IN GOD'S PRESENCE, CONSIDER . . .

What other images, drawn from my own experience, would be fitting symbols of Our Lady?

CLOSING PRAYER

Blessed Mother, you are the great highway to heaven, stretching out across the hills and valleys to make the way straight and smooth on our journey home to your Son.

Mary, the Ark of God

In the Old Testament, the Ark of the Covenant was the place of God's special presence, carried up to Jerusalem. With other Church Fathers, St. John of Damascus saw the Ark as a foreshadowing of Mary, carried up to the heavenly Jerusalem in her assumption.

People of Christ, let's acclaim Mary today in sacred song, acknowledge our own good fortune, and proclaim it! Let's honor her in an evening vigil; let's delight in her purity of soul and body, for she, after God, surpasses all in purity. It's natural for similar things to glory in each other. Let's show our love for her by compassion and kindness towards the poor. For if mercy is the best worship of God, who will refuse to show his mother devotion in the same way?

She opened to us the unspeakable abyss of God's love for us. Through her the old enmity against the Creator is destroyed. Through her our reconciliation with him is strengthened, peace and grace are given to us, men are made the companions of angels, and we, who lived in dishonor, are made the children of God. From her we've plucked the fruit of life. From her we've received the seed of immortality. She's the channel of all our goods. In her, God was Man, and Man was God. What could be more marvelous or more blessed than that?

Youthful souls! With Miriam, the prophetess of old, let's sound our musical instruments—that is, let's put to death the passions of the flesh here on earth, for that's the true spiritual music. Let our souls rejoice in the Ark of God, and the walls of Jericho will fall—I mean the fortresses of the Enemy. Let's dance in spirit with David; today the Ark of God is at rest in heaven.

With Gabriel, the great archangel, let's exclaim, "Hail, full of grace! The Lord is with you. Hail, inexhaustible ocean of grace! Hail, sole refuge in grief! Hail, cure of hearts! Hail, you who through whom death is cast out and replaced by life!"

—St. John of Damascus, *Second Homily on the Dormition*

IN GOD'S PRESENCE, CONSIDER . . .

The Ark of the Old Covenant carried the stone tablets of the Ten Commandments. It also carried some of the manna, the bread that God had sent down from heaven, and the staff of Aaron, the high priest. How do each of these three objects serve as a foreshadowing of Christ in Mary's womb?

CLOSING PRAYER

From a prayer of St. Athanasius: *O Virgin, Ark of the Covenant, clothed with purity instead of gold! You are the Ark in which is found the golden vessel containing the true manna, that is, the Flesh in which God resides.*

Mary, the root preserved from sin

In the Old Testament, the prophet Daniel interprets a dream of the Babylonian king Nebuchadnezzar (see Dan 4:10–18). St. Lawrence Brindisi finds in that dream a foreshadowing of Jesus and Mary.

Great was the happiness of human nature in the Garden of Eden before original sin, as long as man remained in the state of innocence and original justice. Then, human nature was like that tree seen by King Nebuchadnezzar in his dreams. It was tall, with its top touching heaven; wide, with its branches filling the whole world; adorned with the loveliest fronds and flowers and the best of fruits in greatest abundance (see Dan 4:10–12).

But soon, by virtue of the sentence of divine judgment executed by the angel, this tree was stripped of its fruits. With branches and trunk cut off, it was reduced to nothing—or almost nothing; for the command was given that a root with a shoot be preserved safe and intact (see Dan 4:13–15). On account of sin, humanity tumbled from maximum good fortune to maximum misfortune; light was changed into darkness, the bright day into the cloudiest of nights; a full moon went into eclipse.

But from the contagion of that sin, the shoot—that is, Christ—was preserved, as well as the root—that is, Mary—from which that shoot was to rise. We see in the Book of Genesis the root with its shoot preserved; for before a penalty for sin was inflicted on man, it was said to the serpent: "I will put enmity between you and the woman, and between your seed and her seed; she will crush your head" (see Gn 3:15).

—St. Lawrence of Brindisi

IN GOD'S PRESENCE, CONSIDER . . .

In which other dream of an Old Testament figure did the Church Fathers find a foreshadowing of Mary (see Gn 28:10–17)? Have I ever had a dream with symbolic significance that gave me a spiritual insight?

CLOSING PRAYER

Mary, you are the shoot that came forth from the stump of Jesse, in the line of King David; and Jesus is the branch that grew out of that shoot; for the Spirit of the Lord rests mightily upon him, in the perfection of all spiritual gifts (see Is 11:1–3).

Mary: pillar of fire, pillar of cloud

St. Alphonsus tells how the ancient Israelites' journey in the wilderness foreshadowed Our Lady.

St. Cosmas of Jerusalem used to say, "While I keep my hope in you unconquerable, O Mother of God, I shall be safe. I will fight and overcome my enemies with no other buckler than your protection and your all-powerful aid."

All who are so fortunate as to be the servants of this great queen can say the same thing. "O Mother of God, if I hope in you, I most certainly shall not be overcome; for, defended by you, I will pursue my enemies and oppose them with the shield of your protection and your all-powerful help. Then, without doubt, I will conquer!"

James the monk (who was a teacher among the Christians of the East) addressed our Lord this way on the subject of Mary: "You, O Lord, have given us in Mary arms that no force of war can overcome, and a trophy never to be destroyed."

It is said in the Old Testament that God guided His people from Egypt to the land of promise "by day in a pillar of cloud . . . and by night in a pillar of fire" (Ex 13:21). This stupendous pillar, at times as a cloud, at others as fire, says Richard of Saint Lawrence, was a foreshadowing of Mary fulfilling the double ministry she constantly exercises for our good: As a cloud she protects us from the heat of divine justice; and as fire she protects us from the demons.

She protects us as a burning fire; for St. Bonaventure remarks: "As wax melts before the fire, so do the demons lose their power against those souls who often remember the name of Mary, and devoutly invoke it—and still more so, if they also endeavor to imitate her virtues."

—St. Alphonsus Liguori, *The Glories of Mary*

IN GOD'S PRESENCE, CONSIDER . . .

How does imitating Mary's virtues protect us against the Devil? Why are the virtues our spiritual armor against the assault of temptations?

CLOSING PRAYER

Blessed Lady, if I imitate your humility, I will be protected against temptations to pride. If I take on your purity, no impurity will tempt me. And so with every other virtue you display. Help me to cover myself in the spiritual armor of God!

Mary was the perfection God originally intended

Blessed John Henry Newman, a celebrated convert to the Catholic faith, observes that the original righteousness of Adam and Eve, before their fall, was restored in Mary and perfected.

Mary then is a specimen, and more than a specimen, in the purity of her soul and body, of what man was before his fall, and what he would have been, had he risen to his full perfection. It would have been hard, it would have been a victory for the Evil One, had the whole race passed away, nor any one instance in it occurred to show what the Creator had intended it to be in its original state.

Adam, you know, was created in the image and after the likeness of God; his frail and imperfect nature, stamped with a divine seal, was supported and exalted by an indwelling of divine grace. Impetuous passion did not exist in him, except as a latent element and a possible evil; ignorance was dissipated by the clear light of the Spirit; and reason, sovereign over every motion of his soul, was simply subjected to the will of God. No, even his body was preserved from every wayward appetite and affection, and was promised immortality instead of dissolution.

Thus he was in a supernatural state; and, had he not sinned, year after year would he have advanced in merit and grace, and in God's favor, till he passed from paradise to heaven. But he fell; and his descendants were born in his likeness; and the world grew worse instead of better, and judgment after judgment cut off generations of sinners in vain, and improvement was hopeless; "because man was flesh" and "the thoughts of his heart were bent upon evil at all times" (Gn 6:5).

However, a remedy had been determined in heaven. A Redeemer was at hand; God was about to do a great work, and he purposed to do it suitably in Mary. "Where sin abounded, grace was to abound more" (see Rom 5:20).

—Blessed John Henry Newman,
"The Glories of Mary for the Sake of Her Son"

IN GOD'S PRESENCE, CONSIDER . . .

Some claim that "to sin is only human," and if Mary never sinned, she wasn't really human like the rest of us. But isn't it true, instead, to say that God's original intention for humanity was to be sinless—so by being sinless, Mary is in fact the one who shows us what it means to be fully human?

CLOSING PRAYER

O Mary, conceived without sin, pray for us who have recourse to thee.

The world's first love

Archbishop Fulton Sheen explains how the Blessed Mother existed in the mind of God "as an eternal thought before there were any mothers. She is the mother of mothers—she is the world's first love."

All creatures below man correspond to the pattern God has in his mind. A tree is truly a tree because it corresponds to God's idea of a tree. . . . But it is not so with persons. God has to have two pictures of us: One is what we are, and the other is what we ought to be. He has the model, and he has the reality: the blueprint and the edifice, the score of the music and the way we play it. God has to have these two pictures because in each and every one of us there is some disproportion and want of conformity between the original plan and the way we have worked it out. The image is blurred; the print is faded.

For one thing, our personality is not complete in time; we need a renewed body. Then, too, our sins diminish our personality; our evil acts daub the canvas the master Hand designed. Like unhatched eggs, some of us refuse to be warmed by the divine Love, which is so necessary for incubation to a higher level. We are in constant need of repairs; our free acts do not coincide with the law of our being; we fall short of all God wants us to be. . . .

There is, actually, only one person in all humanity of whom God has one picture and in whom there is a perfect conformity between what he wanted her to be and what she is, and that is his own mother. Most of us are a minus sign, in the sense that we do not fulfill the high hopes the heavenly Father has for us. But Mary is the equal sign. The ideal that God had of her, that she is, and in the flesh. The model and the copy are perfect; she is all that was foreseen, planned, and dreamed. The melody of her life is played just as it was written.

—Archbishop Fulton Sheen, *The World's First Love*

IN GOD'S PRESENCE, CONSIDER . . .

Have I ever longed to have the melody of my life "played just as it was written"? Since that's not possible for me as it was for Mary, is it nevertheless possible for God the composer to improvise, finding a way to transform my flat and sharp notes into a new and more beautiful composition?

CLOSING PRAYER

I waited patiently for you, Lord, and you turned to me and heard my cry. You put a new song in my mouth, a song of praise to you! Blessed are those who make you their trust (see Ps 40:1, 3– 4).

God chose Mary to give us his Son

St. Louis teaches us that God the Son comes to us through Mary, and that God takes delight in her.

It was only through Mary that God the Father gave his only-begotten Son to the world. Whatever sighs the patriarchs may have sent forth, whatever prayers the prophets and the saints of the Old Covenant may have offered up to obtain this treasure for four thousand years, it was only Mary who merited it and found grace before God by the force of her prayers and eminence of her virtues. The world was unworthy, says St. Augustine, to receive the Son of God directly from the Father's hands. He gave him to Mary in order that the world might receive him through her.

The Son of God became Man for our salvation. But it happened in Mary and by Mary. God the Holy Spirit formed Jesus Christ in Mary. But it was only after having asked her consent by one of the angelic first ministers of his court.

God the Father communicated to Mary his fruitfulness, to the extent that a mere creature was capable of it, in order that he might give her the power to produce his Son and all the members of his Mystical Body. God the Son descended into her virginal womb as the New Adam into his terrestrial paradise, to take his pleasure there, and to work in secret marvels of grace.

God made Man found his liberty in seeing himself imprisoned in her womb. He made his omnipotence shine forth in letting himself be carried by that humble maiden. He found his glory and his Father's glory in hiding his splendors from all creatures here below, and revealing them to Mary only.

—St. Louis de Montfort, *True Devotion to Mary*

IN GOD'S PRESENCE, CONSIDER . . .

Have I pondered Mary's essential role in God's plan for our salvation? Am I grateful to the Father for choosing her, and grateful to her for saying yes to him?

CLOSING PRAYER

From the *"Salve Regina"*: *Almighty and everlasting God, who by the cooperation of the Holy Spirit prepared the body and soul of the glorious Virgin Mother Mary to become a dwelling place fit for your Son: Grant that as we rejoice in her commemoration, so by her fervent intercession we may be delivered from present evils and from everlasting death.*

How can Mary be our hope?

St. Alphonsus responds to those who object to speaking of Mary as our hope.

Some cannot bear to hear us salute and call Mary our hope: "Hail, our hope!" They say that God alone is our hope, and that he curses those who put their trust in creatures, as the prophet Jeremiah says: "Cursed is the man who trusts in man" (Jer 17:5). Mary, they exclaim, is a creature; and how can a creature be our hope? St. Thomas Aquinas notes that we can place our hope in a person in two ways: as a principal cause or as an intermediate one. For example, those who hope for a favor from a king, hope for it to come from him as lord; but they hope for it to come through his minister or favorite as an intercessor. If the favor is granted, it comes primarily from the king, but it comes also through the instrumentality of the favorite. In this case, then, whoever seeks the favor is right in calling his intercessor his hope.

The King of heaven, being infinite goodness, desires in the highest degree to enrich us with his graces. But because confidence is required on our part, and in order to increase it in us, he has given us his own mother to be our mother and advocate, and to her he has given all power to help us. So he wills that we should rest our hope of salvation and blessing in her.

Those who place their hopes in creatures alone, independently of God, as sinners do; those who, in order to obtain the friendship and favor of a man, don't fear to outrage his divine Majesty: such are most certainly cursed by God, as Jeremiah says. But those who hope in Mary, who as Mother of God is able to obtain graces and eternal life for them, are truly blessed and acceptable to the heart of God. For God desires to see that greatest of his creatures honored, for she loved and honored him in this world more than all men and angels put together.

—St. Alphonsus Liguori, *The Glories of Mary*

IN GOD'S PRESENCE, CONSIDER . . .

When a carpenter uses a hammer to drive a nail, we say that both the carpenter drives the nail and the hammer drives the nail. When God uses Mary to bring us hope through her Son, isn't it appropriate, then, to say both that God gives us hope, and that Mary gives us hope?

CLOSING PRAYER

From a prayer of St. Ephraem: *Hail, Mary, hope of my soul! Hail, certain salvation of Christians! Hail, helper of sinners! Hail, fortress of the faithful and salvation of the world!*

Mary and the Blessed Trinity

St. Louis summarizes the ancient Christian teachings about Mary in her relationship to each Person of the Blessed Holy Trinity.

God the Father gathered all the waters, and he named it the sea (Latin, *mare*). He gathered all his graces, and he called it Mary (Latin, *Maria*). This great God has a most rich treasury in which he's laid up all that he has of beauty and splendor, of rarity and preciousness, including even his own Son. And this immense treasury is none other than Mary, whom the saints have named the Treasure of the Lord, out of whose abundant fullness all people are made rich.

God the Son has communicated to his mother all that he acquired by his life and his death, his infinite merits and his admirable virtues. And he's made her treasurer of all that his Father gave him for his inheritance. It's by her that he applies his merits to his members, and communicates his virtues, and distributes his graces. She's his mysterious channel. She's his aqueduct through which he makes his mercies flow gently and abundantly.

To Mary, his faithful spouse, God the Holy Spirit has communicated his unspeakable gifts. He's chosen her to be the dispenser of all he possesses, in such a way that she distributes to whom she wills, as much as she wills, as she wills, all his gifts and graces. The Holy Spirit gives no heavenly gift to us that he doesn't have pass through her virginal hands. Such has been the will of God, who's willed that we should have everything through Mary. She who was impoverished and humble, and who hid herself even in the abyss of nothingness by her profound humility her whole life long, is now enriched and exalted and honored by the Most High. Such are the sentiments of the Church and the Holy Fathers.

—St. Louis de Montfort, *True Devotion to Mary*

IN GOD'S PRESENCE, CONSIDER . . .

If Mary is the channel through which Christ's gifts flow, have I expressed to her my confidence in her assistance? Have I acknowledged my gratitude for her role in our salvation?

CLOSING PRAYER

From a prayer of Blessed Raymond Jordano: *Blessed Virgin Mary, it is you who teach true wisdom, you who obtain grace for sinners, for you are their advocate. It is you who promise glory to the one who honors you, for you are the treasurer of graces.*

Mary cooperated in our redemption

St. Alphonsus observes that even though Jesus could have redeemed us without any assistance, it was fitting that God chose to have Mary cooperate in our redemption.

St. Bernard says that "as a man and a woman cooperated in our ruin, so it was proper that another man and another woman should cooperate in our redemption; and these two were Jesus and his mother, Mary."

"There is no doubt," observes the saint, "that Jesus Christ alone was more than sufficient to redeem us. But it was more becoming that both sexes should cooperate in repairing an evil that both sexes had shared in causing."

For this reason St. Albert the Great calls Mary "the helper of redemption." And this Blessed Virgin herself revealed to St. Bridget that "as Adam and Eve sold the world for an apple, so did she with her Son redeem it, as it were, with one heart."

This thought is confirmed by St. Anselm, who says that "although God could create the world out of nothing, yet when it was lost by sin, he would not repair the evil without the cooperation of Mary."

For this reason our Lord has justly decreed, that as Mary cooperated in the salvation of man with so much love, and at the same time gave such glory to God, so all men through her intercession are to obtain their salvation. Mary is called the cooperator in our justification; for to her God has entrusted all graces intended for us.

—St. Alphonsus Liguori, *The Glories of Mary*

IN GOD'S PRESENCE, CONSIDER . . .

In what ways is it fitting that God should choose someone to cooperate with his Son in the salvation of the world? How is it especially fitting that the cooperator should be Mary?

CLOSING PRAYER

From a prayer of St. Andrew of Candia: *I salute you, Mary, full of grace; our Lord is with you. I salute you, cause of our joy, through whom the sentence of our condemnation was revoked and changed into one of blessing.*

Divine graces come through Mary's hands

Since all graces are the fruits of Christ's redemptive work, St. Alphonsus reasons, they are contained in the treasure that God entrusted to Mary.

The Mother of God made a tremendous sacrifice of her Son for the salvation of the world. Because of the great merit she acquired by this sacrifice, which she made to God, she was rightly called by St. Augustine "the repairer of the human race"; by St. Epiphanius, "the redeemer of captives"; by St. Anselm, "the repairer of a lost world"; by St. Germanus, "our liberator from our calamities"; by St. Ambrose, "the mother of all the faithful"; by St. Augustine, "the mother of the living"; and by St. Andrew of Crete, "the mother of life."

As Arnold of Chartres says, "The wills of Christ and of Mary were then united, so that both offered the same holocaust. In this way she produced with him the one effect, the salvation of the world." At the death of Jesus, Mary united her will to that of her Son—so much so, that both offered one and the same sacrifice. For this reason the holy abbot says that both the Son and the mother effected human redemption, and obtained salvation for men: Jesus by offering satisfaction for our sins, Mary by obtaining the application of this satisfaction to us.

If Mary, then, having by the merit of her sorrows, and by sacrificing her Son, became the mother of all the redeemed, it is right to believe that through her hands divine graces—and the means to obtain eternal life that are the fruits of the merits of Jesus Christ—are given to men. St. Bernard alludes to this when he says: "When God was about to redeem the human race, he deposited the whole price in Mary's hands." By these words, the saint teaches us that the merits of the Redeemer are applied to our souls by the intercession of the Blessed Virgin. For all graces, which are the fruits of Jesus Christ, were contained in that price of which she had charge.

—St. Alphonsus Liguori, *The Glories of Mary*

IN GOD'S PRESENCE, CONSIDER . . .

What does it mean to say that "the merits of the Redeemer are applied to our souls by the intercession of the Blessed Virgin"?

CLOSING PRAYER

From a prayer of St. Athanasius: *Give ear to our prayers, O most holy Virgin, and be mindful of us. Dispense to us the gifts of your riches, and the abundance of the graces with which you are filled.*

Mary, mother of the recreated world

The creation of God the Father was deadened by human sin. But by becoming a Man, born of the Virgin Mary, God the Son restored that creation. St. Anselm observes that as God is the Father of the created world, Mary is the mother of the recreated world.

Blessed Lady! Sky and stars, earth and rivers, day and night—everything that's subject to the power or use of the human race—rejoice that through you they are in some sense restored to their lost beauty and are endowed with inexpressible new grace. All creatures were dead, so to speak, useless for humanity or for the praise of God who made them. The world, contrary to its true destiny, was corrupted and tainted by the acts of those who served idols. Now all creation has been restored to life and rejoices that it's controlled and given splendor by those who believe in God. The universe rejoices with new loveliness beyond description. Not only does it feel the unseen presence of God himself, its Creator. It also sees him openly, working and making it holy. These great blessings spring from the blessed fruit of Mary's womb.

Through the fullness of the grace that was given you, Mary, dead things rejoice in their freedom, and those in heaven are glad to be made new. Through the Son who was the glorious fruit of your virgin womb, righteous souls who died before his life-giving death rejoice as they are freed from captivity, and the angels are glad at the restoration of their shattered domain.

Lady, full and overflowing with grace, all creation receives new life from your abundance. God, then, is the Father of the created world, and Mary the mother of the recreated world. God is the Father by whom all things were given life, and Mary the mother through whom all things were given new life. For God begot the Son, through whom all things were made, and Mary gave birth to him as the Savior of the world. Without God's Son, nothing could exist; without Mary's Son, nothing could be redeemed.

—St. Anselm of Canterbury, *Virgin Mary, Mother of the Recreated World*

IN GOD'S PRESENCE, CONSIDER . . .

Have I ever considered that in one sense, the Blessed Virgin Mary is the mother not just of Jesus, but of the whole of creation that he redeemed? Do I honor her as my mother?

CLOSING PRAYER

Hail, Mary, full of grace, mother of our Savior, mother of the redeemed, mother of a world recreated! Teach me to be your true child by imitating your faith and holiness.

Through Mary, peace is restored to the world

St. Cyril of Alexandria was the great champion of the title "Mother of God" as a way of affirming that her Son was truly God. This hymn to Our Lady celebrates her role as expressed in that title.

Glory be to you, holy Mother of God, masterpiece of the universe, brilliant star, glory of virginity, scepter of faith, indestructible temple inhabited by him whom immensity cannot contain, Virgin Mother of him who, blessed forever, comes to us in the name of the Lord!

By you the Trinity is glorified, the holy cross celebrated and venerated throughout the universe, the heavens are joyful, the angels tremble with joy, the demons are put to flight, man passes from slavery to heaven.

Through you idolatrous creatures have come to know the incarnate Truth, the faithful have received baptism, churches have been raised over all the world.

By your assistance the Gentiles have been led to repentance.

Finally, through you, the only Son of God, Source of all light, has shone on the eyes of the blind who were sitting in the shadow of death (see Lk 1:79).

But Virgin Mother, who can speak your praises? Let us, however, celebrate them as well as we can, and at the same time adore God your Son, the chaste Bridegroom of the Church, to whom is due all honor and glory now and through all eternity!

—St. Cyril of Alexandria, *Homily Against Nestorius*

IN GOD'S PRESENCE, CONSIDER . . .

Have I ever questioned, or heard others question, the title "Mother of God" for Mary? Do I understand that to deny her that title is to deny that Jesus is God, since she is his mother?

CLOSING PRAYER

A frequent aspiration of St. Francis Xavier: *Mother of God, remember me.*

Our poverty has made you rich, Mary!

Blessed Henry Suso is confident of Mary's willingness to show him compassion, because she became the Mother of God precisely for that purpose.

Consider, mild Queen, consider, chosen one, how you derive all your merits from us poor sinners. What was it that made you the Mother of God, that made you a jewel box in which the Eternal Wisdom came to rest? O Lady, it was the sins of us poor mortals!

How could you be called a mother of graces and compassion if it weren't for our wretchedness, which has need of grace and compassion? Our poverty has made you rich; our crimes have made you noble above all creatures.

So turn this way the eyes of your compassion, which your gentle heart has never turned away from a sinner, from a forlorn mortal! Take me under your protection, for my consolation and confidence are in you.

Who is the sinner—no matter how great his crimes—to whom your overflowing goodness has denied assistance? When my soul seriously reflects within herself, I think it would only be right, if it were possible, that while my eyes wept for joy, my heart should leap out of my mouth! For your name dissolves in my mouth like honey from the honeycomb.

You are called the Mother, the Queen, of Compassion—yes, tender mother; yes, gentle mother of compassion! What a name! How immeasurable is she whose name is so rich in grace! Did the melody of song ever resound so soothingly in an anxious heart as your name resounds in our penitent hearts? At this exalted name, all heads should rightly bow, and all knees should bend.

—Blessed Henry Suso, *Little Book of Eternal Wisdom*

IN GOD'S PRESENCE, CONSIDER . . .

If there were no sinners, there would be no need for a Savior, nor for his mother. Given the mission of Jesus and Mary, can I doubt that they both eagerly desire my salvation? Does that increase my confidence to turn to them?

CLOSING PRAYER

From a prayer of St. Bernard: *Grant, we beg you, almighty God, that your faithful, calling upon the name of the Virgin Mary and rejoicing in her protection, may, by her motherly intercession, be delivered from the evils of the earth and advance to the eternal happiness of heaven.*

You became Mother of God for our sake

St. Anselm reminds Our Lady (and himself) that there's no doubt she will help him reach heaven, since God took human flesh from her, not to condemn sinners, but to save them.

We beg you, most holy Lady, by the favor that God did you in raising you so high as to make all things possible to you with him, to act in such a way that the fullness of grace that you merited may make us partakers of your glory. Strive, most merciful Lady, to obtain for us what God desired for us when he was pleased to become Man in your chaste womb.

Lend us a willing ear. If you deign to pray to your Son for this, he will immediately grant it. It's enough that you will our salvation, and then we are sure to obtain it. But who can restrain your great mercy?

If you, who are our mother, and the Mother of Mercy, don't pity us, what will become of us when your Son comes to judge us? Help us, then, most compassionate Lady, and don't consider the multitude of our sins. Remember always that our Creator took human flesh from you, not to condemn sinners, but to save them.

If you had become Mother of God only for your own advantage, we might say that it mattered little to you whether we were lost or saved. But God clothed himself with your flesh for your salvation, and for that of all men. What will your great power and glory avail us, if you don't make us partakers of your happiness?

Help us, then, and protect us! You know how greatly we stand in need of your assistance. We entrust ourselves to you. Don't let us lose our souls, but make us eternally serve and love your beloved Son, Jesus Christ.

—St. Anselm of Canterbury

IN GOD'S PRESENCE, CONSIDER . . .

Have I ever considered that Mary was chosen to bring Jesus into the world so that I could be among those who are saved? Does this consideration strengthen my faith in her assistance?

CLOSING PRAYER

From a prayer of St. Bernard of Clairvaux: *Grant, blessed one, by the grace you have merited, that the One who through you was graciously pleased to become a partaker in our infirmity and misery, may also, through your intercession, make us partakers in his happiness and glory.*

A prayer to the Lady worthy of all love

St. Alphonsus prays that his love for Mary will become a great flame that consumes his heart.

Queen of Heaven and Earth! Mother of the Lord of the world! Mary, of all creatures the greatest, the most exalted, and the most lovable! It's true that there are many in this world who neither know you nor love you. But in heaven there are many millions of angels, and blessed spirits, who love and praise you continually. Even in this world, how many happy souls are there who burn with your love, and live enflamed with love for your goodness!

If only I also can love you, Lady worthy of all love! If only I can always remember to serve you, to praise you, to honor you, and to influence everyone to love you! You have attracted the love of God the Son; by your beauty, you have, so to speak, torn him from the bosom of his Eternal Father, and induced him to become Man, and be your Son. If that's the case, how can I, a lowly creature of the earth, fail to be enflamed with love of you? No, my most sweet mother! I too will love you much, and will do all that I can to make others love you also.

Accept, then, Mary, the desire that I have to love you, and help me to carry it out. I know how favorably those who love you are looked upon by God. After his own glory, he desires nothing more than yours, and to see you honored and loved by all. From you, Lady, I expect all assistance in gaining the remission of my sins and perseverance. You must assist me at death, and deliver me from purgatory; and, finally, you must lead me to heaven. All this, those who love you hope to receive from you, and they are not misled. I love you with so much affection, and after God, I love you above all other things. So I hope for the same favors.

—St. Alphonsus Liguori, *The Glories of Mary*

IN GOD'S PRESENCE, CONSIDER . . .

What might I say to others that will, as St. Alphonsus says, "influence everyone to love" Mary? What might I do to "make others love" her?

CLOSING PRAYER

Lord, I will speak to you about Mary in your own words: "She is far more precious than jewels. . . . She opens her mouth with wisdom, and the teaching of kindness is on her tongue. . . . Give her the fruit of her hands, and let her works praise her in the gates!" (Prv 31:10, 26, 31).

Your compassion surpasses my sins

St. Alphonsus confesses his sinfulness to our Blessed Mother, but declares his confidence in her mercy.

Mother of holy love, our life, our refuge, and our hope, you well know that your Son Jesus Christ, not content with being himself our perpetual advocate with the Eternal Father, has willed that you too should concern yourself, with him, in obtaining the divine mercies for us. He has decreed that your prayers should aid our salvation, and he has made them so efficacious that they obtain all that they ask.

To you, then, who are the hope of the miserable, this wretched sinner turns his eyes. I trust, Lady, that in the first place through the merits of Jesus Christ, and then through your intercession, I will be saved. Of this I'm confident; and my confidence in you is such that if my eternal salvation were in my own hands, I would place it in yours, for I rely more on your mercy and protection than on all my own works.

My Mother and my hope, don't abandon me, though I deserve that you would do so. See my miseries and, being moved with compassion, help and save me. I admit that I have too often closed my heart, by my sins, against the lights and helps that you have procured for me from our Lord. But your compassion for the miserable, and your power with God, far surpass the number and malice of my sins.

Mary, I trust in you. In this hope I live; in it I desire and hope to die, repeating always, "Jesus is my only hope, and after Jesus, the most Blessed Virgin Mary."

—St. Alphonsus Liguori, *The Glories of Mary*

IN GOD'S PRESENCE, CONSIDER . . .

Do I have the sense that I am, before God, a "wretched sinner"? Or does that sound too harsh, because I consider myself a good person? Should I perhaps ask God to let me see myself as he sees me?

CLOSING PRAYER

From a prayer of St. Alphonsus: *O Queen and Mother of mercy, you dispense graces to all who turn to you with so much generosity, because you are a queen, and with so much love, because you are our most loving mother. I entrust myself to you this day.*

The name of Mary is my love

St. Alphonsus wants to call on Mary's name, not just with an expectation of assistance, but with great love.

Great Mother of God and my Mother, Mary, it's true that I'm unworthy to speak your name. But despite the impurity of my tongue, you love me and desire my salvation. So grant that I may always invoke your most holy and powerful name for my aid, for your name is the help of the living, and the salvation of the dying.

Most pure Mary, most sweet Mary, grant that from now on your name may be the breath of my life. Lady, don't delay to help me when I call upon you. For in all the temptations that assail me, and in all my needs, I'll never cease calling upon you, and repeating again and again, Mary, Mary.

In this way I hope to act during my life, and more especially at death, so that after that last struggle I may eternally praise your beloved name in heaven—O clement, O pious, O sweet Virgin Mary! Mary, most amiable Mary, with what consolation, what sweetness, what confidence, what tenderness, is my soul penetrated simply by calling your name and thinking of you! I thank my Lord and God, who for my good has given you a name so sweet and deserving of love, and at the same time so powerful.

However, my sovereign Lady, I'm not satisfied with only calling your name. I wish to call your name with love. I desire that my love may every hour remind me to call on you, so that I may be able to exclaim with St. Bonaventure, "O name of the Mother of God, you are my love."

My own dear Mary, O my beloved Jesus, may your most sweet names reign in my heart, and in all hearts.

—St. Alphonsus Liguori, *The Glories of Mary*

IN GOD'S PRESENCE, CONSIDER . . .

Do I call on Mary's name, not just with faith and hope, but also with love? Does her name have for me consolation, sweetness, tenderness?

CLOSING PRAYER

From a prayer of St. Alphonsus: *Jesus my Redeemer, and my Mother Mary, when the moment of death comes, when I must breathe forth my soul and leave this world, through your merits, grant that I may then pronounce my last words, and that they may be: "I love you, Jesus; I love you, Mary; to you I give my heart and my soul."*

The figure of the Faith

The celebrated English convert to the Catholic faith, G. K. Chesterton, tells what Mary meant to him before his conversion.

The unconverted world . . . has a very strange notion of the collective unity of Catholic things or thoughts. Its exponents . . . give the most curious lists of things which they think make up the Catholic life; an odd assortment of objects, such as candles, rosaries, incense . . . vestments, pointed windows, and then all sorts of essentials or unessentials thrown in in any sort of order; fasts, relics, penances, or the Pope.

But even in their bewilderment, they do bear witness to a need which is not so nonsensical as their attempts to fulfill it; the need of somehow summing up "all that sort of thing," which does really describe Catholicism and nothing else except Catholicism. . . . Men need an image, single, colored, and clear in outline, an image to be called up instantly in the imagination, when what is Catholic is to be distinguished from what claims to be Christian or even what in one sense is Christian.

Now I can scarcely remember a time when the image of Our Lady did not stand up in my mind quite definitely, at the mention or the thought of all these things. I was quite distant from these things, and then doubtful about these things; and then disputing with the world for them, and with myself against them; for that is the condition before conversion. But whether the figure was distant, or was dark and mysterious, or was a scandal to my contemporaries, or was a challenge to myself—I never doubted that this figure was the figure of the Faith; that she embodied, as a complete human being still only human, all that this Thing had to say to humanity. The instant I remembered the Catholic Church, I remembered her; when I tried to forget the Catholic Church, I tried to forget her.

—G. K. Chesterton, "Mary and the Convert," *The Well and the Shallows*

IN GOD'S PRESENCE, CONSIDER . . .

Have I had an experience similar to that of Chesterton, in that Mary embodies and sums up in some way all that is distinctive about the Catholic faith? Why does Mary play that role for so many Catholics and non-Catholics alike?

CLOSING PRAYER

From a prayer of Venerable Pope Pius XII: *O Virgin, fair as the moon, delight of the angels and saints in heaven, grant that we may become like you and that our souls may receive a ray of your beauty, which does not decline with the years but shines forth into eternity.*

Queen of hell and the demons

To speak of Mary as queen of hell may sound surprising and even confusing. But St. Alphonsus explains.

Not only is the most Blessed Virgin the queen of heaven and of all saints. She is also queen of hell and of all evil spirits. For she overcame them valiantly by her virtues. From the very beginning God foretold the victory and empire that our queen would one day gain over the serpent, when he announced to him that a woman would come into the world to conquer him: "I will put enmity between you and the woman. . . . She will crush your head" (Gn 3:15). And who could this woman, his enemy, be but Mary, who by her fair humility and holy life always conquered him and beat down his strength?

As St. Bernard remarks, this proud spirit, in spite of himself, was beaten down and trampled underfoot by this most Blessed Virgin. Now, as a slave conquered in war, he is forced always to obey the commands of this queen: "Beaten down and trampled under the feet of Mary, the Devil endures a wretched slavery." And she bound him in such a way that this enemy cannot stir so as to do even the least injury to any of those who go to her for protection.

"My children," Mary seems to say, "when the enemy assails you, fly to me. Cast your eyes on me, and be of good heart. Since I am your defender, victory is assured to you." In this way, turning to Mary is a most secure means to conquer all the assaults of hell. For she is even the queen of hell and sovereign mistress of the demons, since she is the one who tames and crushes them. St. Bernardine of Siena expresses the thought this way: "The most Blessed Virgin rules over the regions of hell. She is therefore called the ruling mistress of the demons, because she brings them into subjection."

—St. Alphonsus Liguori, *The Glories of Mary*

IN GOD'S PRESENCE, CONSIDER . . .

What does it mean to say that Mary is queen of hell? What encouragement should I take in knowing that she is "sovereign mistress of the demons," so that they are conquered slaves with no choice but to obey her command?

CLOSING PRAYER

From a prayer of St. John Bosco: *Mary, most powerful Virgin, you are the mighty and glorious protector of the Church. In the midst of our anguish, our struggle, and our distress, defend us from the power of the Enemy, and at the hour of our death receive our soul into heaven.*

Mary's name is a fortified tower

St. Alphonsus reminds us that the very name of Mary is a defense against the assaults of the Evil One.

The Blessed Virgin herself revealed to St. Bridget: "On earth there is no sinner, however devoid he may be of the love of God, from whom the Devil is not obliged to flee immediately, if he invokes her holy name with a determination to repent." On another occasion she repeated the same thing to the saint, saying, "All the demons venerate and fear her name to such a degree, that on hearing it they immediately loosen the claws with which they hold the soul captive."

Our Blessed Lady also told her: "In the same way as the rebel angels fly from sinners who invoke the name of Mary, so also do the good angels approach nearer to righteous souls who pronounce her name with devotion." St. Germanus declares: "Just as breathing is a sign of life, so also is the frequent pronunciation of the name of Mary a sign either of the life of divine grace, or that it will soon come. For this powerful name has in it the virtue of obtaining help and life for him who invokes it devoutly."

To sum up, "This admirable name of our sovereign Lady," says Richard of Saint Lawrence, "is like a fortified tower. If a sinner takes refuge in it, he will be delivered from death; for it defends and saves even the most abandoned." But it is a tower of strength that not only delivers sinners from chastisement, but also defends the righteous from the assaults of hell.

—St. Alphonsus Liguori, *The Glories of Mary*

IN GOD'S PRESENCE, CONSIDER . . .

What does it mean to say that Mary's name is strong and powerful? Why would the demons flee from it?

CLOSING PRAYER

From a prayer of Blessed Raymond Jordano: *Virgin Mother of God, you assist the dying, protecting them against the snares of the Devil; and you help them also after death, receiving their souls and conducting them to the kingdom of the blessed.*

The demons tremble at the name of Mary

St. Alphonsus Liguori elaborates on the power of Mary's name to terrify the powers of darkness.

The demons tremble even if they only hear the name of Mary. St. Bernard declares that "in the name of Mary every knee bows," and "the devils not only fear but tremble at the very sound of that name."

As men fall prostrate with fear if a thunderbolt falls near them, so do the demons if they hear the name of Mary. Thomas à Kempis expresses the same sentiment in this way: "The evil spirits greatly fear the Queen of Heaven, and flee at the sound of her name, as if from fire. At the very sound of the word Mary, they are cast down as if by thunder."

O how many victories have those who turn to Mary gained only by making use of her most holy name! It was in this way that St. Anthony of Padua was always victorious. In this way also so many other lovers of this great queen conquered.

We learn from the history of the missions in Japan that many demons appeared under the form of fierce animals to a certain Christian, to alarm and threaten him. But he addressed them in this way: "I have no arms that you can fear; and if the Most High permits it, do whatever you please with me. In the meantime, however, I take the holy names of Jesus and Mary for my defense." At the very sound of these tremendous names, the earth opened, and the proud spirits cast themselves headlong into it.

St. Anselm, the great archbishop and Doctor of the Church, once declared that he himself "knew and had seen and heard many who had invoked the name of Mary in time of danger, and were immediately delivered."

—St. Alphonsus Liguori, *The Glories of Mary*

IN GOD'S PRESENCE, CONSIDER . . .

What do the demons have to fear about Jesus' and Mary's names? If the demons are so powerful, why do they flee just to hear these names spoken?

CLOSING PRAYER

From a prayer of St. Alphonsus: *Mary, sweet refuge of miserable sinners, when my soul is on the point of leaving this world, drive the enemy from hell far from me, and come and take my soul to yourself, and present it to the eternal Judge.*

A name better than earthly riches

St. Alphonsus wonders: What price could we possibly place on a name like Mary's, so full of graces and eternal benefits?

St. Bernard, enflamed with love, raises his heart to his good mother and says with tenderness, "O great one! O pious one! You who are worthy of all praise, most holy Virgin Mary!

"Your name is so sweet and amiable that it can't be pronounced without enflaming those who do so with love toward you and God. The thought of it need only occur to the mind of those who love you to move them to love you more, and to console them. You can't be named without enflaming their hearts; you can't be thought of by those who love you without filling their minds with joy."

"If riches comfort the poor," says Richard of Saint Lawrence, "because they relieve them in their distress, how much more does your name, O Mary, comfort us than any earthly riches! It comforts us in the anguishes of this life. Your name, O Mary, is far better than riches, because it can better relieve poverty."

In sum, St. Methodius says, "Your name, O Mother of God, is filled with divine graces and blessings." So filled with such graces and blessings is her name, declares St. Bonaventure of Our Lady, that her name "cannot be pronounced without bringing some grace to the one who speaks it devoutly."

—St. Alphonsus Liguori, *The Glories of Mary*

How is Mary's name more precious than wealth? What kind of poverty does it relieve?

CLOSING PRAYER

From a prayer of Blessed Henry Suso: *O most sweet name! O Mary, what must you yourself be, if your name alone is so lovable and gracious!*

The sweetness of Mary's name

St. Alphonsus tells why those who are devoted to Mary take such great pleasure in speaking her name.

Among the other privileges of the name of Mary given to it by God is the peculiar sweetness found in it by the servants of this most holy Lady during life and in death. "Name of Mary!" said St. Anthony of Padua. "Joy in the heart, honey in the mouth, melody to the ear of the devout who seek her assistance!"

It's reported in the life of the Venerable Juvenal Ancina, Bishop of Saluzzo, that in pronouncing the name of Mary his bodily sense of taste experienced so great a sweetness that, after doing so, he licked his lips. We read also that a Lady at Cologne told the Bishop Massilius that as often as she uttered the name of Mary she experienced a taste far sweeter than honey. The bishop imitated her, and he experienced the same thing.

But here I don't intend to speak of that sweetness of the bodily senses, for it's not granted to everyone. I speak instead of that healthful sweetness of consolation, love, joy, confidence, strength, that the name of Mary usually brings to those who pronounce it with devotion.

The Abbot Francone, speaking on this subject, says, "There is no other name after that of the Son, in heaven or on earth, from which pious minds derive so much grace, hope, and sweetness. For there is something so admirable, sweet, and divine in this name of Mary, that when it meets with friendly hearts it breathes into them a fragrance of delightful sweetness. The wonder of this great name is that, even if heard by those who love Mary a thousand times, it's always heard again with renewed pleasure, for they always experience the same sweetness each time it is pronounced."

—St. Alphonsus Liguori, *The Glories of Mary*

IN GOD'S PRESENCE, CONSIDER . . .

What comes to mind when I say Mary's name? Do I take pleasure in talking about her with others?

CLOSING PRAYER

From a prayer of St. Bonaventure: *I ask you, O Mary, for the glory of your name, to come and meet my soul when it is departing this world, and take it into your arms.*

The price of redemption is found in Mary's womb

St. Bonaventure considers what kind of magnificent price had to be paid to purchase so great a redemption as ours.

"Who shall find a valiant woman? Far and from the uttermost coasts is the price of her" (see Prv 31:10). This is the price about which the Apostle Paul speaks: "You were bought with a price. So glorify God in your body" (1 Cor. 6:20).

This price had to be great to redeem the whole world and the entire human race. So it was necessary that the price have both a divine and a human nature. Where is that price found? Nowhere but in the womb of the glorious Virgin. Thus one reads in Isaiah: "Behold, a Virgin shall conceive and bear a son, and shall call his name Emmanuel" (see Is 7:14). "Emmanuel" is translated "God with us."

It was not fitting that a virgin should have as a son anyone but God, nor for God to have as a mother anyone but a virgin. That price, then, could only be found in the Virgin Mary. "Far and from the uttermost coasts": because in him is united highest and lowest, first with last. That price by which the entire human race is redeemed is from afar. Because the lowest is redeemed, it is the highest price; because the last is redeemed, it is the first; and man was the last of the creatures to be made.

Whose is this price? This price by which we are able to reach the kingdom of heaven belongs to this woman, the Blessed Virgin. It is hers, because it is taken from her, offered by her, possessed by her. It is taken from her in the incarnation of the Word; offered by her in the redemption of the human race; possessed by her in attaining the glory of paradise. She brought forth this price, paid this price, and possesses this price.

—St. Bonaventure, *Conferences on the Seven Gifts of the Holy Spirit*

IN GOD'S PRESENCE, CONSIDER . . .

Am I grateful to the Blessed Virgin for her role in the price of my salvation? Do I have a sense of indebtedness to her that urges me to make sure that in my case, that price was not paid in vain?

CLOSING PRAYER

From a prayer of St. Alphonsus: *Receive me and don't reject me, my Mother. The price of my salvation is already paid; my Savior has already shed his blood, which is enough to save an infinity of worlds. This blood has only to be applied to someone such as I am.*

Mary is a fountain of grace

St. Alphonsus encourages us to seek Mary's help by reminding us that she's eager to give it.

What the Venerable Sister Mary Villani saw in a heavenly vision is experienced by many. This servant of God once saw the Mother of God as a great fountain. Many went to the fountain, and from it they carried off the waters of grace in great abundance.

But what then happened? Those who had jars without cracks kept the graces they received. But those who brought broken vessels—that is to say, those whose souls were burdened with sin—received graces, but didn't keep them for long.

In any case, it's certain that even those who are ungrateful sinners and the most miserable daily obtain innumerable graces from Mary.

As those who are devoted to Mary, then, let's rouse ourselves to greater and greater confidence each time we turn to her for graces. So that we may do just that, let's always remember two great powers of this good mother: her great desire to do us good, and the power she has with her Son to obtain what she asks.

As Bernardine de Bustis writes, "Mary desires more earnestly to do us good and grant us graces than we desire to receive them." For Mary's desire to enrich everyone with graces is, so to speak, a part of her nature, and she superabundantly enriches her servants.

—St. Alphonsus Liguori, *The Glories of Mary*

IN GOD'S PRESENCE, CONSIDER . . .

When I seek Mary's help in my life, what kind of "jar" do I bring to receive God's grace from her: a broken one, or one that is whole?

CLOSING PRAYER

From a prayer of St. Augustine: *Through you, Mary, the miserable obtain mercy; the ungracious, grace; sinners, pardon; the weak, strength; the worldly, heavenly things; mortals, life; and pilgrims, their country.*

The glories of Mary are for the sake of Jesus

Mary has a mission to fulfill, declares Blessed John Henry Newman. Her graces and glories are not for her own sake, but for that of her Son.

The glories of Mary are for the sake of Jesus. We praise and bless her as the first of creatures, so that we may confess him as our sole Creator. Mary is exalted for the sake of Jesus. It was fitting that she, as being a creature, though the first of creatures, should have an office of ministry.

She, as others, came into the world to do a work; she had a mission to fulfill. Her grace and her glory are not for her own sake, but for her Maker's; and to her is committed the custody of the Incarnation. This is her appointed office: "A virgin shall conceive, and bear a Son, and they shall call his name Emmanuel" (see Is 7:14). As she was once on earth, and was personally the guardian of her divine Child, as she carried him in her womb, folded him in her embrace, and nursed him at her breast, so now, and to the latest hour of the Church, do her glories and the devotion paid her proclaim and define the right faith concerning him as God and Man.

Every church which is dedicated to her, every altar which is raised under her invocation, every image which represents her, every litany in her praise, every Hail Mary for her continual memory, only remind us that there was One who, though he was all-blessed from all eternity, yet for the sake of sinners "did not shrink from the Virgin's womb." Thus she is the *Turris Davidica*, as the Church calls her, "the Tower of David"; the high and strong defense of the King of the true Israel.

—Blessed John Henry Newman,
"The Glories of Mary for the Sake of Her Son"

IN GOD'S PRESENCE, CONSIDER . . .

Some insist that Mary is too highly honored when churches are dedicated to her, images displayed of her, liturgical praises sung to her, and prayers offered to her. How do these expressions of Marian devotion point ultimately to Jesus?

CLOSING PRAYER

From a prayer of St. Faustina: *Lord, we unite ourselves with your immaculate mother, for then our hymn will be more pleasing to you, because she is chosen from among men and angels. Through her, as through a pure crystal, your mercy was passed on to us.*

Mary's honors defend the truth about her Son

Blessed John Henry Newman observes that God allowed Mary to remain in the background until the divinity of her Son was challenged in the early centuries of the Church. At that time, the attention of the world turned to her as the "Mother of God," for that title defended the truth about his identity.

I have shown you how full of meaning are the truths which the Church teaches concerning the Most Blessed Virgin. Now consider how full of meaning also has been the Church's dispensation of them. You will find that, in this respect, as in Mary's prerogatives themselves, there is the same careful consideration of the glory of him who gave them to her.

You know, when first her Son went out to preach, she kept apart from him; she interfered not with his work. Even when he had gone up on high, yet she, a woman, went not out to preach or teach, she seated not herself in the apostolic chair, she took no part in the priest's office. She only sought her Son humbly in the daily Mass of those who, though her ministers in heaven, were her superiors in the Church on earth. Even when she and they had left this lower scene, and she was a queen upon her Son's right hand, she didn't ask him to publish her name to the ends of the world, or to hold her up to the world's gaze. But she remained waiting for the time when her own glory should be necessary for his.

He indeed had been from the very first proclaimed by holy Church and enthroned in his temple, for he was God. It would have ill befitted the living Oracle of Truth to have withheld from the faithful the very object of their adoration. But it was otherwise with Mary. It was fitting for her, as a creature, a mother, and a woman, to stand aside and make way for the Creator, to minister to her Son, and to win her way into the world's homage by sweet and gracious persuasion. So when his name was dishonored, then it was that she did him service. When Emmanuel was denied, then the Mother of God came forward. When heretics said that God was not incarnate, then was the time for her own honors.

—Blessed John Henry Newman

IN GOD'S PRESENCE, CONSIDER . . .

If Mary was concerned for the honor of her Son—and he, for hers—then so should we be. What is the best way to honor Jesus and Mary, and to cause them to be honored by others?

CLOSING PRAYER

My Lord and my Lady, let there never be cause for someone to say of me, as they once said of your people whose conduct brought scandal, "The name of God is blasphemed among the Gentiles because of you" (Rom 2:24).

Mary's special gifts help her witness to Christ

Blessed John Henry Newman considers how Mary's special gifts, and her special dignity in the Church, are necessary for her to bear proper witness to her Son.

If the Mother of God is to bear witness to Emmanuel, she must be necessarily more than the Mother of God. For consider: A defense must be strong in order to be a defense; a tower must be, like that Tower of David (which is one of her titles), "built with bulwarks"; "a thousand bucklers hang upon it, all the armor of valiant men" (see Sg 4:4).

It would not have sufficed, in order to bring out and impress on us the idea that God is man, had his mother been an ordinary person. A mother without a home in the Church, without dignity, without gifts, would have been, as far as the defense of the Incarnation goes, no mother at all. She would not have remained in the memory or the imagination of men. If she is to witness to and remind the world that God became man, she must be on a high and eminent station for the purpose. She must be made to fill the mind, in order to suggest the lesson.

When she once attracts our attention, then, and not till then, she begins to preach Jesus. "Why should she have such prerogatives," we ask, "unless he is God? And what must he be by nature, when she is so high by grace?"

This is why she has other prerogatives besides, namely, the gifts of personal purity and intercessory power, distinct from her maternity. She is personally endowed so that she may perform her office well; she is exalted in herself so that she may minister to Christ.

—Blessed John Henry Newman,
"The Glories of Mary for the Sake of Her Son"

IN GOD'S PRESENCE, CONSIDER . . .

Why is it necessary for Mary to "attract our attention"? How do her special gifts enable her to bear testimony to Jesus?

CLOSING PRAYER

From a prayer of St. Bernard of Clairvaux: *Grant, O blessed one, by the grace you found, by the privilege you merited, by that mercy to which you gave birth, that the One who, through you, came down to take part in our infirmity and misery may also, through your intercession, make us take part in his happiness and glory.*

Mary's perpetual virginity

In the fourth century, one Scripture interpreter cited a passage in the Gospel of Matthew to claim that Mary gave birth to other children after Jesus. In response, the great Bible scholar St. Jerome showed how the passage doesn't contradict the Church's ancient tradition that Jesus was Mary's only Child.

Joseph had no relations with Mary, the Gospel says, "*until* she had borne a son" (Mt 1:25). In this passage, some people insist, *until* implies a fixed and definite time after which the event that previously didn't take place, now takes place. So this text, they say, means that she had sexual relations *after* she delivered her Son. Such relations were only delayed, not prevented, by her bearing a Child.

Our reply is briefly this. The word *until* in the language of Holy Scripture can have either of two meanings. The Scripture often uses this word to mean a fixed time, as we noted. But frequently the term refers instead to time without limitation, as when the Savior in the Gospel tells the Apostles, "Lo, I am with you always, *until* the close of the age" (Mt 28:20).

Does this mean, then, that the Lord, after the end of the world has come, will forsake His disciples, so that at the very time when they're seated on twelve thrones to judge the twelve tribes of Israel, they'll be abandoned by their Lord? (See Mt 19:28.) Of course not! And I could pile up countless examples of this usage in the Scripture.

In the same sense, then, that we interpret the word *until* in this and other passages, we must interpret what we're told about St. Joseph. St. Matthew simply pointed out a circumstance that might have given rise to some scandal, namely, that Mary didn't have relations with her husband until she delivered her Son. The Evangelist did this so that we might be all the more certain that she—the one with whom Joseph refrained from having relations while there was yet room to doubt the meaning of his dream—did not have relations after her delivery, either.

—St. Jerome, *Against Helvidius*

IN GOD'S PRESENCE, CONSIDER . . .

In ancient times as now, Catholic teaching is sometimes challenged by those who claim that it contradicts Scripture. Have I made good use of Catholic resources for defending my faith so that I'll be prepared when someone challenges the Church's teaching?

CLOSING PRAYER

Lord, the Scripture is your gift to the Church to help us know and follow you. Help me to read the Scripture with the mind of the Church so that I can understand more accurately what it teaches.

The mother was like the Son

St. Ignatius of Loyola reminds us that the Son and the mother bear a resemblance, not just in body, but in soul.

What creature was more like Jesus than Mary? The laws of nature ordain that the son should resemble the mother; the laws of grace ordained beforehand that the mother should possess all the characteristics suitable to the Son. Here recall with profound respect:

First, her immaculate conception, which renders her a stranger to sin and its consequences, and to all the occasions leading to sin. This privilege alone, which separates Mary from the mass of iniquity out of which we have all come, raises her above all the saints as much as the heavens are above the earth.

Second, her heavenly virginity, which causes her to be alarmed at the approach of an angel; which would shrink from divine maternity if the Mother of God would cease to be a virgin; a virginity that the Holy Spirit renders fruitful, making her a mother by a miracle beyond words.

Third, her profound humility that, says a holy Father of the Church, made her merit to become the Mother of God: "Behold," she said, "the handmaid of the Lord. He has regarded the humility of his handmaid. He has exalted the humble. He has filled the hungry with good things" (see Lk 1:38, 48, 52, 53).

Fourth, her perfect charity, which made her so prompt in visiting Elizabeth, so faithful in preserving in her heart the words of life, so attentive at the marriage of Cana, so devoted, so heroic during the labors and sorrows of her Son, so useful to the apostles, so dear to the infant Church.

—St. Ignatius Loyola, *The Spiritual Exercises*

IN GOD'S PRESENCE, CONSIDER . . .

St. Ignatius notes four fundamental ways in which Mary resembles Jesus. In what other ways do I see a resemblance?

CLOSING PRAYER

From a prayer of St. John of Damascus: *Mary, make us worthy of future happiness through the sweet and face-to-face vision of the Word made flesh through you. With him, glory, praise, power, and majesty be to the Father and to the holy and life-giving Spirit, now and forever.*

A throne of divine mercy

The Divine Mercy message didn't begin with our Lord's revelations to St. Faustina Kowalska in the twentieth century. Nearly seven centuries before, St. Alphonsus reports, St. Bonaventure wrote about Mary's role in the Divine Mercy.

"Who can there be in the world," exclaims St. Bonaventure, "who refuses to love this most amiable queen? She is more beautiful than the sun, and sweeter than honey. She is a treasure of goodness, lovable and courteous to all. I salute you, then," continues the enraptured saint, "O my Lady and mother— no, my heart, my soul! Forgive me, Mary, if I say that I love you; for if I am not worthy to love you, at least you are all-worthy to be loved by me."

It was revealed to St. Gertrude that when these words are addressed with devotion to the most Blessed Virgin—"Turn, then, most gracious advocate, thine eyes of mercy toward us"—Mary cannot do otherwise than yield to the demand of anyone who calls on her this way. "Truly, O great Lady," says St. Bernard, "the immensity of your mercy fills the whole earth."

The prophet Isaiah foretold that, together with the great work of the redemption of the human race, a throne of divine mercy was to be prepared for us poor creatures: "And a throne shall be prepared in mercy" (see Is 16:5). What is this throne?

St. Bonaventure answers: "Mary is this throne, at which all—both the righteous and sinners—find the consolations of mercy." He then adds: "For as we have a most merciful Lord, so also we have a most merciful Lady. Our Lord is plentiful in mercy to all who call upon him, and Our Lady is plentiful in mercy to all who call upon her."

As our Lord is full of mercy, so also is Our Lady. And just as the Son doesn't know how to refuse mercy to those who call upon him, neither does the mother.

—St. Alphonsus Liguori, *The Glories of Mary*

IN GOD'S PRESENCE, CONSIDER . . .

What does it mean to say that Mary is her Son's throne? How is the mercy of God at the same time the mercy of his mother?

CLOSING PRAYER

From the "Divine Mercy Chaplet": *Holy God, Holy Mighty One, Holy Immortal One, have mercy on us and on the whole world.*

It was fitting for Mary never to be a slave to Satan

If Mary was to crush Satan's head, St. Alphonsus reasons, it was fitting that she would never have been first subject to him because of sin.

Great indeed was the injury imposed on Adam and all his posterity by his accursed sin. At the same time that he, to his own great misfortune, lost grace, he also forfeited all the other precious gifts with which he had originally been enriched, and drew down upon himself and all his descendants the enmity of God and an accumulation of evils. But from this general misfortune God was pleased to exempt that Blessed Virgin whom he had destined to be the mother of the Second Adam—Jesus Christ—who was to repair the evil done by the first Adam. Now let's see how becoming it was that God should in this way preserve her.

It was fitting that God should preserve Mary from original sin because he destined her to crush the head of that hellish serpent that, by seducing our first parents, brought death upon all men. This our Lord foretold to the serpent: "I will put enmity between you and the woman, and your seed and her seed. She shall crush your head" (see Gn 3:15). But if Mary was to be that valiant woman brought into the world to conquer Lucifer, certainly it was not fitting that he should first conquer her and make her his slave. Instead, it was reasonable that she should be preserved from all stain or even momentary subjection to her opponent. The proud spirit endeavored to infect the most pure soul of this virgin with his venom, as he had already infected the whole human race.

But praised and ever blessed be God! In his infinite goodness, he endowed Mary ahead of time for this purpose with such great grace that, remaining always free from any guilt of sin, she was always able to beat down and confound the Devil's pride.

—St. Alphonsus Liguori, *The Glories of Mary*

IN GOD'S PRESENCE, CONSIDER . . .

Do I take comfort in the knowledge that Mary was never subject to Satan as his slave? Am I grateful for her role in crushing his head?

CLOSING PRAYER

From a prayer of St. Maximillian Kolbe: *O Immaculata, queen of heaven and earth, refuge of sinners and our most loving mother, God has willed to entrust the entire order of mercy to you. I, a repentant sinner, cast myself at your feet.*

The Son of God chose his own mother

If you could choose your own mother, what kind of woman would you choose? The Son of God actually had such a choice, St. Alphonsus reminds us, and Mary had the qualities he was seeking.

It was fitting that the Son of God should preserve Mary from sin, since she was his mother. No other man could choose his mother. But if such a thing could ever be granted to anyone, who would wish for a slave, if he could choose a queen? Who would wish for a servant, if he could choose a noble lady? And if he could choose a friend of God, would he wish for God's enemy?

If, then, the Son of God alone could choose a mother according to his own heart, his own liking, we must consider that he would of course choose one fitting a God. St. Bernard says, "When the Creator of men became Man, he must have selected for himself a mother whom he knew was fitting for him." And since it was fitting that a most pure God should have a mother pure from all sin, he created her spotless.

St. Paul wrote: "The first Adam was of the earth, earthly; the second Adam, Christ, was from heaven, heavenly" (see 1 Cor 15:47). St. Ambrose alludes to these words when he says of Mary: "Christ chose this vessel into which he was about to descend: not of the earth, but from heaven; and he consecrated it a temple of purity." The saint calls the Mother of God "a heavenly vessel," not because Mary wasn't earthly by nature, but because she was heavenly by grace. She was as superior to the angels of heaven in holiness and purity, as she was fit to be the one in whose womb a King of glory was to dwell.

God said to St. Bridget: "Mary was conceived without sin, so that the divine Son might be born of her without sin." Not that Jesus Christ could have contracted sin, but so that he might not be reproached with even having a mother infected with it, who would consequently have been the slave of the Devil.

—St. Alphonsus Liguori, *The Glories of Mary*

IN GOD'S PRESENCE, CONSIDER . . .

The Son of God also chose his foster father, Joseph. What qualities do you think he was looking for in such a man? God's Son also chose just the right time to enter the world. Why do you think he chose that particular time in history?

CLOSING PRAYER

"Blessed be the God and Father of our Lord Jesus Christ, who has blessed us in Christ with every spiritual blessing in the heavenly places, even as he chose us in him before the foundation of the world, that we should be holy and blameless before him" (Eph 1:3–4).

Mary loved God with her whole heart

St. Alphonsus tells us that Mary perfectly fulfilled the greatest commandment: to love God with all her heart.

St. Anselm says that "wherever there is the greatest purity, there is also the greatest charity." The more a heart is pure, and empty of itself, the greater is the fullness of its love toward God. The most holy Mary, because she was all humility and had nothing of self in her, was filled with divine love—so much so that "her love toward God surpassed that of all men and angels," as St. Bernardine writes. For this reason St. Francis of Sales called her the "Queen of Love."

God has indeed given us the precept to love him with our whole hearts: "You shall love the Lord your God with all your heart" (Mt 22:37). But as St. Thomas declares, "This commandment will be fully and perfectly fulfilled by those in heaven alone, and not on earth, where it is fulfilled only imperfectly." On this subject, St. Albert the Great remarks that in a certain sense, it wouldn't have been fitting for God to give a precept that was never to have been perfectly fulfilled. Yet this would have been the case, had not the Mother of God perfectly fulfilled it. Richard of Saint Victor confirms this opinion, saying, "The mother of our Emmanuel practiced virtues in their very highest perfection. Who has ever fulfilled as she did that first commandment, 'You shall love the Lord your God with all your heart'? In her, divine love was so ardent that no defect of any kind could have access to her."

"The love of God," says St. Bernard, "so penetrated and filled the soul of Mary that no part of her was left untouched. She loved with her whole heart, with her whole soul, with her whole strength; and she was full of grace." "Well might even the Seraphim have descended from heaven," says Richard of Saint Victor, "to learn, in the heart of Mary, how to love God."

—St. Alphonsus Liguori, *The Glories of Mary*

IN GOD'S PRESENCE, CONSIDER . . .

When St. Thomas comments that the great command to love God with all that we are will be fully and perfectly fulfilled only in heaven, do his words discourage me or encourage me? Do I find it consoling that at least one person, Our Lady, was able to fulfill the command perfectly even in this life?

CLOSING PRAYER

"Teach me your way, O LORD, that I may walk in your truth; unite my heart to fear your name. I give thanks to you, O LORD my God, with my whole heart" (Ps 86:11–12).

Mary loved her neighbor

Genuine love for God leads inevitably to love for neighbor. St. Alphonsus points out that just as Mary loved God perfectly, she loved her neighbor perfectly.

Love toward God and love toward our neighbor are commanded by the same precept: "And this commandment we have from him, that he who loves God should love his brother also" (1 Jn 4:21). St. Thomas says the reason for this is that whoever loves God, loves all that God loves.

This truth was confirmed for St. Catherine of Genoa one day when she prayed, "Lord, you will that I should love my neighbor. Yet I can love no one but you."

God answered her in these words: "All who love me, love what I love."

But just as there never was, and never will be, anyone who loved God as much as Mary loved him, so there never was, and never will be, anyone who loved her neighbor as much as she did. So great was Mary's charity when she was on earth that she helped the needy without even being asked. That was the case at the marriage feast of Cana, when she told her Son that family's distress: "They have no wine" (Jn 2:3) and asked him to work a miracle.

With what speed did she travel when there was possibility of relieving her neighbor! When she went to the house of Elizabeth to fulfill a charitable role, "Mary went with haste into the hill country" (Lk 1:39). Yet she could never display more fully the greatness of her charity than she did in offering her Son up to death for our salvation. For this reason, St. Anselm exclaims, "Blessed among women, your purity surpasses that of the angels, and your compassion that of the saints!"

—St. Alphonsus Liguori, *The Glories of Mary*

IN GOD'S PRESENCE, CONSIDER . . .

Based only on my attitudes and behavior toward them, would those around me have reason to conclude that I love God?

CLOSING PRAYER

From a prayer of Pope St. John Paul II: *Mary, take from all our hearts the selfishness that sours relationships and keeps us centered only on ourselves. Give us hearts aflame with charity and filled with love. Make us, like the Apostle John who was commended to your care, loving children of our heavenly Father, conscious always of your maternal presence in our lives.*

Mary loves us because her Son died for us

Mary's beloved Son loved us so much that he gave his life for us. What greater reason, St. Alphonsus asks, could she have for loving us as well?

Yet another motive for the love of Mary towards us is this: In us, she beholds what has been purchased at the price of the death of Jesus Christ. If a mother knew that a servant had been ransomed by a beloved son at the price of twenty years of imprisonment and suffering, how greatly would she esteem that servant—even if on this account alone! Mary well knows that her Son came into the world only to save us poor creatures, as he himself proclaimed: "The Son of Man came to seek and to save the lost" (Lk 19:10). And to save us he was pleased even to lay down his life for us, and "became obedient to death" (Phil 2:8). If, then, Mary loved us only a little, she would show that she valued only little the blood of her Son, which was the price of our salvation.

Because all people have been redeemed by Jesus, therefore Mary loves and protects them all. It was she who was seen by St. John in the Apocalypse, clothed with the sun: "And a great sign appeared in heaven: a woman clothed with the sun" (Rv 12:1). She is said to be clothed with the sun because, as there is no one on earth who can be hidden from the heat of the sun—"there is nothing hidden from its heat" (Ps 19:6)—so there is no one living who can be deprived of the love of Mary.

"Who," exclaims St. Antoninus, "can ever form an idea of the tender care that this most loving mother takes of all of us . . . offering and dispensing her mercy to everyone?" For our good mother desired the salvation of all, and she cooperated in obtaining it.

—St. Alphonsus Liguori, *The Glories of Mary*

IN GOD'S PRESENCE, CONSIDER . . .

Someone once said that a thing is worth what the right buyer is willing to pay for it. If God was willing to redeem me at the cost of his Son's lifeblood, what must I be worth to God?

CLOSING PRAYER

Lord, let me never forget the words of St. Paul: "You are not your own; you were bought with a price. So glorify God in your body" (1 Cor 6:19–20).

More reasons why Mary loves us so much

St. Alphonsus observes that Mary has multiple compelling reasons for loving us.

Our mother loves us so much because we were entrusted to her by her beloved Jesus, when he said to her before he died, "Woman, behold your son!" (Jn 19:26). For St. John represented us all. These were our Lord's last words; and the last requests made before death by those we love are always treasured and never forgotten.

In addition, we are extremely dear to Mary on account of the sufferings we cost her. Mothers generally love most those children who have cost them the most suffering and anxiety in preserving their lives. We are those children for whom Mary, in order to obtain for us the life of grace, was obliged to endure the bitter agony of offering her beloved Jesus to die a humiliating death. She had to see him die before her own eyes in the midst of the most cruel and unheard-of torments.

It was then by this great offering of Mary that we were born to the life of grace. We are for that reason her very dear children, since we cost her such great suffering. It is written of the Eternal Father's love toward us, in giving his own Son over to death for us, that "God so loved the world that he gave his only-begotten Son" (Jn 3:16). "In a similar way," observes St. Bonaventure, "we can say of Mary, that she has so loved us that she gave her only-begotten Son for us."

—St. Alphonsus Liguori, *The Glories of Mary*

IN GOD'S PRESENCE, CONSIDER . . .

Do I know a parent who has had to fight long and hard to protect or preserve the life of a child? If so, can I better appreciate St. Alphonsus' claim that such a parent has a fierce and protective love for that child—and that Mary loves us in that way?

CLOSING PRAYER

From a prayer of St. Peter Damian: *I know, O Lady, that you are most loving, and that you love us with an invincible love.*

Mary has shown herself to be your mother

St. Ignatius Loyola recalls all the good reasons we have to call Mary our mother, and to honor her accordingly.

Mary has always shown herself to be your mother. She received you to her heart when Jesus gave you to her as her child. For this reason the Scripture calls Jesus Christ her "firstborn" (see Mt 1:25). You ought to be born in her and by her, after him. She has nourished you, not only by the graces her prayers have obtained for you, but also in a real way by the Body and Blood of her Son given to you in the Eucharist.

She has looked out for you, cared for you, loaded you with favors. All the graces you have received from the Lord have been solicited and obtained by her. This means that your call to the faith, the grace of a Christian education, of a first Communion, the grace of conversion and retreats, the grace that now leads you to give yourself entirely to God—all come to you from Jesus through Mary.

When needed, Mary provides for the defense and salvation of her children extraordinary graces and wonderful miracles. What wonders have caused, sustained, spread everywhere, a confidence among Christian people! What striking proofs of her protection the Church recalls to our memory in solemn feasts and devout practices, enriched by precious indulgences! What titles Christians give her to testify to their gratitude: "Help of Christians, health of the sick, comfort of the afflicted, refuge of sinners, gate of heaven, our life, our sweetness, our hope!" What a multitude of people gather to the places where she is most honored, where she obtains the most assistance to those who call on her! What prayers and acts of thanksgiving are offered at the foot of her altars! In our days, what conquests have been made by Our Lady of Victories! What favors have been bestowed on all hearts devoted to the heart of Mary!

—St. Ignatius Loyola, *The Spiritual Exercises*

IN GOD'S PRESENCE, CONSIDER . . .

What has Mary done for you personally to demonstrate her maternal care? How have you expressed your gratitude for her care?

CLOSING PRAYER

From a prayer of St. Bernard of Clairvaux: *My dear mother, if only I could love you as you love me! Yet I will not cease to do all that I can to honor and love you. My most sweet Lady, obtain for me grace to be faithful to you.*

Mary was the first to adore her Son

St. Peter Julian Eymard, known as the "Apostle of the Eucharist," devoted his life to encouraging Eucharistic adoration and devotion to the Blessed Sacrament. Here he reminds adorers of our Lord that they are following Mary's example.

All Mary's life—taken as a whole—may be summed up in this one word—adoration; for adoration is the perfect service of God, and it embraces all the duties of the creature toward the Creator. It was Mary who first adored the incarnate Word. He was in her womb, and no one on earth knew of it. Oh! How well was our Lord served in Mary's virginal womb! Never has he found a ciborium, a golden vase more precious or purer than was Mary's womb! . . .

At Bethlehem, Mary was the first to adore her divine Son lying in the manger. She adored him with the perfect love of a virgin mother, the love of charity, as says the Holy Spirit. After Mary, St. Joseph, the shepherds, then the Magi came to adore: but it was Mary who opened up that furrow of fire that was to spread over the world. And what beautiful things, what divine things, Mary must have said! For hers was an ardent love whose depths we can never fathom. Mary continued to adore our Lord: first in his hidden life at Nazareth; afterwards in his apostolic life; and finally, on Calvary, where her adoration became intense suffering.

Notice the nature of Mary's adoration. She adored our Lord according to the different states of his life; Jesus' state determined the character of her adoration—her adoration did not stay in a set groove. At one time, she adored God in her womb; at another, as poor and lowly in Bethlehem; again, as laboring at Nazareth; and later on, as evangelizing and converting sinners. She adored him in his sufferings on Calvary by suffering with him. Her adoration was always in keeping with the sentiments of her divine Son, which were clearly revealed to her. Her love brought her into perfect conformity of thought and life with him.

—St. Peter Julian Eymard, *Our Lady of the Most Blessed Sacrament*

IN GOD'S PRESENCE, CONSIDER . . .

Mary has much to teach us about adoring her Son. Do I take time for a regular holy hour before the Blessed Sacrament? Have I asked her to teach me how to adore him worthily?

CLOSING PRAYER

From a prayer of St. Peter Julian Eymard: *O Mary! Teach us the life of adoration. Teach us to see, as you did, all the mysteries and all the graces in the Eucharist.*

Mary was an instrument of redemption

St. John of Damascus speaks to God the Son, declaring all that he accomplished by taking on flesh to redeem us. Then comes an important question: Who was the human instrument God chose to make that redemption possible?

The Father predestined her; the prophets foretold her through the Holy Spirit. His sanctifying power overshadowed her, cleansed her, and made her holy. Then you, Word of the Father, leaving your place in heaven, invited the lowliness of our nature to be united to the immeasurable greatness of your unsearchable nature as God.

You took your flesh from the flesh of the Blessed Virgin. It was given life by a reasoning soul and dwelled in her undefiled and immaculate womb. Creating yourself, and causing her to exist in you, you became perfect Man without ceasing to be perfect God, equal to your Father but taking upon yourself our weakness through unspeakable goodness.

Having become in this way the mediator between God and man, you destroyed our enmity with you. You led back to your Father those who had deserted him, the wanderers back to their home, and those in darkness back to the light. You brought pardon to the contrite and changed mortality into immortality.

You delivered the world from the error of belief in many gods, and you made men the children of God, partakers of your divine glory. You raised the human race, which was condemned to hell, above all power and majesty. And in your Person, it is now seated on the King's eternal throne in heaven.

Who was the instrument of these infinite benefits, beyond all thought and comprehension, if not the mother, ever-virgin, who gave you birth?

—St. John of Damascus, *First Homily on the Dormition*

IN GOD'S PRESENCE, CONSIDER . . .

Does it detract from the glory of God to say that he chose Mary as his instrument in our redemption through Christ? Does it lessen the praise for a potter to say that he chose the finest of clays to create his masterpiece?

CLOSING PRAYER

From a prayer of St. Catherine of Siena: *You, Mary, are the young plant that produced the fragrant flower of the Word, only-begotten of God, because you were the fertile land that was sown with this Word.*

The Holy Spirit made his spouse beautiful

Mary is called the spouse of the Holy Spirit. If an artist could make his bride look the way he could paint her, he would render her as beautiful as possible. So, then, St. Alphonsus reasons, the Spirit made Mary's character exquisitely beautiful.

Since it was fitting that the Father should preserve Mary from sin as his daughter, and the Son as his mother, it was also fitting that the Holy Spirit should preserve her as his spouse. St. Augustine says: "Mary was the only one who merited to be called the mother and the spouse of God." For St. Anselm asserts that "the divine Spirit, the love itself of the Father and the Son, came bodily into Mary. Enriching her with graces above all other creatures, he reposed in her and made her his spouse, the queen of heaven and earth."

When he says that the Holy Spirit came into her bodily, he means with regard to the effect of his coming: for he came to form from her immaculate body the immaculate body of Jesus Christ, as the archangel had already promised her: "The Holy Spirit will come upon you" (Lk 1:35). For this reason, says St. Thomas, "Mary is called the temple of the Lord, and the sacred resting place of the Holy Spirit. For by the operation of the Holy Spirit, she became the mother of the incarnate Word."

Consider this: If an excellent artist had the power to make his bride look the way he could paint her, what pains would he take to render her as beautiful as possible! Who, then, would dare to say that the Holy Spirit did any less with Mary? He was able indeed to make the one who was to be his spouse as beautifully fit for him as possible. So he acted as it was fitting for him to act.

—St. Alphonsus Liguori, *The Glories of Mary*

IN GOD'S PRESENCE, CONSIDER . . .

Anyone who has ever been smitten by the beauty of a loved one—especially a beauty of character—knows the power of that beauty to transform the beholder. In what ways has Mary's beauty of character attracted and transformed me?

CLOSING PRAYER

Spouse of the Holy Spirit, "behold, you are beautiful, my love; behold, you are beautiful!" (Sg 1:15).

Hospital for sinners

St. Alphonsus notes how the healing power God has given Mary has led some to call her a "public infirmary" for the poor.

St. Ephraem, addressing the Blessed Virgin, says, "You are the only advocate of sinners, and of all who are unprotected." Then he salutes her with these words: "Hail, refuge and hospital for sinners!" She is the true refuge, in which alone they can hope for admission and liberty.

St. Basil of Seleucia remarks: "God granted to some who were only his servants such power that not only their touch, but even their shadows, healed the sick who were placed for this purpose in the public streets (see Acts 5:14–16). How much greater power must we suppose, then, has he granted to the one who was not only his handmaid, but also his mother?"

We may indeed say that our Lord has given us Mary as a public infirmary, to which all who are sick, poor, and destitute can be admitted. But now I ask, in hospitals erected expressly for the poor, who have the greatest claim to admission? Certainly the most infirm and those who are in the greatest need.

For this reason, if anyone should find himself devoid of merit and overwhelmed with spiritual infirmities—that is to say, with sin—he can address Mary this way: "Lady, you are the refuge of the sick poor. Don't reject me. Since I'm the poorest and most infirm of all, I have the greatest right to be welcomed by you."

—St. Alphonsus Liguori, *The Glories of Mary*

IN GOD'S PRESENCE, CONSIDER . . .

What do I consider my greatest spiritual infirmities that desperately require healing? Why should I wait any longer to seek a cure from Mary, the "hospital for sinners"?

CLOSING PRAYER

Mary, God has sent you to be "a faithful envoy who brings healing"; the words of your gracious invitation to embrace your Son's salvation are "sweetness to the soul and health to the body" (Prv 13:17; 16:24).

Mary helps an infamous sinner

St. Alphonsus recalls the story of St. Mary of Egypt, whose conversion was enabled in part by seeing a picture of Mary in a church.

At the age of twelve, St. Mary of Egypt ran away from home and went to Alexandria. There she led an infamous life and was a scandal to the whole city. After living for sixteen years in sin, she decided to go to Jerusalem. The Feast of the Holy Cross was being celebrated. Moved by curiosity rather than devotion, she decided to enter the church. But at the door she felt herself repelled by an invisible force. She made several attempts but was unable to enter. Finding her efforts in vain, the unfortunate creature withdrew to a corner of the porch. There, enlightened from above, she understood that it was because of her infamous life that God had repelled her from the church. In that moment she fortunately raised her eyes and beheld a picture of Mary.

As soon as she saw it, she exclaimed, sobbing: "Mother of God, pity a poor sinner! Because of my sins I don't deserve for you to look upon me. But you're the refuge of sinners; for the love of your Son, Jesus, help me! Allow me to enter the church, and I promise to change my life and go do penance wherever you show me." She immediately heard an interior voice, as the Blessed Virgin replied: "Since you turned to me, and you wish to change your life, go; enter the church. It's no longer closed to you." The sinner entered, adored the cross, and wept bitterly. She then returned to the picture and said, "Lady, I'm ready. Where do you want me to go do penance?"

"Cross the Jordan," the Blessed Virgin replied, "and you'll find the place of your rest." So she went to Confession and Communion, and then passed over the river. Finding herself in the desert, she understood that it was the place where she should do penance for her sinful life.

—St. Alphonsus Liguori, *The Glories of Mary*

IN GOD'S PRESENCE, CONSIDER . . .

Are there particular images of Our Lady that inspire me to greater devotion? Have I placed throughout my home images of Jesus, and of Mary and other saints, as reminders of their presence and care for me?

CLOSING PRAYER

Blessed Mother, just as an artist has painted your portrait lovingly to inspire my devotion, so God has created you lovingly as the masterpiece of his creation, to inspire my gratitude and devotion.

Mary will never abandon anyone

Would a mother refuse to apply medicine to her child's infected wounds, simply because they are repulsive? Of course, not, insists St. Alphonsus. In the same way, however revolting our sins may be, Mary will come to apply a remedy.

The multitude of our sins shouldn't lessen our confidence that Mary will grant our petitions when we cast ourselves at her feet. She's the mother of mercy, and mercy wouldn't be needed if there were no one who requires it. On this subject Richard of Saint Lawrence remarks, "As a good mother doesn't hesitate to apply a remedy to her child infected with ulcers, however nauseous and revolting they may be, so also is our good mother unable to abandon us when we turn to her, so that she may heal the wounds caused by our sins, however loathsome they may have made us."

This is exactly what Mary helped St. Gertrude to understand, when she showed herself to her with her mantle spread out to receive all who turn to her. At the same time the saint was told that "angels constantly guard the devotees of this Blessed Virgin from the assaults of hell."

If anyone doubts whether Mary will aid him if he turns to her, Pope Innocent III corrects him with these words: "Who is there that ever, when in the night of sin, turned to this sweet lady without being relieved?" The blessed Eutychian, patriarch of Constantinople, exclaims to Mary, "Who ever faithfully begged your all-powerful aid and was abandoned by you?" Indeed, no one; for she can relieve the most wretched, and save the most abandoned. Such a case certainly never did and never will occur.

Let everyone say, then, with full confidence, in the words of that beautiful prayer addressed to the Mother of Mercy, and commonly attributed to St. Bernard: "Remember, O most pious Virgin Mary, that never was it heard of in any age that anyone having recourse to your protection was abandoned."

—St. Alphonsus Liguori, *The Glories of Mary*

IN GOD'S PRESENCE, CONSIDER . . .

Are there sins in my life that seem like festering wounds, disgusting even to me? Have I asked Mary to apply the healing balm of God's grace, so that I may be healed?

CLOSING PRAYER

From a prayer of St. Alphonsus: *Blessed Lady, my misery, rather than taking away my confidence, increases it, for your compassion is great in proportion to the greatness of my misery. Show yourself full of liberality towards me.*

We are under Mary's protection

St. Ephraem the Syrian marvels at the unparalleled dignity of Mary, and the power God has given her on our behalf.

O immaculate and entirely-pure Virgin Mary, Mother of God, Queen of the Universe, our own good Lady! You are above all the saints, the only hope of the patriarchs, and the joy of the saints. Through you we have been reconciled with our God.

You are the only advocate of sinners, and the secure haven of those who are sailing on the sea of this life. You are the consolation of the world, the ransom of captives, the joy of the sick, the comfort of the afflicted, the refuge, the salvation of the whole world. O great princess, Mother of God, cover us with the wings of your mercy, and pity us.

No other hope but you is given us, most pure Virgin. We are given to you, and consecrated to your service; we bear the name of your servants. Don't allow Lucifer to drag us to hell. Immaculate Virgin, we are under your protection, and therefore we turn to you alone.

I salute you, O peace, O joy, O consolation of the whole world. I salute you, O greatest of miracles, O paradise of delights, secure haven of those who are in danger, fountain of graces, mediatrix of peace between God and men, mother of Jesus our Lord, who is the love of all men and of God, to whom be honor and blessing with the Father and the Holy Spirit.

—St. Ephraem the Syrian

IN GOD'S PRESENCE, CONSIDER . . .

God has given Mary a share in his own power—a greater share than he's given all the other saints. When I'm in physical or spiritual danger, do I ask for her protection?

CLOSING PRAYER

From a prayer of St. Ephraem the Syrian: *Virgin, you who are full of grace, enlighten my understanding, loosen my tongue, that it may sing your praises and especially the angel's greeting, so worthy of you.*

Our Lady leads a man to reconciliation

St. Alphonsus tells how a simple picture of the Blessed Mother brought a man to repent of a vengeful heart.

Our religious Congregation was giving a mission in the diocese of Salerno. There we encountered a man who bore a great hatred toward another man, named Mastrodati, who had offended him.

One of our fathers spoke to him to convince him to be reconciled. But he replied: "Father, have you ever seen me listening to the sermons in the missions? No, and for this very reason, I don't go: I know that I'm damned, but nothing else will satisfy me. I must have revenge."

The priest did all he could to persuade the man to convert. But when he saw that his time was running out, he at last said, "Here, take this picture of our Blessed Lady."

The man at first replied, "Well, of what use is this picture?" But as soon as he took it, he said to the missionary—as if he had never refused to be reconciled—"Father, is anything else required besides reconciliation? I'm willing."

So they made an appointment for the following morning. But when the time came, the man had again changed his mind, and he refused to do anything. The priest offered him another picture, but he refused it.

Nevertheless, after a long time, and with great reluctance, the man took the other picture. Behold! As soon as he took possession of it, he said, "Now let's be quick. Where's Mastrodati?" And he was immediately reconciled with the man, and then went to confession.

—St. Alphonsus Liguori, *The Glories of Mary*

IN GOD'S PRESENCE, CONSIDER . . .

I may not desire revenge against anyone, but is there perhaps someone with whom I need to be reconciled? If so, have I asked Mary to help me approach that person in a spirit of forgiveness?

CLOSING PRAYER

Blessed Mother, help me to forgive as I have been forgiven (see Eph 4:32), and to live in peace with everyone, as far as it depends upon me (see Rom 12:18).

The Devil is tormented by devotion to Mary

St. Alphonsus recalls a story that illustrates yet one more reason for devotion to Mary: It torments the Devil!

A hermit on Mount Olivet kept a devout image of Mary in his room, and said many prayers as he knelt before it. The Devil was unable to endure such devotion to the Blessed Virgin. So he continually tormented the man with impure thoughts.

The harassment was so severe that the poor old hermit, seeing that all his prayers and penances didn't deliver him from those thoughts, one day said to the Enemy: "What have I done to you that you would torment me to death?"

At this the Devil appeared to him and replied, "You torment me much more than I do you. But if you will swear to keep it secret, I will tell you what you must give up for me to stop molesting you."

The hermit took the oath. Then the Devil said: "You must no longer pray before that image that you have in your cell."

The hermit, perplexed at this, went to consult the Abbot Theodore. The abbot told him that he was not bound by his oath, and that he must not cease to entrust himself to Mary in prayer before the image, as he had always done. The hermit obeyed, and the Devil was put to shame and conquered.

—St. Alphonsus Liguori, *The Glories of Mary*

IN GOD'S PRESENCE, CONSIDER . . .

Do I ever experience the Enemy's harassment or distraction when I'm trying to meditate or pray? If I persevere in my devotions, do I eventually win the battle?

CLOSING PRAYER

"Every day," Lord Jesus, with your Blessed Mother beside me, "I will bless you, and praise your name for ever and ever." For "the LORD is near to all who call upon him, to all who call upon him in truth. He fulfills the desire of all who fear him" (Ps 145:2, 18–19).

The Devil wants Mary cast away from the soul

Mary and Jesus are so close, St. Alphonsus insists, that the Devil can't get rid of the Son in someone's life unless he gets rid of the mother as well.

The Devil does his utmost with sinners, so that, after they have lost the grace of God, they may also lose devotion to Mary. When Sarah saw Isaac in company with his half-brother Ishmael, who was teaching him evil habits, she wanted Abraham to drive away both Ishmael and his mother, Hagar (see Gn 21:10). She was not satisfied with having the son turned out of the house, but insisted on having the mother go also. Otherwise, she thought, the son, coming to see his mother, would continue to frequent the house.

In a similar way, the Devil is not satisfied with a soul casting out Jesus Christ, unless it also casts away his mother: "Cast out this woman with her Son." Otherwise, he fears, the mother will again, by her intercession, bring back her Son. "And his fears are well grounded," says the learned scholar Angeli Pacciuchelli; "for the one who is faithful in serving the Mother of God will soon receive God himself by means of his devotion to Mary."

What St. Bernard says is certainly true: "Neither the power nor the will to save us can be lacking to Mary." The power cannot be lacking, for it's impossible that her prayers should not be heard; as St. Antoninus says, "It is impossible that a Mother of God should pray in vain." Neither can the will to save us be lacking, for Mary is our mother, and she desires our salvation more than we can desire it ourselves. Since, then, this is the case, how can it be possible for someone who turns to Mary to be lost? He may be a sinner. But if he entrusts himself to this good mother with perseverance and the intention to change, she will undertake to gain for him light to abandon his wicked state, sorrow for his sins, perseverance in virtue, and in the end, a good death.

—St. Alphonsus Liguori, *The Glories of Mary*

IN GOD'S PRESENCE, CONSIDER . . .

How many people do I know who developed a lively relationship with God through a devotion to Mary? When my devotion to Mary fades, do I find my relationship with God weakening?

CLOSING PRAYER

From a prayer of St. Andrew of Candia: *Holy Virgin, grant me the help of your prayers with God—prayers that stymy my enemies, confound their strategies, and triumph over their strength.*

Mary helps us bear our crosses

St. Alphonsus reminds us that in this world, consolations always come with a cross; but Mary can help us bear the burden.

Our Savior one day appeared to Sister Diomira, a nun in Florence, and said, "Think of me, and love me, and I will think of you and love you." At the same time he presented her with a bouquet of flowers and a cross, signifying through them that the consolations of the saints in this world are always to be accompanied by the cross. The cross unites souls to God.

When St. Jerome Emiliani was a soldier and loaded down with sins, he was imprisoned by his enemies in a tower. There, moved by his misfortunes and enlightened by God to change his life, he turned to the ever-blessed Virgin. From that time forward, by the help of the Mother of God, he began to lead the life of a saint, so much so that he merited once to see the very high place that God had prepared for him in heaven. He became the founder of a religious order, died as a saint, and was canonized by holy Church.

Mary, my sorrowful mother! By the merit of that grief you felt in seeing your beloved Jesus led to death, obtain for me the grace to bear always with patience the crosses that God sends me. Happy indeed shall I be, if only I know how to accompany you with my cross until death.

You with your Jesus—and you were both innocent—have carried a far heavier cross. Shall I, then, a sinner who has deserved hell, refuse to carry mine?

—St. Alphonsus Liguori, *The Glories of Mary*

IN GOD'S PRESENCE, CONSIDER . . .

Which crosses am I bearing just now? How can Mary's example help me to bear those crosses with grace?

CLOSING PRAYER

From a prayer of St. Alphonsus: *Immaculate Virgin, I hope to gain from you the help to bear all crosses with patience.*

Miracles through Mary's intercession

St. Alphonsus challenges skeptics who categorically deny the possibility of miracles in the generations since the Scriptures were written.

Many stories have been told of miracles accomplished through Mary's intervention. But we must note that some people make it a boast that they are free of such notions. They pride themselves on believing that no other miracles have ever taken place than those recorded in the Sacred Scriptures, looking upon all others as tales and old fables.

In this matter it's well to repeat a reasonable observation made by the devout scholar Fr. John Crasset. He notes: "Just as good people easily believe miracles, so are the wicked always ready to ridicule them."

He goes on to say: "It is a weakness to give credit to everything we hear. But on the other hand, the rejection of the possibility of miracles, when they are attested by serious and devout people, suggests one of two attitudes: either lack of faith, because such things are thought to be impossible to God; or presumption, because the credibility of such reliable witnesses is denied."

We normally give credit to a pagan historian from ancient times such as Tacitus or Suetonius. So how can we escape the charge of presumption if we refuse to give credit to writers who are Christian, learned, and proven reliable?

St. Peter Canisius says: "If respectable authors have reported an event with reasonable evidence, and it has not been rejected by learned men, and it is also an account that spiritually edifies our neighbor, then there is less danger in believing and accepting it as true than in rejecting it with a disdainful and presumptuous spirit."

—St. Alphonsus Liguori, *The Glories of Mary*

IN GOD'S PRESENCE, CONSIDER . . .

Do I tend toward skepticism about reported miracles in Christian settings? On the other hand, have I ever witnessed what I would consider to be a miracle, or known someone personally who did?

CLOSING PRAYER

You, Blessed Lady, are yourself a miracle, conceived without sin, and your Son is a miracle, conceived by a virgin. Is there anything impossible for God?

Brought to confession by Mary

St. Alphonsus recalls a story of a husband brought back to confession through a picture of our Blessed Lady.

A woman came to a house of our little religious congregation in this kingdom to let one of the priests know that her husband had not been to Confession for many years. The poor creature could no longer figure how to bring him to his duty. If she mentioned Confession to him, he beat her.

The priest told her to give him a picture of Mary Immaculate. In the evening, the woman once more begged her husband to go to Confession. But as usual, he turned a deaf ear to her entreaties. So she gave him the picture.

Behold! He had scarcely received it from her, when he said, "Well, when will you take me to Confession? For I am willing to go." The wife, on seeing this instantaneous change, began to weep for joy.

In the morning he did indeed come to our church. When the priest asked him how long it had been since he had been to Confession, he answered, "Twenty-eight years." So the priest asked him next what had led him to come that morning.

"Father," he replied, "I was obstinate. But last night my wife gave me a picture of our Blessed Lady. In the same moment, I felt my heart changed—so much so, that during the whole night, every moment seemed a thousand years, so great was my desire to go to Confession."

He then confessed his sins with great contrition, changed his life, and continued for a long time to go frequently to Confession to the same priest.

—St. Alphonsus Liguori, *The Glories of Mary*

IN GOD'S PRESENCE, CONSIDER . . .

Are there particular pictures or other images of Mary that have had special significance for you on a particular occasion or during a particular season in your life? What have they meant to you?

CLOSING PRAYER

From a "Prayer Before an Image of Our Sorrowful Mother": *Most loving mother of my Lord Jesus Christ, behold, poor and sinful, I draw near to your holy image with deep devotion, and beg you to obtain for me the grace to honor and love you with all my strength.*

Call on Mary in temptation

The most common activity of demonic powers is to lead us into temptation. St. Alphonsus reminds us that when we are tempted, we need only call on Mary to send the demons fleeing.

"Glorious indeed, and admirable, is thy name, O Mary!" exclaims St. Bonaventure. "For those who pronounce it at death need not fear all the powers of hell. The demons, on hearing that name, instantly flee, and leave the soul in peace."

The same saint adds: "Men do not fear a powerful hostile army as much as the powers of hell fear the name and protection of Mary."

"You, O Lady," says St. Germanus, "by the simple invocation of your most powerful name, give security to your servants against all the assaults of the enemy."

If only Christians were careful in their temptations to pronounce the name of Mary with confidence, they would never fall. For as Blessed Alan de la Roche remarks, "At the very sound of the words *Hail, Mary!* Satan flies, and hell trembles."

Our Blessed Lady herself revealed to St. Bridget that the enemy flees even from the most abandoned sinners—those who are consequently the furthest from God, and fully possessed by the Devil—if they will only invoke her most powerful name with a true purpose of repentance. "All demons, on hearing this name of Mary, filled with terror, leave the soul." But at the same time our Blessed Lady added: "If the soul does not repent, and wipe out its sins by sorrow, the demons almost immediately return and continue to possess it."

—St. Alphonsus Liguori, *The Glories of Mary*

IN GOD'S PRESENCE, CONSIDER . . .

Do I recognize that Satan is the source of many of the temptations that plague me? Do I keep in mind when I'm being tempted that if I call on Mary, she can help me resist and reject the Enemy's suggestions?

CLOSING PRAYER

From a "Novena to Our Mother of Perpetual Help": *Mother, I fear nothing: not from my sins, because you will obtain pardon for me; nor from the demons, because you are more powerful than all hell together.*

Our Lady of Sorrows saves a youth from the Devil

St. Alphonsus tells how a young man who had sold his soul to the Devil escaped from his clutches through wearing Our Lady's scapular.

A young man in Perugia, I am told, promised the Devil that if he would enable him to attain a sinful goal he had in mind, he would give him his soul. The man then gave the Devil a written contract to this effect, signed in his own blood.

When the crime had been committed, the Devil demanded that the young man keep his promise. For this purpose, he led him to the brink of a well. At the same time, the demon threatened that, if the young man didn't throw himself in, he himself would drag him, body and soul, to hell.

The wretched youth, thinking that it would be impossible to escape from the Devil's hands, climbed up to cast himself in. But terrified at the prospect of death, he told the Devil that he lacked the courage to take the leap. If the demon was determined that the youth must die, he would have to push him in.

The young man wore a scapular of the Sorrows of Mary. So the Devil said, "Take off that scapular, and then I will push you in." But the youth, discovering in the scapular the protection still promised to him by the Mother of God, refused to do so.

Finally, after a heated argument, the Devil departed, filled with humiliation. So the sinner, grateful to his sorrowful mother, went to thank her. Penitent for his sins, he presented a painting of what had taken place, as a votive offering for her altar in the church of Santa Maria la Nuova in Perugia.

—St. Alphonsus Liguori, *The Glories of Mary*

IN GOD'S PRESENCE, CONSIDER . . .

Do I wear a scapular as a sign of my devotion to Mary? If not, have I considered wearing one? Do I recognize that such sacramentals, through the power of the Church's prayers, can dispose me to receive the grace of divine protection from Satan?

CLOSING PRAYER

From a prayer of St. Alphonsus: *Most sorrowful of all mothers, only this thought can console you: Jesus, by his death, conquered hell and opened heaven, which until then had been closed to us; and he has gained so many souls.*

Jesus returns the favor to his mother

Jesus was granted a great favor by his mother, St. Alphonsus observes, when she consented to allow him to take his flesh from her. Now the Son returns the favor by granting her intercessions for us.

St. George of Nicomedia says that Jesus Christ grants all his mother asks, as if to satisfy an obligation under which he placed himself towards her when she consented to give him his human nature. "The Son," he says to Mary, "as if paying a debt, grants all your petitions."

On this same matter the holy martyr St. Methodius exclaims: "Rejoice, rejoice, O Mary, for you have as your debtor that Son who gives to all and receives from none. We are all God's debtors for all that we possess, for all is his gift. But God has been pleased to become your debtor in taking flesh from you and becoming man."

St. Theophilus of Alexandria, in the time of St. Jerome, wrote: "The prayers of his mother are a pleasure to the Son, because he desires to grant all that is granted on her account. In this way he returns to her the favor she did him in giving him his body."

Let's conclude with the words of St. Bonaventure. Considering the great benefit conferred on us by our Lord in giving us Mary for our advocate, he addresses her this way: "O truly immense and admirable goodness of our God, which has been pleased to grant you, O sovereign Mother, to us miserable sinners for our advocate, so that you, by your powerful intercession, may obtain all that you desire for us!"

"O wonderful mercy of our God," he continues, "who, in order that we might not flee because of the sentence that might be pronounced against us, has given us his own mother and the patroness of graces to be our advocate."

—St. Alphonsus Liguori, *The Glories of Mary*

IN GOD'S PRESENCE, CONSIDER . . .

When I think of someone to whom I feel deeply indebted, would my gratitude make me eager to answer that person's request? How eager do I think Jesus is to grant his mother's requests?

CLOSING PRAYER

From a prayer of St. Andrew of Crete: *We beg you, holy Virgin, to grant us the help of your prayers with God; prayers that are more precious than all the treasures of the world; prayers that obtain for us a very great abundance of graces; prayers that confound all enemies.*

Hands filled with mercy and generosity

Don't hesitate to seek Mary's help, counsels St. Alphonsus; in her generosity, she's more eager to grant us graces than we are to receive them!

Do we perhaps fear that Mary doesn't see, or doesn't feel for, our needs? Not at all! She sees and feels them far better than we do ourselves. "There is not one among all the saints," says St. Antoninus, "who can ever feel for us in our miseries, both bodily and spiritual, as does this woman, the most Blessed Virgin Mary." So much so, that wherever she sees misery, she must instantly fly and relieve it with her tender compassion.

The Roman historian Suetonius reports that the Emperor Titus was so eager to render service to those who came to him for help, that when a day passed without his being able to grant a favor, he used to say with sorrow, "I have lost a day; for I have spent it without benefiting anyone."

Now it's probable that Titus spoke in this way more from vanity and the desire to be esteemed, rather than from true charity. But if such a thing were to happen to our Empress Mary, and she had to pass a day without granting a grace, she would speak in the same way Titus did—but from a true desire to serve us, and because she is full of charity.

"Indeed," says the distinguished preacher Bernardine de Bustis, "she is more eager to grant us graces than we are to receive them. Whenever we go to her, we always find her hands filled with mercy and generosity."

—St. Alphonsus Liguori, *The Glories of Mary*

IN GOD'S PRESENCE, CONSIDER . . .

Have I ever found myself eager to help someone who is nevertheless reluctant to ask for help? If that's how Mary is with me, shouldn't I overcome my reluctance and run to her right away?

CLOSING PRAYER

From a prayer of St. Alphonsus: *Lady, pray for me; for you will ask for the graces I need with greater devotion than I can dare to ask for them; and you will obtain far greater graces from God for me than I can presume to seek.*

Help me up when I fall!

St. Alphonsus acknowledges the depth of his sin and weakness, but he runs to Mary to reach out her hand and pull him up.

Mother of God, behold at your feet a miserable sinner, in bondage to hell, who turns to you and trusts in you. I don't deserve that you should even look at me. But because you have seen your Son die for the salvation of sinners, I know that you have the greatest desire to help them.

I hear everyone call you the refuge of sinners, the hope of those who are in despair, and the help of the abandoned. You, then, are my refuge, my hope, and my help. You must save me by your intercession.

Help me, for the love of Jesus Christ. Extend your hand to a miserable creature who has fallen and now entrusts himself to you. I know that your pleasure is to help a sinner to your utmost, so help me, now that you can.

By my sins I have lost divine grace, and with it my soul. I now place myself in your hands. Tell me what I must do to recover the favor of my Lord, and I will immediately do it. He sends me to you so that you may help me. He wills that I should turn to your mercy, so that not only the merits of your Son, but also your intercession, may help me to save my soul.

To you, then, I turn. You who pray for so many others, pray also to Jesus for me. Ask him to pardon me, and he will forgive me. Tell him that you desire my salvation, and he will save me. Show how you can enrich those who trust in you.

—St. Alphonsus Liguori, *The Glories of Mary*

IN GOD'S PRESENCE, CONSIDER . . .

Have I ever fallen and injured myself so that someone had to help me get up again? Have I ever felt that way spiritually? Am I willing to humble myself and ask Mary to help me up again?

CLOSING PRAYER

From a prayer of St. Alphonsus: *O Mother of God, Queen of Angels and hope of men, give ear to one who calls upon you and has recourse to your protection.*

Our Lady provides two friars with lodging

St. Alphonsus tells a story of how the Blessed Virgin rewarded the faithful devotion of two religious who served her.

Two Franciscan friars were going to visit a sanctuary of the Blessed Virgin, when night overtook them in a great forest. They became bewildered and troubled, but they at last discovered a house. They found the door, knocked, and immediately heard someone inside asking who they were. They replied that they were two poor religious brothers who had lost their way in the forest, and they begged at least for shelter, so that they might not be devoured by the wolves. Immediately the doors were thrown open, and two pages richly dressed received them with the greatest courtesy. The religious asked them who resided in that palace. The pages replied that it was a most compassionate Lady. "We would be glad to present her our respects," the friars said, "and thank her for her charity."

"She also wishes to see you," the pages said. They ascended the staircase and entered the Lady's room. She was majestic and most beautiful. She received them with the greatest friendliness and asked them where they were going. They said they were going to visit a certain church of the Blessed Virgin.

"I'll give you a letter before you go," she replied, "which will be of great service to you." They then retired for the night. In the morning the Lady gave them the letter, and they departed. But when they got a short distance from the house, they realized that the letter had no addressee, and when they turned around, they could no longer find the house. Finally, they opened the letter and found that it was from the Virgin Mary, addressed to themselves. She was the Lady who had given them lodging. She exhorted them to continue to serve and love her, for she always would amply reward their devotion, and would help them in life and at death.

—St. Alphonsus Liguori, *The Glories of Mary*

IN GOD'S PRESENCE, CONSIDER . . .

How are Mary's beauty and hospitality in this story suggestive of her virtues and her role in our redemption?

CLOSING PRAYER

In this life and the next, Blessed Mother, let me make my home with you and your Son.

The Church calls us to turn to Mary

St. Alphonsus points to the Church's celebration of Marian feasts and devotions as clear evidence that she invites the faithful to turn often to Our Lady.

Blessed is he who, in the midst of these sorrows, turns often to the comforter of the world, to the refuge of the unfortunate, to the great Mother of God, and devoutly calls upon her and invokes her! The holy Church carefully teaches us, her children, that with attention and confidence we should unceasingly turn to this loving protector. For this purpose, the Church enjoins on us a veneration unique to Mary. And not only this, but she has instituted so many festivals that are celebrated throughout the year in honor of this great queen.

The Church devotes one day in the week, in a special way, to Mary's honor. In the prayers of the Divine Office, all clergy and religious are daily obliged to call upon her in the name of all Christians. Finally, the Church desires that all the faithful should salute this most holy Mother of God three times a day, at the sound of the Angelus bell.

To understand the confidence that the holy Church has in Mary, we need only remember this: In all public calamities, she invariably invites everyone to turn to the protection of this Mother of God, by novenas, prayers, processions, visits to the churches dedicated in her honor, and her images.

And this is what Mary desires; she wishes us always to seek her and invoke her aid. It's not as if she were begging of us the honors and marks of veneration that the Church gives her, for they are in no way in proportion to her merit. But she desires them so that by such means our confidence and devotion may be increased, and she may be able to give us greater assistance and comfort.

—St. Alphonsus Liguori, *The Glories of Mary*

IN GOD'S PRESENCE, CONSIDER . . .

Do I take part enthusiastically in Marian feasts and devotions? Do I recognize that this is one way to deepen my relationship with her as my mother?

CLOSING PRAYER

From the hymn *"O Sanctissima"*: *O most holy, O most loving, sweet Virgin Mary! Beloved mother, undefiled, pray, pray for us. You are solace and refuge, Virgin Mother Mary. Whatever we wish, we hope it through you. Pray, pray for us.*

Celebrate Mary's feasts by imitating her virtues

What's the best way to celebrate Marian feast days? St. Alphonsus suggests that we practice penance and cultivate a virtue.

The best way to celebrate the novenas before Our Lady's feasts is to practice certain interior penances. For example, we can get alone and observe silence. We can refrain from speaking to others impatiently. We can bear challenges and opposition with grace. All these interior penances can be practiced with less danger of vanity and with greater merit.

The most useful spiritual exercise is to resolve from the beginning of the novena to correct some fault into which we fall the most frequently. For this purpose it would be well, when making visits to Our Lady, to ask pardon for past faults, to renew our resolution not to commit them anymore, and to implore Mary's help.

The devotion most dear and pleasing to Mary is to endeavor to imitate her virtues. So it would be well always to commit ourselves to the imitation of some virtue that corresponds with the festival. For example, we can imitate on the Feast of the Immaculate Conception her purity of intention; on her Nativity, renewal of spirit, to throw off lukewarmness; on the Presentation, detachment from something to which we are most attached; on the Annunciation, humility in bearing contempt; on the Visitation, charity toward our neighbor, in giving alms, or at least in praying for sinners; on the Purification, obedience to superiors.

Finally, on the Feast of the Assumption, let's endeavor to detach ourselves from the world, do all we can to prepare ourselves for death, and order each day of our lives as if it will be our last.

—St. Alphonsus Liguori, *The Glories of Mary*

IN GOD'S PRESENCE, CONSIDER . . .

Have I been careful to observe Mary's feast days with some kind of special devotions or penances? If not, how might I celebrate the next Marian day on the Church calendar?

CLOSING PRAYER

Blessed Lady, all days belong to you and your Son. But help us to recall the mysteries of your life and the titles by which we honor you by consecrating your feasts, so that through them, we may consecrate ourselves to your service.

Receive Communion on Mary's feast days

Do I want to honor Mary on her special days? What could honor her more, asks St. Alphonsus, than to unite myself to her Son?

We should receive Holy Communion on Our Lady's feast days, for we cannot honor Mary better than with Jesus. She herself once revealed to a holy soul that we could offer her nothing that was more pleasing to her than Holy Communion. For it's in this holy Sacrament that Jesus gathers the fruit of his passion in our souls.

From this it appears that the Blessed Virgin desires nothing as much as Communion from those who are devoted to her, saying, "Come, eat of my bread, and drink of the wine I have mixed" (Prv 9:5). So after receiving Communion on each of her feast days, we must offer ourselves to the service of this Mother of God, and ask her for the grace to practice whatever virtue or other grace we seek.

It's well every year to choose, among the feasts of the Blessed Virgin, one for which we have the greatest and most tender devotion. Then, for this one, we should make a very special preparation by dedicating ourselves anew, and in a more special way, to her service, choosing her for our sovereign Lady, advocate, and mother.

Finally, we must ask her pardon for all our negligence in her service during the past year, and promise greater faithfulness in the year to come. Then we can conclude by begging her to accept us as her servants, and to obtain for us a holy death.

—St. Alphonsus Liguori, *The Glories of Mary*

IN GOD'S PRESENCE, CONSIDER . . .

Mary's great desire is for us to receive her Son in Holy Communion because of the matchless benefits it brings us. Might it be possible for me to attend Mass more often on weekdays and receive Communion more frequently?

CLOSING PRAYER

O Sacrament most holy! O Sacrament divine! All praise and all thanksgiving be every moment thine!

How to celebrate Marian novenas

What are some specific ways to observe a novena—nine days of special prayer—leading up to one of Our Lady's feast days? St. Alphonsus proposes several possibilities.

Those devoted to Mary are all attention and fervor in celebrating the novenas, or nine days preceding her festivals. And the Blessed Virgin is all love in granting countless and most special graces to them. St. Gertrude one day saw, under Mary's mantle, a band of souls on whom the great Lady was gazing with the most tender affection. She was led to understand that they were persons who, during the preceding days, had prepared themselves with various devotions for the Feast of the Assumption. Here are some devotions that can be used during the novenas before Our Lady's feasts.

First, we can engage in interior prayer in the morning and evening, with a visit to the Blessed Sacrament, adding as well the Our Father, the Hail Mary, and the Glory Be nine times. Second, we can pay Mary three visits by visiting her statue or other image. Each time we are there, we can thank our Lord for the graces he granted her and ask the Blessed Virgin for some special grace.

Third, we can make many acts of love toward Mary (at least fifty or a hundred), and also towards Jesus. For we can do nothing that pleases her more than to love her Son, as she said to St. Bridget: "If you wish to bind yourself to me, love my Son." Fourth, we can read every day of the novena, for a quarter of an hour, some book that talks about her glories.

Fifth, we can perform some bodily penance, such as fasting or abstaining at meals from fruit or some favorite dish; or we can chew some bitter herbs as a penance. On the vigil of the feast we can fast on bread and water. But interior penances are the best of all to practice during these novenas.

—St. Alphonsus Liguori, *The Glories of Mary*

IN GOD'S PRESENCE, CONSIDER . . .

Do I practice any of these devotions or penances during the nine days of a Marian novena? If not, are there some suggestions here I can take to heart?

CLOSING PRAYER

From a prayer of St. John of Damascus: *I salute you, Mary; you are the hope of Christians. Receive the supplication of a sinner who loves you tenderly and honors you in a special way.*

Imitate Mary's charity

St. Alphonsus reminds us that if we want to imitate Mary, we must give ourselves to practicing charity.

"Mary's love for us," says St. Bonaventure, "hasn't diminished now that she's in heaven. It's increased, because she now sees better the miseries of the world. Mary's mercy toward the miserable was great when she was still in exile on earth; but it's far greater now that she reigns in heaven."

Blessed is he, says the Mother of God, who listens to my instructions, pays attention to my love and, in imitation of me, practices it himself toward others: "Happy is the man who listens to me, watching daily at my gates, waiting beside my doors" (Prv 8:34). St. Gregory Nazianzen assures us that "there is nothing by which we can with greater certainty gain the affection of Mary than by charity towards our neighbor."

In the same way that God exhorts us, saying, "Be merciful, even as your Father is merciful" (Lk 6:36), so also Mary seems to say to all her children, "Be merciful, even as your mother is merciful." It's certain that our charity toward our neighbor will be the measure of the mercy that both God and Mary will show us: "Give, and it will be given to you. For the measure you give will be the measure you get back" (Lk 6:38).

St. Methodius used to say, "Give to the poor, and receive paradise." St. John Chrysostom once reflected on these words of Proverbs: "He who is kind to the poor lends to the LORD" (Prv 19:17). He remarked: "He who assists the needy makes God his debtor."

Mother of Mercy, you are full of charity for all. Don't forget my miseries; you see them clearly. Entrust me to God, who denies you nothing. Obtain for me the grace to imitate you in holy charity, toward God as well as toward my neighbor.

—St. Alphonsus Liguori, *The Glories of Mary*

IN GOD'S PRESENCE, CONSIDER . . .

Our devotion to Mary should turn us outward as well as inward. Am I making a regular effort to practice charity, both to strangers and to those I know?

CLOSING PRAYER

From a prayer of Blessed Mother Teresa: *Mary, give me your heart: so beautiful, so pure, so immaculate; your heart so full of love and humility that I may be able to receive Jesus in the Bread of Life and love him as you love him, and serve him in the distressing guise of the poor.*

Imitate Mary's faith

A lively faith is one that puts belief into practice, St. Alphonsus reminds us. It's the kind of faith Our Lady had, and we should imitate it.

We must imitate Mary's faith. But how can we do so? Faith, at the same time that it's a gift, is also a virtue. It's a gift of God in that it's a light infused by him into our souls. But it's a virtue in that the soul must exercise itself to practice it. For this reason, faith is not only to be the rule of our belief, but also the rule of our actions. That's why St. Gregory the Great says, "The one who truly believes is the one who puts what he believes in practice." St. Augustine adds: "You say, 'I believe.' Well, then, do what you say, and that is faith."

This is to have a lively faith, to live according to our belief. "My righteous one shall live by faith" (Heb 10:38). In this way the Blessed Virgin lived very differently from those who don't live in accordance with what they believe, and whose faith is dead, as St. James declares: "Faith, apart from works, is dead" (Jas 2:26). The ancient Greek philosopher Diogenes sought for an honest man on earth. But God, among the many faithful, seems to seek for a real Christian. For only a few have good works; the greater part have only the name of Christian.

To such people as these should be applied the words once addressed by Alexander the Great to a cowardly soldier who was also named Alexander: "Either change your name or change your conduct." For this reason, St. Augustine exhorts us to see things with the eyes of Christians—that is to say, with eyes that look at everything in the light of faith. For as St. Teresa of Avila often said, all sins come from a lack of faith. So let's beg the most holy Virgin, by the merit of her faith, to obtain for us a lively faith: "O Lady, increase our faith."

—St. Alphonsus Liguori, *The Glories of Mary*

IN GOD'S PRESENCE, CONSIDER . . .

When I consider to what extent my faith is expressed in works, would I say that my faith is lively? Lazy? Comatose? Perhaps even dead? Have I asked Mary to increase and enliven my faith?

CLOSING PRAYER

My Lord, even the demons believe in God, and they tremble in fear (see Jas 2:19). Let me believe in such a way that I tremble, not with fear, but with eagerness to do your will, so that by my works I may show my faith (see Jas 2:18).

Mary exercised perfect faith

If we're looking for a perfect model of faith, St. Alphonsus says, we can look to Mary.

The theologian Francisco Suárez teaches that the most holy Virgin had more faith than all men and angels.

She saw her Son in the crib of Bethlehem, yet she believed him to be the Creator of the world. She saw him flee from Herod, yet she believed him to be the King of kings. She saw him born, yet she believed him to be eternal.

She saw him poor and in need of food, yet she believed him to be the Lord of the universe. She saw him lying on straw, yet she believed him to be omnipotent. She observed that he didn't speak, yet she believed him to be infinite wisdom. She heard him weeping, yet she believed him to be the joy of paradise.

And in the end, she saw him in death, despised and crucified; yet even though faith wavered in others, she remained firm in the belief that he was God. On these words of the Gospel, "standing by the cross of Jesus [was] his mother" (Jn 19:25), St. Antoninus says: "Mary stood, supported by her faith, which she retained, firm in the divinity of Christ."

St. Albert the Great assures us that in this moment, "Mary exercised perfect faith. For even when the disciples were doubting, she did not doubt." So Mary merited by her great faith to become "the light of all the faithful," as St. Methodius calls her; and the "queen of the true faith," as she is called by St. Cyril of Alexandria. In fact, in her liturgy, the holy Church herself attributes to the merits of Mary's faith the destruction of all heresies: "Rejoice, O Virgin Mary, for you alone have destroyed all heresies throughout the world."

—St. Alphonsus Liguori, *The Glories of Mary*

IN GOD'S PRESENCE, CONSIDER . . .

Are there particular matters of faith that cause me difficulties or even doubts? Have I asked Mary to help me overcome those difficulties and doubts?

CLOSING PRAYER

Blessed Mother, if "faith is the assurance of things hoped for, the conviction of things not seen" (Heb 11:1), then you are indeed a perfect model of faith, and the mother of all the faithful. Be my mother, and show me how to increase my faith.

Imitate Mary's humility

We can never be true children of Mary, St. Alphonsus warns, if we aren't humble.

On one occasion our Lord showed St. Bridget two ladies. One was all pomp and vanity. "She is Pride," the Lord said. "But the other one you see with her head bent down, courteous toward all, having God alone in mind, and considering herself as no one, is Humility. Her name is Mary." In this revelation, God was pleased to make known to us that the humility of his blessed Mother is so great that she is humility itself.

There can be no doubt, as St. Gregory of Nyssa says of humility, that of all virtues, perhaps none is more difficult to our nature to practice, given that our nature is corrupted by sin. But there is no alternative. We can never be true children of Mary if we aren't humble.

St. Bernard observes: "If you can't imitate the virginity of this humble Virgin, imitate her humility." She detests the proud, and she invites only the humble to come to her, saying, "Whoever is a little one, let him come to me" (see Prv 9:4).

"Mary protects us under the mantle of humility," says Richard of Saint Lawrence. The Mother of God herself explained what her mantle was to St. Bridget, saying, "Come, my daughter, and hide yourself under my mantle; this mantle is my humility."

She then added that the consideration of her humility was a good mantle with which we could warm ourselves. But just as a mantle warms only those who actually wear it, rather than just think about wearing it, "so also her humility is of no avail except to those who endeavor to imitate it. . . . Therefore, my daughter, clothe yourself with this humility."

—St. Alphonsus Liguori, *The Glories of Mary*

IN GOD'S PRESENCE, CONSIDER . . .

In which events and circumstances of her life do I see Mary practicing humility? How can I imitate her?

CLOSING PRAYER

From a prayer of St. Alphonsus: *My Queen, I can never be really your child unless I am humble. But my sins have made me proud. My Mother, supply a remedy. By the merit of your humility, obtain for me that I may be truly humble, and thus become your child.*

Imitate Mary's patience

If Mary is to be our model, says St. Alphonsus, we need to imitate her patience; for it's patience that makes saints.

If we wish to be the children of Mary, we must seek to imitate her in her patience. "For what can enrich us with greater merit in this life," asks St. Cyprian, "and greater glory in the next, than the patient endurance of sufferings?" Just as a hedge of thorns protects a vineyard, God protects his servants from the danger of attaching themselves to the things of this world by encompassing them with tribulations. For this reason, St. Cyprian concludes, it's patience that delivers us from sin and from hell. It's also patience that makes saints: "Let patience have its full effect, that you may be perfect and complete, lacking nothing" (see Jas 1:4). We must bear in peace, not only the crosses that come immediately from God, such as sickness and poverty, but also those that come from other people: persecutions, injuries, and all the rest.

St. John saw all the saints bearing palm branches—the emblem of martyrdom—in their hands: "After this I looked, and behold, a great multitude . . . with palm branches in their hands" (Rv 7:9). These branches mean that all adults who are saved must be martyrs, either by shedding their blood for Christ or by patience. "Rejoice, then!" exclaims St. Gregory. "We can be martyrs without the executioner's sword, if we only maintain patience." "Provided only," as St. Bernard says, "we endure the afflictions of this life with patience and joy."

What fruit will be produced for us in heaven by every pain borne for God's sake! That's why the Apostle Paul encourages us with these words: "For this slight momentary affliction is preparing for us an eternal weight of glory beyond all comparison" (2 Cor 4:17). When our crosses weigh heavily upon us, let's turn to Mary, who is called by the Church "the Comforter of the Afflicted."

—St. Alphonsus Liguori, *The Glories of Mary*

IN GOD'S PRESENCE, CONSIDER . . .

In which areas of my life do I need most to learn the virtue of patience? In particular, which people in my life are challenging me to exercise patience and endurance?

CLOSING PRAYER

From a prayer of St. Alphonsus: *My most sweet Lady, you who were innocent suffered with so much patience. Should I, who deserve condemnation, refuse to suffer? My Mother, I now ask you this favor: not to be delivered from crosses, but to bear them with patience.*

Mary was perfectly obedient to God

Because of her freedom from original sin, St. Alphonsus explains, Our Lady could be more perfectly obedient to God than all the other saints.

When the angel Gabriel announced to Mary God's great plans for her, because of her love for obedience she would call herself only a handmaid: "Behold, I am the handmaid of the Lord" (Lk 1:38). "Yes," says St. Thomas of Villanova, "for this faithful handmaid never, in either thought or word or deed, contradicted the Most High. Instead, having entirely laid aside her own will, she lived always and in all things obedient to that of God."

Mary herself declared that God was pleased with her obedience when she said, "He has regarded the humility of his handmaiden" (see Lk 1:48). For the humility of a servant, properly speaking, consists in prompt obedience.

St. Irenaeus says that by her obedience, the Mother of God repaired the evil done by Eve's disobedience: "As Eve, by her disobedience, caused her own death and that of the whole human race, so did the Virgin Mary, by her obedience, become the cause of her own salvation and of that of all mankind." Mary's obedience was much more perfect than that of all other saints, since all people, on account of original sin, are prone to evil, and find it difficult to do good. But not so the Blessed Virgin.

St. Bernardine writes: "Because Mary was free from original sin, she found no obstacle in obeying God. She was like a wheel, which was easily turned by every inspiration of the Holy Spirit. . . . Her only goal in this world was to keep her eyes constantly fixed on God, to discover his will and, when she had found out what he required, to perform it."

—St. Alphonsus Liguori, *The Glories of Mary*

IN GOD'S PRESENCE, CONSIDER . . .

Is there any area of my life in which am I knowingly disobeying God's will for me? How might I become obedient with Mary's help?

CLOSING PRAYER

From a prayer of Venerable Pope Pius XII: *Through your powerful intercession, O Mary, may minds and hearts find repose in abandoning themselves to the will of the heavenly Father, in the consciousness of their frailty, with faith in divine promises, in the hope of eternal blessings, and in adhering lovingly to your crucified Jesus who has made our crosses his own.*

In Mary, all the virtues of the saints unite

Each saint excels in certain heroic virtues, St. Alphonsus declares, but Mary excels in them all.

In each of the saints there were different graces. As St. Paul says, "there are varieties of gifts" (1 Cor 12:4). Each of the saints, by cooperating with the grace he had received, excelled in some particular virtue: one in saving souls, another in leading a penitential life; one in enduring torments, another in a life of prayer.

This is the reason why the holy Church, in the liturgy celebrating the festivals of the saints, says of each one: "There was not found another one like him." And as in their merits they differ, so do they differ in heavenly glory: "for star differs from star in glory" (1 Cor 15:41). Apostles differ from martyrs, confessors from virgins, the innocent from penitents.

The Blessed Virgin, being full of all graces, excelled each saint in every particular virtue. She was the apostle of the apostles. She was the Queen of Martyrs, for she suffered more than all of them. She was the standard-bearer of virgins and the model of married people. She united in herself perfect innocence and perfect mortification.

In short, Mary united in her heart all the most heroic virtues that any saint ever practiced. All the graces, privileges, and merits of the other saints were all joined in Mary. She possessed them to such a degree that, as St. Basil of Seleucia says, "As the splendor of the sun exceeds that of all the stars united, so does Mary's glory exceed that of all the blessed."

—St. Alphonsus Liguori, *The Glories of Mary*

IN GOD'S PRESENCE, CONSIDER . . .

Which virtue do I think I need most to cultivate? How does Mary provide me a model for that particular virtue?

CLOSING PRAYER

Blessed Lady, just as all the colors of the spectrum, when they converge, form the brilliant white of pure light, so in your soul all the virtues converge, so that you shine with the pure light of heaven.

Mary was poor

St. Alphonsus tells how Mary's detachment from worldly goods allowed her to be content in poverty.

Our most loving Redeemer, so that we might learn from him to despise the things of the world, was pleased to be poor on earth: "Though he was rich," says St. Paul, "for your sake he became poor, so that by his poverty you might become rich" (2 Cor 8:9). For this reason Jesus Christ exhorts each one who desires to be his disciple: "If you would be perfect, go, sell what you possess and give to the poor . . . and come follow me" (Mt 19:21).

Behold Mary, his most perfect disciple, who indeed imitated his example. Out of love for poverty she did not disdain to marry St. Joseph, who was only a poor carpenter. An angel, speaking of Mary, told St. Bridget that "worldly riches were of no more value in her eyes than dirt." At her purification in the temple she didn't offer a lamb, which was the offering prescribed in Leviticus for those who could afford it (see Lv 12:6). Instead, she offered two turtledoves, or two pigeons, which was the offering prescribed for the poor (see Lk 2:24).

In a word, Mary always lived poor, and she died poor. At her death, as far as we know, she left nothing but two poor gowns, to two women who had served her during her life, as it's recorded by two ancient historians. St. Philip Neri used to say that "whoever loves the things of the world will never become a saint." We may add what St. Teresa said on the same subject: "Whoever runs after perishable things will himself perish as well." For this reason Jesus Christ said, "Blessed are the poor in spirit, for theirs is the kingdom of heaven" (Mt 5:3). They are blessed because they desire nothing but God, and in God they find every good. In poverty they find their paradise on earth, as St. Francis did when he exclaimed, "My God and my all."

—St. Alphonsus Liguori, *The Glories of Mary*

IN GOD'S PRESENCE, CONSIDER . . .

Am I content with what I have? Or do I sometimes find myself too attached to possessions? How might I learn to let go?

CLOSING PRAYER

From a prayer of St. Alphonsus: *My most holy Mother, in this world you desired and loved no other good but God. "Draw me after you" (Sg 1:3), my Lady! Detach me from the world, so that I may love him alone, who alone deserves to be loved.*

Mary supports us in the journey of life

Pope Leo XIII recognizes the difficulties of our journey toward heaven, but he's confident that we can reach our destination safely if we hold Mary's hand as we walk.

In Mary we see how a truly good and provident God has established for us a most suitable example of every virtue. As we look upon her and think about her, we are not cast down as though stricken by the overpowering splendor of God's power. On the contrary, attracted by the closeness of the common nature we share with her, we strive with greater confidence to imitate her. If we, with her powerful help, should dedicate ourselves wholly and entirely to this undertaking, we can portray at least an outline of such great virtue and sanctity, and reproducing that perfect conformity of our lives to all God's designs which she possessed in so marvelous a degree, we shall follow her into heaven.

Undaunted and full of courage, let's go on with the pilgrimage we have undertaken, even though the way should be rough and full of obstacles. Amid the trouble and toil, let's not cease to hold out suppliant hands to Mary with the words of the Church: "To thee do we send up our sighs, mourning and weeping in this valley of tears; turn then, most gracious advocate, thine eyes of mercy toward us. . . . Keep our lives all spotless, make our ways secure, till we find in Jesus joys that will endure."

Although she was never subject to the frailty and perversity of our nature, Mary well knows its condition and is the best and most solicitous of mothers. How willingly will she hasten to our aid when we need her; with what love will she refresh us, and with what strength sustain us. For those of us who follow the journey hallowed by the blood of Christ and by the tears of Mary, our entrance into their company and the enjoyment of their most blessed glory will be certain and easy.

—Pope Leo XIII, *Magnae Dei Matris*

IN GOD'S PRESENCE, CONSIDER . . .

Do I sometimes grow weary, wondering whether I'll ever make it home safely to heaven? In times of discouragement, have I learned to lean hard on Mary?

CLOSING PRAYER

From a prayer of Blessed John Henry Newman: *O hope of the pilgrim! Lead us still as you have led; in the dark night, across the bleak wilderness, guide us on to our Lord Jesus; guide us home.*

In heaven Mary is better able to help us

*We should rejoice in Mary's exalted position in heaven, says St. Alphonsus.
Not only should we be glad for her blessedness; we should be grateful that she's
better able to help us there.*

St. Bernardine of Siena teaches, with St. Bernard, that the saints have
a share in the divine glory. But the Blessed Virgin has been, in a certain way, so
greatly enriched with it, that it seems no creature could be more closely united
with God than Mary is: "She has penetrated into the bottom of the deep, and
she seems immersed as deeply as it is possible for a creature in that inaccessible
light." St. Albert the Great confirms this insight, saying that our queen "con-
templates the majesty of God in incomparably closer proximity than all other
creatures."

Let's rejoice, then, with Mary that God has exalted her to so high a throne
in heaven. Let's also rejoice on our own account. For even though our mother is
no longer present with us on earth, having ascended in glory to heaven, yet she's
always with us in affection. In fact, since she's nearer to God there, she knows
better our miseries; her pity for us is greater; and she's better able to help us.

"If Mary's compassion for the miserable was great when she lived on earth,"
says St. Bonaventure, "it's far greater now that she reigns in heaven." In the
meantime, then, let's dedicate ourselves to the service of this queen, to honor
and love her as much as we can. For, as Richard of Saint Lawrence remarks,
"She's not like other rulers, who oppress their vassals with burdens and taxes.
Instead, she enriches her servants with graces, merits, and rewards."

—St. Alphonsus Liguori, *The Glories of Mary*

IN GOD'S PRESENCE, CONSIDER . . .

If I were rescued from a burning house, but my children were still in danger
inside, would I be less likely, or more, to be concerned with helping my children to
safety? Now that Mary is safely in heaven, wouldn't she feel the same way about
her children still in danger on earth?

CLOSING PRAYER

From a prayer of Guarric, Abbot of Igniac: *Mother of Mercy, you who sit on so
lofty a throne and in such close proximity to God, enjoy your fill of the glory of your Jesus; and
send us, your servants, the fragments that are left.*

Jesus and Mary are inseparable

St. Ignatius of Loyola insists that Jesus cannot be separated from Mary; they have been united from the beginning, on earth and in heaven.

The holy soul of Mary is united to the soul of Jesus, which is worthy of our adoration. She conceived him in her heart before receiving him in her bosom, says St. Bernard. She unites herself to him by the most lively faith, the most fiery charity, by her consent, whose memory we revere in the Angelus prayer three times a day, and which joins her with her whole destiny. So Mary is found with Jesus at Bethlehem, in Egypt, in Nazareth, in Jerusalem, and above all on Calvary, where the sword of sorrow pierced her soul when the lance opened the heart of her divine Son.

Jesus ascends to heaven, and Mary is soon placed at his right hand, that is, united with his glory and his all-powerful action in the salvation of the world. She is united to the King of heaven by a union beyond words. Here on earth the Son and the mother are united in the praises of the Fathers of the Church, in the prayers of the Christian liturgy, in the definitions of councils, in the solemnities of the Church. We see Christians honoring, always in union, the incarnation of Jesus, the conception of Mary; the birth of Jesus, the nativity of Mary; the presentation of Jesus, the presentation of Mary; the baptism of Jesus, the purification of Mary; the sufferings of Jesus, the sorrows of Mary; the ascension of Jesus, the assumption of Mary; the sacred heart of Jesus, the holy heart of Mary.

The names of Jesus and Mary live always united in the hearts and the songs of the faithful. Their temples and their altars are always near together, and nothing is more inseparable in their pious remembrances, their confidence, their invocation, their love, than Jesus and Mary.

—St. Ignatius Loyola, *The Spiritual Exercises*

IN GOD'S PRESENCE, CONSIDER . . .

If Jesus and Mary are inseparable, is it possible to embrace one without embracing the other?

CLOSING PRAYER

From a prayer of St. Alphonsus Rodriguez: *Jesus and Mary, my most sweet loves, for you may I suffer; for you may I die. Grant that I may be in all things yours, and in nothing, mine.*

Mary follows our footsteps

Pope Benedict XVI urges those who live without faith, or as if they had no faith, to open themselves to the mystery of God by contemplating Mary.

Some people today live as if they never had to die or as if, with death, everything were over; others, who hold that man is the one and only author of his own destiny, behave as though God did not exist, and at times they even reach the point of denying that there is room for him in our world. Yet the great breakthroughs of technology and science that have considerably improved humanity's condition leave unresolved the deepest searchings of the human soul.

Only openness to the mystery of God, who is Love, can quench the thirst for truth and happiness in our hearts; only the prospect of eternity can give authentic value to historical events and especially to the mystery of human frailty, suffering, and death.

By contemplating Mary in heavenly glory, we understand that the earth is not the definitive homeland for us either, and that if we live with our gaze fixed on eternal goods, we will one day share in this same glory and the earth will become more beautiful. Consequently, we must not lose our serenity and peace even amid the thousands of daily difficulties. The luminous sign of Our Lady taken up into heaven shines out even more brightly when sad shadows of suffering and violence seem to loom on the horizon.

We may be sure of it: From on high, Mary follows our footsteps with gentle concern, dispels the gloom in moments of darkness and distress, reassures us with her motherly hand. Supported by awareness of this, let us continue confidently on our path of Christian commitment wherever Providence may lead us. Let us forge ahead in our lives under Mary's guidance.

—Pope Benedict XVI, "Mary, the Exemplar"

IN GOD'S PRESENCE, CONSIDER . . .

How much room in my everyday life do I give to God? Does my devotion to Mary help to expand that space?

CLOSING PRAYER

From a prayer of Pope St. John Paul II: *Mary, be our mother. Share with us your limitless faith. Take and keep us within your protective arms in a world that has largely lost faith and abandoned hope.*

Mary invites us to give Jesus our hearts

Mary calls us to give ourselves completely to her Son, and St. Alphonsus urges us to accept that invitation.

Let's cease to torment this afflicted mother. And if until now we've grieved her by our sins, let's now do all that she desires. She says, "Return, you transgressors, to the heart" (see Is 46:8). Sinners, return to the wounded heart of my Jesus. Return as penitents, and he will welcome you.

"Flee from him to him," Abbot Guarric imagines her saying, "from the Judge to the Redeemer, from the Tribunal to the Cross." Our Blessed Lady herself revealed to St. Bridget that "she closed the eyes of her Son, when he was taken down from the Cross, but she could not close his arms." Through this, Jesus Christ meant for us to understand that he desired to remain with his arms extended to receive all penitent sinners who return to him.

"World!" continues Mary. "Look! 'Your time is the time of lovers' (see Ez 16:8). Now that my Son has died to save you, it's no longer for you a time of fear, but one of love—a time to love the One who was pleased to suffer so much to show you the love he had for you." "The heart of Jesus was wounded," says St. Bernard, "so that through the visible wound, the invisible wound of love might be seen."

"My Son, in the abundance of love, was pleased that his side should be pierced open, so that he might give you his heart," Mary concludes, in the words of Blessed Raymond Jordano. "So it's only right that you in return should also give him yours."

"And if you desire, children of Mary, to find a place in the heart of Jesus without fear of being rejected, go, go with Mary," says Ubertino da Casale. "For she will obtain the necessary grace for you."

—St. Alphonsus Liguori, *The Glories of Mary*

IN GOD'S PRESENCE, CONSIDER . . .

Is here anything in my life that seems to be keeping me from giving myself wholeheartedly to Jesus? Have I asked Mary's help to overcome it?

CLOSING PRAYER

From a prayer of St. Alphonsus: *Mother, pity me, for instead of loving God, I have greatly offended him. Your sorrows encourage me to hope for pardon. But this isn't enough. I want to love my Lord; and who can better obtain for me this love than you, who are the Mother of Fair Love?*

What do we owe Mary?

We often focus on the help we can receive from Mary. But have we carefully considered what we owe her as our mother? St. Ignatius of Loyola explains.

We owe to our mother love, confidence, imitation, and zeal to spread devotion to her.

First, we owe *love* to her who is the beloved of our Lord; gratitude toward her who has loaded us with benefits; the affection of a child for our mother.

Second, we owe her our *confidence*. Her power and her title of mother were given to her so that our trust in her might be unlimited, so that we might know that she would always be able and willing to help us.

Third, we owe her our *imitation*. She expects from us this proof of true love. Doesn't the child naturally resemble the mother? Let this resemblance in us be the fruit of our efforts, of a careful study and practice of her virtues. Sons of a virgin, let's be pure; sons of the mother of sorrows, let's be faithful to Jesus, even to the Cross.

Fourth, we owe her *zeal* to spread her devotion. A sincere love will produce this zeal. We must praise and defend all the devotional practices authorized by the Church. Her images must be venerated and given to others. We must love to bear her insignia, visit the places where she is honored, take pleasure in singing her praises, prepare for her feasts by penance, and sanctify them by the reception of the holy Eucharist. Let's honor the sacred heart of Mary, and honor it by a special devotion.

—St. Ignatius Loyola, *The Spiritual Exercises*

IN GOD'S PRESENCE, CONSIDER . . .

Have I considered what I owe to Mary as my mother? In what specific ways today can I offer to her what I owe?

CLOSING PRAYER

From a prayer of St. Maximillian Kolbe: *Immaculata, Queen and Mother of the Church, I renew my consecration to you for this day and for always, so that you might use me for the coming of the kingdom of Jesus in the whole world. To this end I offer you all my prayers, actions, and sacrifices of this day.*

God was drawn to Mary's humility

Humility is essential to all the other virtues, St. Alphonsus teaches, and Mary had humility in perfection.

Humility is the foundation of all the virtues, as the holy Fathers of the Church have taught. Let's consider, then, how great was the humility of the Mother of God.

"Humility," says St. Bernard, "is not only the foundation, but also the guardian of virtues." He says this with good reason, for without it no other virtue can exist in a soul. Even if a soul has all the virtues, they all will depart when humility is gone.

On the other hand, as St. Francis de Sales wrote to St. Jane de Chantal: "God so loves humility, that wherever he sees it, he is immediately drawn there."

This beautiful and so necessary virtue was unknown in the world. But the Son of God himself came to earth to teach humility by his own example. He willed that in this virtue in particular, we should endeavor to imitate him: "Learn from me, because I am meek and humble of heart" (see Mt 11:29).

Mary, being the first and most perfect disciple of Jesus Christ in the practice of all virtues, was the first also in the virtue of humility. By it she merited to be exalted above all creatures. It was revealed to St. Matilda that the first virtue the Blessed Mother especially practiced, from her very childhood, was that of humility.

—St. Alphonsus Liguori, *The Glories of Mary*

IN GOD'S PRESENCE, CONSIDER . . .

In which areas of my life do I face the greatest struggles in practicing humility? Have I asked Mary for help specifically in those areas?

CLOSING PRAYER

Lord, "you deliver a humble people, but the haughty eyes you bring down" (Ps 18:27).

Mary knew herself truly

Mary was humble because she had true self-knowledge, St. Alphonsus observes, and she knew her utter dependence on God's grace.

The first effect of humility of heart is a modest opinion of ourselves. Mary always had so humble an opinion of herself that, as it was revealed to St. Matilda, even though she saw herself enriched with greater graces than all other creatures, she never preferred herself to anyone else.

This is not to say, of course, that Mary considered herself a sinner. For humility is truth, as St. Teresa remarks; and Mary knew that she had never offended God. Nor was it that she failed to acknowledge that she had received greater graces from God than all other creatures. For a humble heart always acknowledges the special favors of the Lord, in order to humble itself all the more.

Instead, the Mother of God, by the greater light through which she knew the infinite greatness and goodness of God, also knew her own nothingness. For this reason, more than all others, she humbled herself. Yes, says St. Bernardine, for "the Blessed Virgin always had the majesty of God, and her own nothingness, present to her mind."

When a beggar is clothed with a rich garment that has been given to her, she doesn't pride herself on it in the presence of the giver. Instead, she's humbled, because it reminds her of her own poverty.

In the same way, the more Mary saw herself enriched, the more she humbled herself, remembering that all was God's gift. For this reason, St. Bernardine says: "After the Son of God, no creature in the world was so exalted as Mary, because no creature in the world ever humbled itself so much as she did."

—St. Alphonsus Liguori, *The Glories of Mary*

IN GOD'S PRESENCE, CONSIDER . . .

Have I sometimes labored under a false understanding of what true humility is? Does humility mean denying the gifts I have—or acknowledging, with gratitude, their Giver?

CLOSING PRAYER

Lord, teach me to know myself truly, and to know that there is nothing I have that I didn't receive as a gift from you (see 1 Cor 4:7).

Devotions to Mary should be joined with holiness

Even lavish devotions to Mary, says St. Alphonsus, are useless if they aren't joined to personal holiness.

"The Queen of Heaven is so gracious and generous," says St. Andrew of Crete, "that she rewards her servants with the greatest lavishness for the smallest devotions." But there are conditions to this generosity. When we offer her our devotions, our souls should be free from sin. Otherwise, she might say to us what she said to a wicked soldier, once spoken of by St. Peter Celestine.

This soldier every day performed some devotion in honor of our Blessed Lady. One day he was suffering greatly from hunger, when Mary appeared to him and offered him some most delicious meats. But they were in such a filthy vessel that he couldn't bring himself to taste them.

"I am the Mother of God," the Blessed Virgin then said, "and I have come to satisfy your hunger."

"But, Lady," he answered, "I can't eat out of such a dirty vessel."

"And how," replied Mary, "can you expect me to accept your devotions, offered to me with so defiled a soul as yours?"

On hearing this, the soldier was converted, became a hermit, and lived in a desert for thirty years. At his death, the Blessed Virgin again appeared to him, and took him herself to heaven.

It's been said that it's morally impossible for someone devoted to Mary to be lost. But this statement must be understood to have the condition that he lives either without sin, or at least lives with the desire to abandon it. For then the Blessed Virgin will help him. But if anyone, on the other hand, should sin in the hope that Mary will save him, he would render himself unworthy and unable to enjoy her protection.

—St. Alphonsus Liguori, *The Glories of Mary*

IN GOD'S PRESENCE, CONSIDER . . .

Do I ever find myself practicing exterior devotions to Mary while consciously disobeying God on some matter? What do I hope to gain from such devotions if my heart is in rebellion against God?

CLOSING PRAYER

Mary, help me hide these words in my heart: "The sacrifice of the wicked is detestable; how much more when he brings it with evil intent" (see Prv 21:27).

Through the Holy Spirit

In this prayer, St. Ildephonsus of Spain recognizes the essential role of the Holy Spirit, both in Mary's life and in ours.

Virgin Mary, hear my prayer!
Through the Holy Spirit,
    you became the mother of Jesus.
From the Holy Spirit,
    let Jesus become mine as well.
Through the Holy Spirit,
    your flesh conceived Jesus.
Through the same Spirit,
    let my soul receive Jesus.
Through the Holy Spirit,
    you were able to know Jesus, to have him,
    and to bring him into the world.
Through the Holy Spirit,
Let me come to know Jesus as well.
Filled with the Spirit, Mary,
    you could say, "I am the handmaid of the Lord,
    be it done unto me according to your word."
In the Holy Spirit, despite my lowliness,
    let me speak exalted things about Jesus.
In the Spirit you now adore Jesus as Lord
    and contemplate him as your Son.
In the same Spirit, Mary,
    let me love Jesus.

—St. Ildephonsus of Spain

IN GOD'S PRESENCE, CONSIDER . . .

The Holy Spirit has been called the Person of the Blessed Trinity who is most neglected by Christians. Have I considered the essential role he plays in my life and the life of the Church? Have I asked him to fill me as he filled Mary?

CLOSING PRAYER

With Mary, I pray: Come, Holy Spirit, fill the hearts of your faithful, and kindle in them the fire of your love.

Mary appears to Brother Conrad

The Little Flowers of St. Francis of Assisi collects anecdotes from the lives of the saint and his first followers. In this story, Brother Conrad and Brother Peter discover the sweetness of seeing Our Lady and her Child.

One day, Brother Conrad went into the forest to meditate on God. Brother Peter followed him to see what would happen to him. Brother Conrad began to beg the Virgin Mary, with great fervor and devotion, to obtain from her blessed Son that he might experience something of the sweetness that St. Simeon had experienced on the day of her purification in the temple.

When he had finished this prayer, the Virgin Mary obtained his request, and behold! the Queen of Heaven appeared in great splendor, with her blessed Son in her arms. Approaching Brother Conrad, she placed the holy Child in his arms. He received him most reverently and, embracing him, clasped him to his breast. His heart was overflowing with divine love and inexpressible consolation. Brother Peter, who witnessed this scene at a distance, felt in his soul as well great sweetness and joy.

When the Virgin Mary had departed from Brother Conrad, Brother Peter hurried back to the convent so that he might not be seen. But when Brother Conrad arrived, full of joy and happiness, Brother Peter said to him: "Brother, you've received great consolation today!"

"What are you saying, Brother Peter?" Brother Conrad answered. "How do you know? Have you seen me?"

"I know," answered Brother Peter, "that the Virgin Mary, with her blessed Son, has visited you." And Brother Conrad, because of his great humility, wanted to keep secret the grace with which God had favored him. So he begged Brother Peter to tell no one. From then on, so great was the love between these two brothers that they seemed to have only one heart and soul in all things.

—*The Little Flowers of St. Francis of Assisi*

IN GOD'S PRESENCE, CONSIDER . . .

Mary could have appeared to Brother Conrad without appearing to Brother Peter. Why, do I think, did she reveal herself to both friars, even though Peter had come only to satisfy his curiosity? How did this experience form such a close bond between the two men?

CLOSING PRAYER

From a prayer of St. Ildephonsus: *Mother of God, grant me the grace to unite myself in affection with your Son as my God, and with you as the Mother of my God.*

Mary rescues a priest from sin

St. Alphonsus recounts a story from the life of St. Francis Borgia, when a priest who was desperately in need of repentance receives help from Mary.

"Father," a priest once confessed to an associate of St. Francis Borgia, "I'm a priest and a preacher, but I'm living in sin, and I despair of God's mercy. One day I preached a sermon against those who are obstinate in sin and afterward despair of God's mercy. Then someone came to me for Confession. Having told me all my own sins, he said he despaired of God's mercy. As was my duty, I told him he must change his life and trust in God. On hearing this, the penitent stood up and reproved me, saying: 'You who preach to others, why don't you change your life and trust in God? I am an angel who has come to help you. Change your life, and you will be forgiven.' With these words he disappeared.

"I gave up my sins for a few days, but an occasion presented itself, and I fell again. On another day I was saying Mass, and Jesus Christ, in the Sacred Host, audibly said to me: 'Why do you mistreat me this way, when I treat you so well?' After this I resolved to change my ways, but on the next occasion, I fell again.

"A few hours ago I was in my room when a young man appeared. He drew a chalice from his cloak, and from it a consecrated Host, saying: 'Do you know this Lord whom I hold in my hand? Do you remember the many graces he has granted you? But now receive the punishment due to your ingratitude!' With these words he drew a sword to kill me. I then cried out, 'For the love of Mary, don't kill me, and I will indeed change my life.' He replied, 'This was the only means that could save you. Learn to make a good use of it; it is the last mercy you will receive.' With these words he left me. I immediately came here to entreat you to receive me into your order."

—St. Alphonsus Liguori, *The Glories of Mary*

IN GOD'S PRESENCE, CONSIDER . . .

Is there some sin into which I repeatedly fall, which makes me despair of God's mercy? Have I asked Mary's assistance to overcome that particular habit of sinning?

CLOSING PRAYER

From a "Novena to Our Mother of Perpetual Help": *You are the advocate of the most wretched and abandoned sinners who turn to you. Come then to my aid, dearest Mother, for I entrust myself to you.*

Mary prevents someone from a moral relapse

St. Alphonsus recalls how Our Lady forcefully kept a man who showed her devotion from falling back into sinful habits.

Another wonder involving Our Lady's intercession was reported by Fr. Paul Segneri in the work entitled *Christian Instructed*. The story of a young man being freed from immoral habits through devotion to her was recounted in a homily by Fr. Nicholas Zucchi in Rome. A captain in the congregation, who for many years had carried on an improper relationship with a certain woman, heard the story.

He determined that he also would practice the same devotion, so that he too might be delivered from the horrible chains that bound him as a slave of the Devil. (For it's necessary that sinners have this intention, so that the Blessed Virgin may be able to help them.) So he also gave up his wickedness and changed his life.

But there's still more. After six months, relying too much on his own strength, the captain foolishly went to pay a visit to the woman, to see whether she also had been converted. But when he approached the door of the house, where he was in clear danger of falling back into sin, he was driven back by an invisible power. Suddenly he found himself far away from the house, all the way down the street, and standing in front of his own door.

Through this experience the captain was clearly made to understand that Mary had delivered him from being lost. From this incident, we ourselves may learn a lesson: Our good mother is eager—if we entrust ourselves to her for this purpose—not only to rescue us out of a state of sin, but also to deliver us from the danger of falling back into it.

—St. Alphonsus Liguori, *The Glories of Mary*

IN GOD'S PRESENCE, CONSIDER . . .

Have I ever been prevented from approaching an occasion of sin, only to realize later that heaven had intervened to protect me?

CLOSING PRAYER

Blessed Lady, defend me from me the Enemy of my soul, and when necessary, defend me from myself, so often my own worst enemy.

Two stories of conversion through Mary

St. Alphonsus tells of two men in quite different circumstances who had one thing in common: Through Our Lady's intervention, they were converted.

A man in Germany once fell into a serious sin. Through shame he was unwilling to confess it. But because he was unable to endure the remorse of his conscience, he went to throw himself into a river. Just as he was about to end his life, he hesitated. Weeping, he begged that God would forgive him his sin without his confessing it in the sacrament. One night, in his sleep, he felt someone shake his arm, and he heard a voice saying, "Go to Confession." He went to the church, but he still didn't confess.

On another night he heard the same voice again. He returned to the church, but when he got there, he declared that he would rather die than confess that sin. Yet before returning home, he went to entrust himself to the most Blessed Virgin, whose image was in that church. As soon as he had knelt down, he found himself quite changed. He immediately got up and called a confessor. Weeping bitterly through the grace received from Mary, he made an entire confession of his sins. Afterward he declared that he experienced greater satisfaction than if had he obtained all the treasures of the world.

In another instance, a young nobleman on a sea voyage from Genoa began to read and take much pleasure in an obscene book. A religious priest noticed it and said to him: "Would you like to make a gift to our Blessed Lady?" The young man replied that he would. "Well," the brother answered, "I wish that, for the love of the most holy Virgin, you would give up that book, and throw it into the sea." "Here it is, Father," said the young man. "No," replied the priest, "you yourself must make Mary this gift." He did so. And as soon as he had returned to his hometown, the Mother of God enflamed his heart with divine love.

—St. Alphonsus Liguori, *The Glories of Mary*

IN GOD'S PRESENCE, CONSIDER . . .

Do I see myself in either of these stories? Have I ever felt so ashamed of a particular sin that I let it prevent me from making a sacramental Confession? Have I ever been pressed to give up a sin that I knew kept me from the graces I needed?

CLOSING PRAYER

Mary, Refuge of Sinners, help me make a good Confession.

All things to all people

St. Alphonsus notes that because of Mary's desire to bring mercy to all, she has accommodated herself to the needs of all.

When the Samaritans refused to receive Jesus Christ and his teachings, St. James and St. John asked him whether they should command fire to fall from heaven and devour them. Our Lord replied, "You do not know what manner of spirit you are of" (Lk 9:55). It's as if he were saying, "I am of such a tender and compassionate spirit that I came from heaven to save and not to chastise sinners—yet you wish to see them lost. Fire, indeed, and punishment! Speak no more of chastisements, for such a spirit is not mine."

But of Mary, whose spirit is the same as that of her Son, we can never doubt that she is all-inclined to mercy. As she said to St. Bridget: "I am called the Mother of Mercy, and truly God's own mercy made me so merciful."

For this reason Mary was seen by St. John in the Book of Revelation as clothed with the sun: "And a great sign appeared in heaven, a woman clothed with the sun" (Rv 12:1). Commenting on these words, St. Bernard turns towards the Blessed Virgin and says: "You, Lady, have clothed the sun—that is, the Eternal Word—with human flesh. But he has clothed you with his power and mercy."

"This queen," continues St. Bernard, "is so compassionate and kind, that when a sinner, whoever he may be, entrusts himself to her charity, she doesn't question his merits, or whether he's worthy or unworthy of her attention. She hears and helps everyone." "As a Mother of Mercy," the same saint says in another place, "she has made herself all things to all people. Out of her most abundant charity she has made herself a debtor to the wise and the foolish, to the righteous and to sinners, and opens to all her compassionate heart, so that all may receive of the fullness of its treasures."

—St. Alphonsus Liguori, *The Glories of Mary*

IN GOD'S PRESENCE, CONSIDER . . .

It was St. Paul who famously said, "I have become all things to all men, that I might by all means save some" (1 Cor 9:22). How does this statement apply to Mary as well?

CLOSING PRAYER

Thank you, Blessed Lady, for stooping to our various conditions, and becoming for each of us what we most need: mother or queen, advocate or refuge, warrior or comforter, model or counselor.

True devotion to Mary is interior, tender, and holy

St. Louis de Montfort identifies the first three of five characteristics of a genuine devotion to Mary.

True devotion to Our Lady is *interior*. That is to say, it comes from the spirit and the heart. It flows from the esteem we have of her, the high idea we have formed of her greatness, and the love which we have for her.

True devotion is *tender*; that is to say, full of confidence in her, like a child's confidence in his loving mother. This confidence makes the soul turn to her in all its bodily or mental necessities, with much simplicity, trust, and tenderness.

It implores the aid of its good mother, at all times, in all places, and about all things: in its doubts, that it may be enlightened; in its wanderings, that it may be brought into the right path; in its temptations, that it may be supported; in its weaknesses, that it may be strengthened; in its falls, that it may be lifted up; in its discouragements, that it may be cheered; in its scruples, that they may be taken away; in its crosses, toils, and disappointments of life, that it may be consoled under them. In a word, in all its evils of body and mind, the soul's ordinary refuge is in Mary, without fearing to be troublesomely persistent with her or to displease Jesus Christ.

True devotion to Our Lady is *holy*; that is to say, it leads the soul to avoid sin, and to imitate in the Blessed Virgin particularly her profound humility, her lively faith, her continual prayer, her universal mortification, her divine purity, her ardent charity, her heroic patience, her angelical sweetness, and her divine wisdom. These are the ten principal virtues of the most holy Virgin.

—St. Louis de Montfort, *True Devotion to Mary*

IN GOD'S PRESENCE, CONSIDER . . .

When I pray the Rosary or take part in other Marian devotions, can I honestly say that I meet these first three criteria that St. Louis provides here? If not, which aspects of my devotion do I need to correct or strengthen?

CLOSING PRAYER

Blessed Lady, show me how to cultivate an authentic devotion to you that will lead me most readily to your Son, Jesus. Hail, Mary . . .

True devotion to Mary is constant and disinterested

St. Louis de Montfort identifies the last two of five characteristics of a genuine devotion to Mary.

True devotion to Our Lady is *constant*. It confirms the soul in good, and it doesn't let it easily abandon its spiritual exercises. It makes it courageous in opposing the world in its fashions and maxims, the flesh in its weariness and passions, and the Devil in his temptations. So a person truly devout to our Blessed Lady is neither changeable, irritable, scrupulous, nor timid.

It's not that such a person doesn't fall or change sometimes in the feelings of devotion, or in the amount of devotion itself. But when he falls, he rises again by stretching out his hand to his good mother. If he loses the taste and relish of devotion, he doesn't disturb himself because of that; for the just and faithful devotee of Mary lives on the faith of Jesus and Mary, and not on sentiments and sensibilities.

Finally, true devotion to our Blessed Lady is *disinterested*; that is to say, it inspires the soul not to seek itself but God only, and God in his holy mother. A true devotee of Mary doesn't serve that august queen from a spirit of greed and interest, nor for its own good, whether worldly, bodily, or spiritual; but exclusively because she merits to be served, and God alone in her. He doesn't love Mary precisely because she does him good, or because he hopes in her; but because she's so worthy of love.

It's on this account that he loves and serves her as faithfully in his disgusts and dryness, as in his sweetness and feelings of fervor. He loves her as much on Calvary as he does at the marriage of Cana. Such a devotee of our Blessed Lady, who has no self-seeking in his service of her, is agreeable and precious in the eyes of God and of his holy mother!

—St. Louis de Montfort, *True Devotion to Mary*

IN GOD'S PRESENCE, CONSIDER . . .

When I pray the Rosary or take part in other Marian devotions, can I honestly say that I meet these last two criteria that St. Louis provides here? If not, which aspects of my devotion do I need to correct or strengthen?

CLOSING PRAYER

From a prayer of St. Louis: *I am all yours, and all that I have belongs to you, O my sweet Jesus, through Mary, your holy mother. O heart most pure of the Blessed Virgin Mary, obtain for me from Jesus a pure and humble heart.*

Exterior devotees and fickle devotees to Mary

In contrast to the characteristics of true devotion to Mary, St. Louis de Montfort identifies the signs of a merely exterior and presumptuous devotion.

Exterior devotees to Mary are persons who make all devotion to our Blessed Lady consist in outward practices. They have no taste except for the exterior of this devotion, because they have no interior spirit of their own. They will say quantities of Rosaries with the greatest hastiness; they will hear many Masses distractedly; they will go without devotion to processions; they will enroll themselves in all sorts of confraternities, without amending their lives, without doing any violence to their passions, or without imitating the virtues of that most holy Virgin. They have no love but for the part of devotion that appeals to their senses, without having any relish for its substance. If they don't produce sweet feelings by their practices, they think they are doing nothing. They get all out of joint, throw everything away, or do everything at random. The world is full of these exterior devotees.

The *fickle* devotees to Mary are those who are devout to our Blessed Lady by intervals and whims. Sometimes they are fervent and sometimes lukewarm. Sometimes they seem ready to do anything for her, and then, a little afterwards, they are not like the same people. They begin by taking up all the devotions to her, and enrolling themselves in the confraternities; and then they don't practice the rules faithfully. They change like the moon. They are inconstant and unworthy to be reckoned among the servants of that faithful Virgin whose devotees have for their special graces faithfulness and constancy. It were better for such persons to load themselves with fewer prayers and practices, and to fulfill them with faithfulness and love, in spite of the world, the Devil, and the flesh.

—St. Louis de Montfort, *True Devotion to Mary*

IN GOD'S PRESENCE, CONSIDER . . .

When I pray the Rosary or take part in other Marian devotions, do I ever fall into a mere exterior practice, or a fickle one? If so, how can I make my devotion more interior and constant?

CLOSING PRAYER

Mother of God, I can truly say to you what I say to your Son: "With the faithful, you show yourself faithful; with the blameless, you show yourself blameless; with the pure, you show yourself pure" (see Ps 18:25–26).

Presumptuous devotion to Mary

In contrast to the characteristics of true devotion to Mary, St. Louis de Montfort identifies the signs of a presumptuous devotion.

Presumptuous devotees to Mary are sinners abandoned to their passions, or lovers of the world. Under the fair name of Christians and devotees of our Blessed Lady, they conceal pride, avarice, impurity, drunkenness, anger, swearing, detraction, injustice, or some other sin. They sleep in peace in the midst of their bad habits, without chastising themselves to correct their faults, under the pretext that they are devout to the Blessed Virgin.

They promise themselves that God will pardon them, that they will not be allowed to die without Confession, and that they will not be lost eternally, because they say the Rosary, because they fast on Saturdays, because they belong to the Confraternity of the Holy Rosary, or wear the scapular, or are enrolled in other congregations, or wear the little habit or little chain of Our Lady. They will not believe us when we tell them that their devotion is only an illusion of the Devil, and a pernicious presumption likely to destroy their souls.

They say that God is good and merciful; that he has not made us to condemn us everlastingly; that no man is without sin; that they will not die without Confession; that one good acknowledgment of sin at the hour of death is enough; that they are devout to Our Lady; that they wear the scapular; and that they say daily, without reproach or vanity, seven Our Fathers and Haily Marys in her honor; and that they sometimes say the Rosary and the Office of Our Lady, besides fasting, and other things. Nothing in Christianity is more detestable than this diabolical presumption. For how can we say truly that we love and honor our Blessed Lady, when by our sins we are pitilessly piercing, wounding, crucifying, and outraging Jesus Christ her Son?

—St. Louis de Montfort, *True Devotion to Mary*

IN GOD'S PRESENCE, CONSIDER . . .

When I pray the Rosary or take part in other Marian devotions, do I ever fall into any of the habits, or offer the excuses for sin, that St. Louis tells us are presumptuous? If so, which aspects of my devotion do I need to correct?

CLOSING PRAYER

Lord, *"who can discern his errors? Clear me from hidden faults. Keep back your servant also from presumptuous sins; let them not have dominion over me!" (Ps 19:12–13).*

A mother can never forget her children

St. Alphonsus insists that once we realize that Mary is our mother, with a mother's fierce love for us, we won't doubt her undying concern for us.

Since Mary is our mother, we should consider how great is the love she bears us.

Love toward our children is a necessary impulse of nature. St. Thomas says that this is the reason why the divine law imposes on children the obligation of loving their parents, but gives no express command that parents should love their children. For nature itself has so strongly implanted it in all creatures that—as St. Ambrose remarks—"we know that a mother will expose herself to danger for her children," and even the most savage beasts cannot do otherwise than love their young.

It's said that even tigers, on hearing the cry of their cubs taken by hunters, will go into the sea and swim until they reach the vessel in which they are captured. Since the very tigers, says our most loving mother Mary, can't forget their young, how can I forget to love you, my children? And even, she adds, were such a thing possible as that a mother should forget to love her child, it's not possible that I should cease to love a soul that has become my child: "Can a woman forget her infant, so as not to have pity on the son of her womb? And even if she should forget, yet I won't forget you" (see Is 49:15).

Mary is our mother, not according to the flesh, but by love. So it's only the love that she bears us that makes her our mother. For this reason, someone has said, "She glories in being a mother of love, because she is all love towards us whom she has adopted for her children." And who can ever tell the love that Mary bears us miserable creatures?

—St. Alphonsus Liguori, *The Glories of Mary*

IN GOD'S PRESENCE, CONSIDER . . .

What experiences in my life can I recall that clearly demonstrated my earthly mother's strong love for me? Do those experiences help me to understand my heavenly mother's loving commitment to my present and eternal welfare?

CLOSING PRAYER

From a prayer of St. Alphonsus: *Mary, my Mother, don't abandon me. Never, never cease to pray for me, until you see me safe in heaven at your feet, blessing and thanking you forever.*

Go to Mary to find Jesus

St. Alphonsus reminds us that where the mother is, so too will be the Child.

The sacrifice of Abraham, by which he offered his son Isaac to God, was so pleasing to the divine Majesty that as a reward God promised to multiply his descendants to become like the stars of heaven: "Because you have done this, and have not withheld your son, your only-begotten son, for my sake, I will indeed bless you, and I will multiply your descendants as the stars of heaven" (Gn 22:16–17).

If this is the case, then we must certainly believe that the more noble sacrifice that the great Mother of God made to him of her Jesus was far more pleasing to him. For this reason, then, he has granted that through her prayers the number of the elect would be multiplied—that is to say, increased by the number of her fortunate children. For she considers all those who are devoted to her to be her children, and she protects them as such.

St. Simeon received a promise from God that he would not die until he had seen the Messiah born: "And it had been revealed to him by the Holy Spirit that he should not see death before he had seen the Lord's Christ" (Lk 2:26). But this grace he received only through Mary, for it was in her arms that he found the Savior. Let us, too, then, go to this Mother of God if we wish to find Jesus, and let us go with great confidence.

—St. Alphonsus Liguori, *The Glories of Mary*

IN GOD'S PRESENCE, CONSIDER . . .

What does it mean to seek Jesus by going to his mother? In what ways is she able to show me where to find him?

CLOSING PRAYER

From a "Novena to Our Lady of Good Remedy": *Lady, be ever present to me, and through your intercession, may I enjoy health of body and peace of mind, and grow stronger in the faith and in the love of your Son, Jesus.*

The greatness of Mary's mercy

St. Bernard of Clairvaux preached extensively about Our Lady throughout his life. In this prayer, he praises the depths of the mercy she shows to those who turn to her for help.

Blessed Virgin, did anyone ever call upon you in need yet fail to receive your assistance? Only that kind of person could remain silent about your mercy. But as for us, your poor servants, we rejoice because of all your virtues, but we especially exult in your mercy toward us.

We praise your virginity, and we admire your humility. But your mercy has an even sweeter taste for us sinners. We have a greater love for your mercy; we remember it and call upon it more often.

Who then could measure, Blessed Lady, the length and breadth, the height and depth of your mercy? Its length truly stretches out to the last day, so that you may come to the assistance of all who call upon it. Its breadth spans the whole universe, so that the whole earth is full of your mercy.

Its height is so great that it brought about the restoration of the heavenly city. Its depth accomplished the redemption of those who sat in darkness and in the shadow of death.

Thanks to you, heaven has been filled, hell has been emptied, the ruins of the heavenly Jerusalem have been rebuilt, and the afflicted people living in hope have been given back the life they had lost!

So it is that your charity, so powerful and yet so gentle, gushes forth in abundance, revealing itself tenderly and giving aid effectively.

—St. Bernard of Clairvaux

IN GOD'S PRESENCE, CONSIDER . . .

What is the meaning of mercy? Why is the mercy of Mary an attribute that deserves our special gratitude?

CLOSING PRAYER

From a prayer of St. Alphonsus Liguori: *O holy Mary, my mistress, into your blessed trust and special keeping, into the bosom of your tender mercy, I commend my soul and my body this day, every day of my life and at the hour of my death.*

Mary gathers after the reapers

Missionaries, preachers, and confessors are constantly reaping souls for God, says St. Alphonsus. But the "hard cases" who aren't part of that harvest are a special concern of Mary.

The Scriptures say that in ancient Israel, Boaz allowed Ruth to gather the ears of grain that the reapers had left behind (see Ru 2:3). St. Bonaventure comments, "Just as Ruth found favor with Boaz, so has Mary found favor with our Lord. She too is allowed to gather the ears of grain left by the reapers.

"The reapers followed by Mary are all evangelical laborers, missionaries, preachers, and confessors, constantly reaping souls for God. But some hardened and rebellious souls are left behind even by these. To Mary alone is it granted to gather them by her powerful intercession." Truly unfortunate are they if they don't allow themselves to be gathered even by this sweet Lady. They will indeed be most certainly lost and accursed. But on the other hand, blessed is he who turns to this good mother. "There is not in the world," says the devout abbot, Blessed Louis de Blois, "any sinner, however revolting and wicked he may be, who is despised or rejected by Mary. She can, she will, and she knows how to reconcile him to her most beloved Son, if only he will seek her assistance."

St. Antoninus relates that there was once a sinner at enmity with God, who had a vision in which he found himself before the dread tribunal. The Devil accused him, and Mary defended him. The Enemy produced the catalogue of his sins; it was thrown into the scales of divine justice, and weighed far more than all his good works. But then his great advocate, extending her sweet hand, placed it on the balance, causing it to turn in favor of her devotee. In this way she helped him understand that she would obtain his pardon if he changed his life. And so he did after the vision, and was entirely converted.

—St. Alphonsus Liguori, *The Glories of Mary*

IN GOD'S PRESENCE, CONSIDER . . .

Are there people I know whom I would consider "hard cases," resisting God's grace? Am I myself in some ways a "hard case"? Have I entrusted those people, and myself as well, to Mary's help?

CLOSING PRAYER

From a prayer of St. Alphonsus: *My only hope, Mary, behold a miserable sinner, who asks you for mercy. You are proclaimed and called by the whole Church, and by all the faithful, "the Refuge of Sinners." So you must be my refuge, most sweet Mother of God.*

Mary, ask for me what is best for me

When we don't really know what we should pray for, St. Alphonsus instructs, we can simply ask Mary to pray for whatever she knows to be best for us.

Pray for me, Mary, and entrust me to your Son. You know my miseries and my needs far better than I do. What more can I say?

Have pity on me. I'm so miserable and ignorant that I don't know, nor can I even seek for, the graces that I stand the most in need of.

My most sweet Queen and Mother, seek and obtain for me from your Son those graces that you know to be the most expedient and necessary for my soul. I abandon myself entirely into your hands, and I beg the divine Majesty only that, by the merits of my Savior Jesus, he will grant me the graces that you ask from him for me.

Ask, ask, then, most holy Virgin, whatever you see to be best for me. Your prayers are never rejected. They are the prayers of a mother addressed to a Son who loves you, his mother, so much, and who rejoices in doing all that you desire. For he wishes to honor you more, and at the same time to show you the great love he bears you.

Let's make an agreement, then, my Lady, that while I live confiding in you, you on your part will concern yourself with my salvation.

—St. Alphonsus Liguori, *The Glories of Mary*

IN GOD'S PRESENCE, CONSIDER . . .

Do I have a perplexing situation that leaves me wondering how I should be praying about it? How might I take that situation to Mary and leave it to her to pray for what's best?

CLOSING PRAYER

Blessed Mother, I entrust this situation wholly to you, confident that you will pray for what's best for me, and that Jesus will answer your prayer. Help me to see what it is he wants me to do, and then help me to do it.

Mary comes to the aid of soldiers

St. Alphonsus recalls the story of one soldier who was protected by Our Lady, and another who was healed of a battle wound through her assistance.

Fr. John Crasset reports that a military commander told him how once he was present when a trumpeter of his company received a pistol shot from a man who stood near him. When the trumpeter examined his breast, where he said he was wounded, he found that the ball had been stopped by a scapular of the Blessed Virgin that he wore. It had not even touched the flesh. He took it and showed it to all who were present.

A certain cavalier of the city of Dole in France, named Ansald, received in battle a wound from an arrow. It entered so deep into the jawbone that it wasn't possible to extract the iron point that remained. After four years, the poor man was unable any longer to endure the torment. Being very ill as well, he thought of having the wound reopened so that the surgeons might again try to extract the iron.

So he entrusted himself to the Blessed Virgin and made a vow that if she would grant his prayer, he would every year visit a devout image of Mary found in that place and make an offering of a certain sum of money.

As soon as he made the vow, he felt the iron drop on its own accord into his mouth. On the following day, ill as he was, he went to visit the image. When he placed his offering on the altar, he found himself entirely restored to health.

—St. Alphonsus Liguori, *The Glories of Mary*

IN GOD'S PRESENCE, CONSIDER . . .

In what kinds of danger do I find myself, physical or spiritual, that should lead me to seek Mary's protection? What wounds do I have, physical or spiritual, that need healing?

CLOSING PRAYER

From a prayer of St. Germanus: *Mary, my refuge, my defense, my strength, my hope, obtain for me, by your all-powerful intercession, a place with you in paradise.*

Mary, make me a saint!

St. Alphonsus sums up his prayer intentions when he asks for Mary's help: Make me a saint!

Mother of Mercy, you are so compassionate, and have so great a desire to render service to us poor creatures and to grant our requests! So I, the most miserable of all men, now turn to your compassion, so that you may grant me what I ask.

Others may ask of you what they please: bodily health, and earthly goods and advantages. But I come, Lady, to ask you for whatever you desire for me, and whatever is most like, most pleasing to, your most sacred heart.

You are so humble; obtain for me humility and love of contempt. You were so patient in the sufferings of this life; obtain for me patience in trials. You were all filled with the love of God; obtain for me the gift of his pure and holy love. You were all love towards your neighbor; obtain for me charity toward all, and particularly toward those who are in any way my enemies.

You were entirely united to God's will; help me to conform entirely to the will of God in whatever way he may be pleased to dispose of me. In short, you are the most holy of all creatures. Mary, make me a saint!

Love for me is not lacking on your part. You can do anything, and you have the will to obtain everything for me. The only thing, then, that can prevent me from receiving your graces is either neglect on my part in turning to you, or too little confidence in your intercession. These two things you must obtain for me. These two greatest graces I ask from you; from you I must obtain them; from you I hope for them with the greatest confidence, Mary, my Mother Mary, my hope, my love, my life, my refuge, my help, and my consolation.

—St. Alphonsus Liguori, *The Glories of Mary*

IN GOD'S PRESENCE, CONSIDER . . .

What does it mean to be a saint? What attitudes will keep me from receiving Mary's help to become one?

CLOSING PRAYER

From a prayer of St. Bernard: *O sovereign Lady of all things, saint of saints, splendor of the world, glory of heaven: Acknowledge those who love you; hear us, for your Son honors you by denying you nothing.*

Hail, sweet Mary!

The abbot Venerable Louis de Blois rejoices in the abundant sweetness of the Blessed Virgin.

Hail, sweet Mary! Foreshadowed under many types and images, you were promised by various sayings of the prophets, and the ancient fathers sighed after you with earnest longings. Take me, O my Lady, for your poor servant. Adopt me, my Mother, for your son. Grant that I may be among the number of those who are written in the memory of your virgin heart, whom you teach, direct, cherish, and love.

Hail, sweet Mary! God honored you with so great a privilege as to preserve you free from original sin, and he adorned you with unique graces and precious gifts. O Virgin most renowned! O Virgin most peaceful! O Virgin most pure! You who are the one chosen child among a thousand, don't reject me because of my iniquities, and because I am stained with the filth of sin. Instead, hear me crying out to you in misery. Comfort me, for I earnestly desire you; and help me, for I hope in you.

Hail, sweet Mary! Your birth was for ages desired and expected by the nations. You enlightened the world with a new light, and gladdened it with an unheard-of joy. O tender Virgin of most perfect innocence! Obtain for me true holiness of life. Remove from me whatever is displeasing to your virgin eyes. Have pity on me, O Lady, have pity on me; for your compassion increased with your tender years.

Hail, sweet Mary! The Lord adorned you with every beauty of form, and with all virtues, and made you most lovely. O most elegant, O most graceful Virgin! Adorn my soul, I beg you, with spiritual beauty. Implant in my heart the lively affections of holy chastity, so that I may please you, and give you acceptable service.

—Blessed Abbot Louis de Blois, *The Oratory of the Faithful Soul*

IN GOD'S PRESENCE, CONSIDER . . .

Do I ever experience a sweetness in conversation with Mary—a spiritual delight that spills like honey through my heart? What is it about my Lady that gives me such pleasure?

CLOSING PRAYER

From a prayer of St. Bonaventure: *Mary, you are sweet toward those who love you, and sweet in giving yourself to those who seek you.*

I don't ask for visions or revelations

St. Louis de Montfort realizes that extraordinary spiritual experiences, and even sweet spiritual feelings, are not to be sought out. In his devotion to Mary, he simply asks to be joined with her in glorifying her Son.

Dearly beloved Mother, grant, if it's possible, that I may have no other spirit but yours to know Jesus and his divine will; that I may have no other soul but yours to praise and glorify the Lord; that I may have no other heart but yours to love God with a love as pure and passionate as yours.

I don't ask you for visions, revelations, feelings of devotion, or spiritual pleasures. It's your privilege to see God clearly; it's your privilege to enjoy heavenly bliss; it's your privilege to triumph gloriously in heaven at the right hand of your Son and to hold absolute sway over angels, men, and demons; it's your privilege to dispose of all the gifts of God, just as you wish.

Heavenly Mary, this is the "best part" that the Lord has given you and that will never be taken away from you—and this thought fills my heart with joy. As for my part here below, I want nothing more than what was yours: to believe sincerely even without spiritual pleasures; to suffer joyfully without human consolation; to die continually to myself without pause; and to work zealously and unselfishly for you until death as the humblest of your servants.

The only grace I beg you to obtain for me is that every day and every moment of my life I may say: "Amen, so be it, to all that you did while on earth; amen, so be it, to all that you are now doing in heaven; amen, so be it, to all that you are doing in my soul, so that you alone may fully glorify Jesus in me for time and eternity."

—St. Louis de Montfort, *True Devotion to Mary*

IN GOD'S PRESENCE, CONSIDER . . .

Do I ever seek out extraordinary spiritual experiences or pleasant spiritual feelings? Why are such things of much less importance than a humble encounter with Mary that transforms us into the image of her Son?

CLOSING PRAYER

From a prayer of St. Ignatius of Loyola: *Take, Lord, and receive all my liberty, my memory, my understanding, and my entire will, all I have and call my own. You have given all to me. To you, Lord, I return it. Everything is yours; do with it what you will. Give me only your love and your grace; that is enough for me.*

A beggar before the Queen

St. Alphonsus confesses his own spiritual poverty, yet looks to Mary as the queen who can relieve him of his miserable condition.

Mother of my God, and my Lady, Mary: As a beggar, all wounded and sore, presents himself before a great queen, so I present myself before you, the Queen of Heaven and Earth. From the lofty throne on which you are seated, do not disdain, I implore you, to cast your eyes on me, a poor sinner.

God has made you so rich so that you might assist the poor, and he has appointed you Queen of Mercy so that you might relieve the miserable. Behold me, then, and pity me; behold me, and do not abandon me, until you see me changed from a sinner into a saint. I know well that I merit nothing; worse than that, I deserve, on account of my ingratitude, to be deprived of the graces that I have already received from God through your help. But you, who are the Queen of Mercy, do not seek out merits, but rather miseries, to help the needy. And who is more needy than I am?

Exalted Virgin, well do I know that you, the Queen of the Universe, are already my queen. Yet I am determined to dedicate myself more especially to your service, so that you may make use of me as you please. As St. Bernard said, "Govern me, my Queen, and don't leave me to myself."

Command me! Employ me as you wish, and chastise me when I don't obey. For the chastisements that come from your hands will be to me pledges of salvation. It's worth more to me to be your servant than to be ruler of the earth. Accept me, Mary, for your own, and as your own, take charge of my salvation. I will no longer be mine; to you I give myself.

—St. Alphonsus Liguori, *The Glories of Mary*

IN GOD'S PRESENCE, CONSIDER . . .

Am I willing to admit my spiritual poverty when I come to Mary for assistance? What kinds of spiritual poverty do I need to confess?

CLOSING PRAYER

From a prayer of St. Alphonsus: *My Queen, even if in times past I have served you poorly, and lost so many occasions to honor you, in the future I will be one of your most loving and faithful servants. I am determined that from this day forward no one shall surpass me in honoring and loving you, my most amiable Queen.*

Run, hurry, my Lady!

St. Bonaventure expresses a sentiment often found in the Psalms and familiar to us all: We need heaven's help, and we need it right away!

Run, hurry, my Lady! And in your mercy
    help your sinful servant who calls upon you,
    and deliver him from the hands of the Enemy.
Who will not sigh to you?
We sigh with love and grief,
    for we are oppressed on every side.
How can we do otherwise than sigh to you,
    comfort of those who are miserable,
    refuge of outcasts, ransom of captives?
We are certain that when you see our miseries,
    your compassion will hurry to relieve us.
Our sovereign Lady and our advocate,
    commend us to your Son.
Grant, blessed one,
    by the grace that you have merited,
    that the One who through you
    was graciously pleased to become a partaker
    of our infirmity and misery
    may also through your intercession
    make us partakers of his happiness and glory.

—St. Bonaventure

IN GOD'S PRESENCE, CONSIDER . . .

Am I facing any situations right now in which I need Our Lady's help right away? Am I willing to trust that she knows God's will for the timing of my assistance?

CLOSING PRAYER

From a prayer of St. Bernard: *It's not possible, O Lady, that you would abandon someone who has placed his hopes in you.*

Mary comes immediately to our aid

St. Bonaventure cried out for Mary to come running to help him, but as St. Alphonsus notes, he was in fact confident of her speed. She not only runs; she flies to our assistance.

St. Bonaventure remarks that the biblical figure Ruth, whose name means "seeing and hurrying," was a figure of Mary: "For Mary, seeing our miseries, hurries in her mercy to help us." The spiritual writer Novarini adds: "Mary, in the greatness of her desire to help us, cannot allow delay, for she is in no way a greedy guardian of the graces she has at her disposal as Mother of Mercy. She can't help but shower down immediately the treasures of her generosity on her servants." How prompt is this good mother to help those who call upon her! The compassion of Mary is poured out on everyone who asks for it, even if it should be sought for by no other prayer than a simple Hail Mary.

"In the exercise of her mercy," says this author, "she knows only how to act as God does. Just as he flies at once to the assistance of those who beg his aid—faithful to his promise, 'Ask, and you will receive' (Jn 16:24)—so Mary, whenever someone calls on her, is at once ready to assist the one who prays to her. God has wings when he assists his own, and immediately flies to them; Mary also takes wing when she is about to fly to our aid."

From this we see who the woman was, spoken about in the Book of Revelation, to whom two great eagle's wings were given, so that she might fly to the desert (see Jn 12:14). The author Ribeira explains: "She has the wings of an eagle, for she flies with the love of God." But the blessed Amadeus, more to our purpose, remarks that these wings of an eagle signify "the speed, faster than that of the seraphim, with which Mary always flies to the aid of her children."

—St. Alphonsus Liguori, *The Glories of Mary*

IN GOD'S PRESENCE, CONSIDER . . .

St. Alphonsus suggests that when we're in a pinch, even a simple Hail Mary can bring Our Lady running in a hurry. Have I found that brief prayer effective in temptation, in perplexity, and in danger?

CLOSING PRAYER

A brief prayer of St. Philip Neri: *O Virgin and Mother, grant that I may always remember you.*

Invoke Mary's name for purity

St. Alphonsus reports that Mary's name is an especially powerful weapon against temptations to impurity.

It's well known, and daily experienced by those who seek Mary's assistance, that her powerful name gives the specific strength necessary to overcome temptations against purity. Richard of Saint Lawrence comments on the words of St. Luke: "And the Virgin's name was Mary" (Lk 1:27). He remarks that these two words, "Mary" and "Virgin," are joined together by the Gospel writer, to denote that the name of this most pure Virgin should always be coupled with the virtue of chastity.

For this reason St. Peter Chrysologus says: "The name of Mary is an indication of chastity." He means that when we doubt as to whether we've consented to thoughts against this virtue, if we remember having invoked the name of Mary, we have a certain proof that we haven't sinned.

So let's always take advantage of the beautiful advice given us by St. Bernard, in these words: "In dangers, in perplexities, in doubtful cases, think of Mary, call on Mary; don't let her leave your lips; don't let her depart from your heart." In every danger of forfeiting divine grace, we should think of Mary, and call her name, together with that of Jesus. For these two names always go together.

We must never, then, permit these two most sweet names to leave our hearts, or to be off our lips. For they will give us strength so that we can refuse to yield to all our temptations, and can conquer them instead.

—St. Alphonsus Liguori, *The Glories of Mary*

IN GOD'S PRESENCE, CONSIDER . . .

Do I ever struggle to maintain purity, especially in my thoughts? Have I developed a consistent habit of asking Mary to help me when I'm under assault by the Enemy in this way?

CLOSING PRAYER

Lord, enflame our hearts and our inmost beings with the fiery love of your Holy Spirit, so that we may serve you with chaste bodies and pure minds.

The Memorare

The Memorare is one of the best-known and best-loved of prayers to the Blessed Virgin. Though widely attributed to St. Bernard, it first appeared as part of a longer fifteenth-century prayer, Ad sanctitatis tuae pedes, dulcissima Virgo Maria.

Remember, O most gracious Virgin Mary,
that never was it known
that anyone who fled to thy protection,
implored thy help,
and sought thy intercession,
was left unaided.

Inspired with this confidence,
I fly unto thee,
O Virgin of Virgins, my Mother;
to thee I come,
before thee I stand sinful and sorrowful.

O mother of the Word incarnate!
Despise not my petitions,
but in thy mercy, hear and answer me.

—From *Ad sanctitatis tuae pedes, dulcissima Virgo Maria*

IN GOD'S PRESENCE, CONSIDER . . .

Am I "inspired by the confidence" that so many others have found Mary's assistance to be unfailing? Am I willing to rest in that confidence, however difficult my situation?

CLOSING PRAYER

From a prayer of St. Methodius: *Your name, O Mother of God, is filled with all graces and divine blessings. Deign, we beg you, to remember us in our miseries—we who celebrate your glories and know how great is your goodness!*

The ladder by which God came down into the world

It was Mary's perfect humility, says St. Alphonsus, that became a ladder between heaven and earth.

In admiring Mary's humility, St. Bernard speaks beautifully: "O Lady, how could so humble an opinion of yourself be united in a heart with such great purity, with such innocence, and so great a fullness of grace as you possessed? And how, O Blessed Virgin, did this humility, such great humility, ever take such deep root in your heart, seeing yourself honored and exalted by God in this way? O blessed one, from where did your humility, such great humility, come?"

Lucifer, seeing himself endowed with great beauty, aspired to exalt his throne above the stars, and to make himself like God: "I will ascend to heaven above the stars of God. . . . I will make myself like the Most High" (Is 14:13–14). What would that proud spirit have said, and to what would he have aspired, had he ever been adorned with the gifts of Mary?

The humble Mary didn't act that way. The higher she saw herself raised, the more she humbled herself. St. Bernard concludes that by this admirable humility, Mary rendered herself worthy to be regarded by God with a unique love; worthy to captivate her King with her beauty; worthy to draw, by the sweet fragrance of her humility, the Eternal Son from his rest in the bosom of God into her most pure womb.

The saint says that although this innocent virgin made herself dear to God by her virginity, yet it was by her humility that she rendered herself worthy, as far as a creature can be worthy, to become the mother of her Creator: "Though she pleased by her virginity, she conceived by her humility." St. Jerome confirms this insight, saying: "God chose her to be his mother more on account of her humility than all her other sublime virtues." An ancient author sums it up: "Mary's humility became a heavenly ladder, by which God came down into the world."

—St. Alphonsus Liguori, *The Glories of Mary*

IN GOD'S PRESENCE, CONSIDER . . .

Am I seeking to cultivate the kind of humility that will draw the Son of God down from heaven to make his home in my heart?

CLOSING PRAYER

From a prayer of St. Lawrence Justinian: *Mary, you are the ladder of paradise, the gate of heaven, the most true mediatrix between God and man.*

The land overflowing with milk and honey

Mercy is fruitful, St. Alphonsus assures us, so Mary is like the biblical Promised Land, "flowing with milk and honey."

St. Bernard, speaking of the great compassion of Mary toward us poor creatures, says, "She is the land overflowing with milk and honey promised by God" (see Ex 3:8, 17). For this reason Pope St. Leo the Great observes, "The Blessed Virgin has so merciful a heart, that she deserves not only to be called merciful, but mercy itself."

St. Bonaventure considers that Mary was made Mother of God for the sake of those who are miserable, and that to her is committed the charge of dispensing mercy. He considers as well the tender care she takes of all, and that her compassion is so great that she seems to have no other desire than that of relieving the needy. In light of these considerations, he says that when he looks at her, he seems no longer to see the justice of God, but only the divine mercy, of which Mary is full. "Lady," he concludes, "you are walled in with mercy; your only wish is to show it."

In short, the compassion of Mary is so great toward us, that the Abbot Guarric says, "Her loving heart can never remain a moment without bringing forth its fruits of tenderness." "And what," exclaims St. Bernard, "can ever flow from a source of compassion but compassion itself?"

"What safer refuge," asks the devout Thomas à Kempis, "can we ever find than the compassionate heart of Mary? There the poor find a home; the infirm, a remedy; the afflicted, relief; the doubtful, counsel; and the abandoned, assistance." Wretched indeed would we be if we didn't have this Mother of Mercy, always attentive and eager to meet our needs!

—St. Alphonsus Liguori, *The Glories of Mary*

IN GOD'S PRESENCE, CONSIDER . . .

If I were to take further the analogy of Mary to the Promised Land, what would the milk and honey represent? What would the fruit represent? What other aspects of the Promised Land would provide a useful analogy?

CLOSING PRAYER

Holy Spirit, you have come to your spouse, Mary, saying, "Your lips distill nectar, my bride; honey and milk are under your tongue . . . your shoots are an orchard . . . with all choicest fruits" (Sg 4:11, 13).

A magnet of hearts

St. Alphonsus recalls a nobleman who despaired of his salvation, but found hope in the assistance of Mary.

A certain nobleman despaired of his salvation on account of his many crimes. He was encouraged by a monk to turn to the most Blessed Virgin and, for this purpose, to visit a devout statue of Mary in a particular church. He went there and, on seeing the image, he felt as if she invited him to cast himself at her feet and to have confidence.

When the nobleman hurried to prostrate himself and kiss her feet, Mary extended her hand and gave it to him to kiss. On it he saw written these words: "I will deliver you from those who oppress you," as though she had said, "My son, don't despair, for I will deliver you from the sins and sorrows that weigh so heavily on you."

On reading these sweet words, the poor sinner was filled with such sorrow for his sins and, at the same time, with so ardent a love for God and his tender mother, that he instantly died at the feet of Mary.

How many obstinate sinners does this magnet of hearts draw each day to God! For this is what Mary called herself one day, saying to St. Bridget, "As the magnet attracts iron, so I attract hearts." Yes, even the most hardened of hearts, to reconcile them with God!

We must not suppose that such wonders are extraordinary events; they are in fact everyday occurrences. For my own part, I could relate many similar cases that have occurred in our missions, where certain sinners, with hearts harder than iron, continued that way through all the sermons they heard. But no sooner did they hear the sermon on the mercies of Mary, than they were filled with remorse and returned to God.

—St. Alphonsus Liguori, *The Glories of Mary*

IN GOD'S PRESENCE, CONSIDER . . .

What do I find in Mary that attracts my heart to hers? If I'm tempted to despair of my salvation, do I ask her to restore my hope?

CLOSING PRAYER

From a prayer of St. Bernard: *Mary, you don't abhor a sinner, however loathsome he may be. You don't despise him, if he sighs to you and, repentant, asks your intercession. With your compassionate hand, you deliver him from despair and give him a lively hope.*

Thirsty for the wine of Christ's love

St. Bernard prays to Our Lady using the image of wine, drawing from the Gospel account of her intercessory role at the marriage feast in Cana (see Jn 2:1–12).

To you we cry,
Queen of Mercy!
Return to us,
so that we may behold you
dispensing favors,
bestowing remedies,
giving strength.

Ah, tender mother!
Tell your all-powerful Son
that we have no more wine.
We are thirsty for the wine of his love,
for that marvelous wine
that fills souls with a holy drunkenness,
that sets them on fire,
that gives them the strength
to despise the things of this world
and to seek after heavenly things with passion.

—St. Bernard of Clairvaux

IN GOD'S PRESENCE, CONSIDER . . .

Am I thirsty for the wine of Christ's love? Have I ever felt a "holy drunkenness" because of that love, that fills me with gladness?

CLOSING PRAYER

Pray for us thirsty souls, Blessed Mother, so that when we're filled with the love of your Son, we'll be eager to follow your instruction: "Do whatever he tells you" (Jn 2:5).

Shower us with mercy

St. Anthony of Padua prays to a mother in heaven who overflows with God's grace and showers down his mercy on the world.

Mary, our Queen,
　　Holy Mother of God,
　　we beg you to hear our prayer.
Make our hearts overflow with God's grace
　　and the splendor of heavenly wisdom.
Make them strong with your power
　　and rich in virtue.
Shower down upon us the gift of mercy
　　so that we may gain the forgiveness of our sins.
Help us to live in such a way
　　that we will merit the glory and happiness of heaven.
Let this be granted to us by your Son, Jesus,
　　who has exalted you above the angels,
　　has crowned you as queen,
　　and has seated you with him forever
　　on his glorious throne.

—St. Anthony of Padua

IN GOD'S PRESENCE, CONSIDER . . .

St. Anthony was a brilliant preacher and a Doctor of the Church, but his devotion to Jesus and Mary was quite childlike, as this prayer demonstrates. How might I imitate his childlike simplicity as I approach Our Lady in prayer?

CLOSING PRAYER

From a prayer of St. Alphonsus: *Mary, since you love me, make me like you. You have all power to change hearts, so take mine and change it. Show the world what you can do for those who love you. Make me a saint; make me your worthy child. This is my hope.*

Turn to us, Mother of God!

In making an urgent appeal to the Blessed Virgin, St. Peter Damian focuses on her great power and love for us.

Holy Virgin, Mother of God, help those who ask for your aid. Turn toward us! Have you forgotten us, perhaps, because you have been raised to so close a union with God? Most certainly not! You know well in what danger you left us when you ascended to heaven, and the miserable condition of your servants. No, it wouldn't be fitting for so great a mercy as yours to forget such great misery as ours.

Turn toward us, then, with your power. For he who is powerful has made you sovereign in heaven and on earth. Nothing is impossible to you, for you can raise even those who are in despair to the hope of salvation. The more powerful you are, the greater is your mercy.

Turn also to us in your love. I know, my Lady, that you are all kind, and that you love us with a love that can be surpassed by no other love. How often you appease the wrath of our Judge, when he is on the point of chastising us!

All the treasures of the mercies of God are in your hands. Never cease to benefit us. You seek only an opportunity to save all the miserable, and to shower your mercies upon them. For your glory is increased when, by your means, penitents are forgiven and thus reach heaven.

Turn, then, toward us, so that we also may be able to go and see you in heaven. For the greatest glory we can have will be, after seeing God, to see you, to love you, and to be under your protection. Be pleased, then, to grant our prayer; for your beloved Son desires to honor you by denying you nothing that you ask.

—St. Peter Damian

IN GOD'S PRESENCE, CONSIDER . . .

Have I ever felt that Mary has forgotten me, because she doesn't seem to be answering my prayers? Do I ever doubt her power to help me, or her willingness to do so? How does this prayer encourage me to trust in her faithfulness to me?

CLOSING PRAYER

From a prayer of St. Alphonsus: *Lady, protect me; this is all that I ask of you. If you protect me, I fear nothing. I don't fear the evil spirits; for you are more powerful than all of them. I don't fear my sins; for you, by one word, can obtain their full pardon from God.*

A prayer to be changed from sinners into saints

Is Mary less concerned for sinners on earth, now that she has left them behind for a glorious throne in heaven? Not at all, St. Alphonsus insists. She loves us now more than ever.

O great, exalted, and most glorious Lady, prostrate at the foot of your throne we venerate you from this valley of tears. We rejoice at your immense glory, with which our Lord has enriched you. And now that you are enthroned as Queen of Heaven and Earth, don't forget us, your poor servants.

Don't disdain, from the high throne on which you reign, to cast your eyes of mercy on us miserable creatures. The nearer you are to the Source of graces, the greater is the abundance in which you procure those graces for us. In heaven you see more plainly our miseries, so you must have compassion on us and help us all the more.

Make us your faithful servants on earth, so that we may one day bless you in heaven. On this day of your coronation, on which you were made Queen of the Universe, we also consecrate ourselves to your service. In the midst of your great joy, console us also by accepting us as your servants.

You are our mother. Most sweet Mother, most amiable Mother, your altars are surrounded by many people. Some ask to be cured of a disorder, some to be relieved in their needs, some for an abundant harvest, and some for success in litigation. But we ask you for graces more pleasing to your heart.

Obtain for us that we may be humble, detached from the world, resigned to the divine will. Obtain for us the holy fear of God, a good death, and paradise. Lady, change us from sinners into saints. Work this miracle, which will redound more to your honor than if you restored sight to a thousand blind persons, or raised someone from the dead.

Most beautiful Queen, we have no pretensions to see you on earth, but we do desire to go to see you in paradise. It is you who must obtain for us this grace, and we hope for it with confidence.

—St. Alphonsus Liguori, *The Glories of Mary*

IN GOD'S PRESENCE, CONSIDER . . .

In what ways does Mary's exalted position in heaven make her better able to assist us on earth?

CLOSING PRAYER

From a prayer of St. Alphonsus: *Through you, Mary, I hope for salvation. I don't ask for riches, honors, or earthly goods. I seek only the grace of God, love toward your Son, the accomplishment of his will, and his heavenly kingdom, so that I may love him eternally.*

Help for despairing sinners

Are you convinced that your sins and weaknesses keep you from Mary's assistance? St. Alphonsus urges you to overcome your fears; she'll help you as soon as you ask.

In the revelations of St. Bridget, Mary is called "the star preceding the sun." This image helps us to understand that when devotion toward the Mother of God begins to manifest itself in a soul that's in a state of sin, it's a certain mark that before long, God will enrich it with his grace.

The devout Benedictine abbot, Blessed Louis de Blois, declares that "Mary is the only refuge of those who have offended God, the asylum of all who are oppressed by temptation, calamity, or persecution. This mother is all mercy, kindness, and sweetness, not only to the righteous, but also to despairing sinners. As soon as she sees them coming to her, and seeking her help from their hearts, then she aids them, welcomes them, and obtains their pardon from her Son.

"Mary doesn't know how to despise anyone, however unworthy he may be of mercy. So she denies her protection to no one. She consoles everyone, and as soon as she is called upon, she helps the one who invokes her.

"By her sweetness, she often awakens and draws to her devotion those sinners who are the most at enmity with God and the most deeply plunged in the lethargy of sin. Then, by the same means, she arouses them effectively, and prepares them for grace. In this way she renders them fit for the kingdom of heaven.

"God has created his beloved daughter of so compassionate and sweet a disposition that no one can fear to turn to her. It's impossible for anyone to perish who attentively, and with humility, cultivates devotion towards the Mother of God."

—St. Alphonsus Liguori, *The Glories of Mary*

IN GOD'S PRESENCE, CONSIDER . . .

Do I avoid asking Mary's assistance because I think my sins are too offensive to her? Am I willing to admit my need for her help and then seek it?

CLOSING PRAYER

From a prayer of St. Bonaventure: *Mary, if you are the Queen of Mercy, and I am the most miserable of sinners, it follows that I am the first of your subjects. How, then, my Lady, could you do anything but extend your mercy on my behalf?*

A prayer for Mary's help to obtain heaven

Though we may legitimately ask Our Lady's help in countless matters, St. Alphonsus here focuses on the most important matter of all: obtaining heaven.

Queen of Paradise, you reign above all the choirs of angels, and you are the nearest of all creatures to God. Greeting you from this valley of tears, I beg you to turn your compassionate eyes toward me, for in whichever direction they turn, they dispense graces.

See, Mary, in how many dangers I am now, and will be as long as I live in this world—in danger of losing my soul, of losing heaven and God. In you, Lady, I've placed my hope. I love you, and I sigh to go soon to see you and praise you in heaven.

Mary, when will be that happy day on which I'll see myself safe at your feet, and contemplate my mother, who has done so much for my salvation? When will I kiss that hand that has delivered me so many times from hell, and has dispensed to me so many graces—when, on account of my sins, I deserved instead to be hated and abandoned by all?

My Lady, in this life I've been very ungrateful to you. But if I get to heaven, I'll no longer be ungrateful. There I'll love you as much as I can in every moment for all eternity, and I'll make amends for my ingratitude by blessing and thanking you forever.

I thank God with my whole heart, who gives me firm confidence in the blood of Jesus Christ and in you. Beg your Son Jesus, as I also beg him, by the merits of his passion, to preserve and always increase this confidence in me, and I will be saved.

—St. Alphonsus Liguori, *The Glories of Mary*

IN GOD'S PRESENCE, CONSIDER . . .

Am I aware of the spiritual dangers that constantly surround me and threaten to turn me away from heaven? Have I sought Mary's help in overcoming those dangers?

CLOSING PRAYER

From a prayer of St. Alphonsus: *Mary, my most dear mother, into how many evils would I have fallen, if with your compassionate hand you hadn't so often helped me through the dangers into which I almost fell! Continue, O my hope, to preserve me from hell, and from the sins into which I may still fall.*

A prayer to Mary for perseverance

St. Alphonsus realizes that he's always in danger of falling away from God's grace. So he asks Our Lady to help him stand firm in temptations.

Queen of Heaven, I was once a miserable slave of the enemy of my soul. But now I dedicate myself to you, to be your servant forever. I offer myself to honor you and serve you during my whole life. Accept me; don't refuse me as I deserve.

My Mother, in you I've placed all my hopes; from you, I expect every grace. I bless and thank God, who in his mercy has given me this confidence in you, which I consider a pledge of my salvation. But I'm miserable, because I've fallen before but didn't turn to you. I now hope that, through the merits of Jesus Christ and your prayers, I've obtained pardon.

Even so, I may again lose divine grace; the danger isn't past. My enemies don't sleep. How many new temptations I still have to conquer!

My most sweet Lady, protect me, and don't let me become their slave again. Help me at all times. I know that you'll help me, and that with your help I'll conquer, if I entrust myself to you.

But this is what I fear: I fear that in the time of danger I may neglect to call upon you, and thus be lost. I ask you, then, for this grace: Obtain for me that, when hell assaults me, I may always turn to you, saying, "Mary, help me!" My Mother, don't permit me to lose my God.

—St. Alphonsus Liguori, *The Glories of Mary*

IN GOD'S PRESENCE, CONSIDER . . .

Am I too confident of my perseverance in grace until the end? On the other hand, do I constantly fear that I will be lost? Have I asked Mary to help me avoid both presumption and despair?

CLOSING PRAYER

From a prayer of St. Thomas Aquinas: *My Queen and Mother, by your most powerful intercession, grant that I may persevere in love for your Son and for you until death, and after death be escorted by you to the kingdom of the blessed.*

Mary wants us to love God as she does

We are lacking in our love for God, St. Alphonsus declares. So we must ask Mary for a share of her perfect love of God.

Since Mary loves God so much, what she requires most of those who turn to her is that they also should love him to their utmost. She said to St. Bridget, "Daughter, if you desire to bind me to yourself, love my Son." Mary desires nothing more than to see her beloved, who is God, loved.

Because Mary was all on fire with the love of God, all who love and approach her are enflamed by her with this same love. She makes them like herself. For this reason St. Catherine of Siena called Mary "the bearer of fire," the bearer of the flame of divine love. If we also desire to burn with these blessed flames, we must endeavor always to draw nearer to our mother by our prayers and the affections of our souls.

Mary, Queen of Love, of all creatures the most loveable, the most beloved, and the most loving (as St. Francis de Sales addressed you), my own sweet mother! You were always and in all things enflamed with love towards God. Reach down, then, to bestow at least a spark of it on me.

You interceded with your Son for the wedding couple whose wine had failed: "They have no wine" (Jn 2:3). Won't you pray for us as well, in whom is lacking the love of God—the God we are under such obligation to love? Say also, "They have no love," and obtain for us this love.

—St. Alphonsus Liguori, *The Glories of Mary*

IN GOD'S PRESENCE, CONSIDER . . .

Does my love for God sometimes grow cold? Do I wish that my love for God was more passionate? Have I asked Mary to set me aflame with the fire of her divine love?

CLOSING PRAYER

From a prayer of St. Alphonsus: *To love God—this is the only grace for which we ask. Mother, by the love you bear for Jesus, graciously hear and pray for us.*

A prayer to Mary for two graces

St. Alphonsus asks the Blessed Virgin to grant him two graces. In the end, they are really just one: the grace to love and serve God forever.

Greatest and most sublime of all creatures, most sacred Virgin, I salute you from this earth! I'm a miserable and unfortunate rebel against my God; I who deserve chastisements, not favors; justice, and not mercy.

Lady, I don't say this because I doubt your compassion. I know that the greater you are, the more you glory in being benevolent. I know that you rejoice that you're so rich, because in this way you're enabled to help us poor miserable creatures. I know that the greater the poverty of those who turn to you, the more you exert yourself to protect and save them.

My Mother, it was you who one day wept over your Son who died for me. Offer, I beg you, your tears to God, and by these obtain for me true sorrow for my sins. On that day, sinners afflicted you so much; and I, by my great sins, have done the same.

Obtain for me, Mary, that at least from this day forward I may not continue to afflict you and your Son by my ingratitude. What would your sorrow avail me if I continued to be ungrateful to you? To what purpose would your mercy have been shown me, if again I was unfaithful and lost?

No, my Queen, don't permit it; you've supplied for all my shortcomings. You obtain from God what you wish. You grant the prayers of all.

I ask of you two graces; I expect them from you, and I won't be satisfied with less. Obtain for me that I may be faithful to God, and no more offend him, and love him during the remainder of my life as much as I have offended him.

—St. Alphonsus Liguori, *The Glories of Mary*

IN GOD'S PRESENCE, CONSIDER . . .

If I could ask Mary for just two graces, what would they be? If only one, what would it be?

CLOSING PRAYER

From a prayer of St. Alphonsus: *Mary, you ask of me that I would love your God, and I ask of you that you would obtain this love for me, to love him always. This is all that I desire.*

To Jesus Through Mary

St. Alphonsus Liguori emphasizes that we must never think of Jesus as a severe Judge to be feared. But if the fact that Jesus is God as well as Man should intimidate us, he has given us his mother to lead us to him.

What must a sinner do who has the misfortune to be the enemy of God? He must find a mediator who will obtain pardon for him, and who will enable him to recover the lost friendship of God.

"Be comforted, you unfortunate soul, you who have lost your God," says St. Bernard. "Your Lord himself has provided you with a Mediator, and this is his Son Jesus, who can obtain for you all that you desire. He has given you Jesus for a Mediator; and what is there that such a Son cannot obtain from the Father?"

Then the saint exclaims: "Why should this merciful Savior, who gave his life to save us, ever be thought severe? Why should men believe him to be terrifying who is all love? You distrustful sinners, what do you fear?

"If your fear arises from having offended God, know that Jesus has fastened all your sins on the Cross with his own lacerated hands, and having satisfied divine justice for them by his death, he has already wiped them away from your souls."

The words of St. Bernard continue: "They imagine him rigorous, who is all compassion; terrifying, who is all love. What do you fear, you of little faith? With his own hands he has fastened your sins to the Cross."

"But if by chance," adds the saint, "you fear to turn to Jesus Christ because the majesty of God in him overawes you—for though he became Man, he did not cease to be God—and you desire another advocate with this divine Mediator, then go to Mary. For she will intercede for you with the Son, who will most certainly hear her. And then he will intercede with the Father, who can deny nothing to such a Son."

—St. Alphonsus Liguori, *The Glories of Mary*

IN GOD'S PRESENCE, CONSIDER . . .

Do I ever see Jesus as a Judge whose severity keeps me from approaching him? If so, how might I seek Mary's help to approach her Son with confidence?

CLOSING PRAYER

Blessed Mother, take me by the hand, and lead me to your Son; teach me how to seek his face and walk with him every day of my life.

Mary, be the mistress of all that is mine

*In the affairs of his life, St. Louis is much more confident of Mary's wisdom
and competence than his own. So he asks her to take charge of all that he is
and all that he has.*

Hail, Mary, beloved daughter of the Eternal Father! Hail, Mary, admirable mother of the Son! Hail Mary, faithful spouse of the Holy Spirit!

Hail, Mary, my dear mother, my loving mistress, my powerful sovereign! Hail, my joy, my glory, my heart, and my soul!

You are all mine by mercy, and I am all yours by justice. But I am not yet sufficiently yours. I now give myself wholly to you without keeping anything back for myself or others. If you still see in me anything that does not belong to you, I beg you to take it and to make yourself the absolute mistress of all that is mine. Destroy in me all that may be displeasing to God. Root it out and bring it to nothing; place and cultivate in me everything that is pleasing to you.

May the light of your faith dispel the darkness of my mind. May your profound humility take the place of my pride. May your sublime contemplation check the distractions of my wandering imagination. May your continuous sight of God fill my memory with his presence. May the burning love of your heart enflame this lukewarm heart of mine. May your virtues take the place of my sins. May your merits be my only adornment in the sight of God and make up for all that is lacking in me.

—St. Louis de Montfort, *True Devotion to Mary*

IN GOD'S PRESENCE, CONSIDER . . .

How, in practical terms, would I go about placing Mary in charge of my affairs? Might it require a frequent turning to her in prayer for wisdom, and a frequent reference to her example as my model of conduct?

CLOSING PRAYER

From a prayer of St. John of Damascus: *I implore you, Mary, deliver me from the burden of my sins, dispel the darkness of my mind, banish earthly affections from my heart, repress the temptations of my enemies, and so rule my whole life that by your means and under your guidance I may attain the eternal happiness of heaven.*

A prayer to make Mary the Lady of the home

St. Alphonsus offers a prayer for parents to pray if they seek to make Mary the Lady of their family and home.

Most Blessed Virgin, immaculate Queen and our Mother Mary, refuge and consolation of all miserable creatures: Prostrate before your throne, with my whole family, I choose you for my Lady, mother, and advocate with God. I dedicate myself, with all who belong to me, forever to your service. And I beg you, Mother of God, to receive us into the number of your servants, by taking us all under your protection, helping us in life, and still more at the hour of our death.

Mother of Mercy, I appoint you as Lady and ruler of my whole house, of my relations, of my interests, and of all my affairs. Don't refuse to take charge of them; dispose of all as it pleases you. Bless me, then, and all my family, and don't permit any of us to offend your Son.

Defend us in temptations, deliver us from dangers, provide for us in our necessities, counsel us in our doubts, comfort us in our afflictions, assist us in our infirmities, especially in the sorrows of death. Never allow the Devil to glory in having in his chains any of us who are now consecrated to you. Rather, grant that we may go to heaven to thank you, and together with you to praise and love Jesus our Redeemer for all eternity.

—St. Alphonsus Liguori, *The Glories of Mary*

IN GOD'S PRESENCE, CONSIDER . . .

Have I asked Mary to become the Lady of our house and to take charge of my family's affairs?

CLOSING PRAYER

From a prayer of St. Ephraem of Syria: *O Lady, don't cease to watch over us. Preserve and guard us under the wings of your compassion and mercy. For, after God, we have no hope but in you.*

Love Mary as the saints have loved her

St. Alphonsus recalls some of the saints who have had a passionate devotion to Mary.

How much does the love of this good mother exceed that of all her children! Let them love her as much as they will; yet Mary will always be the most loving among lovers. Let them love her like St. Stanislaus Kostka, who loved this dear mother so tenderly that in speaking of her, he moved all who heard him to love her. He even created new words and new titles with which to honor her name. When he said her office, the Rosary, or other prayers, he did so with the same expressions and gestures of affection that he would have had if he had been speaking face to face with Mary. When the *Salve Regina* was sung, his whole soul and countenance were all enflamed with love.

Let us love Mary like St. Philip Neri, who was filled with consolation at the mere thought of Mary, and so called her his delight. Let us love her like St. Bonaventure, who called her not only his Lady and mother but also—in order to show the tenderness of his affection—even called her his heart and soul. Let us call her our beloved, like St. Bernardine of Siena, who daily went to visit a devotional picture of Mary, and there, in tender conversations with his queen, declared his love.

Let us love Mary like St. Aloysius Gonzaga, whose love for Mary burned so unceasingly that whenever he heard the sweetest name of his mother mentioned, his heart was instantly enflamed, and his countenance lit up with a fire that was visible to all. Let us love her like St. Francis Solano who, as if gone mad with love for Mary (but with a holy madness), would sing before her picture, and accompany himself on a musical instrument, saying that like worldly lovers, he serenaded his most sweet queen. To sum up: Let us do, or desire to do, all that it is possible for a lover to do, who intends to make his affection known to the person loved.

—St. Alphonsus Liguori, *The Glories of Mary*

IN GOD'S PRESENCE, CONSIDER . . .

St. Philip called Mary his delight; St. Bonaventure, his heart and soul. What special name would I give her to show my affection?

CLOSING PRAYER

From a prayer of St. Anselm: *May my heart faint and my soul melt and be consumed with your love, O my beloved Savior Jesus, and my dear mother Mary!*

Mary, olive branch of forgiveness

St. Gertrude the Great was a visionary whose passionate devotion to the Sacred Heart of Jesus gave her a deep love for his mother. Here, she humbly asks for Mary's tender motherly care.

Hail, Mary, Queen of Mercy,
olive branch of forgiveness,
through whom we receive the medicine
that heals our mortal sickness,
the balsam of pardon;
Virgin mother of the divine Offspring,
through whom the grace of heavenly light
has been shed upon us,
the sweet-scented son of Israel!
Through your Son, your only Child,
who stooped to become
the Brother of mankind,
you have become
the true Mother of us all.
For the sake of his love, take me,
all unworthy as I am,
into your motherly care.
Sustain, preserve, and enlighten my conversion;
be for all eternity my incomparable cherished mother,
tenderly caring for me throughout my earthly life,
and enfolding me in your arms at the hour of my death.

—St. Gertrude the Great

IN GOD'S PRESENCE, CONSIDER . . .

What might St. Gertrude mean when she asks Mary to "sustain, preserve, and enlighten [her] conversion"? Does this petition suggest that conversion is a lifelong endeavor?

CLOSING PRAYER

From a "Novena to Our Lady of Good Remedy": *Come to the aid of all who call upon you; extend your maternal protection to us. We depend on you, dear mother, as helpless and needy children depend on a tender and caring mother.*

A prayer to Mary of thanksgiving and hope

St. Alphonsus is always careful to include praise and thanksgiving along with his petitions to Our Lady.

O my soul, see what a sure hope of salvation and eternal life our Lord has given you, by having in his mercy inspired you with confidence in the patronage of his mother! And he has done this despite the many times when, by your sins, you have merited his displeasure and hell. Thank your God, and thank your protector Mary, who has condescended to take you under her mantle.

O yes, I do thank you, my most loving mother, for all you have done for me—I who am deserving of hell. And from how many dangers have you delivered me, O Queen! How many inspirations and mercies have you obtained for me from God! What service, what honor, have I ever rendered you, that you should do so much for me?

I know that it is only your goodness that has compelled you. Even if I were to shed my blood and give my life for you, it would be too little in comparison with all that I owe you. For you have delivered me from eternal death. You have enabled me, as I hope, to recover divine grace. To you, in short, I owe all I have.

My most amiable Lady, poor wretch that I am, I can make you no return but that of always loving and praising you. Don't disdain to accept the tender affection of a poor sinner, who is enflamed with love for your goodness. If my heart is unworthy to love you, because it is impure and filled with earthly affections, it is you who must change it. Change it, then. Bind me to my God, and bind me so that I may never more have it in my power to separate myself from his love.

—St. Alphonsus Liguori, *The Glories of Mary*

IN GOD'S PRESENCE, CONSIDER . . .

When I approach Mary in prayer, do I spend all my time asking for favors? Or do I also take the time to thank and praise her for her kindness to me?

CLOSING PRAYER

From a prayer of St. Bonaventure: *O Mary, may my heart never cease to love you, and my tongue never cease to praise you.*

Mary's sincere devotees will never perish

St. Alphonsus insists that those whose devotion to Mary is genuine have a firm hope of salvation.

It is impossible for someone who turns to Mary, who is faithful in honoring and entrusting himself to her, to be lost. To some this proposition may appear, at first sight, exaggerated. But anyone to whom this might seem to be the case, I would beg to suspend his judgment, and, first of all, read what I have to say on this subject.

When we say that it is impossible for a devotee of Mary to be lost, we must not be understood as speaking of those who take advantage of this devotion so that they may sin more freely. For this reason, those who disapprove of the great praises bestowed on the mercy of this most Blessed Virgin, because it causes the wicked to take advantage of it to sin with greater freedom, do so without foundation. For such people who practice that kind of presumption deserve chastisement, and not mercy, for their rash confidence.

Our claim is therefore to be understood of those devotees of Mary who, with a sincere desire to change, are faithful in honoring and entrusting themselves to the Mother of God. It is, I say, morally impossible that such as these should be lost.

St. Bonaventure says, "O Lady, whoever honors you will be far from damnation." And this will still be the case, St. Hilary observes, even should the person in the past have greatly offended God. "However great a sinner he may have been previously," says the saint, "if he shows himself devout to Mary, he will never perish."

—St. Alphonsus Liguori, *The Glories of Mary*

IN GOD'S PRESENCE, CONSIDER . . .

Do I consider myself a faithful devotee of Mary? If so, is my devotion genuine, or is it, as St. Alphonsus says, an occasion for a false confidence while I continue to sin freely?

CLOSING PRAYER

From a prayer of St. Germanus: *My Lady, my refuge, my life, my help, my defense, my strength, my joy, my hope: Grant that I may one day be with you in heaven. I know that, being the Mother of God, you can, if you will, obtain this grace for me.*

To you, Mary, I entrust my life

St. Aloysius Gonzaga died quite young from caring for plague victims, but when his final hour came, he had long before entrusted both his life and his death to Mary.

O holy Mary, my mistress,
into your blessed trust and special blessing,
into the bosom of your tender mercy,
this day,
every day of my life,
and at the hour of my death,
I commend my soul and body.

To you I entrust
all my hopes and consolations,
all my trials and miseries,
my life and the end of my life,
that through your most holy intercession
and your merits,
all my actions may be ordered and disposed
according to your will
and that of your divine Son.

—St. Aloysius Gonzaga

IN GOD'S PRESENCE, CONSIDER . . .

Do I maintain a lively awareness that this day could be my last? Have I entrusted both this day and my last day to the Mother of God?

CLOSING PRAYER

From "The Seven Dolors of Mary at the Death of Jesus": *O Mary, befriend me when I take leave of my friends, and my soul is about to part from my body in the bitterness of death, so that the Enemy may have no power over me.*

Gain for us the grace to turn to your Son

St. Bernard's prayer beautifully expresses the intimate connection between devotion to Mary and devotion to Jesus, and the meaning of the celebrated motto: "To Jesus through Mary."

Blessed Lady, you found grace; you brought forth Life;
you became the mother of salvation.
Gain for us the grace to turn to your Son through you.
Through you, let us be received by the One
who through you gave himself to us.
Let your wholesomeness make reparation with him
for the fault of our corruption;
and let your humility, so pleasing to God,
gain forgiveness for our vanity.
Let your abundant charity cover the multitude of our sins,
and let your glorious fruitfulness
conceive in us a fruitfulness of merits.
Reconcile us to your Son, entrust us to him, and present us to him.
Blessed Virgin, by the grace you found with God,
by the favor you merited,
by the mercy he has granted you,
gain for us this favor:
Let the One who, through you,
came down to share our weakness and affliction,
make us share, through you, his glory and blessedness—
Jesus Christ, your Son, our Lord,
who is above all, God forever blessed!

—St. Bernard of Clairvaux

IN GOD'S PRESENCE, CONSIDER . . .

In my devotion to Mary, do I always keep in mind that in the end, my goal is for her to bring me to Jesus?

CLOSING PRAYER

From a prayer of St. Alphonsus Liguori: *Jesus wills that I should turn to you, Mary, not only so that his blood may save me, but also so that your prayers may assist me in this great work, for your glory, and for his own, since you are his mother.*

Mary, Temple of God

St. Francis of Assisi, with characteristic exuberance, sings a joyful hymn to the Virgin Mary that celebrates many of her traditional titles.

Holy Virgin Mary, there is none like you
among all the women born into the world!
Daughter and handmaid of the heavenly Father, the almighty King,
mother of our most high Lord Jesus Christ,
Spouse of the Holy Spirit,
pray for us to your most holy Son, our Lord and Master.
Hail, holy Lady, most noble Queen,
Mother of God, Mary ever-virgin!
You were chosen by the heavenly Father,
who has been pleased to honor you
with the presence of his most holy Son
and the Holy Spirit, the divine Advocate.
You were blessed with the fullness of grace and goodness.
Hail, Temple of God, his dwelling place,
his masterpiece, his handmaid!
Hail, Mother of God! I venerate you for the holy virtues that,
through the grace and enlightenment of the Holy Spirit,
you bring into the hearts of your devoted ones
to change them from unfaithful Christians
into faithful children of God.

—St. Francis of Assisi

IN GOD'S PRESENCE, CONSIDER . . .

Which of the titles for Mary found in this hymn seems to hold the richest meaning for me? What is my favorite title for Mary, and why?

CLOSING PRAYER

From a prayer of St. Andrew of Candia: *I salute you, O temple of the glory of God, sacred dwelling of the King of heaven. You are the reconciliation of God with men. I salute you, O mother of our joy!*

Holy Mary

Blessed John Henry Newman examines the fundamental meaning of holiness in order to understand the title "Holy Mary."

By holiness we mean the absence of whatever sullies, dims, and degrades a rational nature; all that is most opposite and contrary to sin and guilt. In his mercy, God has communicated in various measures his great attributes to his rational creatures, and first of all, as being most necessary, holiness. Thus Adam, from the time of his creation, was gifted, over and above his nature as man, with the grace of God, to unite him to God, and to make him holy. Grace is therefore called holy grace; being holy, it is the connecting principle between God and man. Adam in paradise might have had knowledge, and skill, and many virtues; but these gifts did not unite him to his Creator. It was holiness that united him.

When man fell and lost this holy grace, he had various gifts still adhering to him. He might be, in a certain measure, true, merciful, loving, and just; but these virtues did not unite him to God. What he needed was holiness; therefore the first act of God's goodness to us in the Gospel is to take us out of our unholy state by means of the Sacrament of Baptism, and by the grace then given us to reopen the communications, so long closed, between the soul and heaven.

We see then the force of Our Lady's title, when we call her *"Holy* Mary." When God would prepare a human mother for his Son, this was why he began by giving her an immaculate conception. He began, not by giving her the gift of love, or truthfulness, or gentleness, or devotion, though according to the occasion she had them all. But he began his great work before she was born; before she could think, speak, or act, by making her *holy,* and thereby, while on earth, a citizen of heaven. Nothing of the deformity of sin was ever hers.

—Blessed John Henry Newman, *Meditations and Devotions*

IN GOD'S PRESENCE, CONSIDER . . .

My baptism, as Blessed John affirms, brought me into a state of holiness, of reconciliation and thus reconnection with God. But my sins can once again diminish and damage that connection. Am I making frequent use of the sacrament of Reconciliation as a remedy? Do I ask Mary to help me make a good Confession?

CLOSING PRAYER

From a prayer of St. Athanasius: *Give ear to our prayers, O most holy Virgin, and be mindful of us. Distribute to us the gifts of your riches, and the abundance of the graces with which you are filled.*

Mary, Mother of God

At first sight, says Blessed John Newman, calling Mary the "Mother of God" seems impossible. But its meaning is clarified when we consider the identity of her Son.

The "Mother of the Creator" is a title which, of all others, we should have thought it impossible for any creature to possess. At first sight we might be tempted to say that it throws into confusion our primary ideas of the Creator and the creature, the Eternal and the temporal, the Self-subsisting and the dependent. Yet on further consideration we shall see that we cannot refuse the title to Mary without denying the divine Incarnation—that is, the great and fundamental truth of revelation, that God became man.

And this was seen from the first age of the Church. Christians were accustomed from the first to call the Blessed Virgin "the Mother of God," because they saw that it was impossible to deny her that title without denying St. John's words: "The Word" (that is, God the Son) "was made flesh" (see Jn 1:14).

What can be more consoling and joyful than the wonderful promises which follow from this truth, that Mary is the Mother of God? The great wonder, namely, that we become the brethren of our God; that, if we live well, and die in the grace of God, we shall all of us hereafter be taken up by our incarnate God to that place where angels dwell; that our bodies shall be raised from the dust, and be taken to heaven; that we shall be really united to God; that we shall be partakers of the divine nature (see 2 Pt 1:4); that each of us, soul and body, shall be plunged into the abyss of glory which surrounds the Almighty; that we shall see him, and share his blessedness, according to the text: "Whosoever shall do the will of my Father that is in heaven, the same is my brother, and sister, and mother" (see Mt 12:50).

—Blessed John Henry Newman, *Meditations and Devotions*

IN GOD'S PRESENCE, CONSIDER . . .

Have I ever considered that, when I call Mary both the Mother of God and my mother, I'm saying that I have God the Son for my Brother? Do I find consolation and hope in that truth?

CLOSING PRAYER

From a prayer of St. (Padre) Pio of Pietrelcina: *May the mother of Jesus and our mother, always smile on your spirit, obtaining for it, from her most holy Son, every heavenly blessing.*

Mary's greatest title is "Mother of God"

St. Alphonsus explains why the saints agree that one of Mary's titles far exceeds, in greatness and dignity, all the others.

To understand fully the greatness to which Mary was exalted, it would be necessary to understand fully the sublimity and greatness of God. It should be enough, then, to say simply that God made this Blessed Virgin his mother, to understand that God could not have exalted her more than he did exalt her. Arnold of Chartres rightly asserts that God, by becoming the Son of the Blessed Virgin, "established her in a rank far above that of all the saints and angels."

If this is the case, then we have more than sufficient reason not to be surprised when we see that the writers of the sacred Gospels, who have so fully recorded the praises of a John the Baptist and of a Mary Magdalene, yet say so little of the precious gifts of Mary. St. Thomas of Villanova observes that "it was sufficient for them to say of her, 'the one of whom was born Jesus.'"

"What more could you wish the evangelists to have said of the greatness of this Blessed Virgin?" continues the saint. "Isn't it enough that they declare that she was the Mother of God? In these few words they recorded the greatest, the whole, of her precious gifts. And since the whole was contained in those words, it was unnecessary to go into detail."

St. Anselm agrees: "When we say of Mary that she is the Mother of God, this alone transcends every greatness that can be named or imagined after that of God." Peter of Celles, on the same subject, adds: "Address her as Queen of Heaven, sovereign mistress of the angels, or any other title of honor you may please. But you can never honor her so much as by simply calling her the Mother of God."

—St. Alphonsus Liguori, *The Glories of Mary*

IN GOD'S PRESENCE, CONSIDER . . .

Have I ever considered that the Gospel writers say so little about Mary, not because she was unimportant, but because her exalted status was revealed in the simple declaration that she was the mother of Jesus?

CLOSING PRAYER

From a prayer of St. Germanus: *You who are the Mother of God, the lover of men, hear and grant my prayers, and fulfill my petition.*

Mary, Advocate of Sinners

Do you need a patron to represent you in the divine court? St. Alphonsus says let Mary be your advocate.

Perhaps there may be a sinner who, though not doubting Mary's power, might doubt her compassion—fearing that she might be unwilling to help him on account of the greatness of his sins. If so, let him take courage from the words of St. Bonaventure:

"The great, the special privilege of Mary, is that she is all-powerful with her Son. . . . But to what purpose would Mary have such great power if she didn't care for us?

"No! We must not doubt, but be certain, that she is our most loving advocate, and the one who is the most solicitous for our welfare, to the same degree that her power with God exceeds that of all the saints. And let us always thank our Lord and his divine mother for that."

"And who, O Mother of Mercy," exclaims St. Germanus, in the joy of his heart, "who, after your Jesus, is as tenderly solicitous for our welfare as you are? Who defends us in the temptations with which we are afflicted as you defend us? Who, like you, undertakes to protect sinners, fighting in their behalf?"

"Therefore," he adds, "your patronage, O Mary, is more powerful and loving than anything of which we can ever form an idea."

Mary takes care of all, even of sinners. Indeed, she glories in being called in a special way their advocate, as she herself declared to the venerable Sister Mary Villani, saying: "After the title of Mother of God, I rejoice most in that of Advocate of Sinners."

—St. Alphonsus Liguori, *The Glories of Mary*

IN GOD'S PRESENCE, CONSIDER . . .

If I should imagine I'm in court, standing before the judge, I can hear him read aloud the charges against me, all of which are true. Then my advocate steps forward to speak for me and to appeal to the judge's mercy—and that advocate is the mother of the judge! What do I think the judge will say?

CLOSING PRAYER

From "Remember, O Virgin Mother": *Remember, O Virgin Mother of God, when you will stand before the face of the Lord, to speak favorable things in our behalf, so that he may turn away his indignation from us.*

Mary, Mother of Fair Love

St. Alphonsus celebrates the love of a mother unlike any other.

The Church applies to Mary these words of the Book of Sirach: "I am the mother of fair love" (see Sir 24:18). A commentator, explaining them, says that the Blessed Virgin's love renders our souls beautiful in the sight of God, and also makes her, as a most loving mother, receive us as her children, "since she is all love towards those whom she has adopted in this way." St. Bonaventure says to her: "Don't you love us and seek our welfare far more—without comparison!—than any earthly mother?"

Blessed are those who live under the protection of so loving and powerful a mother! The prophet David, although Mary was not yet born, sought salvation from God by dedicating himself as a son of Mary, and prayed to God this way: "Save the son of your handmaid" (Ps 86:16). "Of what handmaid?" asks St. Augustine. He replies: "Of the one who said, 'Behold the handmaid of the Lord'" (Lk 1:38).

"Who would ever dare," asks St. Robert Bellarmine, "to snatch these children from the bosom of Mary, when they have taken refuge there? What power of hell, or what temptation, can overcome them, if they place their confidence in the patronage of this great mother, the Mother of God, and their mother?"

There are some who say that when the mother whale sees her young in danger, either from storms or predators, she opens her mouth so they can swim inside her to be protected. This is precisely what the devotional writer Luigi Novarini asserts of Mary: "When the storms of temptations rage, the most compassionate mother of the faithful, with maternal tenderness, protects them as if in her own bosom, until she has brought them into the harbor of salvation."

—St. Alphonsus Liguori, *The Glories of Mary*

IN GOD'S PRESENCE, CONSIDER . . .

In what ways has Mary shown herself to be the "Mother of Fair Love" in my life? How has her love helped to make my soul beautiful like hers?

CLOSING PRAYER

From a prayer of St. Bonaventure: *As a mother loves her children and attends to their welfare, so you love us and procure our happiness, O most sweet Queen!*

Mary, Mother of Hope

Mary gives birth to a holy hope in our hearts, St. Alphonsus observes, both by her example of hope, and by her powerful intercession.

We rightly and reasonably call the Blessed Virgin our hope, trusting, as St. Robert Bellarmine says, "that we shall obtain, through her intercession, what we couldn't obtain by our own unaided prayers." "We pray to her," says the learned scholar Francisco Suárez, "so that the dignity of the intercessor may supply for our own unworthiness. . . . To implore the Blessed Virgin in such a spirit is not distrust in the mercy of God, but fear of our own unworthiness."

It's not without reason, then, that the holy Church, using the words of Sirach, calls Mary "the mother of holy hope" (see Sir 24:18). She is the mother who gives birth to holy hope in our hearts: not to the hope of the vain and transitory goods of this life, but of the immense and eternal goods of heaven.

Before the Divine Word took flesh in the womb of Mary, he sent an archangel to ask her consent, because he willed that the world should receive the incarnate Word through her, and that she should be the source of every good. For this reason, St. Irenaeus remarks that as Eve was seduced, by a fallen angel, to flee from God, so Mary was led to receive God into her womb, obeying a good angel. In this way, by her obedience, Mary repaired Eve's disobedience and became her advocate, and that of the whole human race. "As the human race was bound to death through a virgin, it is saved through a virgin."

—St. Alphonsus Liguori, *The Glories of Mary*

IN GOD'S PRESENCE, CONSIDER . . .

In what ways has Mary given birth to hope in my life? How has her model of hope inspired me to put my full confidence in God?

CLOSING PRAYER

From a prayer of Pope St. John Paul II: *Mary, Mother of Hope, accompany us on our journey! Teach us to proclaim the living God; help us to bear witness to Jesus, the one Savior.*

Mary, Mother of Mercy

St. Alphonsus explains why it seems that Mary has no other desire or concern than to grant us mercy.

A demon-possessed person was once being exorcised, and the exorcist questioned the demon about what Mary did. The demon replied, "She descends and ascends." By this it meant that this benevolent Lady is constantly descending from heaven to bring graces to men, and re-ascending to obtain the divine favor for our prayers. With good reason, then, St. Andrew Avellino used to call the Blessed Virgin the "Heavenly Commissioner," for she is continually carrying messages of mercy and obtaining graces for all, for the just and for sinners alike.

The royal prophet, King David, said: "The eyes of the LORD are toward the righteous" (Ps 34:16). "But the eyes of the Lady," says Richard of Saint Lawrence, "are on the righteous and on sinners. For the eyes of Mary are the eyes of a mother; and a mother not only watches her child to prevent it from falling, but when it has fallen, she picks it up." Jesus himself revealed this to St. Bridget, for one day he allowed her to hear him addressing his holy mother with these words: "My Mother, ask of me whatever you wish." And in this way her Son is constantly addressing Mary in heaven, taking pleasure in gratifying his beloved mother in all that she asks. But what does Mary ask? St. Bridget heard her reply: "I ask mercy for sinners." It's as if she had said, "My Son, you have made me the Mother of Mercy, the refuge of sinners, the advocate of the miserable; and now you tell me to ask what I desire. What can I ask except mercy for them?

"O Mary," says St. Bonaventure, with deep feeling, "you are so full of mercy, so attentive in relieving the wretched, that it seems that you have no other desire, no other concern."

—St. Alphonsus Liguori, *The Glories of Mary*

IN GOD'S PRESENCE, CONSIDER . . .

In what current matters am I seeking God's mercy because of my personal weaknesses and failures? Do I recognize that Mary's constant prayer for me is to receive that mercy from God?

CLOSING PRAYER

From the *Salve Regina*: *Hail, Holy Queen, Mother of Mercy, our life, our sweetness, and our hope. To thee do we cry, poor banished children of Eve! To thee do we cry, mourning and weeping in this valley of tears!*

Mary, House of Gold

The traditional Marian title "House of Gold" may seem an unlikely one. But Blessed John Henry Newman explains why it's fitting for the beautiful, precious mother in whom God chose to make his home.

Why is Mary called "House of Gold"? Gold is the most beautiful, the most valuable, of all metals. Silver, copper, and steel may in their way be made good to the eye, but nothing is so rich, so splendid, as gold. We have few opportunities of seeing it in any quantity; but anyone who has seen a large number of bright gold coins knows how magnificent is the look of gold.

Mary is called golden because her graces, her virtues, her innocence, her purity, are of that transcendent brilliancy and dazzling perfection, so costly, so exquisite, that the angels cannot, so to say, keep their eyes off her any more than we could help gazing upon any great work of gold. But observe further: She is a golden house, or I will rather say, a golden palace.

Let us imagine we saw a whole palace or large church all made of gold, from the foundations to the roof. Such, in regard to the number, the variety, the extent of her spiritual excellences, is Mary. But why called a house or palace? And whose palace?

She is the house and the palace of the great King, of God himself. Our Lord, the coequal Son of God, once dwelt in her. He was her Guest; no, more than a guest, for a guest comes into a house as well as leaves it. But our Lord was actually born in this holy house. He took his flesh and his blood from this house, from the flesh, from the veins of Mary.

Rightly then was she made to be of pure gold, because she was to give of that gold to form the body of the Son of God. She was golden in her conception, golden in her birth. She went through the fire of her suffering like gold in the furnace, and when she ascended on high, she was, in the words of our hymn, "above all the angels in glory untold, standing next to the king in a vesture of gold."

—Blessed John Henry Newman, *Meditations and Devotions*

IN GOD'S PRESENCE, CONSIDER . . .

The beauty and precious value of gold is reflected in many common expressions: "good as gold," "golden opportunity," "a heart of gold," "the Golden Rule." In what ways do I find Mary to be "golden" in beauty and value?

CLOSING PRAYER

Mary, Queen of Heaven, I will acclaim you in the words of the psalmist: "The daughter of the King is decked in her chamber with golden-woven robes!" (Ps 45:13–14).

Mary, Virgin of Virgins

St. Alphonsus presents Mary to us as the model of chastity and purity.

Ever since the fall of Adam, when the bodily senses became rebels against reason, chastity is of all the virtues the one most difficult to practice. St. Augustine notes: "Of all the combats in which we're engaged, the most severe are those of chastity. Its battles take place daily, but victory is rare."

May God be ever praised, however, who in Mary has given us a great example of this virtue. "With good reason," says Richard of Saint Lawrence, "Mary is called the Virgin of Virgins. For she, without the counsel or example of others, was the first who offered her virginity to God." In this way she brought all virgins who imitate her to God, as David had already foretold: "After her shall virgins be brought to the King" (see Ps 45:15).

"Without counsel and without example." Yes; as St. Bernard says: "O Virgin, who taught you to please God by virginity, and to lead an angel's life on earth?" St. Sophronius replies, "God chose this most pure Virgin for his mother, so that she might be an example of chastity to all." This is why St. Ambrose calls Mary "the standard-bearer of virginity."

The Blessed Virgin inspired all who looked at her with chaste thoughts. This is confirmed by St. Thomas, who says that the beauty of the Blessed Virgin was an incentive to chastity in all who beheld her. St. Jerome declared it was his opinion that St. Joseph actually remained a virgin by living with Mary. Writing against the heretic Helvidius, who denied Mary's virginity, he says: "You say that Mary did not remain a virgin. I say that, not only did she remain a virgin, but also that Joseph preserved his virginity through Mary."

St. John of Damascus says that Mary "is pure, and a lover of purity." So she cannot endure those who are unchaste. But whoever turns to her will certainly be delivered from this vice, if he only pronounces her name with confidence.

—St. Alphonsus Liguori, *The Glories of Mary*

IN GOD'S PRESENCE, CONSIDER . . .

Are the words of St. Augustine true in my life? "Of all the combats in which we're engaged, the most severe are those of chastity. Its battles take place daily, but victory is rare." If so, do I turn to Mary to help me win these battles?

CLOSING PRAYER

From a prayer of St. Alphonsus: *Sovereign Lady, obtain for us the grace always to turn to you in our temptations, and always to invoke you, saying, "Mary, Mary, help us!"*

Mary, Help of Christians

This popular traditional prayer appeals to Mary under her title "Help of Christians." The prayer's scope is universal, asking for her help not just in personal affairs, but also for the Pope, the whole Church, the conversion of sinners, and even the souls in purgatory.

O Mother of Mercy, Help of Christians,
most faithful minister of divine providence,
treasurer of all graces,
remember that never in the world
has it been heard that you have left without comfort
anyone who has come to you with true devotion.
For this reason, trusting in your tender pity
and in your most generous providence,
I bend low before you,
praying that you would hear my prayer.
Obtain for me a holy provision for the future,
namely, graces for all my spiritual and temporal needs.
I fervently recommend to your loving motherly heart
our holy Church, the Sovereign Pontiff,
the conversion of sinners, the spread of the Catholic faith,
and those souls chosen by our Lord
who are suffering the tormenting flames of purgatory,
that they may soon be comforted
with eternal refreshment.

—Traditional

IN GOD'S PRESENCE, CONSIDER . . .

How often do I pray for the Pope . . . the universal Church . . . the conversion of sinners . . . the souls in purgatory? Might I ask Mary to help me keep in mind all these, whose needs are so great?

CLOSING PRAYER

From a prayer of Pope St. John Paul II: *O Virgin mother, guide and sustain us so that we might always live as true sons and daughters of the Church of your Son. Enable us to do our part in helping to establish on earth the civilization of truth and love, as God wills it, for his glory.*

Mary, Seat of Wisdom

Mary's Son was Wisdom himself. As the mother in whose womb he was carried and in whose lap he sat as a Child, she is called "Seat of Wisdom." But Blessed John Henry Newman insists that the name tells us even more about her.

Mary has one particular title in her litany because the Son of God, who is also called in Scripture the Word and Wisdom of God, once dwelt in her. Then, after she gave him birth, he was carried in her arms and seated in her lap in his first years. Thus, being as it were the human throne of him who reigns in heaven, she is called the "Seat of Wisdom."

But the possession of her Son lasted beyond his infancy. He was under her rule, as St. Luke tells us, and lived with her in her house, till he went forth to preach—that is, for at least a whole thirty years (see Lk 2:51–52). And this brings us to a reflection about her.

If such close and continued intimacy with her Son created in her a sanctity inconceivably great, the knowledge which she gained during those many years from his conversation of present, past, and future, must also have been large, and profound, and diversified, and thorough. So even though she was a poor woman without human advantages, she must in her knowledge of creation, of the universe, and of history have excelled the greatest of philosophers; and in her theological knowledge, the greatest of theologians; and in her prophetic discernment, the most favored of prophets.

Our Lady, Seat of Wisdom, pray for us!

—Blessed John Henry Newman, *Meditations and Devotions*

IN GOD'S PRESENCE, CONSIDER . . .

If I had lived with Jesus for thirty years as Mary did, what questions might I have asked him? What might I have sought to learn from him about God and the universe he had created?

CLOSING PRAYER

From a prayer of St. Thomas Aquinas: *Mary, Seat of Wisdom, I choose you as my guardian and patron of my studies. Obtain for me the grace of the Holy Spirit, so that I can understand more quickly, retain more readily, and express myself more fluently. May the example of my life serve to honor you and your Son, Jesus.*

Mary, Mother of Faith

Through Mary's faith, St. Alphonsus declares, her divine Son was conceived, and our salvation was secured.

As the Blessed Virgin is the mother of holy love and hope, she is also the Mother of Faith: "I am the mother of beautiful love, of fear, of knowledge, and of holy hope" (Sir 24:18). With good reason do these words apply to her, for as St. Irenaeus says, "The evil done by Eve's disbelief was remedied by Mary's faith."

This is confirmed by the ancient writer Tertullian. He says that because Eve, contrary to the assurance she had received from God, believed the serpent, she brought death into the world. But our queen believed the angel when he said that she, remaining a virgin, would become the mother of God. In doing so, she brought salvation into the world.

As St. Augustine says, "When Mary consented to the incarnation of the Eternal Word, by means of her faith she opened heaven to men." Richard of Saint Lawrence, commenting on the words of St. Paul that "the unbelieving husband is sanctified by the believing wife" (1 Cor 7:14), observes: "Mary is the believing woman by whose faith the unbelieving Adam and all his posterity are saved."

It was because of Mary's faith that Elizabeth called the holy Virgin blessed: "Blessed is she who believed that there would be a fulfillment of what was spoken to her from the Lord" (Lk 1:45). St. Augustine adds: "Mary was blessed more by receiving the faith of Christ than by conceiving the flesh of Christ."

—St. Alphonsus Liguori, *The Glories of Mary*

IN GOD'S PRESENCE, CONSIDER . . .

Is my faith being tested right now by doubts or difficult circumstances? Have I asked Mary to share her faith with me?

CLOSING PRAYER

Blessed Mother, I thank you that through your faith, you became the mother of our Lord Jesus Christ, the One who is "the pioneer and perfecter of our faith" (Heb 12:2).

Mary, Lovable Mother

What exactly makes Mary so lovable? What is it about her that charms and attracts all who come to know her? Blessed John Henry Newman explains.

Mary is called the "Lovable Mother" because she was without sin. Sin is something odious in its very nature, and grace is something bright, beautiful, attractive. There is a vast difference between the state of a soul such as that of the Blessed Virgin, which has *never* sinned, and a soul, however holy, which has once had upon it Adam's sin. For, even after baptism and repentance, it suffers necessarily from the spiritual wounds which are the consequence of that sin.

Now, whatever lack of amiableness, sweetness, attractiveness, really exists in holy men arises from the *remains* of sin in them, or again from the lack of a holiness powerful enough to overcome the defects of nature, whether of soul or body. But as to Mary, her holiness was such that if we saw her and heard her, we should not be able to tell to those who asked us anything about her except simply that she was angelic and heavenly. Of course her face was most beautiful. But we would not be able to recollect whether it was beautiful or not; we would not recollect any of her features, because it was her beautiful sinless soul, which looked through her eyes, and spoke through her mouth, and was heard in her voice, and compassed her all about—when she was still, or when she walked, whether she smiled, or was sad—her sinless soul: This it was which would draw all those to her who had any grace in them, any remains of grace, any love of holy things.

There was a divine music in all she said and did—in her mien, her air, her deportment, that charmed every true heart that came near her. Her innocence, her humility and modesty, her simplicity, sincerity, and truthfulness, her unselfishness, her unaffected interest in everyone who came to her, her purity—it was these qualities which made her so lovable.

—Blessed John Henry Newman, *Meditations and Devotions*

IN GOD'S PRESENCE, CONSIDER . . .

In which of the people I know do I recognize the qualities that make Mary so lovable? Do I possess any of these qualities myself, at least in some measure? How might I deepen these qualities in myself, with Mary's help?

CLOSING PRAYER

From a prayer of St. Germanus: *My sovereign Lady, delight of my soul, heavenly dew quenching my burning thirst, liquid flowing from God into my parched heart, bright light in the midst of my soul's darkness: Listen to my prayers.*

Mary, Our Lady of Victory

Mary isn't just our mother and queen; she's a mighty warrior who fights the powers of darkness on our behalf. Her humble obedience to God has overthrown Satan's arrogant revolt.

O Queen of Angels, Bane of Devils!
The proud spirits of wickedness
were humiliated by your perfect humility;
their rebellion was scattered by your perfect obedience.
Your *fiat* overthrew Eve's baleful consent to the ancient Serpent,
crushing his head, exposing his deceits,
and healing the wounds inflicted by his venom,
through the Son you conceived,
Jesus Christ, our Lord.

Come to our aid, Our Lady of Victory!
When the battle rages,
when our strength fails,
when the Enemy wounds us,
when defeat seems certain:
With your mantle, cover and protect us;
with your bright banner above us, dispel the darkness;
so that we may rally again in combat
through the invincible power of your Son.

Then, when our warfare is complete, and our victory won,
lead us from the battlefield to his glorious throne,
so that we may join you there
in a glad song of everlasting triumph!

—Paul Thigpen

IN GOD'S PRESENCE, CONSIDER . . .

The lives of the saints offer striking examples of Mary's powerful defense of Christians when they were under assault, both spiritually and otherwise. What battles do I face today in which I need to call on her assistance?

CLOSING PRAYER

From a "Prayer to Our Lady of Victory": *O Mary, powerful Virgin, you are the mighty and glorious protector of the Church; you are the marvelous help of Christians; you are terrifying as an army in battle array!*

Mary, Consoler of the Afflicted

Blessed John Henry Newman explains that Mary can console us in adversity because she herself has suffered affliction. She knows especially the hardships of dealing with difficult people.

St. Paul says that his Lord comforted him in all his tribulations, so that he also might be able to comfort those who are in distress, by the encouragement which he received from God (see 2 Cor 1:4). This is the secret of true consolation: Those are able to comfort others who, in their own case, have been much tried, and have felt the need of consolation, and have received it. So of our Lord himself it is said: "In that he himself hath suffered and been tempted, he is able to help those also that are tempted" (see Heb 2:18).

This too is why the Blessed Virgin is the comforter of the afflicted. We all know how special a mother's consolation is, and we are allowed to call Mary our mother from the time that our Lord from the Cross established the relation of mother and son between her and St. John. And she especially can console us because she suffered more than mothers in general.

After our Lord's ascension, she was sent out into foreign lands almost as the apostles were, a sheep among wolves. In spite of all St. John's care of her, which was as great as was St. Joseph's in her younger days, more than all the saints of God she was a stranger and a pilgrim upon earth, in proportion to her greater love of him who *had* been on earth, and had gone away. Just as, when our Lord was an infant, she had to flee across the desert to the pagan Egypt; so when he had ascended on high, she had to go on shipboard to the pagan city of Ephesus, where she lived and died.

You who are in the midst of rude neighbors or scoffing companions, or of wicked acquaintances, or of spiteful enemies, and are helpless: Invoke the aid of Mary by the memory of her own sufferings among the pagan Greeks and the pagan Egyptians.

—Blessed John Henry Newman, *Meditations and Devotions*

IN GOD'S PRESENCE, CONSIDER . . .

Do I face adversity "in the midst of rude neighbors or scoffing companions, or of wicked acquaintances, or of spiteful enemies"? Do I seek comfort in the presence and help of Mary, my consoling mother?

CLOSING PRAYER

From "Thirty Days' Prayer to the Blessed Virgin": *Hope and comfort of dejected and desolate souls, you are the mother of mercies, the sweet consoler and only refuge of the needy and the orphan, of the desolate and afflicted.*

Mary, the Awesome Virgin

The awe that is struck in human hearts by angelic visitors cannot compare to the awe and wonder we should feel in Mary's presence. Blessed John Henry Newman tells why.

The holy Daniel, when St. Gabriel appeared to him, "fainted away, and lay in a consternation, with his face close to the ground" (see Dan 8:17). When this great archangel came to Zechariah, the father of St. John the Baptist, he too was troubled, and fear fell upon him (see Lk 1:12). But it was otherwise with Mary when the same St. Gabriel came to her. She was overcome indeed, and troubled at his *words*, because, humble as she was in her own opinion of herself, he addressed her as "full of grace" (see Lk 1:28). But she was able to bear the sight of him.

Hence we learn two things: first, how great a holiness was Mary's, seeing she could endure the presence of an angel, whose brightness smote the holy prophet Daniel even to fainting and almost to death; and secondly, since she is so much holier than that angel, and we so much less holy than Daniel, what great reason we have to call her the *Virgo Admirabilis*, the Wonderful, the Awesome Virgin, when we think of her unspeakable purity!

There are those who are so thoughtless, so blind, so groveling as to think that Mary is not as much shocked at willful sin as her divine Son is, and that we can make her our friend and advocate, even though we go to her without contrition at heart, without even the wish for true repentance and resolution to amend. As if Mary could hate sin less, and love sinners more, than our Lord does! No. She feels a sympathy for those only who wish to *leave* their sins; else, how should she be without sin herself? No. If even to the best of us she is, in the words of Scripture, "fair as the moon, bright as the sun, and *terrible as an army set in array*" (see Sg 6:10), what is she to the impenitent sinner?

—Blessed John Henry Newman, *Meditations and Devotions*

IN GOD'S PRESENCE, CONSIDER . . .

Like Jesus, Mary loves sinners, but hates sin. Do I ever approach her for help without genuine contrition, or even the desire to repent and change?

CLOSING PRAYER

From a prayer of St. Alphonsus Liguori: *Mary, I abandon myself into your hands. Only tell me what you would have me do, and obtain for me the strength to do it; for I am resolved to do all that depends on me to recover God's grace. I take refuge under your mantle.*

Mary, the Mystical Rose

Blessed John Henry Newman proposes that Mary is called the "mystical" (or "hidden") rose because after her assumption, her body has been hidden from us in heaven.

Mary is the queen of spiritual flowers; and therefore she is called the rose, for the rose is fitly called of all flowers the most beautiful. But moreover, she is the *mystical*, or *hidden*, rose; for "mystical" means "hidden." How is she now "hidden" from us more than are other saints? What does this unique title mean, which we apply to her specially? It is this: If her body was not taken into heaven, where is it? How did it come to be hidden from us? Why don't we hear of her tomb as being here or there? Why aren't pilgrimages made to it? Why can none of her relics be produced, as they can for the saints in general?

Isn't it even a natural instinct which makes us reverent towards the places where our dead are buried? We bury our great men honorably. Christians from the earliest times went from other countries to Jerusalem to see the holy places. And when the time of persecution was over, they paid still more attention to the bodies of the saints. Thus, from the first to this day, it has been a great feature and characteristic of the Church to be most tender and reverent towards the bodies of the saints. Now, if there was anyone who more than all would be preciously taken care of, it would be Our Lady. Why then do we hear nothing of the Blessed Virgin's body and its separate relics? Why is she thus the *hidden* rose? Is it conceivable that they who had been so reverent and careful of the bodies of the saints and martyrs should neglect her—the one who was the Queen of Martyrs and the Queen of Saints, who was the very mother of our Lord?

It is impossible. Why then is she thus the *hidden* rose? Plainly because that sacred body is in heaven, not on earth.

—Blessed John Henry Newman, *Meditations and Devotions*

IN GOD'S PRESENCE, CONSIDER . . .

Some have challenged the Church's teaching that Mary was assumed into heaven, both body and soul, noting that the doctrine was not formalized by the Church until modern times. How might Blessed John's insights about the absence of her relics from the very beginning show the matter in a new light?

CLOSING PRAYER

Mary, Mystical Rose, hidden from our sight: Grant that I, too, may be hidden with you, with Christ at the right hand of God.

Mary, Tower of Ivory

The popular term "ivory tower" refers to a disinterest in, a disconnectedness with, the world. But as Blessed John Henry Newman explains, calling Mary the "Tower of Ivory" means something quite different from that, for it symbolizes her strength and beauty.

A tower is a structure which rises higher and more conspicuous than other objects in its neighborhood. Thus, when we say a man "towers" over his fellows, we mean to signify that they look small in comparison to him. This quality of greatness is displayed in the Blessed Virgin.

Though she suffered more keen and intimate anguish at our Lord's passion and crucifixion than any of the Apostles because she was his mother, yet consider how much more noble she was amid her deep distress than they were. When our Lord underwent his agony, they slept for sorrow. They could not wrestle with their deep disappointment and despondency; they could not master it; it confused, numbed, and overcame their senses. And soon after, when St. Peter was asked by bystanders whether he was one of our Lord's disciples, he denied it. Nor was he alone in this cowardice. The Apostles, one and all, forsook our Lord and fled, though St. John returned. No, still further, they even lost faith in him, and thought all the great expectations which he had raised in them had ended in a failure.

In this courage and generosity in suffering she is, as compared with the Apostles, fittingly imaged as a *tower*. But towers, it may be said, are huge, rough, heavy, obtrusive, graceless structures, for the purposes of war, not of peace; with nothing of the beauty, refinement, and finish which are conspicuous in Mary. It is true: Therefore she is called the Tower of *Ivory*, to suggest to us, by the brightness, purity, and exquisiteness of that material, how transcendent is the loveliness and the gentleness of the Mother of God.

—Blessed John Henry Newman, *Meditations and Devotions*

IN GOD'S PRESENCE, CONSIDER . . .

Mary's extraordinary strength was most clearly revealed in her powers of long-suffering and endurance. In what ways am I being called even now to exhibit these virtues in my life? Have I asked for Mary's help to be strong as she was strong?

CLOSING PRAYER

Mary, Tower of Ivory, just as you stood strong beside your Son as he died on the Cross, now stand by me in my trials, and grant me a share of your courage, which is beautiful to behold.

Mary, Queen of Martyrs

Though Mary never suffered a bodily martyrdom, Blessed John Henry Newman insists that her soul suffered a worse sort of martyrdom.

Why is Mary called the Queen of Martyrs? She never had any blow, or wound, or other injury to her consecrated person. How can she be exalted over those whose bodies suffered the most ruthless violence and the keenest torments for our Lord's sake? She is, indeed, Queen of All Saints, of those who "walk with Christ in white, for they are worthy" (see Rv 3:4); but how is she queen of those "who were slain for the Word of God, and for the testimony which they held" (see Rv 6:9)?

To answer this question, it must be recollected that the pains of the soul may be as fierce as those of the body. Bad men who are now in hell, and the elect of God who are in purgatory, are suffering only in their souls, for their bodies are still in the dust; yet how severe is that suffering! And perhaps most people who have lived long can bear witness in their own persons to a sharpness of distress which was like a sword cutting them, to a weight and force of sorrow which seemed to throw them down, though bodily pain there was none.

What an overwhelming horror it must have been for the Blessed Mary to witness the passion and the crucifixion of her Son! Her anguish was, as holy Simeon had announced to her, at the time of that Son's presentation in the temple, a sword piercing her soul. If our Lord himself could not bear the prospect of what was before him, and was covered in the thought of it with a bloody sweat, his soul thus acting upon his body, doesn't this show how great mental pain can be? Thus is she most truly the Queen of Martyrs.

—Blessed John Henry Newman, *Meditations and Devotions*

IN GOD'S PRESENCE, CONSIDER . . .

Have I ever experienced anguish so sharp, grief so heavy, that physical pain could not compare with such suffering? How might Mary come to my aid in such a situation? How might I come to the aid of others who suffer this way?

CLOSING PRAYER

Sometimes I must say with the prophet Jeremiah, "O LORD, behold my affliction! . . . Look and see if there is any sorrow like my sorrow. . . . For these things I weep; my eyes flow with tears" (Lam 1:9, 12, 16). But unlike Jeremiah, I need not say, "a comforter is far from me," for your mother is near me to console me.

Prayer to Mary, Queen of Martyrs

This popular traditional prayer asks for the grace to become a companion of Our Lady's sorrowful heart at the foot of the Cross.

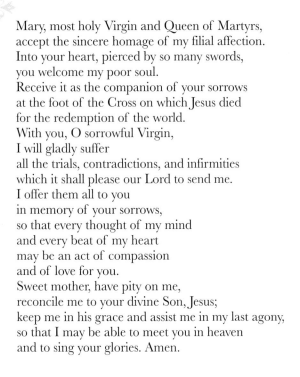

Mary, most holy Virgin and Queen of Martyrs,
accept the sincere homage of my filial affection.
Into your heart, pierced by so many swords,
you welcome my poor soul.
Receive it as the companion of your sorrows
at the foot of the Cross on which Jesus died
for the redemption of the world.
With you, O sorrowful Virgin,
I will gladly suffer
all the trials, contradictions, and infirmities
which it shall please our Lord to send me.
I offer them all to you
in memory of your sorrows,
so that every thought of my mind
and every beat of my heart
may be an act of compassion
and of love for you.
Sweet mother, have pity on me,
reconcile me to your divine Son, Jesus;
keep me in his grace and assist me in my last agony,
so that I may be able to meet you in heaven
and to sing your glories. Amen.

—Traditional

IN GOD'S PRESENCE, CONSIDER . . .

When I am in anguish, especially over the suffering of a loved one, does it comfort me to know that Mary can fully sympathize with my pain, and pray for me accordingly?

CLOSING PRAYER

From "Thirty Days' Prayer to the Blessed Virgin": *Where can I flee for more secure shelter, amiable mother of my Lord and Savior Jesus Christ, than under the wings of your maternal protection?*

Mary, Vessel of Devotion

Blessed John Henry Newman illustrates the meaning of devotion, and shows how Our Lady overflowed with devotion to her son.

To be *devout* is to be devoted. We know what is meant by a devoted wife or daughter. It is one whose thoughts center in the person so deeply loved, so tenderly cherished. She follows him about with her eyes; she is ever seeking some means of serving him; and if her services are very small in their character, that only shows how intimate they are, and how unceasing. And especially if the object of her love be weak, or in pain, or near to die, still more intensely does she live in his life, and know nothing but him.

This intense devotion towards our Lord, forgetting self in love for him, is displayed in St. Paul, who says: "I know nothing but Jesus Christ and him crucified" (see 1 Cor 2:2). And again, "I live, [yet] now not I, but Christ liveth in me; and [the life] that I now live in the flesh, I live in the faith of the Son of God, who loved me, and delivered himself for me" (see Gal 2:20).

But great as was St. Paul's devotion to our Lord, much greater was that of the Blessed Virgin: because she was his mother, and because she had him and all his sufferings actually before her eyes, and because she had the long intimacy of thirty years with him, and because she was from her special sanctity so unspeakably near to him in spirit. When, then, he was mocked, bruised, scourged, and nailed to the Cross, she felt as keenly as if every indignity and torture inflicted on him was struck at herself. She could have cried out in agony at every pang of his. This is called her compassion, or her suffering with her Son, and it arose from this that she was the "Vessel of Devotion" unlike any other.

—Blessed John Henry Newman, *Meditations and Devotions*

IN GOD'S PRESENCE, CONSIDER . . .

Am I devoted to Jesus and his mother in the sense described here? In what practical ways do I show my devotion?

CLOSING PRAYER

From a prayer of St. Bridget: *O Lady, by the love that you bear for Jesus, help me to love him.*

Mary, Vessel of Honor

Mary was a martyr, but in her soul, not her body. Blessed John Henry New-man observes that for the sake of her great honor, she was spared by her Son the bodily dishonor that he and other martyrs had to endure.

St. Paul calls elect souls "vessels of honor": of honor, because they are elect or chosen; and vessels, because, through the love of God, they are filled with God's heavenly and holy grace (see 2 Tim 2:20–21). How much more, then, is Mary a Vessel of Honor by reason of her having within her, not only the grace of God, but the very Son of God, formed as regards his flesh and blood out of her!

But this title "Vessel of Honor," as applied to Mary, admits of a further and special meaning. She was a martyr without the rude dishonour which accompanied the sufferings of martyrs. The martyrs were seized, hauled about, thrust into prison with the vilest criminals, and assailed with the most blasphemous words and foulest speeches which Satan could inspire. No, such was the unutterable trial also of the holy women, young ladies, the spouses of Christ, whom the heathen seized, tortured, and put to death. Above all, our Lord himself, whose sanctity was greater than any created excellence or vessel of grace—even he, as we know well, was buffeted, stripped, scourged, mocked, dragged about, and then stretched, nailed, lifted up on a high cross, to the gaze of a brutal multitude.

But he who bore the sinner's shame for sinners spared his mother, who was sinless, this supreme indignity. Not in the body, but in the soul, she suffered. True, in his agony she was agonized; in his passion she suffered a fellow passion; she was crucified with him; the spear that pierced his breast pierced through her spirit. Yet there were no visible signs of this intimate martyrdom. She stood up, still, collected, motionless, solitary, under the cross of her Son, surrounded by angels, and shrouded in her virginal sanctity from the notice of all who were taking part in his crucifixion.

—Blessed John Henry Newman, *Meditations and Devotions*

IN GOD'S PRESENCE, CONSIDER . . .

What is meant by Mary's "intimate martyrdom"? Can you think of other possible reasons why God willed that Mary be spared bodily harm?

CLOSING PRAYER

From a prayer of St. Alphonsus Liguori: *You know, most sweet Mother of God, how much your blessed Son desires our salvation. You know all that he endured for this purpose. Show now that you love your beloved Son; by this love I beg you to assist me.*

Mary, Virgin Most Prudent

We know little of Mary's everyday life. But Blessed John Henry Newman reminds us that she doubtless would have had numerous practical obligations, and in performing them perfectly, she would have needed that most practical of virtues, prudence.

It may not appear at first sight how the virtue of prudence is connected with the trials and sorrows of Our Lady's life. Yet there is a point of view from which we are reminded of her prudence by those trials. It must be recollected that she is not only the great example of the contemplative life, but also of the practical; and the practical life is at once a life of penance and of prudence, if it is to be well discharged.

Now Mary was as full of external work and hard service as any Sister of Charity at this day. Of course her duties varied according to the seasons of her life, as a young maiden, as a wife, as a mother, and as a widow. But still her life was full of duties day by day and hour by hour.

As a stranger in Egypt, she had duties towards the poor pagans among whom she was thrown. As a dweller in Nazareth, she had her duties towards her kinsfolk and neighbors. She had her duties, though unrecorded, during those years in which our Lord was preaching and proclaiming his kingdom. After he had left this earth, she had her duties towards the Apostles, and especially toward the Evangelists. She had duties towards the martyrs, and to the confessors in prison; to the sick, to the ignorant, and to the poor.

All her acts were perfect, all were the best that could be done. Now, always to be awake, guarded, fervent, so as to be able to act not only without sin, but in the best possible way, in the varying circumstances of each day, denotes a life of untiring mindfulness. But of such a life, prudence is the presiding virtue. It is, then, through the pains and sorrows of her earthly pilgrimage that we are able to invoke her as "Virgin Most Prudent."

—Blessed John Henry Newman, *Meditations and Devotions*

IN GOD'S PRESENCE, CONSIDER . . .

Do I tend to view my everyday obligations as competing with my spiritual life, or as providing me a chance to practice the virtue of prudence? When I'm uncertain about the wisest course of action, do I ask myself what would Jesus and Mary do?

CLOSING PRAYER

Virgin, Most Prudent, Mary, Mother of the Church, pray for us.

Mary, the second and better Eve

Since ancient times, Christian teachers have noted both the parallels and the contrasts between Eve and Mary. Blessed John Henry Newman sums up the traditional teaching about Mary as the "second and better Eve."

Eve had a part in the fall of man, though it was Adam who was our representative, and whose sin made us sinners. It was Eve who began, and who tempted Adam. It was fitting then in God's mercy that, as the woman began the *destruction* of the world, so woman should also begin its *recovery*, and that, as Eve opened the way for the fatal deed of the first Adam, so Mary should open the way for the great achievement of the second Adam, even our Lord Jesus Christ, who came to save the world by dying on the Cross for it. Hence Mary is called by the holy Fathers a second and a better Eve, as having taken that first step in the salvation of mankind which Eve took in its ruin.

How, and when, did Mary take part, and the initial part, in the world's restoration? It was when the angel Gabriel came to her to announce to her the great dignity which was to be her portion. It was God's will that she should undertake *willingly* and with *full understanding* to be the mother of our Lord, and not to be a mere passive instrument whose maternity would have no merit and no reward.

The higher our gifts, the heavier our duties. It was no light thing to be so intimately near to the Redeemer of men, as she experienced afterwards when she suffered with him. Therefore, weighing well the angel's words before giving her answer to them, first she asked whether so great an office would be a forfeiture of that virginity which she had vowed. When the angel told her no, then, with the full consent of a full heart, full of God's love to her and her own lowliness, she said, "Behold the handmaid of the Lord; be it done unto me according to thy word."

—Blessed John Henry Newman, *Meditations and Devotions*

IN GOD'S PRESENCE, CONSIDER . . .

What does it mean to say "the higher our gifts, the heavier our duties"? What gifts have I been given that oblige me to heavier duties?

CLOSING PRAYER

Mary, teach me how to say yes to God, to consent to his will with a whole heart, so that I too might crush the head of the serpent in my life.

Mary, Star of the Sea

Our Lady has long been called by the title "Star of the Sea." Just as ancient mariners navigated by the stars, St. Bernard observes, Christians can find their way safely home to heaven if they follow her lovely, shining example of holiness and faith.

Mary is the distinguished and bright shining star, lifted up above this great broad sea, gleaming with merits, giving light by her example. If you're caught between storms and tempests, tossed about in the flood of this world, instead of walking on dry land, keep your eyes fixed on the glow of this star, unless you want to perish, overwhelmed by the tempest!

If the winds of temptations surge, if you run aground on the shoals of troubles, look to this star, call upon Mary! If you're tossed by the winds of pride or ambition or detraction or jealousy, look to this star, call upon Mary!

If anger or greed or the allurements of the flesh dash against the boat of your mind, look to Mary! And if you're troubled by the enormity of your sins, ashamed by the foulness of your conscience, terrified by the horror of Judgment Day, so that you begin to be swallowed up in the pit of sadness, the abyss of despair—think of Mary!

In dangers, in straits, in perplexity, think of Mary, call upon Mary. Let her name be always in your mouth and in your heart. And if you would ask for and obtain the help of her prayers, don't forget the example of how she lived. If you follow her, you won't go astray. If you pray to her, you won't despair. If you think of her, you won't be lost. If you cling to her, you won't fall. If she protects you, you won't fear. If she's your guide, you won't grow weary. If she's favorable to you, you'll reach your goal.

—St. Bernard of Clairvaux, *Super missus est*

IN GOD'S PRESENCE, CONSIDER . . .

What storms threaten to overwhelm me just now? What winds of temptation are buffeting me? What shoals of troubles present me with dangers? Have I looked to Mary for help?

CLOSING PRAYER

From a "Prayer to Our Lady of Mount Carmel": *O most beautiful flower of Mount Carmel, fruitful vine, splendor of heaven, Blessed Mother of the Son of God, immaculate Virgin, help me in this, my need. O Star of the Sea, help me, and show me in this that you are my mother.*

O Stella Maris!

In darkness and in doldrums, in storms and in shallows, we cry out to Our Lady Stella Maris, Star of the Sea, for safety and certainty in our voyage home to her Son.

O brilliant star above the sea, our beacon to eternity,
whose beams beyond the surging wave draw all to him who came to save:
To heaven's harbor, through the night, *O Stella Maris*, be our light!

When darkness deepens, storms assail, when charity and courage fail,
when hope gives way to doubt and fear, with deadly shallows lying near:
Illumine us, our faith increase; *O Stella Maris*, star of peace!

When doldrums gently lull to sleep, when comforts slow the course we keep;
when we forget our destiny and, aimless, drift upon the sea;
when siren songs tempt us to roam, *O Stella Maris*, lead us home!

For all uncertain on their way, for all whose maps have led astray,
with compass lost or found untrue, whose hearts, unknowing, cry to you:
Point heavenward above the tide; *O Stella Maris*, be our guide!

—Paul Thigpen

IN GOD'S PRESENCE, CONSIDER . . .

Do I ask Mary's help, not only when I'm afraid or in danger, but also when pleasant temptations beckon me to stray?

CLOSING PRAYER

Blessed Lady, Star of the Sea, radiant beacon guiding us to your glorious Son, pray for us that the light of faith will shine through us, and that Jesus Christ, the Dawn from on high, will rule among us in the splendor of holiness.

Mary, Refuge of Sinners

St. Alphonsus explains the ancient origins of the Marian title "Refuge of Sinners."

One of the titles of Mary that is the most encouraging to poor sinners, under which the Church teaches us to invoke Mary in the Litany of Loreto, is that of "Refuge of Sinners." In Judea in ancient times there were cities of refuge, in which criminals who fled there for protection were exempt from the punishments that they had deserved. Today these cities are not so numerous; there is but one, and that is Mary, of whom the psalmist says, "Glorious things are spoken of you, O city of God!" (Ps 87:3).

But this city differs from the ancient ones in this respect: In the ancient cities, not all kinds of criminals could find refuge, nor was the protection extended to every class of crime. But under the mantle of Mary all sinners, without exception, find refuge for every sin that they may have committed, provided only that they go there to seek for this protection.

"To all who fly to me," says St. John of Damascus, speaking in the name of our queen, "I am the city of refuge."

A devout author exhorts all sinners to take refuge under the mantle of Mary, exclaiming, "Flee, Adam and Eve, and all you their children, who have outraged God! Flee, and take refuge in the bosom of this good mother. Don't you know that she is our only city of refuge?"

—St. Alphonsus Liguori, *The Glories of Mary*

IN GOD'S PRESENCE, CONSIDER . . .

Am I willing to admit the depth and breadth of my own sin and weakness? Am I willing to run to Mary as a refuge God has given for my healing?

CLOSING PRAYER

"Prayer in Honor of Our Lady, Refuge of Sinners": *Almighty and merciful God, who appointed the blessed, ever-virgin Mary to be the refuge and help of sinners, grant that under her protection we may be delivered from all guilt, and obtain the happiness that your mercy brings.*

Mary, Mirror of Virtue

St. Ambrose of Milan offers a meditation on Our Lady, reflecting on how her sinlessness would have shaped her thoughts, words, attitudes, and conduct.

Let the life of Mary be like a mirror, in which is reflected the form of virtue and the beauty of chastity. In her you can find your pattern of life, for she demonstrates clearly the rules of virtue: what you must correct in yourselves, what you must embrace, and what you must hold firmly.

She was virgin, not only in body, but also in mind. She never stained the integrity of her mind through deception. She was humble of heart, serious in conversation, wise in thought, brief in words, earnest in study. She didn't rest her hope on uncertain riches, but on God who answers the prayers of the poor.

She was diligent in work and restrained in speech. She looked to God as the Judge of her thoughts, not to other people. She sought to avoid injury to all and to have goodwill toward everyone. She respected her elders and didn't envy her peers. She avoided boasting; she acted reasonably; she loved virtue.

When did she ever bring pain to her parents even by as much as a look? When did she ever quarrel with her neighbors? When did she despise the lowly? When did she turn away from those in need? She avoided gatherings that would have made a generous heart blush, or sent a modest soul fleeing.

There was nothing gloomy in her eyes, nothing pushy in her words, nothing unbecoming in her conduct. She didn't run around acting silly. Her voice wasn't rude.

In short, her outward appearance was the image of her soul, a reflection of everything honorable.

—St. Ambrose of Milan, *On Virginity*

IN GOD'S PRESENCE, CONSIDER . . .

How do I think Our Lady would think, speak, and act in the circumstances I'll face today? How might I keep her example in mind?

CLOSING PRAYER

Mary, Mirror of Virtue, help me find in you my pattern for life..

Mary, Mirror of Justice

If Mary is called a Mirror of Justice, whose justice did she reflect? Blessed John Henry Newman observes that it was the justice of her Son, with whom she lived so closely.

When Our Lady is called the "Mirror of Justice," it is meant to say that she is the mirror of sanctity, holiness, supernatural goodness. But what is meant by calling her a *mirror*? A mirror is a surface which reflects, such as still water, polished steel, or a looking glass.

What did Mary reflect? She reflected our Lord—but *he* is infinite *sanctity*. She then, as far as a creature could, reflected his divine sanctity, and therefore she is the *Mirror* of Sanctity, or as the Litany says, of *Justice*.

Do we ask how she came to reflect his sanctity? It was by living with him. We see every day how alike people get to each other who live with those they love.

All of us perceive this; we are witnesses to it with our own eyes and ears—in the expression of their features, in their voice, in their walk, in their language, even in their handwriting, they become like each other; and so with regard to their minds, as in their opinions, their tastes, their pursuits. And again doubtless in the state of their souls, which we do not see, whether for good or for bad.

Now, consider that Mary loved her divine Son with an unutterable love; and consider too she had him all to herself for thirty years. Don't we see that, as she was full of grace before she conceived him in her womb, she must have had a vast incomprehensible sanctity when she had lived close to God for thirty years? A sanctity of an angelical order, reflecting back the attributes of God with a fullness and exactness of which no saint upon earth, or hermit, or holy virgin, can even remind us. Truly then she is the *Mirror* of Divine *Perfection*.

—Blessed John Henry Newman, *Meditations and Devotions*

IN GOD'S PRESENCE, CONSIDER . . .

When I look in a mirror, I see both the best and the worst of my appearance. Might Mary serve as a mirror for me in a second sense in that, when I look at her moral perfection, I see more clearly my own flaws in comparison?

CLOSING PRAYER

Mary, Mirror of Justice, most holy, most wise, pray for us who seek to follow your example and the example of your Son.

Mary, Mother of the Church

St. Louis de Montfort teaches us that Mary is our mother in the order of grace, the Mother of the Church. Since she's the mother of Christ, the Head of the Mystical Body, then she's also the mother of all that Body's members.

Just as in the natural and bodily generation of children there are a father and a mother, so in the supernatural and spiritual generation there are a Father, who is God, and a mother, who is Mary. All the true children of God have God for their Father and Mary for their mother. Whoever doesn't have Mary for his mother doesn't have God for his Father.

The first human born in Mary is the Man-God, Jesus Christ. The others are mere men and women, the children of God and Mary by adoption. If Jesus Christ, the Head of the human race, is born in her, then the members of that Head ought also to be born in her, as a necessary consequence.

One and the same mother doesn't bring forth into the world the head of a child's body without its members, or the members without the head. This would be a monster of nature. In the same way, in the order of grace the Head, Jesus Christ, and the members of his Body, the Church, are born of the same mother. If a member of the Mystical Body of Jesus were born of any other mother than Mary, who has produced the Head, he would not be a member of Jesus Christ, but simply a monster in the order of grace.

—St. Louis de Montfort, *True Devotion to Mary*

IN GOD'S PRESENCE, CONSIDER . . .

Do I see Mary as my spiritual mother? What might it mean for my devotional life to approach her daily as my mother?

CLOSING PRAYER

From a prayer of Pope St. John Paul II: *To you, mother of the human family and of the nations, we confidently entrust the whole of humanity, with its hopes and fears. Do not let it lack the light of true wisdom. Guide its steps in the ways of peace. Enable all to meet Christ, the Way and the Truth and the Life.*

Two occasions when Mary became our mother

We typically think of Jesus' words from the Cross, "Behold your mother!" (Jn 19:27) as the moment when we all became her spiritual children. But St. Alphonsus points to two other occasions when Mary became our spiritual mother.

On two occasions, according to the holy Fathers of the Church, Mary became our spiritual mother. The first, according to St. Albert the Great, was when she merited to conceive in her virginal womb the Son of God. St. Bernardine of Siena tells us that "when at the Annunciation the most Blessed Virgin gave the consent which was expected by the Eternal Word before becoming her Son, she from that moment asked God for our salvation with intense ardor, and took it to heart in such a way, that from that moment, as a most loving mother, she bore us in her womb." Abbot St. William writes in the same sense, saying, "Mary, in bringing forth Jesus, our Savior and our Life, brought forth many to salvation. By giving birth to Life itself, she gave life to many."

The second occasion on which Mary became our spiritual mother, and brought us forth to the life of grace, was when she offered to the Eternal Father the life of her beloved Son on Mount Calvary, with such bitter sorrow and suffering. St. Augustine declares that "as she then cooperated by her love in the birth of the faithful to the life of grace, she became the spiritual mother of all who are members of the one Head, Christ Jesus."

St. William says that "Mary, in order that she might save many souls, exposed her own to death." He means that to save us, she sacrificed the life of her Son. And who but Jesus was the soul of Mary? He was her life, and all her love. For this reason the prophet Simeon foretold that a sword of sorrow would one day pierce her own most blessed soul (see Lk 2:35). And it was precisely the lance that pierced the side of Jesus, who was the soul of Mary. It was at this moment that this most Blessed Virgin brought us forth by her sorrows to eternal life.

—St. Alphonsus Liguori, *The Glories of Mary*

IN GOD'S PRESENCE, CONSIDER . . .

What does it mean to me to realize that Mary is not just my "adopted" mother, but my spiritual mother, who spiritually bore me in her womb? Does that realization lead to a greater sense of intimacy with her?

CLOSING PRAYER

From a prayer of St. Alphonsus: *The name "Mother" consoles and fills me with tenderness, and reminds me of my obligation to love you, Mary. This name excites me to great confidence in you. When my sins and the divine justice fill me most with consternation, I am all consoled at the thought that you are my mother.*

Run to your mother!

When small children are in danger, to whom do they run and call for help? To their mother, of course! And so should we, says St. Alphonsus.

Our Blessed Lady herself in a vision addressed these words to St. Bridget: "Just as a mother, if she saw her son surrounded by the swords of his enemies, would use every effort to save him, so will I. And I will do this for all sinners who seek my mercy." For this reason, in every engagement with the powers of hell we will always certainly conquer by turning to the Mother of God for help, who is also our Mother, repeating again and again: "We fly to your patronage, O holy Mother of God! We fly to your patronage, O holy Mother of God!" How many victories the faithful have gained over hell by turning to Mary for help with this short but most powerful prayer!

Be of good heart, then, all you who are children of Mary. Remember that she accepts as her children all those who choose to be so. Rejoice! Why do you fear to be lost, when such a mother defends and protects you? St. Bonaventure observes: "Say, then, O my soul, with great confidence: 'I will rejoice and be glad; for whatever the judgment to be pronounced on me may be, it depends on and must come from my Brother and Mother.' . . . In this way each one who loves this good mother, and relies on her protection, should stir himself to confidence, remembering that Jesus is our Brother, and Mary our Mother."

Children have always on their lips their mother's name, and in every fear, in every danger, they immediately cry out, "Mother! Mother!" Most sweet Mary! Most loving Mother! This is precisely what you desire: that we should become children, and call on you in every danger, and at all times turn to you, because you desire to help and rescue us, as you have rescued all who have turned to you.

—St. Alphonsus Liguori, *The Glories of Mary*

IN GOD'S PRESENCE, CONSIDER . . .

What fears or dangers do I face today that should send me running to my spiritual mother and asking her protection?

CLOSING PRAYER

From the *Sub Tuum Praesidium: We flee to your patronage, O holy Mother of God. Do not despise our petitions in our needs, but deliver us always from all dangers, O glorious and Blessed Virgin!*

Mary, Morning Star

Blessed John Henry Newman considers why a star—and in particular, the morning star—is such a fitting symbol of Mary.

What is the nearest approach in the way of symbols, in this world of sight and sense, to represent to us the glories of that higher world which is beyond our bodily perceptions? What are the truest tokens and promises here, poor though they may be, of what one day we hope to see hereafter, as being beautiful and rare? Whatever they may be, surely the Blessed Mother of God may claim them as her own. And so it is. Two of them are ascribed to her as her titles, in her Litany—the stars above, and flowers below. She is at once the *Rosa Mystica* (Mystical Rose) and the *Stella Matutina* (Morning Star). And of these two, both of them well suited to her, the Morning Star becomes her best, and that for three reasons.

First, the rose belongs to this earth, but the star is placed in high heaven. Mary now has no part in this lower world. No change, no violence from fire, water, earth, or air, affects the stars above; and they show themselves, ever bright and marvelous, in all regions of this globe, and to all the tribes of men.

Next, the rose has but a short life; its decay is as sure as it was graceful and fragrant in its noon. But Mary, like the stars, abides forever, as lustrous now as she was on the day of her assumption; as pure and perfect, when her Son comes to judgment, as she is now.

Finally, it is Mary's prerogative to be the Morning Star, which heralds in the sun. She does not shine for herself, or from herself, but she is the reflection of her Redeemer and ours, and she glorifies him. When she appears in the darkness, we know that he is close at hand.

—Blessed John Henry Newman, *Meditations and Devotions*

IN GOD'S PRESENCE, CONSIDER . . .

The morning star is not only a herald of the sun; it's actually a planet that shines, not with its own light, but the light of that same sun, reflected. Today, are there situations in which I can imitate Mary by pointing to Jesus and reflecting his light?

CLOSING PRAYER

If "the heavens are telling the glory of God, and the firmament proclaims his handiwork" (Ps 19:1), how much more, my Lady, do you declare his glory, bright Morning Star who shines down from heaven!

Mary, Most Faithful Virgin

Blessed John Henry Newman examines the meaning of faithfulness, as it applies to Mary, to all God's servants, and to God himself.

One title of the Blessed Virgin is *Virgo Fidelis*, "Most Faithful Virgin." The word *faithfulness* means loyalty to a superior, or exactness in fulfilling an engagement. In the latter sense it is applied even to Almighty God himself who, in his great love for us, has promised to limit his own power in action by his word of promise and his covenant with his creatures. He has given his word that, if we will take him for our portion and put ourselves into his hands, he will guide us through all trials and temptations, and bring us safe to heaven. And to encourage and inspirit us, he reminds us, in various passages of Scripture, that he is the *faithful* God, the *faithful* Creator.

And so, his true saints and servants have the special title of "faithful," as being true to him as he is to them; as being simply obedient to his will, zealous for his honor, observant of the sacred interests which he has committed to their keeping. Thus Abraham is called the "faithful"; Moses is declared to be "faithful in all his house"; David, on this account, is called the "man after God's own heart"; St. Paul returns thanks that God accounted him faithful; and at the last day, God will say to all those who have well employed their talents, "Well done, good and faithful servant."

Mary, in like manner, is preeminently faithful to her Lord and Son. Let no one for an instant suppose that she is not supremely zealous for his honor or, as those who are not Catholics fancy, that to exalt her is to be unfaithful to him. Her true servants are still more truly his. Well as she rewards her friends, she would deem him no friend, but a traitor, who preferred her to him. As he is zealous for her honor, so is she for his. He is the Fount of grace, and all her gifts are from his goodness.

—Blessed John Henry Newman, *Meditations and Devotions*

IN GOD'S PRESENCE, CONSIDER . . .

Some claim that to honor and serve Mary is to be unfaithful to her Son. How might I explain to them that "her servants are still more truly his"?

CLOSING PRAYER

From a prayer of Blessed John Henry Newman: *Mary, teach us ever to worship your Son as the one Creator, and to be devout to you as the most highly favored of creatures.*

Mary, Model of Virtue

If we truly love Mary, St. Alphonsus insists, we will imitate all her virtues.

St. Augustine says that to obtain the favor of the saints with more certainty, and in greater abundance, we must imitate them. For when they see us practice their virtues, they are more roused to pray for us. So as soon as the Queen of Saints and our principal advocate, Mary, delivers a soul from Lucifer's grasp and unites it to God, she desires for it to begin imitating her. Otherwise, she can't enrich it with the graces she would desire, because it's so opposed to her in conduct.

Whoever loves either is like the person loved or endeavors to become like that person. As the well-known proverb says, "Love either finds or makes what is like it." For this reason, St. Sophronius urges: "My beloved children, serve Mary, whom you love; for you then truly love her, if you endeavor to imitate the one you love." Richard of Saint Lawrence says, "Those who strive to imitate Mary's life are and can call themselves her true children." "Let the child, then," concludes St. Bernard, "endeavor to imitate his mother, if he desires her favor. For Mary, seeing herself treated as a mother, will treat him as her child."

There is little recorded in the Gospels of Mary's virtues in detail. But when we learn from them that she was "full of grace" (Lk 1:28), this alone tells us that she possessed all virtues to a heroic degree. "The other saints excelled," says St. Thomas, "each in some particular virtue: one in chastity, another in humility, another in mercy. But the Blessed Virgin excelled in all, and is given as a model of all." St. Ambrose agrees: "Mary was such that her life alone was a model for all." Then he concludes: "Let the virginity and life of Mary be for you as a faithful image, in which the form of virtue is resplendent. From that image, learn how to live, what to correct, what to avoid, and what to retain."

—St. Alphonsus Liguori, *The Glories of Mary*

IN GOD'S PRESENCE, CONSIDER . . .

What does it mean to say that "love either finds or makes what is like it"? How do I see that principle illustrated in my life?

CLOSING PRAYER

From a prayer of Venerable Pope Pius XII: *Our eyes are fixed on you in admiration, immaculate Virgin; you who are loved by the heavenly Father above all others! Obtain for us from your divine Son the grace to reflect your sublime virtues in our conduct, according to our age and condition in life.*

Mary, Mother of Oil

Why would Our Lady be called "Mother of Oil?" St. Alphonsus explains.

The words of the biblical Book of Sirach have been applied to Mary: "like a beautiful olive tree on the plain" (see Sir 24:14). For just as from the olive, only oil—a symbol of mercy—is extracted, so from the hands of Mary, only graces and mercy proceed. For this reason the venerable Fr. Louis de Ponte says, "Mary may properly be called the Mother of Oil, since she is the Mother of Mercy."

When we go, then, to this good mother for the oil of her mercy, we can't fear that she'll deny it to us, as the wise virgins in the Gospel story did to the foolish ones, saying, "Perhaps there may not be enough for us and for you" (Mt 25:9). Oh, no! For she is indeed rich in this oil of mercy; as St. Bonaventure assures us, "Mary is filled with the oil of compassion." Hugh of Saint Victor declares: "You, Blessed Virgin, are full of grace, and indeed so full, that the whole world may draw of this overflowing oil. While the prudent virgins in the Gospel story provided oil in vessels with their lamps, you, most prudent Virgin, have borne an overflowing and inexhaustible Vessel. With the oil of mercy streaming from this Vessel, you replenish the lamps of all."

But why, I ask, is this beautiful olive tree said to stand in the midst of the plain, and not rather in the midst of a garden, surrounded by a wall and hedges? The same Hugh of Saint Victor tells us that this is the case so that "all may see her, and all may go to her for refuge." This beautiful explanation is confirmed by St. Antoninus, who says: "All can go to, and gather the fruit of, an olive tree that is exposed in the midst of a plain. In the same way, all—both righteous and sinners—can turn to Mary, to obtain her mercy."

—St. Alphonsus Liguori, *The Glories of Mary*

IN GOD'S PRESENCE, CONSIDER . . .

Oil is an ancient symbol of many things: abundance, healing, the Holy Spirit, election by God, and consecration to God. In fact, "Christ" literally means "the one anointed" by oil. How do these symbolic associations enrich our understanding of Mary as the Mother of Oil?

CLOSING PRAYER

From a Father of the Council of Ephesus: *Hail, Mary, Mother of God! You are the lamp that is never extinguished. Through you, the oil of gladness reaches us.*

Mary, Queen of Angels

The Church has long affirmed that the angels are arranged in a hierarchy of ranks. Blessed John Henry Newman tells why Mary stands as queen above that hierarchy.

The great title "Queen of Angels" may be fitly connected with the maternity of Mary, that is, with the coming upon her of the Holy Spirit at Nazareth after the angel Gabriel's annunciation to her, and with the consequent birth of our Lord at Bethlehem. She, as the mother of our Lord, comes nearer to him than any angel; nearer even than the seraphim who surround him and cry continually, "Holy, Holy, Holy!"

We know our Lord came to set up the kingdom of heaven among men; and hardly was he born when he was assaulted by the powers of the world who wished to destroy him. Herod sought to take his life, but he was defeated by St. Joseph's carrying his mother and him off into Egypt. But St. John in the Apocalypse tells us that Michael and his angels were the real guardians of mother and Child, then and on other occasions.

First, St. John saw in a vision "a woman clothed with the sun, and with the moon under her feet, and on her head a crown of twelve stars"; and when she was about to be delivered of her Child there appeared "a great red dragon," that is, the evil spirit, ready "to devour her son" when he should be born (see Rv 12:1–4). The Son was preserved by his own divine power, but next the evil spirit persecuted her. St. Michael, however, and his angels came to the rescue and prevailed against him. "There was a great battle," says the sacred writer; "Michael and his angels fought with the dragon, and the dragon fought and his angels; and that great dragon was cast out, the old serpent, who is called the Devil" (see Rv 12:7–9). Now, as then, the Blessed Mother of God has hosts of angels who do her service; and she is their queen.

—Blessed John Henry Newman, *Meditations and Devotions*

IN GOD'S PRESENCE, CONSIDER . . .

The demonic powers are enemies of Mary, and they are my enemies as well. When they come to tempt, confuse, or buffet me, do I call on the Queen of Heaven and her hosts to defend me?

CLOSING PRAYER

From a prayer of a Bernardine sister: *Queen of Heaven, send down your holy angels, so that under your command and by your power, they may pursue the evil spirits, encounter them on every side, resist their bold attacks, and drive them from here into the abyss of hell.*

Mary is exalted above the angels

As glorious as the angels may be, St. Alphonsus observes, God has placed her above them, the Queen Mother at the right hand of King Jesus.

Rightly does the Church sing in her liturgy, that because Mary loved God more than all the angels, "the Mother of God has been exalted above them all in the heavenly kingdom." Yes, "she was exalted above the angels," says the Abbot Guarric, "so that she sees no one above her but her Son," the Only-begotten of the Father. For this reason, the learned Gerson asserts that, as all the orders of angels and saints are divided into three hierarchies (according to St. Thomas and St. Denis), so Mary in herself constitutes a hierarchy apart, the most sublime of all, and next to that of God. St. Antoninus adds that just as the mistress is, without comparison, above her servants, so also is "Mary, who is the sovereign Lady of the angels, exalted incomparably above the angelic hierarchies." To understand this, we need only know what King David said: "At your right hand stands the queen" (Ps 45:9).

It's certain, as St. Ildephonsus says, that Mary's good works incomparably surpassed in merit those of all the saints. So her reward must have surpassed theirs in the same proportion: "Just as the One she bore was incomprehensible, so is the reward that she merited and received incomprehensibly greater than that of all the saints."

As the Apostle Paul writes, it's certain that God rewards according to merit; "he will render to every man according to his works" (Rom 2:6). So it's also certain, as St. Thomas teaches, that the Blessed Virgin, "who was equal to and even superior in merit to all men and angels, was exalted above all the heavenly orders." "In short," adds St. Bernard, "let us measure the unique grace that she acquired on earth, and then we can measure the unique glory that she obtained in heaven." For "according to the measure of her grace on earth is the measure of her glory in the kingdom of the blessed."

—St. Alphonsus Liguori, *The Glories of Mary*

IN GOD'S PRESENCE, CONSIDER . . .

The more exalted Mary's position, the greater is her power to assist us. What is it that I'm facing today that presses me most to seek her help?

CLOSING PRAYER

From a prayer of a Bernardine sister: *Most holy Mother, send your angels to defend us and to drive the cruel enemy from us. All you holy angels and archangels, help and defend us.*

The angels welcome their queen into heaven

During her life on earth, the angels no doubt stayed close to Mary and her Son. When she went home to heaven, St. Alphonsus concludes, they must have welcomed her with joyous celebration and praise.

Watch as Mary enters that blessed country of heaven in her assumption! The ancient Christian teacher Origen imagines the scene: At her entrance, the heavenly spirits, seeing her so beautiful and glorious, ask the angels coming with her, with united voices of exultation, "Who is that coming up from the wilderness, flowing with delights, leaning upon her Beloved?" (See Sg 8:5.)

Who can be this creature, so beautiful, who comes from the wilderness of the earth—a place of thorns and tribulation? Yet this one comes pure and rich in virtue, leaning on her beloved Lord, who is graciously pleased to accompany her himself with such great honor. Who is she? The angels accompanying her answer: "She is the mother of our King; she is our queen, and the blessed one among women; full of grace, the saint of saints, the beloved of God, the immaculate one, the dove, the fairest of all creatures."

Then all the blessed spirits begin to bless and praise her, singing as the Jews did to Judith, but with far more reason: "'You are the glory of Jerusalem; you are the joy of Israel; you are the honor of our people' (see Jdt 15:9). So, then, our Lady and our Queen, you are the glory of paradise, the joy of our country, the honor of us all.

"Be always welcome; be always blessed! Behold your kingdom. Behold us as well, who are your servants, always ready to obey your commands." All the angels then come to salute her. In reply, she, the great queen, thanks all for the assistance they have given her on earth. Most especially she thanks the archangel Gabriel, who was the happy ambassador, the bearer of all her glories, when he came to announce to her that she was the chosen Mother of God.

—St. Alphonsus Liguori, *The Glories of Mary*

IN GOD'S PRESENCE, CONSIDER . . .

Am I in the habit of thanking the angels who have helped me, as Mary did? Do I regularly express my gratitude especially to my guardian angel and to St. Michael for so often coming to my defense, even when I'm not aware that the Enemy is threatening?

CLOSING PRAYER

Queen of Heaven, you have made your home with the angels; now make your home in our hearts.

Mary is fearful to the demons

St. Alphonsus reminds us that even though we may be terrified by the demons, the demons themselves are terrified by Mary.

How the demons of hell tremble at the very thought of Mary, and of her majestic name! St. Bonaventure declares: "O, how fearful is Mary to the devils!" The saint compares these enemies to those of whom Job speaks: "They dig through houses in the dark. If the morning suddenly appears, it is to them the shadow of death" (Job 24:16–17). Thieves go out and rob houses in the dark; but as soon as morning dawns, they flee, as if they beheld the shadow of death.

"In precisely this way," St. Bonaventure continues, "the demons enter a soul in the time of darkness"; meaning, when the soul is in the obscurity of ignorance. They dig through the house of our mind when it is in the darkness of ignorance.

But then he adds, "If suddenly they are overtaken by the dawn—that is, if the grace and mercy of Mary enters the soul—its brightness instantly dispels the darkness, and puts the hellish enemies to flight, as if they were fleeing from death." How blessed are those who always invoke the beautiful name of Mary in their conflicts with hell!

In confirmation of this reality, it was revealed to St. Bridget: "God has rendered Mary so powerful over the demons that, as often as they assault a devout believer who calls on this most Blessed Virgin for help, she at a single glance instantly terrifies them. They flee far away, preferring to have their pains redoubled rather than see themselves subject in this way to the power of Mary."

—St. Alphonsus Liguori, *The Glories of Mary*

IN GOD'S PRESENCE, CONSIDER . . .

Is there any situation I am facing now that seems to bear the fingerprints of the Enemy of my soul? Have I called on Mary to send the Enemy fleeing?

CLOSING PRAYER

Queen of Angels, illuminate the dark rooms of my mind and heart, so that the Enemy will have no place to enter and make mischief.

Mary's name is a fortified tower

St. Alphonsus declares that the name of Mary, like the name of Jesus, is powerful in spiritual battle.

The Blessed Virgin herself revealed to St. Bridget: "On earth there is no sinner, however devoid he may be of the love of God, from whom the Devil is not obliged to flee immediately, if he invokes her holy name with a determination to repent." On another occasion she repeated the same thing to the saint, saying, "All the demons venerate and fear her name to such a degree, that on hearing it they immediately loosen the claws with which they hold the soul captive."

Our Blessed Lady also told her: "In the same way as the rebel angels fly from sinners who invoke the name of Mary, so also do the good angels approach nearer to righteous souls who pronounce her name with devotion." St. Germanus declares: "Just as breathing is a sign of life, so also is the frequent pronunciation of the name of Mary a sign either of the life of divine grace, or that it will soon come. For this powerful name has in it the virtue of obtaining help and life for him who invokes it devoutly."

To sum up, "This admirable name of our sovereign Lady," says Richard of Saint Lawrence, "is like a fortified tower. If a sinner takes refuge in it, he will be delivered from death; for it defends and saves even the most abandoned." But it is a tower of strength that not only delivers sinners from chastisement, but also defends the righteous from the assaults of hell.

—St. Alphonsus Liguori, *The Glories of Mary*

IN GOD'S PRESENCE, CONSIDER . . .

What does it mean to say that Mary's name is strong and powerful? Why would the demons flee from it?

CLOSING PRAYER

Your name, Mary, like the name of your Son, "is a strong tower; the righteous run into it and are safe" (see Prv 18:10).

What is the Immaculate Conception?

Blessed John Henry Newman lays out in clear terms the meaning of the doctrine of the Immaculate Conception.

Since the fall of Adam, all mankind, his descendants, are conceived and born in sin. That sin which belongs to every one of us, and is ours from the first moment of our existence, is the sin of unbelief and disobedience by which Adam lost paradise. We, as the children of Adam, are heirs to the consequences of his sin, and have forfeited in him that spiritual robe of grace and holiness which he had given him by his Creator at the time that he was made. In this state of forfeiture and disinheritance we are all of us conceived and born; and the ordinary way by which we are taken out of it is the sacrament of Baptism.

But Mary *never* was in this state; she was by the eternal decree of God exempted from it. From eternity, God, the Father, Son, and Holy Spirit, decreed to create the race of man, and, foreseeing the fall of Adam, decreed to redeem the whole race by the Son's taking flesh and suffering on the Cross. In that same incomprehensible, eternal instant, in which the Son of God was born of the Father, was also the decree passed of man's redemption through him. He who was born from Eternity was born by an eternal decree to save us in time, and to redeem the whole race. And Mary's redemption was determined in that special manner which we call the Immaculate Conception.

It was decreed, not that she should be *cleansed* from sin, but that she should, from the first moment of her being, be *preserved* from sin; so that the Evil One never had any part in her. Therefore she was a child of Adam and Eve as if they had never fallen; she did not share with them their sin; she inherited the gifts and graces (and more than those) which Adam and Eve possessed in paradise.

—Blessed John Henry Newman, *Meditations and Devotions*

IN GOD'S PRESENCE, CONSIDER . . .

What does it mean for my relationship with Mary to know that she was preserved from all sin? How does knowing that strengthen my confidence in following her as a model of holiness?

CLOSING PRAYER

From a prayer of Blessed John: *Virgin most pure, conceived without original sin, Mary, pray for us.*

To be preserved from sin is the greater honor

Which is more honorable, St. Alphonsus asks: to fall and be rescued, or never to have fallen in the first place? The latter is more honorable, of course, and so it was with Mary.

A person may be redeemed in two ways, as St. Augustine teaches us: One is to be raised up after he has fallen. The other is to be prevented from falling in the first place. And the second way is without a doubt the most honorable.

"The one who is prevented from falling is more honorably redeemed than the one who, after falling, is raised up," says the learned teacher Francisco Suárez. "For in this way the injury or stain that the soul always contracts by falling is avoided. This being the case, we ought certainly to believe that Mary was redeemed in the more honorable way, the way that was more fitting for the Mother of God."

As St. Bonaventure remarks, "We should believe that the Holy Spirit, as a very special favor, redeemed and preserved Mary from original sin by a new kind of sanctification, and he did this in the very moment of her conception—not that sin was in her, but that it otherwise would have been."

On the same subject, Cardinal Nicholas of Cusa elegantly remarks: "Others had Jesus as a liberator, but to the most Blessed Virgin, he was a pre-liberator." By this he means that all others had a Redeemer who delivered them from the sin with which they were already defiled. But the most Blessed Virgin had a Redeemer who preserved her—because he was her Son—from ever being defiled by sin in the first place.

—St. Alphonsus Liguori, *The Glories of Mary*

IN GOD'S PRESENCE, CONSIDER . . .

Does Mary's sinlessness make her seem unapproachable? Or does it make me more confident that she'll receive me with a holy mercy?

CLOSING PRAYER

From a prayer of St. Ildephonsus: *Give a mother's milk to your Creator, Mary; nurse the One who made you, and who made you in such a way that he could be fittingly made from you.*

A fitting dwelling for the Lord

St. Alphonsus considers the reasons why God would preserve from all sin the mother of his Son.

When speaking of Mary for the honor of our Lord Jesus, whom she merited to have for her Son, St. Augustine insists he would not even consider the possibility of sin in her. "For we know," he says, "that through the One who was clearly without sin, whom she merited to conceive and bring forth, she received grace to conquer all sin."

Therefore, as St. Peter Damian observes, we must consider it certain that "the incarnate Word chose for himself a fitting mother—one of whom he would not have to be ashamed." St. Proclus observes: "He dwelt in a womb that he had created free from all that might be to his dishonor."

It was no shame to Jesus Christ when he heard himself contemptuously called by others "the son of Mary," implying that he was the son of a poor woman (see Mt 13:55). For he came into this world to give us an example of humility and patience. But on the other hand, it would undoubtedly have been a disgrace if he could have heard the Devil say, "Wasn't his mother a sinner? Wasn't he born of an evil mother, who was once our slave?"

Indeed, God, who is Wisdom itself, knew well how to prepare himself a fitting dwelling in which to reside on earth. For it was not fitting that a holy God should choose himself a dwelling that was not holy: "Holiness befits your house, O LORD" (Ps 93:5).

—St. Alphonsus Liguori, *The Glories of Mary*

IN GOD'S PRESENCE, CONSIDER . . .

Why was it fitting for God the Father to create a mother for his Son who was sinless? Why would God want him to take his flesh from a sinless woman, and to be raised by her?

CLOSING PRAYER

From a "Novena to Our Lady of Good Remedy": *Virgin, we honor you. You are the beloved daughter of the Most High God, the chosen Mother of the Incarnate Word, the Immaculate Spouse of the Holy Spirit, the Sacred Vessel of the Most Holy Trinity.*

God made Mary a worthy habitation for his Son

For the honor of his Son, St. Alphonsus insists, God the Father built a perfect home, spotless and flawless.

Here is the most important reason why it was fitting for the Eternal Father to keep Mary, his daughter, unspotted by Adam's sin. As St. Bernardine of Siena remarks, it was fitting because he destined her to be the mother of his only-begotten Son: "You were preordained in the mind of God, before all creatures, that you might conceive God himself as man."

If, then, for no other purpose than the honor of his Son, who was God, it was reasonable that the Father should create Mary free from every stain. The angelic St. Thomas says: "Holiness is to be attributed to those things that are ordained for a God." For this reason, when King David was planning the temple in Jerusalem, on a scale of magnificence fitting God, he said, "For the house will not be prepared for man, but for the LORD God" (1 Chr 29:1).

How much more reasonable is it, then, to suppose that the Sovereign Architect, who destined Mary to be the mother of his own Son, adorned her soul with all most precious gifts, so that she might be a dwelling worthy of a God! The holy Church herself, in the following prayer, assures us that God prepared the body and soul of the Blessed Virgin, so as to be a worthy dwelling on earth for his only-begotten Son: "Almighty and eternal God, by the cooperation of the Holy Spirit, you prepared the body and soul of the glorious virgin and mother Mary, so that she might become a worthy habitation for your Son."

—St. Alphonsus Liguori, *The Glories of Mary*

IN GOD'S PRESENCE, CONSIDER . . .

If I were building new a home for my child, wouldn't I want it to be without stain or damage? Wouldn't God the Father want to do the same for his beloved Son?

CLOSING PRAYER

From a prayer of St. John of Damascus: *Watch over us, O Queen, the dwelling place of our Lord. Lead and govern all our ways as you wish and save us from our sins. Lead us into the calm harbor of God's will.*

Mary reversed the course of the ages

In Mary, Blessed John Henry Newman tells us, the tradition of evil handed down from our first parents was broken, so that Light could enter the darkness.

Kings of the earth, when they have sons born to them, immediately scatter some large bounty, or raise some high memorial. They honor the day, or the place, or the heralds of the auspicious event, with some corresponding mark of favor. Nor did the coming of Emmanuel change the world's established custom. It was a season of grace and wonder, and these were to be exhibited in a special manner in the person of his mother.

The course of ages was to be reversed; the tradition of evil was to be broken; a gate of light was to be opened amid the darkness, for the coming of the Just: A Virgin conceived and bore him. It was fitting, for his honor and glory, that she who was the instrument of his bodily presence should first be a miracle of his grace. It was fitting that she should triumph, where Eve had failed, and should "bruise the serpent's head" (see Gn 3:15) by the spotlessness of her sanctity.

In some respects, indeed, the curse was not reversed. Mary came into a fallen world and resigned herself to its laws. She, as also the Son she bore, was exposed to pain of soul and body, she was subjected to death. But she was not put under the power of sin. As grace was infused into Adam from the first moment of his creation, so that he never had experience of his natural poverty, till sin reduced him to it, so was grace given from the first in still ampler measure to Mary, and she never incurred, in fact, Adam's deprivation. She began where others end, whether in knowledge or in love. She was from the first clothed in sanctity, destined for perseverance, luminous and glorious in God's sight, and incessantly employed in meritorious acts, which continued till her last breath.

—Blessed John Henry Newman,
"The Glories of Mary for the Sake of Her Son"

IN GOD'S PRESENCE, CONSIDER . . .

What does it mean to say that in Mary, "the course of ages was to be reversed"? Why was it fitting for God's honor and glory that "she who was the instrument of his bodily presence should be the first miracle of his grace"?

CLOSING PRAYER

From a prayer of Blessed John: *The Most High came in weakness, not in power; and he sent you, Mary, a creature, in his stead, with a creature's beauty and luster suited to our state.*

Mary was without even a venial sin

In order to make Mary a mother worthy of her Son, St. Alphonsus observes, God preserved her even from venial sins.

Given that Mary was worthy to be the Mother of God, "what excellency and what perfection was there that was not fitting for her?" asks St. Thomas of Villanova. St. Thomas Aquinas, the "Angelic Doctor" of the Church, writes: "When God chooses anyone for a particular dignity, he renders him fit for it. So God, having chosen Mary for his mother, also by his grace rendered her worthy of this highest of all dignities. The Blessed Virgin was divinely chosen to be the Mother of God, so we cannot doubt that God had fitted her by his grace for this dignity. In fact, we are assured of it by the angel: 'For you have found favor with God. Behold, you will conceive in your womb and bear a Son.'"

From this truth, the saint argues that "the Blessed Virgin never committed any actual sin, not even a venial one. Otherwise, she would not have been a mother worthy of Jesus Christ. For the disgrace of the mother would also have been the disgrace of the Son, for he would have had a sinner for his mother."

A venial sin doesn't deprive a soul of God's grace. So if Mary, on account of a single venial sin, wouldn't have been a mother worthy of God, how much more unworthy would she have been, had she contracted the guilt of original sin, which would have made her an enemy of God and a slave of the Devil?

—St. Alphonsus Liguori, *The Glories of Mary*

IN GOD'S PRESENCE, CONSIDER . . .

If Mary was preserved from even venial sins, does that mean she can't sympathize with us in our struggles against sin? Or does it mean that she can help us more perfectly, because her love for us and her wisdom about what we need is perfect?

CLOSING PRAYER

From the Liturgy of St. Basil: *To you, O woman full of grace, the angelic choirs and the human race, all creation rejoices! O sanctified temple, mystical paradise, and glory of virgins!*

God was able to preserve Mary from sin

Was it too difficult for God to preserve Mary from all sin? Not at all, says St. Alphonsus; all things are possible for him.

St. Thomas of Villanova says, "Nothing was ever granted to any saint that did not shine in a much higher degree in Mary from the very first moment of her existence." And as it is true that "there is an infinite difference between the Mother of God and the servants of God," according to the celebrated saying of St. John of Damascus, we must certainly suppose, according to the teaching of St. Thomas Aquinas, that "God conferred privileges of grace in every way greater on his mother than on his servants."

St. Anselm, the great defender of the immaculate Mary, takes up the question: "Was the wisdom of God unable to form a pure dwelling, and to remove every stain of human nature from it?" Is it really possible that God couldn't prepare a clean habitation for his Son by preserving it from the common contagion of sin?

"God could preserve angels in heaven spotless," St. Anselm continues, "in the midst of the devastation that surrounded them. Was he then unable to preserve the mother of his Son and the Queen of Angels from the common fall of men?"

Here I may add that, since God could grant Eve the grace to come into the world immaculate, then couldn't he grant the same favor to Mary? Yes, indeed! God could do it, and did it. For on every account "it was becoming," as St. Anselm says, "that this virgin, on whom the Eternal Father intended to bestow his only-begotten Son, should be adorned with such purity that it exceeded not only that of all men and angels, but also any purity that can be conceived after that of God."

St. John of Damascus speaks in still clearer terms. He says: "Our Lord had preserved the soul, together with the body, of the Blessed Virgin in that purity which was fitting for the one who was to receive a God into her womb. Since he is holy, he reposes only in holy places."

—St. Alphonsus Liguori, *The Glories of Mary*

IN GOD'S PRESENCE, CONSIDER . . .

Does it seem impossible to me that God could preserve a human being from all sin? If so, do I recognize that I am trying to limit God's power?

CLOSING PRAYER

Nothing is impossible for you, Lord God. I praise you for the masterpiece of your creation, the immaculate mother of your Son.

A prayer to Immaculate Mary

St. Alphonsus rejoices in the sinless beauty of Our Lady, and the power it has to draw us to imitate her holiness.

My immaculate Lady! I rejoice with you on seeing you enriched with such great purity. I thank, and resolve always to thank, our common Creator for having preserved you from every stain of sin. I wish that the whole world knew you and acknowledged you as that beautiful Dawn that was always illumined with God's light; as that chosen Ark of salvation, free from the common ship-wreck of sin.

Most sweet, most amiable, immaculate Mary, you who are so beautiful in the eyes of your Lord: Don't despise to cast your compassionate eyes on the wounds of my soul, loathsome as they are. Behold me; pity me; heal me.

O beautiful loadstone of hearts, draw my miserable heart to yourself. You, who from the first moment of your life appeared pure and beautiful before God, pity me—I who not only was born in sin, but have again since Baptism stained my soul with crimes. What grace will God ever refuse you? For he chose you for his daughter, his mother, and spouse, and so preserved you from every stain.

Grant that I may always remember you; and may you never forget me. The happy day, when I will go to behold your beauty in paradise, seems like a thousand years away—so much do I long to praise and love you more than I can now do, my mother, my queen, my beloved, most beautiful, most sweet, most pure, immaculate Mary.

—St. Alphonsus Liguori, *The Glories of Mary*

IN GOD'S PRESENCE, CONSIDER . . .

How does Mary's sinless condition make her beautiful to us? How does this beauty draw us to imitate her holiness?

CLOSING PRAYER

From a prayer of Blessed John Henry Newman: *Your very face and form, dear mother, speak to us of the Eternal; not like earthly beauty, dangerous to look upon, but like the Morning Star, which is your emblem, bright and musical, breathing purity, telling of heaven, and infusing peace.*

Mary, the gate of all grace

Blessed Henry Suso lavishes the heavenly queen's beauty with praise, declaring his confidence that her petitions will not be denied by the King.

You, O Queen, are the gate of all grace, the door of compassion that was never yet closed. Heaven and earth will pass away before you will permit anyone who earnestly seeks your assistance to depart from you without obtaining it. Behold, for this very reason you are the one my soul first has in view when I awake, and the last in view when I lie down to sleep.

How could anything that your pure hands present before God and commend to him—however small it may be in itself—be rejected? So take, then, O take the smallness of my works, and present it to God almighty, so that in your hands it may appear to be something in his eyes.

You are the pure vessel of red gold, melted down with graces, inlaid with precious emeralds, and sapphires, and all virtues, whose unique appearance in the sight of the heavenly King surpasses that of all other creatures. How infinitely pleasing in his eyes, above all mortals, is your delicate and love-inspiring beauty, before which all other beauty fades like a glowworm fades before the brightness of the sun!

What overflowing grace you have found before him for yourself and for us mortals who are without grace! How could, how can, then, the heavenly king deny you anything?

—Blessed Henry Suso, *Little Book of Eternal Wisdom*

IN GOD'S PRESENCE, CONSIDER . . .

How might my days be brighter and sweeter if they were more like Blessed Henry's days: With Mary the first person I think of when I awake, and the last person I have in mind as I lay down to sleep?

CLOSING PRAYER

My Lady, let me say to you what the psalmist said to my Lord: "My mouth praises you with joyful lips, when I think of you upon my bed, and meditate on you in the watches of the night; for you have been my help; and in the shadow of your wings I sing for joy" (Ps 63:5–7).

My soul, step joyfully forth!

Blessed Henry Suso urges his dejected soul, burdened with sins, to take heart and go to Mary for help.

When our poor souls are in the narrow prison house of unfathomable sorrow of heart, and we can stir neither here nor there, nothing remains for us except to lift up our miserable eyes to you, O chosen Queen of Heaven! For this reason, this day I and all penitent hearts salute you, you mirror reflecting the brightness of the Eternal Sun, you hidden treasure of infinite compassion!

You exalted spirits, you pure souls, stand forth, extol and praise, commend and exult in the ravishing paradise of all delight, the sublime queen! For I am not worthy to do so, unless in her goodness she should consent to allow me.

Mary—you chosen bosom friend of God, you fair, golden crown of Eternal Wisdom—permit me, a poor sinner, even me in my weakness, to speak to you a little in confidence. With a trembling heart, shame-faced, with dejected eyes, my soul falls down before you. You mother of all graces, I think that neither my soul nor any other sinful soul requires permission or a passport to turn to you.

Aren't you the immediate mediatrix of all sinners? The more reasonable a soul is, the more reasonable it seems to her that she should have free access to you. The deeper she is in wickedness, the more reason she has to press forward to you.

Therefore, my soul, step joyfully forth! If your great crimes drive you away, her unfathomable goodness invites you to draw near.

For this reason, Mary—you sole consolation of sinful hearts, you sole refuge of guilty mortals, to whom so many a wet eye, so many a wounded heart is raised up—be a gracious mediatrix and channel of reconciliation between me and the Eternal Wisdom!

—Blessed Henry Suso, *Little Book of Eternal Wisdom*

IN GOD'S PRESENCE, CONSIDER . . .

Do I have days when the weight of my sins makes me reluctant even to seek mercy from God? Does Blessed Henry's prayer encourage me to "step joyfully forth" to seek Mary's help anyway?

CLOSING PRAYER

From "Thirty Days' Prayer to the Blessed Virgin": *O Mary Immaculate, we honor your precious name of Mother of Confidence. It fills our hearts to overflowing with the sweetest consolation and moves us to hope for every blessing from you.*

My Lady, my refuge

St. Germanus cries out in confidence to the pure and powerful mother who can answer his prayers and keep him in safety.

My Lady!
My refuge, life, and help,
my armor and my boast,
my hope and my strength:
Grant that I may enjoy
the gifts of your Son,
unspeakable, beyond understanding,
your God and our God,
in the heavenly kingdom.
For I know with certainty
that you have power to do as you will,
since you are mother of the Most High.
Therefore, Lady most pure, I beg you
that I may not be disappointed in my hopes,
but may obtain them, Spouse of God,
who bore the One who is the hope of all,
our Lord Jesus Christ,
true God and Master of all things,
visible and invisible,
to whom belongs all glory, honor, and power,
now and always and through endless ages.

—St. Germanus

IN GOD'S PRESENCE, CONSIDER . . .

St. Germanus expresses his firm faith in Mary's power and willingness to help him. But as the prayer concludes, in whom, does he affirm, is his faith ultimately placed, who makes her loving assistance possible?

CLOSING PRAYER

From a prayer of St. Alphonsus Liguori: *You are the Refuge of Sinners, so you are my refuge. To you I entrust my soul and my eternal salvation. Receive me as your servant, and as your servant protect me always, and especially at the time of my death. You with your powerful intercession must save me!*

Jesus the sun, Mary the moon

St. Alphonsus concludes that if Jesus is the Sun of justice, as the prophet Malachi called him, then Mary is the moon reflecting his light.

In the first chapter of the Book of Genesis, we read that "God made the two great lights, the greater light to rule the day, and the lesser light to rule the night" (Gn 1:16).

The Dominican biblical commentator Cardinal Hugh of Saint-Cher says that "Christ is the greater light to rule the just, and Mary the lesser light to rule sinners." He means that the sun is a figure of Jesus Christ, "the Sun of justice" (see Mal 4:2), whose light is enjoyed by the just who live in the clear day of divine grace. But the moon is a figure of Mary, by whose means those who are in the night of sin are enlightened.

Since Mary is this favorable light, and has been made so for the benefit of poor sinners, if anyone is so unfortunate as to fall into the night of sin, what is he to do? Pope Innocent III replies: "Whoever is in the night of sin, let him cast his eyes on the moon: Let him implore Mary."

Since he has lost the light of the sun of justice by losing the grace of God, let him turn to the moon, and beseech Mary. She will certainly give him light to see the misery of his state, and strength to leave it without delay. As St. Methodius says, "By the prayers of Mary, almost innumerable sinners are converted."

—St. Alphonsus Liguori, *The Glories of Mary*

IN GOD'S PRESENCE, CONSIDER . . .

Does my life have seasons when I seem to be in a dark night of sin, doubt, or confusion, and the light of the Lord is difficult to find? That's the time to look to Mary, whose gentle face reflects the Lord's light to illuminate my darkness.

CLOSING PRAYER

When the Sun of righteousness seems hidden from my view below the horizon, Mary, catch the bright rays of light from his face, and reflect them into my eyes, so that I can see through the darkness, and walk through it safely toward the dawn.

Let no one lament over paradise lost

Blessed Henry Suso exults in the marvelous work of redemption, and Mary's role in it. We've lost one paradise, yes; but we've gained two more, infinitely more wonderful!

Mary, how often have you put to flight the hostile powers of wicked spirits! How often have you allayed the angry justice of the severe Judge! How often have you obtained from him grace and consolation! How shall we ever acknowledge such great goodness?

If all angelic tongues, all pure spirits and souls, if heaven and earth and all that is contained in them, cannot properly praise her merits, her ravishing beauty, her graciousness and immeasurable dignity, then what shall we sinful hearts be able to do? Let's do our best, and express to her our acknowledgment, our thanks. For indeed, her great kindness doesn't look at the smallness of the gift; it looks at the purity of the intention.

Sweet Queen, with what justice can all women rejoice in your sweet name! For the first Eve was cursed that she ever ate of the bitter fruit of the tree of knowledge. But blessed is the second Eve, for she brought us again the sweet fruit of heaven.

Let no one lament over paradise. One paradise we lost, but we have won two others. For isn't she a paradise in whom grew the fruit of the living Tree, in whom all delight and joy are contained together? And isn't he also a paradise above every paradise, in whom the dead live again, if only they taste his fruit from whose hands, feet, and side the living fountains flow to water the whole earth—the fountains of inexhaustible mercy, immeasurable wisdom, overflowing sweetness, fervent love, the fountains of eternal life? Truly, Lord, whoever tastes of this fruit, whoever has drunk of this fountain, knows that these two gardens of paradise far surpass the earthly paradise.

—Blessed Henry Suso, *Little Book of Eternal Wisdom*

IN GOD'S PRESENCE, CONSIDER . . .

What—or rather, who—are the two "new paradises" we've gained to replace the one we lost? What are the fruits and fountains of the new Eden?

CLOSING PRAYER

My Lady, take me by the hand, and lead me to the new paradise that God has prepared, with "the water of life, bright as crystal, flowing from the throne of God and the Lamb," and "the tree of life, with its . . . fruit . . . and the leaves of the tree . . . for the healing of the nations" (Rv 22:1–2).

Mary's parents, Joachim and Anne

St. John of Damascus summarizes an ancient tradition about Mary's parents, Joachim and Anne.

Joachim and Anne were the parents of Mary. Joachim kept as strict a watch over his thoughts as a shepherd over his flock, having them entirely under his control. For the Lord God led him as a sheep, and he lacked none of the best things. When I say "the best things," I mean the good things that are desired by those who possess true knowledge, delighting in God; things that are spiritually fruitful to their possessors: namely, virtues. They bear fruit in due season—that is, in eternity—and they will reward with eternal life those who have labored worthily and persevered, as far as possible, to acquire them. First comes the labor, then eternal happiness follows.

Joachim always shepherded his thoughts. He made them lie down in the green pastures of contemplation on the words of sacred Scripture. Made glad by the restful waters of divine grace, withdrawn from foolishness, he walked in the path of righteousness (see Ps 23:1–3).

Meanwhile, Anne, whose name means "grace," was no less a companion in her life than a wife, blessed with all good gifts, though afflicted with sterility, as a mystical symbol of the world's situation at that time. In fact, grace at that time remained sterile, not being able to produce fruit in the souls of men. So men degenerated, becoming worse and worse. There was no one with understanding, no one who sought after God.

Then his divine goodness, taking pity on the work of his hands and wishing to save it, put an end to that mystical barrenness of holy Anne. She gave birth to a child whose equal had never been created and never can be. The end of her barrenness showed clearly that the world's sterility would cease, and that the withered trunk would be crowned with vigorous and mystical life.

—St. John of Damascus, *First Homily on the Dormition*

IN GOD'S PRESENCE, CONSIDER . . .

What lessons in holiness can I learn from Joachim and Anne? Is there any area of my life that seems spiritually sterile? Have I asked Mary to help me become fruitful in that area?

CLOSING PRAYER

St. Joachim and St. Anne, gracious parents of Our Lady and grandparents of our Savior, teach us by your example to be patient in hope, firm in charity, and fruitful in faith.

Rejoice! Mary was born for us

We should celebrate Mary's nativity, St. Alphonsus declares, because she came into the world full of grace, not only for her own glory, but also for our benefit.

St. Thomas Aquinas teaches that "God gives each person grace in proportion to the dignity for which he destines him." St. Paul teaches us the same thing when he says that God "has made us fit ministers of the New Testament" (see 2 Cor 3:6)—that is, the apostles received gifts from God in proportion to the greatness of the office with which they were charged. St. Bernardine of Siena adds, "It is an established principle in theology, that when a person is chosen by God for any position, he receives not only the qualities necessary for it, but even the gifts that he needs to sustain that position in a fitting way."

Now Mary was chosen to be the Mother of God. So it was quite fitting that God should adorn her, in the first moment of her existence, with an immense grace, and one of an order that is superior to that of all other human beings and angels. For that grace had to correspond with the immense and most high dignity to which God exalted her.

St. Peter Damian says: "Just as the light of the sun far surpasses that of the stars, so that in the daylight they are no longer visible—it overwhelms them, and it's as if they weren't even there—so does the great Virgin Mother surpass in holiness the whole court of heaven." Let's rejoice, then, with our beloved infant Mary, who was born so holy, so dear to God, and so full of grace. Let's rejoice, in fact, not only on her account, but also on our own. For she came into the world full of grace, not only for her own glory, but also for our benefit.

—St. Alphonsus Liguori, *The Glories of Mary*

IN GOD'S PRESENCE, CONSIDER . . .

Do I celebrate Mary's birthday? How do these insights help me to grasp more firmly the significance of that day?

CLOSING PRAYER

From a "Novena to Maria Bambina": *Holy child Mary, obtain for me a great devotion to you, the first creature of God's love.*

Mary was born a saint

Our Lady's immaculate conception, St. Alphonsus reasons, means that she was born already a saint.

It's indeed right to celebrate with festivity and universal joy the birth of our infant Mary. For she first saw the light of this world a baby, it is true, with regard to age, but she was already great in merit and virtue. Mary was born a saint, and a great saint. But to form an idea of the greatness of her sanctity, even at this early point in her life, we must consider the greatness of the first grace with which God enriched her.

To begin with, it is certain that Mary's soul was the most beautiful that God had ever created. After, of course, the work of the incarnation of the Eternal Word, this was the greatest work, and most worthy of himself, that an omnipotent God ever did in the world. St. Peter Damian calls it "a work surpassed only by God." The grace that the Blessed Virgin received exceeded not only that of each particular saint, but of all the angels and saints put together. And she received this grace, exceeding that of all men and angels together, in the first instant of her immaculate conception.

Mary was chosen by God to be the mother of the divine Word. For this reason, observes the theologian Denis the Carthusian, "as she was chosen to an order superior to that of all other creatures, it's reasonable to suppose that from the very beginning of her life, gifts of a superior order were conferred upon her. These would have been such gifts that they incomparably surpassed those granted to all other creatures." Indeed, it can't be doubted that when the Person of the Eternal Word was, in God's decrees, predestined to become man, a mother was also destined for him, from whom he was to take his human nature. And this mother was our infant Mary.

—St. Alphonsus Liguori, *The Glories of Mary*

IN GOD'S PRESENCE, CONSIDER . . .

What extraordinary challenges would Joachim and Anne have faced in trying to rear a child who never sinned, given that they themselves, though holy people, were not sinless?

CLOSING PRAYER

From a "Novena to Maria Bambina": *Holy child Mary, mystical dawn, gate of heaven, you are my trust and hope.*

A prayer to the infant Mary

St. Alphonsus imagines himself speaking to the Blessed Virgin when she was just a baby, as he looks forward to the day when she will conceive the holy Son of God.

Holy and heavenly infant Mary, you who are the destined mother of my Redeemer and the great mediatrix of miserable sinners: Pity me. Behold at your feet another ungrateful sinner who turns to you and asks your compassion.

It's true that for my ingratitude to God and to you, I deserve that God and you should abandon me. But I've heard, and I believe it to be true—knowing the greatness of your mercy—that you don't refuse to help anyone who entrusts himself to you with confidence.

Most exalted creature in the world! Since this is the case, and since there is no one but God above you—compared with you, the greatest saints of heaven are little—saint of saints, Mary, abyss of charity and full of grace: Help a miserable creature who by his own fault has lost God's favor.

I know that you are so dear to God that he denies you nothing. I know also that your pleasure is to use your greatness for the relief of miserable sinners. Show, then, how great is the favor that you enjoy with God, by obtaining for me a divine light and flame so powerful that I may be changed from a sinner into a saint.

In this way, detaching myself from every earthly affection, divine love may be enkindled in me. Do this, Lady, for you're able do it. Do it for the love of God, who has made you so great, so powerful, and so compassionate. This is my hope.

—St. Alphonsus Liguori, *The Glories of Mary*

IN GOD'S PRESENCE, CONSIDER . . .

If you could hold the infant Mary in your arms and speak to her, what would you say?

CLOSING PRAYER

From a "Novena to Maria Bambina": *O powerful advocate, from your cradle stretch out your hand and support me on the path of life. Make me serve God with ardor and constancy until death, and so reach eternity with you.*

Consecration to the child Mary

Alluding to the ancient tradition that Mary consecrated herself to God when she was quite young, St. Alphonsus laments the fact that his own childhood was not consecrated that way.

Beloved Mother of God, most amiable child Mary! You presented yourself in the temple, and with readiness and without reserve you consecrated yourself to the glory and love of God. If only I could offer you, this day, the first years of my life, to devote myself without reserve to your service, my holy and most sweet Lady!

But it's now too late to do this. Unfortunate creature that I am, I've lost so many years in servitude to the world and my own caprices, and I've lived in almost entire forgetfulness of you and of God. Woe to the time when I didn't love you! Even so, it's better to begin late than not at all. Behold, Mary, this day I present myself to you, and I offer myself without reserve to your service for the long or short time that I still have to live in this world. In union with you I renounce the pursuit of all created things, and I devote myself entirely to the love of my Creator.

I consecrate my mind to you, my Queen, so that it may always think of the love that you deserve; my tongue, to praise you; my heart, to love you. Accept, most holy Virgin, the offering that this miserable sinner now makes you. Accept it, I beg you, by the consolation that your heart experienced when you gave yourself to God in the temple. But since I'm entering your service late, it's only reasonable that I should multiply my acts of homage and love, in order to compensate for lost time. Help my weakness with your powerful intercession, Mother of Mercy, by obtaining perseverance for me from your Son, Jesus, and strength to be always faithful to you until death. In this way, always serving you in life, I may praise you in paradise for all eternity.

—St. Alphonsus Liguori, *The Glories of Mary*

IN GOD'S PRESENCE, CONSIDER . . .

Do I ever regret not coming to love and serve God sooner than I did? If so, how can I now make up for lost time?

CLOSING PRAYER

From a "Novena to Maria Bambina": *Holy child Mary of the royal house of David, Queen of the Angels, mother of grace and love, I greet you with all my heart. Obtain for me the grace to love the Lord faithfully during all the days of my life.*

With Mary's fiat, God became man

When the angel spoke to Mary, declares St. Alphonsus, the world breathlessly awaited her yes to God. The salvation of the human race depended upon her fiat.

Our Lord would not become Mary's Son without her previous consent. So the angel speaks, and in humility she hesitates to respond. But why this delay, Mary? "The angel awaits your reply," says St. Bernard; "and we also—on whom the sentence of condemnation weighs so heavily—we await the word of mercy."

We, who are already condemned to death, are waiting. "Behold, the price of our salvation is offered to you; we will be instantly delivered if you consent," continues St. Bernard. Behold, mother of us all, the price of our salvation will be the divine Word, made man in you. In that same moment in which you accept him for your Son, we will be delivered from death. For your Lord himself desires your consent.

"Answer then, sacred Virgin!" says an ancient writer. "Why do you delay in giving life to the world?" Reply quickly, Lady! No longer delay the salvation of the world, which now depends upon your consent.

But see, Mary already answers. She replies to the angel: "Behold, I am the handmaid of the Lord; let it be to me according to your word" (Lk 1:38). What more beautiful, more humble, or more prudent answer could all the wisdom of men and angels together have invented, had they reflected for a million years?

A powerful answer, which rejoiced heaven, and brought an immense sea of graces and blessings into the world! The answer had scarcely fallen from the lips of Mary, when it drew the only-begotten Son of God from the bosom of his Eternal Father, to become man in her most pure womb!

Yes, indeed; for as soon as she had uttered these words, "the Word became flesh" (Jn 1:14), the Son of God became also the Son of Mary. "O powerful fiat!" exclaims St. Thomas of Villanova. "O effective fiat! O fiat to be venerated above every other fiat! For with a fiat, God created light, heaven, earth; but with Mary's fiat, God became man, like us."

—St. Alphonsus Liguori, *The Glories of Mary*

IN GOD'S PRESENCE, CONSIDER . . .

In what circumstances of my life is God waiting to hear my fiat, my "let it be," giving my consent to his will?

CLOSING PRAYER

Lord, I am your servant; let it be done to me according to your word and your will.

Imitate Mary's response at the Annunciation

Blessed John Henry Newman counsels us to learn this lesson from Mary: Grow in holiness through the everyday challenges of life, so that it won't be necessary for God to purify us through great adversity.

Observe the lesson which we gain for ourselves from the history of the Blessed Virgin: that the highest graces of the soul may be matured in private, and without those fierce trials to which the many are exposed for their sanctification. The aids which God gives under the gospel covenant have power to renew and purify our hearts, without uncommon providences to discipline us into receiving them. God gives his Holy Spirit to us silently; and the silent duties of every day (it may be humbly hoped) are blest to bring about the sufficient sanctification of thousands, whom the world knows not of. The Blessed Virgin is a reminder of this; and it is consoling as well as instructive to know it.

When we quench the grace of Baptism, then it is that we need severe trials to restore us. This is the case of the multitude, whose best estate is that of chastisement, repentance, supplication, and absolution, again and again. But there are those who go on in a calm and unswerving course, learning day by day to love him who has redeemed them, and overcoming the sin of their nature by his heavenly grace, as the various temptations to evil successively present themselves.

Of these undefiled followers of the Lamb, the blessed Mary is the chief. Strong in the Lord, and in the power of his might, she "staggered not at the promise of God through unbelief" (see Rom 4:20); she believed when Zechariah doubted—with a faith like Abraham's she believed and was blessed for her belief, and had the fulfillment of those things which were told her by the Lord.

—Blessed John Henry Newman,
"The Reverence Due to the Virgin Mary"

IN GOD'S PRESENCE, CONSIDER . . .

Do I try to grow in holiness quietly, daily, and incrementally, asking God frequently for his grace? Or must some great adversity send me to my knees before I will beg God for assistance?

CLOSING PRAYER

Lord, let me be still before you with my mother, Mary; let me pray with the psalmist: "My heart is not lifted up, my eyes are not raised too high. But I have calmed and quieted my soul, like a child quieted at its mother's breast" (see Ps 131:1–2).

Why the angel showed reverence to Mary

St. Thomas Aquinas examines the reasons why the angel Gabriel showed such reverence to Mary, saying, "Hail!"

In ancient times it was an especially great event when an angel appeared to men, so that men might show them reverence, for they deserve the greatest praise. It was written in praise of Abraham that he received angels hospitably and that he showed them reverence. But it was never heard that an angel showed reverence to a human being until he saluted the Blessed Virgin, saying reverently, "Hail." The reason why in ancient times the angel did not reverence man, but man the angel, is that the angel was greater than man, in three respects. First, with respect to dignity, since the angel is of a spiritual nature, but man is of a corruptible nature, subject to death and decay. It was not then fitting that a spiritual and incorruptible creature should show reverence to a corruptible creature, namely, man.

Second, with respect to closeness with God. For the angel is a close assistant to God. But man is like an outsider, put at a distance from God through sin. Thus it was fitting that man should reverence the angel as one close to and familiar with the King. Third, the angel was preeminent because of the fullness of the splendor of divine grace. For angels partake most fully of the divine light. Therefore the angel always appears with light. But men, although they partake something of the light of grace, it is but little, and with obscurity.

For these reasons, it was not fitting that the angel should show reverence to a human being until someone should be found in human nature who exceeded the angels in those three respects. And this was the Blessed Virgin. In order to indicate that she exceeded him in these three things, the angel said, "Hail."

—St. Thomas Aquinas, "On the Angelic Salutation"

IN GOD'S PRESENCE, CONSIDER . . .

Do I show reverence to Mary? Does my attitude toward her display the honor and love that is due to the Mother of God and my mother?

CLOSING PRAYER

From a hymn ascribed to Venantius Fortunatus: *Hail, Mary, you who are "blest, in the message Gabriel brought; blest, by the work the Spirit wrought; from whom the great Desire of earth took human flesh and human birth!"*

Mary exceeds the angels in fullness of grace

St. Thomas Aquinas explores the ways in which Mary is truly "full of grace," as the angel declared.

The Blessed Virgin exceeded the angels in fullness of grace. It was to indicate this that the angel showed her reverence, saying, "full of grace," as if to say, "I will show you reverence because you excel me in the fullness of grace."

He says that the Blessed Virgin is full of grace with respect to three things. First, with respect to her soul, which has every fullness of grace. For the grace of God is given for two reasons, namely, in order to act well, and to avoid evil. And with respect to these two, the Blessed Virgin had most perfect grace. For more than any other holy person save Christ alone, she avoided all sin. The Blessed Virgin is also an example of all virtues. So she is full of grace both with respect to actions and with respect to the avoidance of evil.

Second, she was full of grace with respect to the overflow of soul to flesh or body. For it is a great thing for the saints to have enough grace to sanctify their soul; but the soul of the Blessed Virgin was so full that from it grace flowed into her body, in order that with it she might conceive the son of God.

Third, she was full of grace with respect to grace's distribution to all men. For it is a great thing in any saint that he has so much grace that it is enough for the salvation of many. But when enough is had for the salvation of all the men in the world, this is the greatest, and so it is with Christ and with the Blessed Virgin. She is full of grace, then, and exceeds the angels in fullness of grace.

—St. Thomas Aquinas, "On the Angelic Salutation"

IN GOD'S PRESENCE, CONSIDER . . .

If Our Lady is truly "full of grace," why do I sometimes hesitate to approach her for a share in that grace?

CLOSING PRAYER

From a prayer of St. Germanus: *Who could know God, if it were not for you, most holy Mary? Who could be saved? Who would be preserved from dangers? Who would receive any grace, if it were not for you, Mother of God, full of grace?*

Mary, you have found grace

With a keen attention to detail, St. Albert the Great notes carefully the importance of the angel's declaration that Mary had "found" grace with God (see Lk 1:30).

"Do not be afraid, Mary,
for you have found favor with God."
For behold, Mary,
you have found grace,
you have not taken it
as Lucifer tried to do.
You have found grace,
you have not lost it
as Adam did.
You have found favor with God
because you desired and sought it.
You have found uncreated Grace:
that is, God himself
became your Son,
and with that Grace
you have found and obtained
every uncreated good.

—St. Albert the Great

IN GOD'S PRESENCE, CONSIDER . . .

What does it mean to "find grace"? Must we actively seek it in order to find it? How can Mary help us "find grace" with God?

CLOSING PRAYER

From a prayer of St. Peter Chrysologus: *Mary, you have found grace, but how great a grace! It was such that it filled you; and so great was its fullness, that it could be poured down as a torrent on every creature.*

Blessed is the fruit of your womb!

St. Thomas Aquinas carefully examines, in his usual systematic way, the meaning of St. Elizabeth's declaration: "Blessed is the fruit of your womb!"

The sinner sometimes seeks in a thing what he cannot obtain there, while the righteous man obtains it. Thus Eve sought in the fruit, but did not find there, all the things that she desired. But the Blessed Virgin finds in her fruit, Jesus, everything that Eve desired. For Eve desired three things from the fruit.

The first was what the Devil falsely promised her, that they would be as gods, knowing good and evil (see Gn 3:5). And he lies because he is a liar, and the father of lies. Eve was not made like God when she ate the fruit, but instead she was made unlike God, because by sinning she lost her salvation from God and was expelled from paradise. But this is precisely what the Blessed Virgin and all Christians find in the fruit of her womb, because by Christ they are united with and made like God (see 1 Jn 3:2).

The second thing that Eve desired in the fruit was pleasure, because it was good to eat. But she did not find it and immediately knew that she was naked, and felt sorrow instead. In the fruit of the Virgin, however, we find sweetness and salvation.

Third, the fruit of Eve was beautiful in appearance. But more beautiful is the fruit of the Virgin on whom the angels desire to gaze, because he is the splendor of his Father's glory.

Eve could not find in her fruit what no sinner can find in his sin. Therefore, what we desire, we should seek in the fruit of the Virgin Mary. Here is a fruit blessed by God, because he has so filled him with every grace that it comes to us by showing him reverence. The Virgin is blessed, but far more blessed is the fruit of her womb, Jesus.

—St. Thomas Aquinas, "On the Angelic Salutation"

IN GOD'S PRESENCE, CONSIDER . . .

Have you found it to be true in your experience that "the sinner sometimes seeks in a thing what he cannot obtain there, while the righteous man obtains it"? What examples of this principle would you offer?

CLOSING PRAYER

From the Salve Regina: Turn then, most gracious advocate, thine eyes of mercy toward us, and after this our exile, show unto us the blessed Fruit of thy womb, Jesus.

"Behold the handmaid of the Lord!"

St. Alphonsus finds in Mary's response to the angelic greeting an expression of her great humility.

Let's consider the great humility of the Blessed Virgin in her answer to the angel Gabriel. She was fully enlightened as to the greatness of the dignity of a Mother of God. She had already been assured by the angel that she was this happy mother chosen by our Lord. But with all this, she in no way rises in her own estimation. She doesn't stop to rejoice in her exaltation. Instead, she sees on the one side her own nothingness, and on the other the infinite majesty of God, who chose her for his mother. So she acknowledges how unworthy she is of so great an honor, but she won't oppose God's will in the least matter. When her consent is asked, then, what does she do? What does she say?

Within herself, she sees nothing, yet she's all enflamed at the same time by the ardor of her desire to unite herself still more closely with God. So abandoning herself entirely to the divine will, she replies, "Behold the handmaid of the Lord." Behold the slave of the Lord, obliged to do whatever her Lord commands. As if she meant to say: Since God chooses me for his mother—I who have nothing of my own—and since all that I have is his gift, who can ever think that he chose me on account of my own merits?

"Behold the handmaid of the Lord." What merit can a slave ever have, that she should become the mother of her Lord? "Behold the handmaid of the Lord." May the goodness of God alone be praised, and not his slave, since it is all his goodness, that he fixes his eyes on so lowly a creature as I am, to make her so great. O great humility of Mary, which makes her little to herself, but great before God! Unworthy in her own eyes, but worthy in the eyes of that immense Lord whom the world cannot contain.

—St. Alphonsus Liguori, *The Glories of Mary*

IN GOD'S PRESENCE, CONSIDER . . .

What is true humility? In what areas of my life do I struggle to cultivate humility?

CLOSING PRAYER

From a prayer of St. Alphonsus: *O most pure Virgin Mary, I venerate your most holy heart, which was the delight and resting place of God, your heart overflowing with humility, purity, and divine love.*

Why did Gabriel's words trouble Mary?

St. Alphonsus considers the various possible reasons why the angelic greeting to Our Lady would have troubled her.

"Whoever exalts himself will be humbled, and whoever humbles himself will be exalted" (Mt 23:12). These are the words of our Lord, and they cannot fail. When God determined to become man, he had to choose a mother on earth, and he sought among women for the one who was not just the most holy, but the most humble.

It was revealed to St. Elizabeth of Hungary that on the day of the Annunciation, the humble Virgin Mary was in prayer in her poor little cottage. She is sighing and begging God to send the Redeemer, with prayers more fervent than ever, and with desires more ardent than ever. Then the archangel Gabriel arrives, the bearer of the great message. He enters and salutes her, saying: "Hail, full of grace; the Lord is with you; blessed are you among women" (see Lk 1:28). Hail, Virgin, full of grace! For you were always full of grace above all other saints. The Lord is with you, because you're so humble. You are blessed among women, for all others fell under the curse of sin. But you, because you are the mother of the Blessed One, are and always will be blessed and free from every stain.

But what does the humble Mary reply to a greeting so full of praises? Nothing. She remains silent, but reflecting upon it, she's concerned: "But she was greatly troubled at the saying, and considered in her mind what sort of greeting this might be" (Lk 1:29). Why was she troubled? Did she fear it was a hallucination? Was it her virginal modesty that caused her to be disturbed at the sight of a man, as some suppose, in the belief that the angel appeared under a human form? No, the text is clear: "She was greatly troubled at the saying." Her trouble, then, arose entirely from her humility, which was disturbed at the sound of praises so far exceeding her own lowly estimate of herself.

—St. Alphonsus Liguori, *The Glories of Mary*

IN GOD'S PRESENCE, CONSIDER . . .

How do I respond to words of praise from others? Do I imitate the humility of Mary?

CLOSING PRAYER

From a prayer of St. Bernard of Clairvaux: *You, Mary, are the beautiful garden in which God has planted all the flowers that adorn the Church—among others, the violet of your humility, the lily of your purity, the rose of your charity. With whom can we compare you, O mother of grace and beauty?*

God waited for Mary's consent

When Gabriel announced that Mary had been chosen to bear God's Son, did she really have a choice in the matter? Fr. Frederick W. Faber considers the matter.

Mary's created spirit was busied in adoration when the Uncreated came, and took his Flesh and Blood, and dwelt within her. Yet his coming was not abrupt. He sent his messenger before he came himself.

But what is the special purpose for which the messenger has come? To ask in the name of God for Mary's consent to the Incarnation. The Creator will not act in this great mystery without his creature's free consent. Her freedom shall be a glorious reflection of his own ineffable freedom in the act of creation.

The Omnipotent stands on ceremony with his feeble, finite creature. He has already raised her too high to be only a blind instrument. Moreover, the honor of his own assumption of a created nature has an interest in the liberty in which creation will grant him what he requires. He would not come claiming his rights or using his prerogatives.

It was an awful moment. It was fully in Mary's power to have refused. Impossible as the consequences seem to make it, the matter was with her, and never did a free creature exercise its freedom more freely than she did that night.

How the angels must have hung over the moment! With what adorable delight and unspeakable satisfaction the Holy Trinity awaited the opening of her lips! It was the fiat of the one whom God had called out of nothingness, and whose own fiat was now to be music to his ears—creation's echo to that fiat of his at whose irresistible sweetness creation itself sprang into being!

—Fr. Frederick W. Faber, *Bethlehem*

IN GOD'S PRESENCE, CONSIDER . . .

Mary had a choice: to say yes to God, or to refuse him. We have the same choice, which we make many times, in many ways, every day. Which choice will I make today?

CLOSING PRAYER

Lord God, thank you for creating me with the great dignity of a free will, a will that is never more free than when it rests in your will. I kneel beside my Lady, and join my feeble fiat to hers: "Let it be done to me according to your word."

Let it be to me according to your word

St. John of Damascus ponders the intentions behind Mary's words to Gabriel at the Annunciation.

"Hail, full of grace, the Lord is with you" (Lk 1:28). Mary considered what this greeting might mean. Then the angel said to her: "Do not be afraid, Mary, for you have found favor with God" (Lk 1:30). In fact, she who was worthy of grace had found it. She found grace, the one who had done the deeds of grace, and had reaped its fullness. She found grace, the one who brought forth the Source of grace, and was a rich harvest of grace.

"You shall conceive in your womb and bear a Son, and you will call his name Jesus" (Lk 1: 31). What did she, who is true wisdom, reply? She did not imitate our first mother Eve, but rather avoided Eve's lack of caution. Appealing to the facts of nature to support her, she answered the angel: "How can this be, since I have no husband?" (Lk 1:34). What you say is impossible, for it goes beyond the natural laws laid down by the Creator. I will not be called a second Eve and disobey the will of my God. If you aren't speaking godless things, explain the mystery by saying how it is to be accomplished.

Then the messenger of truth answered her: "The Holy Spirit will come upon you, and the power of the Most High will overshadow you. Therefore the Child to be born will be called holy, the Son of God" (Lk 1:35). What has been prophesied is not subservient to the laws of nature. For God, the Creator of nature, can alter its laws. Then she, listening in holy reverence to that sacred name that she had always desired, signified her obedience in words full of humility and joy: "Behold, I am the handmaid of the Lord. Let it be to me according to your word" (Lk 1:38).

—St. John of Damascus, *First Homily on the Dormition*

IN GOD'S PRESENCE, CONSIDER . . .

When the angel announced to Zechariah that his wife would bear a son, he asked, "How shall I know this?" (Lk 1:18), and suffered for his unbelief. How did Mary's question to Gabriel differ from his? Was her response an expression of doubt, or a request for clarification?

CLOSING PRAYER

Mary, Seat of Wisdom, you replied to the angel with prudence, and responded to God with humility. Pray for us to have a generous share in your humility, which is the soil in which true prudence grows.

The Word was made flesh

In a lyrical, exquisitely beautiful portrayal of that moment when the Blessed Virgin conceived, Fr. Frederick Faber tells how, beyond all expectations, "the creature has added a fresh liberty to the Creator."

That Mary should have any choice at all is a complete revelation of God in itself. How a creature so encompassed and cloistered in grace could have been free in any sense to do what was less pleasing to God is a mystery that no theology to be met with has ever yet satisfactorily explained. Nevertheless, the fact is beyond controversy. She has this choice, with the uttermost freedom in her election, in some most real sense of freedom. But who could doubt what the voice would be that would come up out of such abysses of grace as hers! There had not yet been on earth, nor in the angels' world, an act of adoration so nearly worthy of God as that consent of hers, that conformity of her deep lowliness to the magnificent and transforming will of God. But another moment, and there will be an act of adoration greater far than that.

Now God is free. Mary has made him free. The creature has added a fresh liberty to the Creator. She has unchained the decrees, and made the sign, and in their procession, like mountainous waves of light, they broke over her in floods of golden splendor. The eternal Sea bathed the queenly creature all around, and the divine pleasure rolled above her in majestic peals of soft mysterious thunder. And a God-like shadow fell upon her for a moment, and Gabriel had disappeared, and without shock, or sound, or so much as a tingling stillness, God in a created nature sat in his immensity within her bosom, and the eternal will was done, and creation was complete.

Far off a storm of jubilee swept far-flashing through the angelic world. But the mother heard not, heeded not. Her head sank upon her bosom, and her soul lay down in a silence that was like the peace of God. The Word was made flesh.

—Fr. Frederick William Faber, *Bethlehem*

IN GOD'S PRESENCE, CONSIDER . . .

How is Mary's conception itself "an act of adoration greater far" than her consent to become the Mother of God? Can we ever know in this life the depths of the mystery of "the Word made flesh"?

CLOSING PRAYER

From a hymn attributed to St. Ephraem: *Today the One who founded and dwells in the heavens has made his abode on earth, so that man, the earth-bound, may find a new home in heaven.*

Mary hoped in God

Mary demonstrated her hope, St. Alphonsus points out, when she saw St. Joseph's anxiety.

Hope takes its rise in faith. For God enlightens us by faith to know his goodness and the promises he has made, so that by this knowledge we may rise by hope to the desire of possessing him. Since Mary had the virtue of faith to its highest degree, she also had hope to the same degree of excellence. She could say with David, "But for me it is good to be near my God, to put my hope in the LORD God" (see Ps 73:28). Mary was indeed that faithful spouse of the Holy Spirit, of whom it was said, "Who is that coming up from the wilderness, flowing with delights, leaning on her beloved?" (See Sg 8:5.)

For Mary was always perfectly detached from earthly affections, looking upon the world as a wilderness. So in no way did she rely either on creatures or on her own merits. Instead, she relied only on divine grace, in which was all her confidence. And so she always advanced in the love of God.

The most holy Virgin gave a clear indication of the greatness of her hope in God when she saw the anxiety of her holy spouse St. Joseph. Unable to account for her miraculous pregnancy, he was troubled at the thought of leaving her: "Joseph . . . resolved to send her away quietly" (Mt 1:19). It seemed necessary at that point for her to reveal the hidden mystery to St. Joseph. But no! As Cornelius à Lapide says, in his commentary on these words of the Gospel: "The Blessed Virgin was unwilling to reveal this secret to Joseph, because she might seem to be boasting of her gifts. So she resigned herself to the care of God, in the confident hope that he would guard her innocence and reputation."

—St. Alphonsus Liguori, *The Glories of Mary*

IN GOD'S PRESENCE, CONSIDER . . .

How might I demonstrate today in a concrete way my hope in God to do for me what's best?

CLOSING PRAYER

From a "Novena to Our Lady of Hope": *I pray, dearest Mother, that through your most powerful intercession my heart may be filled with holy hope, so that in life's darkest hour I may never fail to trust in God my Savior, but by walking in the way of his commandments, I may merit to be united with him, and with you in the eternal joys of heaven.*

A meditation on the Visitation

St. Alphonsus explains that St. Elizabeth knew what we should know: Whenever Mary comes, she brings her Son.

Jesus was the fruit of Mary, as St. Elizabeth told her: "Blessed are you among women, and blessed is the fruit of your womb!" (Lk 1:42). Whoever, then, desires the fruit must go to the tree; whoever desires Jesus must go to Mary; and whoever finds Mary will most certainly find Jesus.

St. Elizabeth saw that the most Blessed Virgin had come to visit her in her own house. Not knowing how to thank her, and filled with humility, she exclaimed: "And why is this granted me, that the mother of my Lord should come to me?" (Lk 1:43).

But we may ask how this could be. Didn't St. Elizabeth already know that not only Mary, but also Jesus, had entered her house? Why then does she say that she is unworthy to receive the mother, and not rather that she is unworthy to receive the Son, who had come to visit her?

The reason is this: The saint knew full well that when Mary comes, she brings Jesus. So it was sufficient to thank the mother without naming the Son.

"She is like ships of the merchant; she brings her bread from afar" (see Prv 31:14). Mary was this fortunate ship that brought us Jesus Christ from heaven, who is the living Bread that comes down from heaven to give us eternal life, as he himself says: "I am the living bread which came down from heaven; if any one eats of this bread, he will live forever" (Jn 6:51).

—St. Alphonsus Liguori, *The Glories of Mary*

IN GOD'S PRESENCE, CONSIDER . . .

What does it mean to say that "when Mary comes, she brings Jesus"? Have I gone to Mary to understand and receive her Son more fully?

CLOSING PRAYER

Mary, I will humbly ask with St. Elizabeth: "Why is this granted to me, that the mother of my Lord should come to me?" (Lk 1:42–43). Though I could never merit such a grace, I will embrace it with gratitude.

Mary hurried to bring graces to Elizabeth's house

Just as Mary went to bring blessings to her cousin's house, St. Alphonsus points out, so she hurries to bring blessings to every home that receives her.

A family that is visited by a royal personage considers itself fortunate, on account of both the honor that comes from such a visit, and the benefits that may be hoped to come from it later. But the soul that is visited by the Queen of the World, the most holy Virgin Mary, should consider itself still more fortunate. For she can't help but fill with riches and graces those blessed souls whom she deigns to visit with her favors.

In Old Testament times, a home was blessed when visited by the Ark of God (see 1 Sam 13:14). How much greater blessings, then, will enrich those who receive a loving visit from this living Ark of God—for such was the Mother of God! This truth was abundantly experienced by the house of St. John the Baptist. As soon as Mary had entered it, she heaped graces and heavenly blessings on the whole family. For this reason, the Feast of the Visitation is commonly called the feast of "Our Blessed Lady of Graces."

After the Blessed Virgin heard from the archangel Gabriel that her kinswoman St. Elizabeth was six months pregnant, she was enlightened within by the Holy Spirit. He showed Mary that the incarnate Word, who had become her Son, was pleased then to manifest to the world the riches of his mercy in the first graces that he desired to impart to all that family. So without delay, according to St. Luke, "Mary arose and went with haste to the hill country" (Lk 1:39). Rising from the quiet of contemplation to which she was always devoted, and leaving her beloved solitude, she immediately set out for the home of St. Elizabeth. "Love bears all things" (1 Cor 13:7) and won't allow delay; as St. Ambrose remarks on this Gospel passage, "The Holy Spirit knows nothing of slow undertakings." So without even considering the difficulty of the journey, this tender Virgin immediately undertook it.

—St. Alphonsus Liguori, *The Glories of Mary*

IN GOD'S PRESENCE, CONSIDER . . .

What kind of blessings is my home most in need of today? Have I asked Mary's help in bringing those blessings to my family?

CLOSING PRAYER

Blessed Mother, I consecrate my home to you and to your Son. Come quickly to bring us the blessings and graces that we need to live as a family of his true disciples.

Visit the poor house of my soul

St. Alphonsus urges Our Lady to come visit his soul in the same way she visited St. Elizabeth, bringing abundant graces with her.

Immaculate and Blessed Virgin, I will always thank my Lord for having granted me the grace to know you. Oh, my Queen! You hurried so quickly to visit St. Elizabeth, and in that way you sanctified her dwelling. Deign, then, to visit, and visit quickly, the poor house of my soul.

Oh, hurry! For you well know, and far better than I do, how poor it is, and with how many maladies it's afflicted: with disordered affections, evil habits, and sins committed, all of which are pernicious diseases that will lead me to eternal death. You can enrich my soul, Treasurer of God, and you can heal all its infirmities.

Visit me, then, in life, and visit me especially at the moment of death, for then, more than ever, I'll need your help. Indeed, I don't expect you to visit me on this earth with your visible presence, as you've visited so many of your servants. For they weren't as unworthy and ungrateful as I am.

Even so, I'll be satisfied to see you in the kingdom of heaven, there to be able to love you more, and thank you for all that you've done for me. For now, I'll be satisfied if you'll visit me with your mercy. Your prayers are all that I desire.

—St. Alphonsus Liguori, *The Glories of Mary*

IN GOD'S PRESENCE, CONSIDER . . .

In what specific ways today does "the poor house of my soul" need repairs? Am I satisfied to have Mary visit me invisibly with her graces, as long as I'm able in the end to see her and her Son when I go to live with them forever?

CLOSING PRAYER

From a prayer of St. Alphonsus: *O my Mother, extend your hand to a poor creature who has fallen and asks your help. Were I a saint, I need not seek your mercy; but because I am a sinner, I flee to thee, I turn to you; in you I confide.*

The first fruits of redemption passed through Mary

St. Alphonsus explains how Mary's visit to St. Elizabeth reveals that the very first fruits of her Son's redemption came through her as a channel, and all the other fruits have come to us in the same way.

When Mary reached the house of her kinswoman, she greeted her cousin Elizabeth (see Lk 1:40). St. Ambrose here remarks that Mary was the first to greet her. But Mary's visit was not at all like the visits of worldly people, which for the most part consist in ceremony and outward show, devoid of all sincerity. Instead, Mary's visit brought with it a heap of graces. The moment she entered that dwelling, at her first greeting, Elizabeth was filled with the Holy Spirit; and St. John the Baptist, the son in her womb, was cleansed from original sin and sanctified. For this reason, the unborn child gave a sign of joy by leaping in his mother's womb. He wished in this way to manifest the grace he had received by means of the Blessed Virgin.

St. Elizabeth declared this was true: "When the voice of your greeting came to my ears, the child in my womb leaped for joy" (Lk 1:44). In this way, as Bernardine de Bustis remarks, in virtue of Mary's greeting St. John received the grace of the Spirit of God that sanctified him: "The voice of the greeting, entering her ears, descended to the child, and by its power he received the Holy Spirit."

All these first fruits of Christ's redemption passed through Mary as the channel through which grace was communicated to John the Baptist; the Holy Spirit to his mother, Elizabeth; the gift of prophecy to his father, Zechariah; and so many other blessings to the whole house. If these were the first graces we know about that the Eternal Word granted on earth after his incarnation, it's quite correct to believe that from then on, God made Mary the universal channel, as she is called by St. Bernard, through which all the other graces would pass that our Lord is pleased to dispense to us.

—St. Alphonsus Liguori, *The Glories of Mary*

IN GOD'S PRESENCE, CONSIDER . . .

What does it mean to say that "God made Mary the universal channel . . . through which all the other graces would pass that our Lord is pleased to dispense to us"? Why is it fitting for her to be this channel?

CLOSING PRAYER

From the "Litany of the Blessed Virgin Mary, Mediatrix of All Grace":

O Lord Jesus Christ, our Mediator with the Father, graciously grant that whoever goes to you in search of blessings may be gladdened by obtaining them all through her.

The Visitation shows us the effects of the Spirit

St. Frances de Sales points out how the visitation of Mary to Elizabeth demonstrates the effects of the Holy Spirit's presence and activity.

Our Lady went to visit St. Elizabeth; but this visit was not useless nor like those which women of the world very often make solely for ceremony, to testify the deepest affections which they do not feel, and during them they frequently gossip about each other so that they come away with guilty consciences. Our Lady's visitation was not like this, for she went to serve her cousin. Their conversations were far from idle—rather, my God, how holy, pious, and devout! That visit filled the whole family of Zechariah with the Holy Spirit. Now the principal effects of the Holy Spirit are those which he produced in St. Elizabeth; you can easily understand this if you have also received him.

The first thing St. Elizabeth did was to humble herself profoundly for, seeing the Virgin, she exclaimed, "But who am I that the mother of my Lord should come to me? This is the first fruit of the grace of God, humility. When grace visits the soul, it inclines itself to efface itself in the awareness of the divine Goodness and its own nothingness and deficiency. Secondly, Elizabeth said: "O how blest is she who trusted!" And then: "Blest are you among women, and blest is the fruit of your womb." By this you see the second effect of the Holy Spirit is to make us remain firm in the faith and to confirm that of others; then to return to God, acknowledging that he is the source of all graces.

In the third place, Elizabeth said that her baby leapt in her womb for joy; and this is the third mark of the visit of the Holy Spirit—interior conversion, the change to a better life. St. John was sanctified; likewise whoever received the Holy Spirit is wholly transformed in God. If, then, you wish to know if you have received him, examine your works, for it is by them that we know the answer.

—St. Francis de Sales, *Sermon for the Feast of the Visitation*

IN GOD'S PRESENCE, CONSIDER . . .

Do I see in my own life the effects of the Holy Spirit's presence and activity that St. Francis points out? Do I try to imitate these qualities of Mary?

CLOSING PRAYER

From a prayer of Blessed Raymond Jordano: *You, most sweet Virgin, have found grace with God, for you were preserved from the stain of original sin, were filled with the Holy Spirit, and conceived the Son of God. Most humble Virgin, you received all these graces not for yourself only, but also for us, so that you might assist us in all our needs.*

The Visitation shows Mary's humility and charity

St. Frances de Sales shows how the visitation of Mary to Elizabeth illustrates the truth that humility and charity go together.

Our Lady was not satisfied with having humbled herself before the divine Majesty, for she well knew that humility and charity are not in their perfection until they are transmitted to their neighbor. From the love of God proceeds love of neighbor, and the great apostle says that the greatness of your love for your brothers will be directly proportioned to the greatness of your love for God (see Rom 13:8; Gal 5:14; Eph 5:1–2). St. John teaches us this when he writes: "How can it be that you love God, whom you do not see, if you do not love your neighbor, whom you do see" (1 Jn 4:20)?

If we then wish to prove that we do indeed love God, and if we wish others to believe us when we assure them of this, we must love our brothers well, serve them, and assist them in their necessities. Now the holy Virgin, knowing this truth, set out promptly, says the evangelist, proceeding in haste into the hill country of Judah (see Lk 1:30), into the town of Hebron or, as others say, Jerusalem (it matters little), to serve her cousin Elizabeth in her advanced age and pregnancy.

In this she manifested great humility and charity; for as soon as she saw herself Mother of God, she humbled herself to the point of immediately setting out on the road to go help and assist that good woman.

—St. Francis de Sales, *Sermon for the Feast of the Visitation*

IN GOD'S PRESENCE, CONSIDER . . .

Do I imitate Mary by allowing my love for God to overflow in works of love for others? Have I seen the connection of humility and charity in others who provide me models of holiness?

CLOSING PRAYER

From a prayer of St. Methodius: *Most holy Mother of God, you have greater goodness and greater charity than all the other saints, and freer access to God than any of them, for you are his mother.*

Truly, blessed are you among women

St. Sophronius offers an abundance of reasons why St. Elizabeth could rightly say to Mary, "Blessed are you among women."

Truly, Mary, blessed are you among women, for you have turned Eve's curse into a blessing; and Adam, who before now stood under a curse, has been blessed because of you.

Truly, blessed are you among women, because through you, the blessing of the Father has shone down on men, setting them free of the ancient curse.

Truly, blessed are you among women, because through you your ancestors have found salvation; for you were to bear the Savior who would win salvation for them.

Truly, blessed are you among women, for without seed you have borne fruit, giving birth to the One who gives blessings to the whole world and redeems it from the curse that had brought forth thorns.

Truly, blessed are you among women, because, though you are a woman by nature, you have become, in truth, the Mother of God.

If the One you bear is truly God made flesh, then rightly do we call you the Mother of God, for you have indeed given birth to God.

—St. Sophronius

IN GOD'S PRESENCE, CONSIDER . . .

If I were to create my own list of reasons why I can rightly call Mary "blessed among women," what would they be?

CLOSING PRAYER

Mary, truly you are blessed, for you are poor in spirit and meek, merciful and pure in heart, and you have mourned. You are a peacemaker who has hungered and thirsted for righteousness in every soul; you have been persecuted for righteousness' sake, and slandered for the sake of your Son. Now you rejoice and are glad, for great is your reward in heaven! (See Mt 5:3–12.)

"All generations will call me blessed!"

St. Alphonsus recounts the many ways in which Mary's prophecy about herself have come true.

How many who were once proud have become humble by devotion to Mary! How many who were ruled by passion have become restrained! How many in the midst of darkness have found light! How many who were in despair have found confidence! How many who were lost have found salvation by the same powerful means!

All this, Mary clearly foretold in the house of Elizabeth, in her own sublime canticle: "Behold, henceforth all generations will call me blessed!" (Lk 1:48). And St. Bernard, interpreting her words, says, "All generations call you blessed, because you have given life and glory to all nations; for in you sinners find pardon, and the righteous find perseverance in the grace of God."

For this reason, the devout monk Lanspergius has our Lord address the world in this way: "Men, poor children of Adam, who live surrounded by so many enemies and in the midst of so many trials! Endeavor to honor my mother and yours in a special way. For I've given Mary to the world, so that she may be your model, and so that from her you may learn to lead good lives. I've given her also to be a refuge to which you can flee in all your afflictions and trials. I've made this daughter of mine in such a way that no one need fear or have the least reluctance to turn to her. For this purpose I've created her of such a kind and compassionate disposition that she doesn't know how to despise anyone who takes refuge with her, nor can she deny her favor to anyone who seeks it. The mantle of her mercy is open to all, and she allows no one to leave her feet without consoling him." May the immense goodness of our God be ever praised and blessed for having given us such a great, such a tender, such a loving mother and advocate!

—St. Alphonsus Liguori, *The Glories of Mary*

IN GOD'S PRESENCE, CONSIDER . . .

According to St. Alphonsus, what are the ways in which Mary's prophecy has been fulfilled? Why do I call her blessed?

CLOSING PRAYER

Blessed Mother, in you have the ancient words about a valiant woman been fulfilled through all generations: "Her children will rise up and call her blessed!" (See Prv 31:10, 28.)

Virgin, wholly marvelous

St. Ephraem the Syrian, known as "the harp of the Holy Spirit," composed some of the most beautiful hymns of the ancient Church. This hymn, composed for the Feast of the Nativity, celebrates Mary's dignity as the mother of our Lord.

Virgin, wholly marvelous,
who didst bear God's Son for us,
worthless is my tongue and weak
of thy purity to speak.
Who can praise thee as he ought?
Gifts, with every blessing fraught,
gifts that bring the gifted life,
thou didst grant us, maiden-wife.
God became thy lowly Son,
made himself thy little One,
raising men to tell thy worth
high in heav'n as here on earth.
Heav'n and earth, and all that is,
thrill today with ecstasies,
chanting glory unto thee,
singing praise with festal glee.
Cherubim with fourfold face
are no peers of thine in grace;
and the six-winged seraphim
shine, amid thy splendor, dim.
Purer art thou than are all
heav'nly hosts angelical,
who delight with pomp and state
on thy beauteous Child to wait.

—St. Ephraem the Syrian

IN GOD'S PRESENCE, CONSIDER . . .

Has familiarity with the Christmas story dulled my sense of wonder over what actually happened that night? Have I taken time to ponder what it means for me that God himself became one of us—and chose Mary for his mother?

CLOSING PRAYER

From a late medieval Christmas prayer: *Mother of God, who wrapped your little, sweet Babe in clothes, and between two beasts in a crib laid him in hay, pray for me that my naked soul may be wrapped in fear and love of my Lord God.*

In Christ's nativity, our treasure was hidden

St. Bernard insists that great spiritual treasure was hidden from the world in the events surrounding the nativity of our Lord: the immaculate nature of his mother, the sinless nature of the Child, the untold riches of God's mercy.

O miraculous novelty! The curse of Eve is reversed in the Virgin, for she brought forth her Son without pain or sorrow. The curse has been changed into a blessing.

You only, Mary, are blessed among women! Blest, not cursed! You alone are free from the universal curse! And no wonder that Jesus gave no sorrow to his mother in childbirth, since he himself bore all the sorrows of the world, as Isaiah says: "Truly he has carried our sorrows" (Is 53:4).

There are two things from which our weak human nature shrinks: pain and shame. Christ came to take both from us, and this he did by accepting both of these in his own person. And to give us the fullest confidence in this deliverance, he first freed his mother from both pain and shame.

Our treasure was hidden. The immaculate nature of the mother was hidden in the rite of purification according to the Law. The innocence of the Child was hidden in the customary rite of circumcision. So hide, then, Mary, hide the brightness of the new Sun! Place him in the manger; wrap your Infant in swaddling clothes, for his humble wrap is our riches.

The rags of our Savior are more precious than royal purple, and his poor manger is more glorious than the gilded thrones of kings. The poverty of Christ is greater riches than all this world's wealth. For what is richer or more precious than the humility by which heaven is bought and divine grace is obtained?

—St. Bernard of Clairvaux, *On the Miraculous Nature of the Nativity*

IN GOD'S PRESENCE, CONSIDER . . .

In what ways are God's spiritual riches hidden from the eyes of the world today? In what ways are they hidden in my life?

CLOSING PRAYER

Lord Jesus Christ, you are "the image of the invisible God"; and though your divinity was hidden from the world in your birth, in you "all the fullness of God was pleased to dwell" (Col 1:15, 19).

On Christmas Eve, before the Blessed Sacrament

Though some would object to Marian devotion as a part of Eucharistic adoration, "where the Child is, there too will be the mother."

Mother of God, Ark of the Covenant,
tabernacle of the Lord, throne of the Most High,
vessel of the Almighty, treasury of the Most Precious,
home of the Most Holy!

Your sacred shadow falls across this room,
where gold and crystal—poor images of you at best—
embrace your beloved Son in sweet stillness.

In the silence I hear you hum a lullaby of adoration, comfort;
for where the Child is, there too will be the mother.

I have woven him a blanket of my praises:
ragged and rough, soiled and smelling of earth.
Take it, my Lady, and hem it round with your prayers;
wash it with your tears, smooth it out with your graces,
sprinkle it with the fragrance of your glory.

Only then will it be a fit covering for my Lord,
the Son of Mary,
the Son of God.

—Paul Thigpen

IN GOD'S PRESENCE, CONSIDER . . .

Jesus and Mary shared a deep spiritual union throughout his life on earth, and she is seated close by at his right hand in glory even now. Even in the presence of the Blessed Sacrament, how could we possibly separate Jesus from his mother?

CLOSING PRAYER

From a prayer of St. Margaret Mary Alacoque: *Mary, obtain for us the grace to understand, even just a little, the love of Jesus Christ in the Blessed Sacrament.*

Presenting Jesus in the temple fulfilled the law

When Mary offered her firstborn Son in the temple, St. Alphonsus tells us, it was much more than the fulfillment of a ritual obligation. She was offering him up to God as a sacrifice—and herself as well.

In the Old Testament law there were two instructions concerning the birth of firstborn sons. The first was that the mother was to remain ritually unclean, confined to her house for forty days. After that, she was to go purify herself in the temple. The other instruction was that the parents of the firstborn son were to take him to the temple and offer him there to God.

On this day the most Blessed Virgin obeyed both these instructions. Although Mary was not bound by the law of purification, since she was always a virgin and always pure, yet her humility and obedience made her wish to go like other mothers to purify herself. At the same time, she obeyed the second instruction to present and offer her Son to the Eternal Father. "And when the time came for their purification, according to the law of Moses, they brought him up to Jerusalem to present him to the Lord" (Lk 2:22). But the Blessed Virgin didn't offer Jesus as other mothers offered their sons. Others offered them to God, but they knew that this offering was simply a legal ceremony. By redeeming the children, they made them their own, without fear of having again to offer them up to death.

Mary, however, actually offered her Son up to death. She knew for certain that the sacrifice of the life of Jesus which she then made would one day actually be consummated on the altar of the Cross. In this way Mary, by offering the life of her Son, because of the love she had for him, actually came to sacrifice her own entire self to God. Leaving aside, then, all other considerations into which we might enter on the many mysteries of the Feast of the Presentation, we do well to consider the greatness of the sacrifice that Mary made of herself to God in offering him on this day the life of her Son.

—St. Alphonsus Liguori, *The Glories of Mary*

IN GOD'S PRESENCE, CONSIDER . . .

Does Mass attendance sometimes feel like the mere fulfillment of a ritual obligation? How might I learn more about the meaning of that ritual so that when I take part in the Mass, I can make more of a conscious offering of myself to God?

CLOSING PRAYER

From the "Chaplet to the Mother of the Most Holy Eucharist": *Hail Mary, O mother of the most holy Eucharist! Help me to believe completely, help me to love completely, help me to live what I believe and love completely.*

Mary's obedience in presenting Jesus in the temple

St. Francis de Sales explains how Mary wasn't obliged to follow the laws for her purification, but submitted to them anyway to avoid scandalizing others.

Our Lady and sacred mistress was not afraid of disobeying the laws of purification, because she was in no way obliged to the Law, which was not made for her or her Son. Rather, she feared the shadow of disobedience. For though she, being all pure, had no need of being purified, if she had not come to the temple to offer our Lord and be purified, some may have wished to investigate why she had not done as the rest of women.

Thus she comes today to the temple to remove all suspicion from men who might have wondered about her. She comes also to show us that we ought not to be satisfied with avoiding sin, but that we must avoid even the shadow of sin. Neither must we stop at the resolution not to commit such and such a sin; rather, we must fly even from the occasions that could serve as a temptation to fall into it.

She also teaches us not to be satisfied with the testimony of a good conscience, but to take care to remove every suspicion in others that will make them unedified by us or by our conduct. I say this for certain people who, being resolved not to commit some sins, are not careful enough to avoid the suggestion that they would willingly commit them if they dared.

Oh, how this example of most holy obedience that our Lord and Our Lady give us should incite us to submit ourselves absolutely and without any reservation to the obedience of all that is commanded us and, not satisfied with that, to observe also the things that are counseled in order to make us more pleasing to the divine Goodness!

—St. Francis de Sales, *Sermon for the Feast of the Purification*

IN GOD'S PRESENCE, CONSIDER . . .

Do I imitate Mary's obedience? Am I careful to avoid even the appearance of sin, so that I won't scandalize others?

CLOSING PRAYER

From a prayer of St. Louis de Montfort: *O my Savior, grant that, doing willingly what is ordained for us, and endeavoring to believe it is best, we may spend our whole lives in continual obedience, and thus secure for ourselves your grace in time, and your glory for all eternity.*

God received Mary's consent to Jesus' death

St. Alphonsus explains that when Mary presented Jesus in the temple, she was giving her consent to God's plan for him to die for the world.

The Eternal Father had already determined to save man, who was lost by sin, and to deliver him from eternal death. But because God willed at the same time that his divine justice should not be defrauded of a worthy and due satisfaction, he didn't spare the life of his Son, who had already become man to in order redeem man. Instead, the Father willed that his Son should pay with the utmost rigor the penalty that men had deserved. "He who did not spare his own Son but gave him up for us all" (Rom 8:32). The Father sent the Son to earth, then, to become man. And he destined for his Son a mother, and willed that this mother should be the Blessed Virgin Mary.

God did not will that his divine Word should become her Son before she had given her express consent to accept him. In the same way, he also did not will that Jesus should sacrifice his life for the salvation of men without Mary's concurring assent. In this way, together with the sacrifice of the life of the Son, the mother's heart might also be sacrificed. St. Thomas teaches that motherhood gives a woman a special right over her children. For this reason, since Jesus in himself was innocent and undeserving of punishment, it seemed fitting that he should not be condemned to the Cross as a victim for the sins of the world without the consent of his mother. In this way, she would voluntarily offer him to death when she presented him in the temple.

From the moment she became the mother of Jesus, Mary consented to his death. Yet God willed that on this day she should make a solemn sacrifice of herself, by offering her Son to him in the temple, sacrificing his precious life to divine justice. And now we begin to see how much this sacrifice cost her, and what heroic virtue she had to practice, when she herself assented to the sentence by which her beloved Jesus was condemned to death.

—St. Alphonsus Liguori, *The Glories of Mary*

IN GOD'S PRESENCE, CONSIDER . . .

If I have children, have I imitated Mary's example by presenting them to God and consecrating them to his service? Do they know that they have been consecrated this way?

CLOSING PRAYER

Mary, help me make a precious gift of my children to our Lord, entrusting them to his care, and seeking to help them fulfill his mission for their lives.

Mary would gladly have suffered instead of Jesus

St. Alphonsus notes that Mary would willingly have taken her Son's place in suffering, but she was obedient to God's will and plan.

Consider how much it must have cost Mary, and what strength of mind she had to exercise, in this act by which she sacrificed the life of so amiable a Son on the Cross. Behold, then, the most fortunate of mothers, because she is the Mother of God. Yet at the same time, she was of all mothers the most worthy of compassion. For she was the most afflicted, in that she saw her Son destined to endure the Cross from the day on which he was given to her.

What mother could accept a child, knowing that she would afterward lose him miserably by a shameful death—knowing, even more, that she herself would be present and see him die this way? Yet Mary willingly accepts this Son on so hard a condition. And not only does she accept him; she herself offers him to death on the day of his presentation in the temple, with her own hand, sacrificing him to divine justice. St. Bonaventure says that the Blessed Virgin would have accepted the pains and death of her Son far more willingly for herself. But to obey God, she made the great offering of the divine life of her beloved Jesus. She overcame, but with overwhelming grief, the tender love that she bore him.

"Could it have been so," St. Bonaventure comments, "she would willingly have endured all the torments of her Son in his place. But it pleased God that his only-begotten Son should be offered for the salvation of the human race." For this reason, in this offering, Mary had to do herself more violence, and was more generous, than if she had offered herself to suffer all that her Son was to endure. In this way, she surpasses all the martyrs in generosity. For the martyrs offered their own lives, but the Blessed Virgin offered the life of her Son, whom she loved and esteemed infinitely more than her own life.

—St. Alphonsus Liguori, *The Glories of Mary*

IN GOD'S PRESENCE, CONSIDER . . .

Am I grateful to, and supportive of, parents who must generously accept the possibility that their children could die in fulfillment of a necessary mission as soldiers, law enforcement officers, or emergency personnel? Have I asked Mary to be with them in their anxious moments?

CLOSING PRAYER

Father, with my Blessed Mother, I will let your peace, which surpasses all understanding, guard my heart and mind in Christ Jesus (see Phil 4:7).

Mary knew Jesus would be spoken against

St. Alphonsus explains how St. Simeon's prophecy was fulfilled that Jesus would be spoken against.

St. Simeon said to Mary in the temple: "Behold, this Child is set . . . for a sign that is spoken against" (Lk 2:34). It was revealed to St. Teresa that even though the Blessed Mother already knew that the life of her Son would be sacrificed for the salvation of the world, at this time she learned more specifically and in greater detail the sufferings and cruel death that awaited her poor Son. She knew that he would be spoken against, and this in every way.

He would be spoken against in his teaching. Instead of being believed, he would be considered a blasphemer for teaching that he was the Son of God. This was what the impious Caiaphas declared him to be when he said: "He has uttered blasphemy . . . he deserves death" (Mt 26:65–66). He was spoken against in his reputation. For he was of noble, even royal, descent, yet he was despised as a peasant: "Is not this the carpenter's son?" (Mt 13:55). He was wisdom itself, yet he was treated as ignorant: "How is it that this man has learning, when he has never studied?" (Jn 7:15). He was considered a madman: "He is mad, why listen to him?" (Jn 10:20).

They thought him a drunkard, a glutton, and a friend of sinners (see Lk 7:34); a sorcerer (Mt 9:34); a heretic, and possessed by an evil spirit (Jn 8:48). In a word, Jesus was considered so notoriously wicked that, as the Jews said to Pilate, no trial was necessary to condemn him: "If this man were not an evildoer, we would not have handed him over" (Jn 18:30). In short, Jesus was spoken against and persecuted in his body and in his life. For he was tortured in all his sacred limbs: in his hands, his feet, his face, his head, and in his whole body. Drained of his blood, an object of scorn, he died of torments on a shameful cross.

—St. Alphonsus Liguori, *The Glories of Mary*

IN GOD'S PRESENCE, CONSIDER . . .

Am I ever spoken against because of my Catholic faith or moral standards? Do I take consolation in knowing that both Jesus and Mary were spoken against for doing the will of God?

CLOSING PRAYER

Lord Jesus, I will "rejoice and be glad" when others "utter all kinds of evil against" me on your account (see Mt 5:11–12).

Mary knew the prophecies of her Son's suffering

Mary was familiar with the Old Testament prophecies about the Messiah, St. Alphonsus insists. So she knew all too well what lay ahead for her Son.

Compassion for the sufferings of this most beloved Son was the sword of sorrow that was to pierce the heart of the mother, as St. Simeon exactly foretold: "And a sword will pierce through your own soul" (Lk 2:35). Already the most Blessed Virgin, as St. Jerome says, was enlightened by the Sacred Scriptures. She knew the sufferings that the Redeemer was to endure in his life, and still more at the time of his death.

She fully understood from the prophets that he was to be betrayed by one of his disciples, as David foretold: "Even my bosom friend in whom I trusted, who ate of my bread, has lifted his heel against me" (Ps 41:9). He was to be abandoned by them: "Strike the shepherd, that the sheep may be scattered" (Zec 13:7). She knew well the contempt, the spitting, the blows, the derisions he was to suffer from the people: "I gave my body to those who struck me, and my cheeks to those who pulled out the beard; I hid not my face from shame and spitting" (Is 50:6).

She knew that he was to become the reproach of men, and the outcast of the most degraded of the people, so as to be saturated with insults and injuries: "But I am a worm, and no man; scorned by men, and despised by the people" (Ps 22:7). She knew that at the end of his life, his most sacred flesh would be torn and mangled by scourges: "But he was wounded for our transgressions; he was bruised for our iniquities" (Is 53:5). She knew that he was to be pierced by nails: "They have pierced my hands and feet" (Ps 22:16). He would be considered a villain: "He was numbered with the transgressors" (Is 53:12). And finally, hanging on a cross, he was to die for the salvation of men: "They [shall] look on him whom they have pierced" (Zec 12:10).

—St. Alphonsus Liguori, *The Glories of Mary*

IN GOD'S PRESENCE, CONSIDER . . .

Do I know the Scriptures well enough to realize what challenges the future holds for me as a faithful follower of Jesus? Do I also know the scriptural promises made to me? (See Mt 5:1–12.)

CLOSING PRAYER

Father, whatever the future holds, "I know whom I have believed, and I am sure he is able to guard until that Day what has been entrusted to me" (2 Tim 1:12).

All her joy was changed to sorrow

The presentation of Jesus in the temple should have been a joyful time for his parents. But St. Alphonsus points out that the joy became sorrow when St. Simeon revealed the Child's future.

In this valley of tears, every man is born to weep, and all must suffer, by enduring the evils that take place every day. But how much greater would be the misery of life, if we also knew the future evils that await us! "Unfortunate, indeed, would be the situation of someone who knows the future," says the pagan Roman philosopher Seneca; "he would have to suffer everything by anticipation." Our Lord shows us this mercy. He conceals the trials that await us so that, whatever they may be, we may endure them only once. But he didn't show Mary this compassion.

God willed her to be the Queen of Sorrows, and in all things like his Son. So she always had to see before her eyes, and continually to suffer, all the torments that awaited her. And these were the sufferings of the passion and death of her beloved Jesus.

For in the temple, St. Simeon, having received the divine Child in his arms, foretold to her that her Son would be a sign for all the persecutions and oppositions of men. "Simeon blessed them and said to his mother, "Behold, this Child is set . . . for a sign that is contradicted (and a sword will pierce through your own soul also), that thoughts out of many hearts may be revealed" (see Lk 2:34–35).

The Blessed Virgin herself told St. Matilda that, at this prophecy of St. Simeon, "all her joy was changed into sorrow." Jesus our King and his most holy mother didn't refuse, for love of us, to suffer such cruel pains throughout their lives. So it's reasonable that we, at least, should not complain if we have to suffer something.

—St. Alphonsus Liguori, *The Glories of Mary*

IN GOD'S PRESENCE, CONSIDER . . .

Am I grateful to God that he doesn't reveal the future to me? Do I recognize that it's a grace to live by Jesus' words, "Do not be anxious about tomorrow, for tomorrow will be anxious about itself. Let the day's own trouble be sufficient for the day"? (See Mt 6:34.)

CLOSING PRAYER

"Search me, O God, and know my heart! Try me, and know my anxious thoughts! And see if there be any hurtful way in me, and lead me in the way everlasting!" (See Ps 139:23–24.)

The sorrow of the flight into Egypt

When St. Joseph received instructions in a dream for the Holy Family to flee to Egypt, Mary knew that St. Simeon's prophecy of her sorrows was beginning to be fulfilled. St. Alphonsus explains.

The stag, wounded by an arrow, carries the pain with him wherever he goes, because he carries with him the arrow that has wounded him. In the same way, after the sad prophecy of St. Simeon, the Mother of God always carried her sorrow with her in the continual remembrance of the passion of her Son. Her Son was himself that arrow in the heart of Mary. And the more lovable he appeared to her, the more deeply did the thought of losing him by so cruel a death wound her heart. Consider the sword of sorrow that wounded Mary, in the flight into Egypt with her infant Jesus from the persecution of Herod.

Herod, having heard that the expected Messiah was born, foolishly feared that he would deprive him of his kingdom. For this reason St. Fulgentius, reproving Herod for his folly, addresses him this way: "Why are you troubled, Herod? This King who is born comes not to conquer kings by the sword, but to bring them under his rule wonderfully by his death." The impious Herod waited to hear from the holy Magi where the King was born, so that he might take his life. But finding himself deceived, he ordered all the infants who could be found in the neighborhood of Bethlehem to be put to death. Then it was that the angel appeared in a dream to St. Joseph, telling him: "Rise, take the Child and his mother, and flee to Egypt" (Mt 2:13). So St. Joseph immediately, on that very night, made the instruction known to Mary; and taking the infant Jesus, they set out on their journey (see Mt 2:14).

St. Albert, speaking on Mary's behalf, says: "O God, must he who came to save men now flee from men?" At that time the afflicted mother knew that already the prophecy of Simeon concerning her Son had begun to come true.

—St. Alphonsus Liguori, *The Glories of Mary*

IN GOD'S PRESENCE, CONSIDER . . .

Doesn't the world still have its Herods—government officials here and abroad who fear the political implications of the gospel and are hostile to Christians? Do I pray and take other action to counter their influence?

CLOSING PRAYER

From a prayer of Venerable Pope Pius XII: *Mary, Mother of Divine Love, stir up and confirm in the hearts of those who govern nations a clear notion of their responsibility, and of their duty to foster religion, morality, and the common good.*

Sinners are like Herod's men pursuing Jesus

If we think Herod's men are villains because they sought out the baby Jesus to kill him, St. Alphonsus urges us to consider how even now our sins also persecute him and afflict his mother.

The most holy Virgin one day appeared to Blessed Collette, a Franciscan nun, and showed her the infant Jesus in a basin, torn to pieces. Mary then said: "This is how sinners continually treat my Son, renewing his death and my sorrows. My daughter, pray for them, so that they may be converted."

To this we may add another vision, which the venerable Sr. Joanna of Jesus and Mary, a Franciscan nun, also had. She was one day meditating on the infant Jesus persecuted by Herod. She heard a great noise, like the sound of armed men pursuing someone. Immediately she saw before her a most beautiful Child, who, all out of breath and running, exclaimed: "My Joanna, help me, conceal me! I'm Jesus of Nazareth; I'm fleeing from sinners, who persecute me and want to kill me as Herod did. Save me!"

Mary, even after your Son has died at the hands of men who persecuted him to death, these ungrateful men have not yet ceased persecuting him by their sins, and they continue to afflict you, sorrowful Mother! My God, I too have been one of these.

My most sweet Mother, obtain for me tears to weep over such ingratitude. By the sufferings you endured in your journey to Egypt, assist me in the journey I now undertake toward eternity. In that way, I may in the end be united with you in loving my persecuted Savior in the kingdom of the blessed.

—St. Alphonsus Liguori, *The Glories of Mary*

IN GOD'S PRESENCE, CONSIDER . . .

The Magi sought the infant Jesus to worship him; Herod's soldiers sought him to kill him. Today, which will I be: my Lord's worshipper, or his persecutor?

CLOSING PRAYER

Lord, I will obey your command: "Seek the Lord while he may be found, call upon him while he is near; let the wicked forsake his way, and the unrighteous man his thoughts; let him return to the Lord, that he may have mercy on him, and to our God, for he will abundantly pardon" (Is 55:6–7).

Sufferings in the flight to Egypt

In an age of fast and comfortable travel, we may forget just how difficult the Holy Family's flight to Egypt would have been. St. Alphonsus provides details.

Anyone can imagine what Mary must have suffered on the journey to Egypt. The distance was great. Most authors agree that it was three hundred miles, so that it was a journey of upwards of thirty days. The road was, according to St. Bonaventure's description of it, "rough, unknown, and rarely traveled." It was in the winter season, so they had to travel in snow, rain, and wind, through rough and dirty roads. Mary was then about fifteen years of age—a delicate young woman, unaccustomed to such journeys. They had no one to serve them. As St. Peter Chrysologus says, "Joseph and Mary had no male or female servants; they were themselves both masters and servants."

O God, what a touching sight must it have been to have beheld that tender virgin, with her newborn Babe in her arms, wandering through the world! "But how," asks St. Bonaventure, "did they obtain their food? Where did they sleep at night? How were they lodged?" What can they have eaten but a piece of hard bread, either brought by St. Joseph or begged as alms? Where can they have slept on such a road (especially on the two hundred miles of desert, where there were neither houses nor inns, as authors relate), unless they slept on the sand or under a tree in a wood, exposed to the air and the dangers of robbers and wild beasts, with which Egypt abounded? Had anyone met them, the three greatest persons in the world, he would have thought them to be three poor wandering beggars.

—St. Alphonsus Liguori, *The Glories of Mary*

IN GOD'S PRESENCE, CONSIDER . . .

When I think of the Holy Family's miserable condition as they journeyed to Egypt, does it make me feel more compassion for the hungry and homeless people of my day? What might Mary want me to do for them?

CLOSING PRAYER

From a prayer of Blessed Pope Paul VI: *Look down with maternal clemency, most Blessed Virgin, upon all your children. Heed the anguish of so many people, fathers and mothers of families who are uncertain about their future and beset by hardships and cares.*

Take the Child and his mother

St. Alphonsus insists that the Holy Family's exile in Egypt should teach us that we, too, must live as pilgrims here on earth.

Having fled to Egypt, the Holy Family resided there. Let's consider the great poverty they must have suffered during the seven years which, according to some teachers, they spent there. They were foreigners unknown, without revenues, money, or family, barely able to support themselves by their humble efforts. "As they were destitute," says St. Basil, "it's evident that they must have labored hard to provide themselves with the necessities of life." In addition, Landolph of Saxony has written (and let this be a consolation for the poor), that "Mary lived there in the midst of such poverty that at times she had not even a bit of bread to give to her Son when, compelled by hunger, he asked for it."

After the death of Herod, the angel again appeared to St. Joseph in a dream, directing him to return to Judea (see Mt 2:19–20). St. Bonaventure, speaking of this return, considers how much greater the Blessed Virgin's sufferings must have been because Jesus had grown so much. He was then about seven years of age, so "he was too big to be carried, and not strong enough to walk without assistance."

The sight of Jesus and Mary wandering as fugitives through the world teaches us that we also must live as pilgrims here below, detached from the goods that the world offers us, and which we must soon leave to enter eternity: "For we have here no lasting city, but we seek the city which is to come" (Heb 13:14). It also teaches us to embrace crosses, for without them we cannot live in this world. Whoever wishes to feel less the sufferings of this life must go in company with Jesus and Mary: "Take the Child and his mother" (Mt 2:13). All sufferings become light, and even sweet and desirable, to him who by his love bears this Son and this Mother in his heart. Let's love them, then; let's console Mary by welcoming in our hearts her Son, whom men even now continue to persecute by their sins.

—St. Alphonsus Liguori, *The Glories of Mary*

IN GOD'S PRESENCE, CONSIDER . . .

When I imagine the Holy Family's exile in Egypt, what do I think would have been the most difficult aspect of their life in a foreign land? What lessons might I learn from them about being detached from the goods of this world?

CLOSING PRAYER

Mary, how were you able to "sing the Lord's song in a foreign land" (see Ps 137:4)? Only because the Lord was in exile with you, and the song you sang was his lullaby.

Mary merited by grace to be Jesus' mother

What does it mean to say that Mary merited to be the Mother of God? Weren't her privileges a gift of grace? St. Alphonsus explains.

Mary was not only the mother, but the worthy mother, of our Savior. She is called such by all the holy fathers. St. Bernard says to her, "You alone were found worthy to be chosen as the one in whose virginal womb the King of kings should have his first dwelling."

St. Thomas of Villanova says, "Before she conceived, she was already fit to be the Mother of God." In fact, the holy Church herself attests that Mary merited to be the mother of Jesus Christ, speaking in her liturgy of "the Blessed Virgin, who merited to bear in her womb Christ our Lord."

St. Thomas Aquinas explains these words this way: "The Blessed Virgin is said to have merited to bear the Lord of all: not that she merited his Incarnation, but that she merited, by the graces she had received, such a degree of purity and sanctity, that she was fit to be the Mother of God."

Mary could not merit the Incarnation of the Eternal Word, but by divine grace she merited such a degree of perfection that it rendered her worthy to be the Mother of a God. According to St. Peter Damian, "Her unique sanctity, the effect of grace, merited that she alone should be judged worthy to receive a God" into her womb.

—St. Alphonsus Liguori, *The Glories of Mary*

IN GOD'S PRESENCE, CONSIDER . . .

Merits aren't rewards from God that are earned apart from his grace, but rather rewards that are fitting for the work of grace he has accomplished in us. In what fitting ways has God blessed me through the work of grace he has accomplished in my life?

CLOSING PRAYER

Lord God, "I praise you, for I am wondrously made. Wonderful are your works" of grace in my life, far beyond all I deserve! (See Ps 139:14.)

Mary's hidden life in Nazareth

The Gospels are silent about the life of Jesus between the ages of about twelve and thirty. St. John Paul II explores the meaning of Mary's "hidden life" with him, as these years are called, before his public ministry began.

During the years of Jesus' hidden life in the house at Nazareth, Mary's life too is "hid with Christ in God" (see Col 3:3) through faith. For faith is contact with the mystery of God. Every day Mary is in constant contact with the ineffable mystery of God made man, a mystery that surpasses everything revealed in the Old Covenant.

From the moment of the Annunciation, the mind of the Virgin-Mother has been initiated into the radical "newness" of God's self-revelation and has been made aware of the mystery. She is the first of those "little ones" of whom Jesus will say one day: "Father . . . you have hidden these things from the wise and understanding and revealed them to babes" (see Mt 11:25). For "no one knows the Son except the Father" (Mt 11:27).

If this is the case, how can Mary "know the Son"? Of course she does not know him as the Father does; and yet she is the first of those to whom the Father "has chosen to reveal him" (see Mt 11:26–27; 1 Cor 2:11). If though, from the moment of the Annunciation, the Son—whom only the Father knows completely, as the One who begets him in the eternal "today" (see Ps 2:7)—was revealed to Mary, she, his mother, is in contact with the truth about her Son only in faith and through faith!

She is therefore blessed, because "she has believed" (see Lk 1:45) and continues to believe day after day amidst all the trials and the adversities of Jesus' infancy, and then during the years of the hidden life at Nazareth, where he "was obedient to them" (Lk 2:51).

—St. John Paul II, *Redemptoris Mater*

IN GOD'S PRESENCE, CONSIDER . . .

Mary knew her Son better than any other human being, and she no doubt treasured in her heart and memory the things he said and did during the "hidden" years. If you could ask her about any event or aspect of his life during that time, what would you ask?

CLOSING PRAYER

Lord, let me join Mary in her hiddenness with you; let me say to Jesus in the words of the psalmist: "In you I have hidden! Teach me to do your will, for you are my God" (see Ps 143:9–10).

Jesus was obedient to His mother

While other virgins follow the Lamb of God (see Rv 14:4), St. Alphonsus reminds us, the Lamb followed Mary.

So great is the authority that mothers possess over their sons that even if they are monarchs, and have absolute dominion over every person in their kingdom, yet never can mothers become the subjects of their sons.

It is true that Jesus now in heaven sits at the right hand of the Father. He has supreme dominion over all, and also over Mary. Nevertheless, it will always be true that for a time, when he was living in this world, Jesus was pleased to humble himself and to be subject to Mary, as we are told by St. Luke: "And he was obedient to them" (Lk 2:51). Even more, says St. Ambrose, Jesus Christ—having deigned to make Mary his mother—inasmuch as he was her Son, he was truly obliged to obey her.

For this reason, says Richard of Saint Lawrence, while of all other virgins we must say that they "follow the Lamb wherever he goes" (Rv 14:4), of the Blessed Virgin Mary we can say that the Lamb followed her, having become subject to her as his earthly mother.

Mary, now in heaven, can no longer command her Son as she did when he was a boy on earth. Nevertheless, her prayers are always the prayers of a mother, and consequently most powerful to obtain whatever she asks. "Mary," says St. Bonaventure, "has this great privilege, that with her Son she above all the saints is most powerful to obtain whatever she wills."

Why is this true? Precisely because they are the prayers of a mother. Jesus is pleased in this way to honor his beloved mother, who honored him so much during her life, by immediately granting all that she asks or desires.

—St. Alphonsus Liguori, *The Glories of Mary*

IN GOD'S PRESENCE, CONSIDER . . .

When I recall how tenderly a loving son obeys his mother, I have some sense of the point St. Alphonsus is making: Mary no longer commands Jesus as a boy. But he has never lost his affection for her and his desire to fulfill her requests, which are all just and gracious. Does this recollection inspire me to bring my petitions to Mary?

CLOSING PRAYER

From a prayer of Blessed Guerric of Igny: *Continue, Mary, to dispose with confidence of the riches of your Son; act as queen, mother, and spouse of the King; for to you belongs dominion and power over all creatures!*

Jesus, remember your mother's immeasurable love

Blessed Henry Suso imagines the fond playfulness of mothers with their children, and asks, in that light, how Mary's Son could ever possibly deny her request.

Exalted Lady of heaven and earth, arise now and be to us a mediatrix who obtains grace from your tender Child, the Eternal Wisdom. And you, Eternal Wisdom, will you deny me anything? Even as I present you before your heavenly Father, so I present your tender mother before you.

Look at her mild eyes that so often looked kindly on you. Behold those fair cheeks that she so often pressed affectionately to your infant face. Look at her sweet mouth that used to kiss you so fondly and tenderly again and again. Look at her pure hands that so often took care of you.

O goodness above all goodness! How can you deny anything to her who nursed you so affectionately and carried you in her arms; who laid you to rest, awakened you, and tenderly reared you? O Lord, let me remind you of all the love you ever experienced from her in the days of your childhood, when you sat in her motherly lap, and with playful eyes laughed so pleasantly and tenderly in her face, with the immeasurable love you had for her above all creatures!

Think, too, of the heart-rending woe that her maternal heart endured with you under the beam of your miserable cross, where she saw you in the agony of death, and when her heart and soul so many times died in sorrow and distress with you. Lord, I beg you, for her sake, grant me every means of shaking off my sins, of acquiring your grace, and never losing it again.

—Blessed Henry Suso, *Little Book of Eternal Wisdom*

IN GOD'S PRESENCE, CONSIDER . . .

When I think of the tender moments between mother and child that every family can recall, I can imagine Mary and Jesus enjoying many such moments, with a mutual love beyond all telling. With that bond between them, what must be the Son's reply when the mother asks a favor on my behalf?

CLOSING PRAYER

From a prayer of St. Bernard of Clairvaux: *We raise our eyes to you, Queen of the World. We must appear before our Judge after so many sins; who will appease him? No one can do it better than you can, holy Lady, who has loved him so much, and by whom you are so tenderly beloved.*

What did Jesus and Mary talk about?

Blessed John Henry Newman speculates about the subjects of conversation between Mary and Jesus during the thirty years he lived with her.

What was the grand theme of conversation between Mary and her Son but the nature, the attributes, the providence, and the works of Almighty God? Wouldn't our Lord be ever glorifying the Father who sent him? Wouldn't he unfold to her the solemn eternal decrees, and the purposes and will of God? Wouldn't he from time to time enlighten her in all those points of doctrine which have been first discussed and then settled in the Church from the time of the Apostles till now, and all that shall be till the end—no, these, and far more than these? All that is obscure, all that is fragmentary in revelation, would, so far as the knowledge is possible to man, be brought out to her in clearness and simplicity by him who is the Light of the world.

The same was true of the events which are to come. God spoke to the prophets: We have his communications to them in Scripture. But he spoke to them in figure and parable. There was one, Moses, to whom he vouchsafed to speak face to face: "If there be among you a prophet of the LORD," God says, "I will appear to him in a vision, and I will speak to him in a dream. But it is not so with my servant Moses. . . . For I will speak to him mouth to mouth, and plainly, and not by riddles and figures does he see the LORD" (see Num 12:6–7).

This was the great privilege of the inspired lawgiver of the Jews; but how much was it below the privilege of Mary! Moses had the privilege only now and then, from time to time. But Mary, for thirty continuous years, saw and heard him. And all through that time she was face to face with him, and able to ask him any question which she wished explained, knowing that the answers she received were from the Eternal God, who neither deceives nor can be deceived.

—Blessed John Henry Newman, *Meditations and Devotions*

IN GOD'S PRESENCE, CONSIDER . . .

What would be my own speculations about the subjects of conversation between Jesus and Mary? What conversations would I like to have been present for?

CLOSING PRAYER

Blessed Virgin, "to you it has been given to know the secrets of the kingdom of God" (Lk 8:10). "O the depths of the riches and wisdom and knowledge of God!" (Rom 11:33).

Mary searches for Jesus in Jerusalem

St. Alphonsus ponders the anxiety Mary must have felt when she was searching for three days before she found young Jesus in the temple.

In the second chapter of his Gospel, St. Luke tells us that every year at the Passover feast, the Blessed Virgin used to visit the temple with her spouse, St. Joseph, and Jesus. When her Son was twelve years of age, she went as usual, and when she returned, Jesus remained in Jerusalem. Mary didn't at once realize it, thinking he was traveling in the company of others.

When she reached Nazareth, we may imagine, she asked around for her Son. But since she didn't find him, she immediately returned to Jerusalem to look for him. She found him only after three days.

Now let's imagine what anxiety this afflicted mother must have experienced in those three days when she was searching everywhere for her Son and asking for him, like the spouse in the Song of Songs: "Have you seen him whom my soul loves?" (Sg 3:3). But she learned nothing of his whereabouts.

The Old Testament patriarch Reuben once said about his brother Joseph: "The lad is gone; and I, where shall I go?" (Gn 37:30). Consider how far greater must have been the tenderness with which Mary could have repeated those words, overcome by fatigue, yet without having found her beloved Son! "My Jesus is gone, and I no longer know what to do to find him; but where shall I go without my treasure?"

Weeping continually, with how much truth could she have repeated with King David, during those three days, "My tears have been my food day and night, while men say to me continually, 'Where is your God?'" (Ps 42:3).

—St. Alphonsus Liguori, *The Glories of Mary*

IN GOD'S PRESENCE, CONSIDER . . .

If Mary knows what it's like to suffer such anxiety, surely she can understand why I also struggle with anxiety at times. Have I asked her to help me find peace in the midst of those struggles?

CLOSING PRAYER

"Have mercy on me, O God. . . . When I am afraid, I put my trust in you. In God, whose word I praise, in God I trust without fear" (Ps 56:1, 3–4).

When God seems far away

Mary suffered great sorrow when she couldn't find the boy Jesus for three days. St. Alphonsus says we can learn from the way she suffered in those days how we ourselves can suffer yet have peace.

The sorrow of Mary at losing the boy Jesus for a while should serve as a consolation to those souls who are desolate because they no longer enjoy, as they once enjoyed, the sweet presence of their Lord. They may weep, but they should weep in peace, as Mary wept over the absence of her Son. And let them take courage, not fearing that on this account they have lost God's favor. For God himself assured St. Teresa that "no one is lost without knowing it, and no one is deceived without wishing to be deceived."

If our Lord withdraws himself from the sight of a soul that loves him, that doesn't mean he has departed from the heart. He often conceals himself from a soul, so that the soul may seek him with a more ardent desire and greater love. But whoever wishes to find Jesus must seek him, not amid the delights and pleasures of the world, but amid crosses and mortifications, as Mary sought him. As Mary said to her Son, "we sought you sorrowing" (Lk 2:48). "Learn, then, from Mary," says the ancient spiritual writer Origen, "to seek Jesus."

In addition, we should imitate Mary in that she would seek no other good in this world than Jesus. Job was not unhappy when he lost all that he possessed on earth—riches, children, health, and honors—and even descended from a throne to a dunghill. But because he had God with him, he was happy even then. St. Augustine says, "Job had lost what God had given him, but he still had God himself." On the other hand, truly miserable and unhappy are those souls who have lost God. If Mary wept over the absence of her Son for three days, how much more should sinners weep, who have lost divine grace? For this is the effect of sin: It separates the soul from God.

—St. Alphonsus Liguori, *The Glories of Mary*

IN GOD'S PRESENCE, CONSIDER . . .

Am I convinced that even when I suffer great loss, though I have lost what God has given me, I still have God himself? When I lose even the sense of God's nearness, am I able to seek him, trusting that he is close by me even then?

CLOSING PRAYER

"O my God, I cry by day, but you do not answer; and by night, but find no rest. Yet you are holy. . . . In you our fathers trusted; they trusted, and you delivered them. . . . Be not far from me, for trouble is near, and there is none to help" (Ps 22:2–4, 11).

How Mary demonstrated hope in God

St. Alphonsus observes that in all the events of Mary's life recorded in the Gospels, we find that she demonstrated a firm hope in God the Father and in her Son.

Mary showed her confident hope in God when she knew that the time for the birth of our Lord approached. For she was driven from even the lodgings of the poor in Bethlehem, and obliged to bring forth her Son in a stable, "because there was no place for them in the inn" (Lk 2:7). She didn't speak a single word of complaint. Instead, abandoning herself to God, she trusted that he would assist her there. The Mother of God also showed how great was her confident hope in Divine Providence when she received notice from St. Joseph that they must flee into Egypt. On that very night she undertook a long journey to a strange and unknown country without provisions, without money, accompanied only by her infant Jesus and her poor spouse, who "rose and took the Child and his mother by night, and departed to Egypt" (Mt 2:14).

Yet even more did she show her confident hope when she asked her Son for wine at the marriage feast of Cana. For when she had said, "They have no wine," Jesus answered her, "Woman, what have you to do with me? My hour has not yet come" (Jn 2:3–4). This answer seemed to be a refusal. But Mary had such great confidence in the divine goodness that she urged the servants to do whatever her Son told them, because she was certain that the favor would be granted (see Jn 2:5). And indeed, it happened: Jesus Christ ordered the vessels to be filled with water, then changed it into wine.

Let's learn, then, from Mary to have the confident hope in God that we should always have—especially in the great affair of our eternal salvation. Though it's truly a matter in which we must cooperate, yet it's from God alone that we must hope for the grace necessary to obtain it. We must put no trust in our own strength, and say with the Apostle Paul: "I can do all things through him who strengthens me" (Phil 4:13).

—St. Alphonsus Liguori, *The Glories of Mary*

IN GOD'S PRESENCE, CONSIDER . . .

What is hope, and how does it differ from faith? In which areas of my life right now do I need most to imitate Mary's virtue of hope?

CLOSING PRAYER

From a prayer of Pope St. John Paul II: *Dawn of a new world, show yourself the Mother of Hope and watch over us!*

How Mary demonstrated humility

St. Alphonsus points out that several biblical accounts of Mary's conduct reveal her humble spirit.

It's a part of humility to serve others. Consider how Mary didn't hesitate to go and serve Elizabeth for three months. For this reason, St. Bernard says: "Elizabeth wondered that Mary should have come to visit her. But still more admirable is that she came not to be ministered to, but to minister."

Those who are humble are retiring, and choose the last places. St. Bernard remarks that this is why Mary, when wishing to speak to her Son when he was preaching in a house, would not of her own accord enter. Instead, she "remained outside, and did not avail herself of her maternal authority to interrupt him" (see Mt 12:46).

For the same reason, when she was with the Apostles awaiting the coming of the Holy Spirit, she took the lowest place, as St. Luke notes: "All these with one accord devoted themselves to prayer, together with the women and Mary the mother of Jesus" (Acts 1:14). It's not that St. Luke was ignorant of the Mother of God's merits, on account of which he should have named her in the first place. Rather, she had taken the last place among the Apostles and the women. For this reason, he described them all in the order in which they were. That's why St. Bernard says, "Rightly has the last become the first, who being the first of all became the last."

Finally, those who are humble love to be disdained rather than praised. So we don't read that Mary showed herself in Jerusalem on Palm Sunday, when her Son was received by the people with so much honor. Instead, at the death of her Son, she didn't shrink from appearing on Calvary. She didn't fear the dishonor that would come to her when it was known that she was the mother of the One who was condemned to die an infamous death as a criminal.

—St. Alphonsus Liguori, *The Glories of Mary*

IN GOD'S PRESENCE, CONSIDER . . .

Can I think of other episodes from Mary's life that demonstrate her humility? What practical lessons can I learn from her about how to practice humility?

CLOSING PRAYER

From a prayer of St. John Neumann: *O Mary, Mother of Mercy, pray to your divine Son for me, a poor sinner; beg him to make me humble. My pride, my self-esteem, my vanity are always against me. I struggle against them, and yet I allow them to surprise and deceive me so often.*

A lesson from the wedding at Cana

St. Alphonsus notes that Mary's action at the wedding feast at Cana shows how she wants to help us even before we ask for her help.

Mary, even when living in this world, showed at the marriage feast of Cana the great compassion that she would afterwards exercise toward us in our necessities. Even now it compels her to have pity on us and assist us, even before we ask her to do so. This good mother's compassion is so great, and the love she bears us is so great, that she doesn't even wait for our prayers before she comes to assist us. Richard of Saint Victor remarks that her love for us is so tender, that in our needs she anticipates our prayers, and her mercy is more prompt to help us than we are to ask her aid: "The heart of Mary is so filled with compassion for poor sinners, she no sooner sees our miseries than she pours her tender mercies upon us. Neither is it possible for this kind queen to see the need of any soul without immediately assisting it."

In the second chapter of St. John we read that at this feast the compassionate mother saw the embarrassing situation in which the bride and bridegroom found themselves, and that they were quite ashamed at seeing the wine fail. So she listened only to the dictates of her compassionate heart, which could never behold the afflictions of others without feeling for them. Without being asked, she begged her Son to console them simply by laying their distress before him: "They have no wine" (Jn 2:3).

No sooner had she done so, than our Lord, in order to satisfy everyone present, and still more to console the compassionate heart of his mother who had asked the favor, worked the well-known miracle by which he changed the water, brought to him in jars, into wine. From this, the spiritual writer Luigi Novarini argues: "If Mary, unasked, is so prompt to help the needy, how much more so will she be to help those who call upon her and ask for her help?"

—St. Alphonsus Liguori, *The Glories of Mary*

IN GOD'S PRESENCE, CONSIDER . . .

Are there concerns in my life right now that I haven't yet brought to Mary in prayer? Might she already be intervening in those matters before I ask for her help?

CLOSING PRAYER

Lord Jesus, I must confess that in some areas of my life, I "have no wine." I am empty, thirsty, dry. Through your Blessed Mother's intercession, fill the stone jar of my heart to overflowing with your life-giving water, and turn the water into the wine of gladness in your love.

Jesus' reply to Mary at Cana

When Jesus replied to Mary's comment about the wine running out at the wedding feast, was he at first refusing her request? Not at all, says St. Alphonsus. He explains.

From the time that Mary came into the world, her only thought, after seeking the glory of God, was to help those in need. And even then she enjoyed the privilege of obtaining whatever she asked. This we know from what occurred at the marriage feast of Cana in Galilee. When the wine failed, the most Blessed Virgin was moved to compassion at the sight of the affliction and shame of the bride and bridegroom. So she asked her Son to relieve it by a miracle, telling him: "They have no wine" (Jn 2:3). Jesus answered: "Woman, what have you to do with me? My hour has not yet come" (Jn 2:4). Note here that our Lord seemed to refuse his mother the favor she asked. He seemed to be saying, This is not the time for me to work a miracle; the time will be when I begin to preach, and when miracles will be required to confirm my doctrines. And yet Mary, as if the favor had already been granted, asked those in attendance to fill the jars with water, for they would be immediately satisfied. And so it was. For Jesus, to satisfy his mother, changed the water into the best wine.

But how could this be? Since the time for working miracles was that of the public life of our Lord, how could it be that, contrary to the divine decrees, this miracle was worked? Actually, in this there was nothing contrary to the decrees of God. For even though, generally speaking, the time for miracles had not come, yet from all eternity God had determined by another decree that nothing that she asked should ever be refused to the Mother of God. St. Thomas Aquinas says that by the words, "My hour has not yet come," Jesus Christ intended to show that, had the request come from anyone else, he would not then have complied with it. But because it came to him from his mother, he could not refuse it.

—St. Alphonsus Liguori, *The Glories of Mary*

IN GOD'S PRESENCE, CONSIDER . . .

Are there times in my life when Jesus seems to be refusing my request for his help? In those times, how might I act in faith, as Mary did, as if the favor has already been granted?

CLOSING PRAYER

Father, help me not to have anxiety about anything. Instead, by prayer and supplication with thanksgiving, I will make my requests known to you. I will trust that your peace, which passes all understanding, will keep my heart and mind (see Phil 4:6–7).

"Blessed is the womb that bore you!"

Pope St. John Paul II explains what to some is a puzzling remark of our Lord with regard to his mother.

The Gospel of Luke records the moment when "a woman in the crowd raised her voice" and said to Jesus: "Blessed is the womb that bore you, and the breasts that you sucked!" (Lk 11:27). These words were an expression of praise of Mary as Jesus' mother according to the flesh. Probably the mother of Jesus was not personally known to this woman; in fact, when Jesus began his messianic activity, Mary did not accompany him but continued to remain at Nazareth. One could say that the words of that unknown woman in a way brought Mary out of her hiddenness.

Through these words, there flashed out in the midst of the crowd, at least for an instant, the gospel of Jesus' infancy. This is the gospel in which Mary is present as the mother who conceives Jesus in her womb, gives him birth, and nurses him: the nursing mother referred to by the woman in the crowd. Thanks to this motherhood, Jesus, the Son of the Most High (see Lk 1:32), is a true Son of Man. He is "flesh," like every other man; he is "the Word who became flesh" (see Jn 1:14). He is of the flesh and blood of Mary!

But to the blessing uttered by that woman upon her who was his mother according to the flesh, Jesus replies in a significant way: "Blessed rather are those who hear the word of God and keep it" (Lk. 11:28). He wishes to divert attention from motherhood understood only as a fleshly bond, in order to direct it towards those mysterious bonds of the spirit which develop from hearing and keeping God's word.

—Pope St. John Paul II, *Redemptoris Mater*

IN GOD'S PRESENCE, CONSIDER . . .

Is Jesus actually dismissing the suggestion, as some would insist, that he has a special relationship with Mary? Or does his comment simply refocus the crowd's attention on the criteria for discipleship that Mary so perfectly modeled?

CLOSING PRAYER

Mary, I will say to you with St. Elizabeth: "Blessed is she who believed that there would be a fulfillment of what was spoken to her" (Lk 1:45).

The Magnificat of the ages begins

Pope St. John Paul illuminates further our Lord's response to the woman who cried out, "Blessed is the womb that bore you, and the breasts that you sucked!" (Lk 11:28).

Is Jesus thereby distancing himself from his mother according to the flesh? Does he perhaps wish to leave her in the hidden obscurity which she herself has chosen? If this seems to be the case from the tone of those words, one must nevertheless note that the new and different motherhood which Jesus speaks of to his disciples refers precisely to Mary in a very special way.

Is not Mary the first of "those who hear the word of God and do it" (see Lk 11:28)? And therefore does not the blessing uttered by Jesus in response to the woman in the crowd refer primarily to her? Without any doubt, Mary is worthy of blessing by the very fact that she became the mother of Jesus according to the flesh ("Blessed is the womb that bore you, and the breasts that you sucked"), but also and especially because already at the Annunciation she accepted the word of God, because she believed it, because she was obedient to God, and because she "kept" the word and "pondered it in her heart" (see Lk 1:38, 45; 2:19, 51) and by means of her whole life accomplished it.

Thus we can say that the blessing proclaimed by Jesus is not in opposition, despite appearances, to the blessing uttered by the unknown woman, but rather coincides with that blessing in the person of this Virgin Mother, who called herself only "the handmaid of the Lord" (Lk 1:38). If it is true that "all generations will call her blessed" (see Lk 1:48), then it can be said that the unnamed woman was the first to confirm unwittingly that prophetic phrase of Mary's Magnificat and to begin the Magnificat of the ages.

—Pope St. John Paul II, *Redemptoris Mater*

IN GOD'S PRESENCE, CONSIDER . . .

What does it mean to "hear the word of God and keep it"? Is there some command in God's Word that I presently have trouble keeping? How can Mary's example help me keep it?

CLOSING PRAYER

With all generations I will call you blessed, Mary; for above all other disciples of your Son, you have most perfectly heard the Word of God and kept it.

Mary prepares to see Jesus crucified

St. Alphonsus recounts St. Bridget's vision of the hours during which Mary prepared to watch her Son die.

The Blessed Virgin revealed to St. Bridget that when the time of the passion of our Lord was approaching, her eyes were always filled with tears as she thought of her beloved Son, whom she was about to lose on earth. The prospect of that approaching suffering caused her to be seized with fear, so that a cold sweat covered her whole body. When the appointed day finally came, Jesus went in tears to say goodbye to his mother before he went to his death. St. Bonaventure, contemplating Mary on that night, says: "You spent it without sleep, and while others slept, you remained watching in vigil."

In the morning the disciples of Jesus Christ came to this afflicted mother, one to bring her one account, the other another. But all were tidings of sorrow, confirming in her the prophecy of Jeremiah: "She weeps bitterly in the night, tears on her cheeks; she has none to comfort her [of] all her friends" (Lam 1:2). Some then came to relate to her the cruel treatment of her Son in the house of Caiaphas. Others came to tell of the insults he had received from Herod. Finally—to come to our point, I omit all the rest—St. John came and announced to Mary that Pilate had already most unjustly condemned Jesus to die on the Cross. I say unjustly, for as St. Leo remarks, "This unjust judge condemned him to death with the same lips with which he had declared him innocent."

"Afflicted mother," said St. John, "your Son is already condemned to death. He has already gone out, bearing his cross, on his way to Calvary," as the saint afterwards reported in his Gospel: "He went out, and bearing his own cross, to the place called the place of a skull" (Jn 19:17). "Come," said St. John, "if you want to see him, and say a last goodbye, in some street through which he must pass."

—St. Alphonsus Liguori, *The Glories of Mary*

IN GOD'S PRESENCE, CONSIDER . . .

Have I ever had to say a final goodbye to someone I loved dearly? Have I entrusted that loved one into the care of our Blessed Mother?

CLOSING PRAYER

Sorrowful Mother, help me prepare for the last goodbye I must say to each of my loved ones, when I commit them into your tender care.

Mary did not plead with Pilate

Mary refrained from appearing before Pilate to plead for Jesus' life, notes St. Alphonsus; she appeared publicly only to be with Jesus at the Cross. Why was she silent the whole time?

Why was Mary silent during the passion of Jesus, when he was unjustly accused? Why did she say nothing to Pontius Pilate, who was somewhat inclined to set him at liberty, knowing, as he did, his innocence? Yet she appeared in public only to attend the great sacrifice to be accomplished on Calvary. She accompanied her beloved Son to the place of execution, and she was with him from the first moment, when he was nailed to the Cross. She was there until she saw him die, and the sacrifice was consummated. Why was Mary silent as she endured all this? Because she did all this to complete the offering that she had made of her Son to God in the temple, when he was still an Infant.

To understand the violence that Mary had to allow herself to suffer in this sacrifice, it's necessary to understand the love that this mother bore to Jesus. Generally speaking, the love of mothers is so tender toward their children that, when their children are at the point of death, and there is fear of losing them, it causes them to forget all their faults and defects, and even the injuries they may have received from them. It makes them suffer an inexpressible grief.

Even so, the love of these mothers is a love divided among other children, or at least among other creatures. But Mary had an only Son, and he was the most beautiful of all the sons of Adam—most amiable, for he had everything to make him so: He was obedient, virtuous, innocent, holy. Suffice it to say, he was God. Again, this mother's love wasn't divided among other objects. She had concentrated all her love on this only Son. Nor did she fear to be excessive in loving him; for this Son was God, who merits infinite love. And this was precisely the Son who became the victim which she of her own free will had to sacrifice to death.

—St. Alphonsus Liguori, *The Glories of Mary*

IN GOD'S PRESENCE, CONSIDER . . .

Have I ever had to remain silent in order to obey God, even though everything inside me wanted to cry out? If so, does that experience help me understand more deeply the sacrifices Mary made?

CLOSING PRAYER

Holy Mary, show me how to treasure silence, and how to cultivate discretion. Teach me to pray with the psalmist, "Set a guard over my mouth, O LORD, keep watch over the door of my lips" (Ps 141:3).

Mary follows Jesus to Calvary

Would Jesus have tried to keep his mother from following him to Calvary because of his desire to protect her? St. Alphonsus and others imagine what might have happened.

When Margaret, the daughter of St. Thomas More, met her father on the way to his execution as a martyr, she could only exclaim, "Father! Father!" and fall fainting at his feet. But Mary, at the sight of her Son on his way to Calvary, does not faint. No—for it's not fitting, as Fr. Francisco Suarez remarks, that this mother should lose the use of her reason. Nor does she die, for God has reserved her for a greater grief.

But even though she doesn't die, her sorrow is enough to have caused her a thousand deaths. The mother wants to embrace her Son, as St. Anselm says, but the guards thrust her aside with insults, and urge the suffering Lord forward. So Mary follows him. Holy Virgin, where are you going? To Calvary. And can you trust yourself to behold the One who is your life hanging on a cross?

St. Lawrence Justinian imagines Jesus saying: "Stop, my Mother! Where are you going? Where do you want to come? If you come where I go, you'll be tortured with my sufferings, and I with yours." But even though the sight of her dying Jesus is to cost her such bitter sorrow, the loving Mary will not leave him. The Son moves forward, and the mother follows, to be crucified with her Son as well.

"We pity even wild beasts," as St. John Chrysostom writes; if we were to see a lioness following her cub to death, the sight would move us to compassion. Shouldn't we, then, be moved to compassion as well to see Mary follow her immaculate Lamb to death? We must pity her, then, and also accompany her and her Son, by bearing with patience the cross that our Lord has given us.

—St. Alphonsus Liguori, *The Glories of Mary*

IN GOD'S PRESENCE, CONSIDER . . .

What does it mean to "accompany" Mary and Jesus to Calvary? What cross has the Lord given me, which I must bear with patience?

CLOSING PRAYER

From a prayer of Pope St. John Paul II: *Mary, humble servant of God Most High . . . you were the servant of redemption, standing courageously at the foot of the Cross, close to the Suffering Servant and Lamb, who was sacrificing himself for love of us.*

Mary draws near to Jesus on the Cross

Think of the good reasons, St. Alphonsus urges, why Mary could have chosen not to be present for her Son's crucifixion. Yet she was there, enduring the outrage, shame, and horror, because of her surpassing love for her Son.

We must now witness a new kind of martyrdom: a mother condemned to see an innocent Son, and one whom she loves with the whole affection of her soul, cruelly tormented and put to death before her own eyes: "Standing by the cross of Jesus [was] his mother" (Jn 19:25). St. John believed that in these words he had said enough of Mary's martyrdom. Consider her at the foot of the Cross in the presence of her dying Son, and then see if there could be any sorrow like her sorrow. Consider the sword that transfixed the heart of Mary.

As soon as our agonized Redeemer had reached the Mount of Calvary, the executioners stripped him of his clothes. They pierced his hands and feet "not with sharp but with blunt nails," as St. Bernard says, to torment him more. Then they fastened him on the Cross. Having crucified him, they erected the Cross and left him there to die.

The executioners left him. But not Mary. She drew nearer to the Cross, to be present at his death. "But what did it avail you, O Lady," says St. Bonaventure, "to go to Calvary, and see this Son die? Shame might well have kept you away, for his disgrace was yours, because you were his mother. At the very least, the horror of witnessing such a crime as the crucifixion of God by his own creatures might well have prevented you from going there."

But the same saint answers: "Your heart wasn't thinking then of its own sorrows, but of the sufferings and death of your dear Son." So of course you would be there yourself, Mary, at least to have compassion on him. "True mother," says the abbot St. William, "most loving mother, whom not even the fear of death could separate from your beloved Son!"

—St. Alphonsus Liguori, *The Glories of Mary*

IN GOD'S PRESENCE, CONSIDER . . .

Are there times when I desperately want to avoid a situation because it appalls me or grieves me so deeply that I can hardly bear to be present—yet I refuse to run away, because of my love for someone involved? In such a situation, do I call on Mary for wisdom, courage, and strength?

CLOSING PRAYER

Blessed Mother, no doubt there are times when my sin and weakness appall and grieve you, yet you remain with me. In your great love, help me to be purified and strengthened.

At the foot of the Cross

In this poignant lament, St. Anselm grieves with Our Lady as she stands at the foot of the Cross.

My most merciful Lady,
how can I speak of the fountains of tears
that flowed from your most pure eyes
when you beheld before you your only Son,
bound, beaten, and wounded?
What do I know of the flood
that flowed over your face, unlike any other,
when you beheld your Son, your Lord, and your God,
innocent, yet stretched out upon the Cross,
when the Flesh of your flesh
was viciously slaughtered by wicked men?
How can I understand what sobbing
shook your most pure breast
when you heard the words,
"Woman, behold your son,"
and to the disciple, "Behold, your Mother,"
when you received as your son
the disciple in place of the Master,
the servant in place of the Lord?

—St. Anselm of Canterbury

IN GOD'S PRESENCE, CONSIDER . . .

Imagining Our Lady's suffering as she watched her Son die can give me a clearer idea of how very much she sacrificed for me. What might I have said to her if I had stood with her below the Cross?

CLOSING PRAYER

From "Thirty Days' Prayer to the Blessed Virgin": *Through that sword of sorrow that pierced your tender heart while your only Son suffered death and shame on the Cross, take pity, I beg you, on my poverty and need; have compassion on my anxieties and cares; assist and comfort me in all my infirmities and miseries.*

Mary could grant no relief to her Son

Mothers are anxious to provide for the relief of their children when they suffer. So imagine Mary's grief, St. Alphonsus says, when she was unable to relieve her Son's suffering on the Cross.

Mothers ordinarily shrink from the presence of their dying children. But when a mother is obliged to witness such a scene, she procures all possible relief for her child. She arranges his bed, so that he may be more at ease; she administers refreshments to him. In this way, the poor mother soothes her own grief.

Most afflicted of all mothers! Mary, you must witness the agony of your dying Jesus, yet you can't grant him relief. Mary hears her Son exclaim, "I thirst!" But she can't even give him a drop of water to refresh him in that great thirst. She can only say, as St. Vincent Ferrer remarks, "My Son, I have only the water of tears." She sees how on that bed of torture her Son, suspended by three nails, can find no repose. She would clasp him in her arms to give him relief, or at least to let him die there if she could. But she can't. "In vain," says St. Bernard, "did she extend her arms; they sank back empty on her breast."

She beholds that poor Son, who in his sea of grief seeks consolation, but in vain. For who among men will console him, since all were enemies? Even on the Cross he is taunted and blasphemed on all sides: "And those who passed by derided him, wagging their heads" (Mt 27:39). Some say to his face, "If you are the Son of God, come down from the Cross" (v. 40). Others, "He saved others; he cannot save himself. If he is the King of Israel, let him come down now from the Cross" (v. 42). Our Blessed Lady herself said to St. Bridget, "I heard some say that my Son was a thief; others, that he was an impostor; others, that no one deserved death more than he did. And every word was a new sword of grief to my heart."

—St. Alphonsus Liguori, *The Glories of Mary*

IN GOD'S PRESENCE, CONSIDER . . .

Is there anyone I know who is suffering, whom I seem unable to help? Have I asked Mary to go to the aid of that person?

CLOSING PRAYER

Blessed Mother, hurry to all those who suffer alone, not because they have no one who desires to relieve their pain, but because their pain seems beyond relief. Be close to them and show yourself to them, for your presence is a healing balm.

Jesus suffered most to see his mother's grief

Mary's grief beside the Cross was like a living death, insists St. Alphonsus; and her Son's greatest sufferings came from watching her sorrow.

The afflicted mother saw her Jesus suffering on every side. She desired to comfort him, but could not. And what grieved her the most was to see that she herself, by her presence and sorrow, increased the sufferings of her Son.

"The grief that filled Mary's heart," says St. Bernard, "like a torrent flowed into and grieved the heart of Jesus. So much so, that Jesus on the Cross suffered more from compassion for his mother than from his own torments."

The saint then speaks in the voice of our Blessed Lady: "I stood with my eyes fixed on him, and his on me. And he grieved more for me than for himself." Then, speaking of Mary beside her dying Son, he says: "She lived dying, without being able to die. Near the cross of Christ, his mother stood half-dead, without speaking. Dying, she lived; living, she died; nor could she die, for death was her very life."

The biographer of blessed Baptista Varani of Camerino writes that Jesus Christ himself one day spoke to her about this. He assured her that when he was on the Cross, so great was his affliction at seeing his mother at his feet in such bitter anguish that compassion for her caused him to die without consolation. The blessed Baptista, being supernaturally enlightened about the greatness of this suffering of Jesus, exclaimed, "Lord, tell me no more of this sorrow of yours, for I can no longer bear it!"

—St. Alphonsus Liguori, *The Glories of Mary*

IN GOD'S PRESENCE, CONSIDER . . .

Have I ever experienced the anguish of watching a loved one in agony, while being unable to relieve that loved one's pain? Does such an experience help me to understand more deeply how Jesus could have died from grief for his mother?

CLOSING PRAYER

Jesus, for the sake of that agony you experienced on Calvary when you saw your mother grieving beneath the Cross, grant me a happy death, so that, loving Mary and you on earth, I may come to love you eternally in heaven.

"Behold your mother!"

Because of Mary's ardent desire to aid in our salvation, St. Alphonsus declares, Jesus made her on Calvary the mother of our souls.

Our most loving mother Mary was always, and in all things, united to the will of God. "And for this reason," says St. Bonaventure, "when she saw the love of the Eternal Father toward men to be so great that, in order to save them, he willed the death of his Son; and, on the other hand, when she saw the love of the Son in wishing to die for us; in order to conform herself to this abundant love of both the Father and the Son toward the human race, she also with her entire will offered, and consented to, the death of her Son, in order that we might be saved."

It is true that, according to Isaiah's prophecy, Jesus—in dying for the redemption of the human race—chose to be alone. But seeing the ardent desire of Mary to aid in the salvation of man, he disposed it so that she, by the sacrifice and offering of the life of her Jesus, should cooperate in our salvation, and thus become the mother of our souls. This our Savior indicated when, before breathing his last, he looked down from the Cross upon his mother and upon the disciple St. John, who stood at its foot.

First addressing Mary, he said, "Behold your Son" (Jn 19:26). In effect, he was saying, "Behold, the whole human race, which by the offering you make of my life for the salvation of all, is even now being born into the life of grace."

Then, turning to the disciple, he said, "Behold your mother" (Jn 19:27). "By these words," says St. Bernardine of Siena, "Mary, by reason of the love she bore them, became the mother not only of St. John, but of all men."

—St. Alphonsus Liguori, *The Glories of Mary*

IN GOD'S PRESENCE, CONSIDER . . .

What does it mean to say that Mary "also with her entire will offered, and consented to, the death of her Son, in order that we might be saved"? How agonizing would that consent have been?

CLOSING PRAYER

From "The Seven Dolors of Mary at the Death of Jesus": *Eternal Father, we offer you the blood, the passion, and the death of Jesus Christ, the sorrows of Mary most holy, and of St. Joseph, in satisfaction for our sins, in aid of the holy souls in purgatory, for the needs of holy mother Church, and for the conversion of sinners.*

Jesus gave you Mary as your mother

As he was dying on the cross, Jesus gave Mary to John as his mother, and in doing so, he gave her to us all. St. Ignatius Loyola urges us to ponder carefully the circumstances surrounding this gift so that we can more fully appreciate it.

Mary has been given you as a mother. Consider, then, in your heart all the circumstances of this gift. First, she was given to you by Jesus Christ, God and Master of all creatures, from whom comes all power, paternal and maternal; by Jesus Christ the God-Savior, who had already sacrificed for you the body and lavished the blood he derived from Mary. Having nothing more to give you but her, he bestows her on you as a complement of all his gifts.

Second, she is given to you in the clearest terms, the strongest, the most precise, to enable you to realize what they mean: "Behold your mother." Jesus said, in showing the bread, "This is my body," and the bread became his Body. Pointing to his mother, he says, "Behold your mother"; and Mary immediately became our mother.

Third, she was given to you under the most serious and solemn circumstances. Jesus, while dying, makes his final arrangements and indicates his last will. Alone of all the disciples, the beloved John is present to receive in the name of all Christians the last gift that their divine Master makes to them.

Fourth, she is given to you to be "your mother." Feel these words at the bottom of your heart. Recall to yourself that man does not live by bread alone; that his soul as well as his body has a life to receive and support. It is in this supernatural order that Mary is your mother; if you live to grace, it is through her. The principle of this spiritual life is in Jesus; but Mary's is the bosom that bore you, the milk that nourished you, the maternal heart that always loves its children even when ungrateful.

—St. Ignatius Loyola, *The Spiritual Exercises*

IN GOD'S PRESENCE, CONSIDER . . .

What does it mean to say that Mary is our mother "in this supernatural order"? How is it that Mary's bosom bore us, her milk nourished us, and her maternal heart always loves us?

CLOSING PRAYER

From a prayer of St. Anselm: *What dignity, O Virgin, could be more highly prized than to be the mother of those of whom Christ deigned to be Father and Brother?*

Mary receives the body of Jesus

St. Alphonsus describes St. Bridget's vision of Mary's petition to receive the body of her Son.

The Mother of God herself revealed to St. Bridget: "When the spear was drawn out from Jesus' side, the point appeared red with blood. Then, seeing the heart of my most dear Son pierced, it seemed to me as if my own heart was also pierced." An angel told the same saint that "the sufferings of Mary were so great, it was only through a miraculous intervention by God that she didn't die." In her other sorrows, she at least had her Son to have compassion on her. But now doesn't even have him to pity her.

The afflicted mother, fearing that other injuries might still be inflicted on her Son, begged Joseph of Arimathea to obtain the body of her Jesus from Pilate, so that at least in death she might guard and protect it from further outrage. Joseph went and told Pilate about the grief and desires of this afflicted mother. St. Anselm believes that compassion for the mother softened the heart of Pilate and moved him to grant her the body of the Savior. Jesus was then taken down from the Cross.

Most sacred Virgin, after you have given your Son to the world for our salvation, with such great love, see how the world now returns him to you. But in what condition do you receive him? He was all fair and beautiful; but now there is no more beauty in him; he is all disfigured. His appearance enamored everyone; now he excites horror in all who see him.

"How many swords," says St. Bonaventure, "pierced the poor mother's soul" when she received the body of her Son from the Cross! We need only consider the anguish it would cause any mother to receive into her arms the body of her lifeless son.

—St. Alphonsus Liguori, *The Glories of Mary*

IN GOD'S PRESENCE, CONSIDER . . .

Mary has given me her Son. How have I received him? How have I treated, or mistreated him?

CLOSING PRAYER

From the Stabat Mater Dolorosa: *Mary, let me mingle tears with thee, mourning him who mourned for me, all the days that I may live.*

Mary watches as Jesus is buried

St. Alphonsus imagines the scene as Jesus is laid in the tomb, and Mary looks on in unspeakable grief.

Mary, with the body of her Son locked in her arms, was absorbed in grief. The holy disciples, fearful that the poor mother might die of grief, approached her to take the body from her arms, to bear it away for burial. This they did with gentle and respectful force, and having embalmed it, they wrapped it in a linen cloth already prepared. On this shroud, which is still preserved at Turin, our Lord was pleased to leave to the world an impression of his sacred body.

The disciples then bore him to the tomb. They first of all raised the sacred body on their shoulders, and then the mournful procession set forth. Choirs of angels from heaven accompanied it. The holy women followed, and with them the afflicted mother also followed her Son to the place of burial. When they had reached the appointed place, "how willingly would Mary have buried herself alive there with her Son, had that been his will!"—this she herself revealed to St. Bridget. But that was of course not God's will. Many authors say that she accompanied the sacred body of Jesus into the sepulcher, and according to Baronius, there the disciples also deposited the nails and the crown of thorns. In raising the stone to close up the entrance, the holy disciples of the Savior had to approach our Blessed Lady, saying: "Now, Lady, we must close the sepulcher. Forgive us, look once more at your Son, and bid him a last goodbye."

The afflicted Mother must have replied: "My beloved Son, shall I see you no more? Then, on this last occasion to see you, receive my last goodbye, the goodbye of your dear mother; and receive also my heart, which I leave buried with you." "The Blessed Virgin," writes St. Fulgentius, "would have fervently desired to bury her soul with the body of Christ." And this Mary herself revealed to St. Bridget, saying: "I can truly say that at the burial of my Son, one tomb contained two hearts."

—St. Alphonsus Liguori, *The Glories of Mary*

IN GOD'S PRESENCE, CONSIDER . . .

What does it mean to say that when Jesus was buried, "one tomb contained two hearts"?

CLOSING PRAYER

Lord of life, in death you remained hidden from the world. Teach us to hide ourselves there with you, grieving over our sins so that we may one day rejoice in our resurrection with you to eternal life.

Mary, this is your night

These words of Pope St. John Paul II, prayed during an Easter vigil Mass, ask Mary to give us a share in the faith and hope in her Son that sustained her as she waited to see him alive once again.

O Mary,
this is truly *your night!*
As the last lights of the Sabbath are extinguished,
and the fruit of your womb rests in the earth,
your heart too keeps watch!
Your faith and your hope look ahead.
Behind the heavy stone,
they already detect the empty tomb;
behind the thick veil of darkness,
they glimpse the dawn of the Resurrection.
Grant, O Mother, that we too may keep watch in the silence of
    the night,
believing and hoping in the Lord's word.
Thus shall we meet, in the fullness of light and life,
Christ, the first fruits of the risen,
who reigns with the Father and the Holy Spirit,
for ever and ever.
Queen of Heaven, rejoice, alleluia!

—Pope St. John Paul II

IN GOD'S PRESENCE, CONSIDER . . .

Is there in my life a "heavy stone" or a "thick veil of darkness" beyond which I must look for the Lord with faith and hope? Does Mary's example inspire me to hold on until the day when my faith and hope are rewarded?

CLOSING PRAYER

As I wait, my Lord, for the stone to roll away, and for the dawn to break on my darkness, I wait in faith and hope, because your mother waits alongside me.

Queen of Heaven, rejoice!

The composer of this traditional hymn is unknown, but one legend says that the sixth-century Pope St. Gregory the Great heard angels chant the first three lines one Easter morning in Rome while he walked barefoot in a great religious procession. He then added the fourth line himself.

O, Queen of Heaven, rejoice! Alleluia!
For he whom you merited to bear, alleluia,
has arisen as he said, alleluia!
Pray for us to God, alleluia!
Rejoice and be glad,
O Virgin Mary, alleluia!
For the Lord has risen indeed, alleluia!

Let us pray:
O God, who, through
the resurrection of your Son,
our Lord Jesus Christ,
vouchsafed to fill the world with joy,
grant, we beseech you,
that through his virgin mother, Mary,
we may lay hold
of the joys of everlasting life.
Through the same Christ our Lord.

—*Regina caeli*

IN GOD'S PRESENCE, CONSIDER . . .

Imagine being with Mary when she receives the news that Jesus is risen! Might he perhaps have appeared to her, before all the others, in an encounter so private that it wasn't recorded in the Gospels?

CLOSING PRAYER

At the Cross, Blessed Mother, you wondered, "Is there any sorrow like my sorrow?" (Lam 1:12). Now at the empty tomb you can rightly ask, "Is there any joy like my joy?"

Mary in the upper room at Pentecost

Pope St. John Paul II explains how Mary's role at Pentecost, and in the life of the Church ever since, is essential.

Among those who devoted themselves to prayer in the upper room, preparing to go "into the whole world" after receiving the Spirit, some had been called by Jesus gradually from the beginning of his mission in Israel. Eleven of them had been made apostles, and to them Jesus had passed on the mission which he himself had received from the Father. . . .

Mary did not directly receive this apostolic mission. . . . But she was in the upper room, where the apostles were preparing to take up this mission with the coming of the Spirit of Truth: She was present with them. In their midst Mary was "devoted to prayer" as the "mother of Jesus" (see Acts 1:13–14), of the crucified and risen Christ. . . . Now, at the first dawn of the Church, at the beginning of the long journey through faith which began at Pentecost in Jerusalem, Mary was with all those who were the seed of the "new Israel." She was present among them as an exceptional witness to the mystery of Christ. . . .

Mary belongs indissolubly to the mystery of Christ, and she belongs also to the mystery of the Church from the beginning, from the day of the Church's birth. At the basis of what the Church has been from the beginning, and of what she must continually become from generation to generation, in the midst of all the nations of the earth, we find the one "who believed that there would be a fulfillment of what was spoken to her from the Lord" (Lk 1:45). It is precisely Mary's faith which marks the beginning of the new and eternal covenant of God with man in Jesus Christ; this heroic faith of hers "precedes" the apostolic witness of the Church, and ever remains in the Church's heart, hidden like a special heritage of God's revelation.

—Pope St. John Paul II, *Redemptoris Mater*

IN GOD'S PRESENCE, CONSIDER . . .

Jesus didn't designate his mother as one of his apostles, yet she played a critical role in the life of the Church through her witness to her Son. What role can my witness to him play in the life of my parish and my community?

CLOSING PRAYER

Holy Spirit, you came in tongues of fire upon Mary and the Apostles at Pentecost. Renew my heart, so that it blazes with love for Jesus and zeal for the mission he has given me.

Mary's life after Jesus' ascension into heaven

How did Mary spend her time in the years after her Son's departure to heaven? St. Alphonsus speculates.

After the ascension of Jesus Christ, Mary remained on earth to give her attention to the spreading of the Faith. For this reason, the disciples of our Lord turned to her. She solved their doubts, comforted them in their persecutions, and encouraged them to labor for the glory of God and the salvation of redeemed souls. Mary willingly remained on earth, knowing that it was the will of God for her to do so, and for the good of the Church. But she must have felt the pain of being far from the presence and sight of her beloved Son, who had ascended to heaven. "Where your treasure is, there will your heart be also" (Lk 12:34), said the Redeemer. Where anyone believes his treasure and his happiness to be, there he always holds firmly the love and desires of his heart.

Mary loved no other good than Jesus. Since he was in heaven, all her desires were in heaven. Johannes Tauler says: "Heaven was the room of the heavenly and most Blessed Virgin Mary. Since she was there with all her desires and affections, she made it her continual home. "Her school was eternity, for she was always detached and free from possessions that pass away. Her teacher was divine truth, for her whole life was guided by this alone. Her book was the purity of her own conscience, in which she always found occasion to rejoice in the Lord.

"Her mirror was God, for she never allowed any thoughts into her soul except for those that were transformed into and clothed with God, so that she might always conform herself to his will. Her adornment was devotion, for she focused her attention solely on her interior sanctification, and she was always ready to fulfil the divine commands. Her rest was union with God, for he alone was her treasure, and the resting place of her heart."

—St. Alphonsus Liguori, *The Glories of Mary*

IN GOD'S PRESENCE, CONSIDER . . .

How might I learn from Mary to make heaven my home, eternity my school, divine truth my teacher, and God my mirror and my rest?

CLOSING PRAYER

From a prayer of Venerable Pope Pius XII: *Mary, crystal fountain of faith, bathe our minds with the eternal truths! Fragrant lily of all holiness, captivate our hearts with your heavenly perfume! Conqueror of evil and death, inspire in us a deep horror of sin!*

Why I love you, Mary!

*These concluding lines of the last poem of St. Thérèse of Lisieux were writ-
ten as she was dying of tuberculosis. Speaking to Mary, she suggests that
Jesus himself will tell the saints in heaven the story of her life after his resurrection. She hopes to be there soon to hear it.*

Henceforth your shelter in your woe was John's most humble dwelling;
the son of Zebedee replaced the Son whom heaven adored.
Naught else the Gospels tell us of thy life, in grace excelling;
it is the last they say of you, sweet mother of my Lord!
But oh! I think that silence means that, high in heaven's glory,
when time is past, and to their house your children safe are come,
the Eternal Word, my Mother dear, himself will tell your story,
to charm our souls—your children's souls—in our eternal home.
Soon I shall hear that harmony, that blissful, wondrous singing;
soon, unto heaven that waits for us, my soul shall swiftly fly.
O you who came to smile on me at dawn of life's beginning,
come once again to smile on me. Mother! the night is nigh.
I fear no more your majesty, so far removed above me,
for I have suffered sore with you: now hear me, Mother mild!
Oh, let me tell you face to face, dear Mary! how I love you;
and say to you for evermore: I am your little child.

—St. Thérèse of Lisieux, "Why I Love You, Mary!"

IN GOD'S PRESENCE, CONSIDER . . .

What events do I imagine might have taken place in the final years of Mary's
life, after the Day of Pentecost? What relationship do I think she might have had
with the Apostles and the other disciples of her Son?

CLOSING PRAYER

From a prayer of St. Vincent Pallotti: *Queen of the Apostles, we are confident
that through God's mercy and the infinite merits of Jesus Christ, you who are our mother will
obtain for us the strength of the Holy Spirit as you obtained it for the community of the Apostles
gathered in the upper room.*

God calls Mary home

St. Alphonsus considers how Mary might have spent her time between her Son's ascension and her assumption into heaven, longing to be reunited with him.

According to some writers, the most holy virgin consoled her loving heart during the time of painful separation after Jesus ascended into heaven by visiting the holy places of Palestine, where her Son had been during his life. She frequently visited at one time the stable at Bethlehem, where her Son was born; at another, the workshop of Nazareth, where her Son had lived so many years poor and despised; now the Garden of Gethsemane, where her Son began his passion; then the praetorium of Pilate, where he was scourged; and the spot on which he was crowned with thorns.

But Mary visited most frequently the Mount of Calvary, where her Son died, and the Holy Sepulcher, in which she had finally left him. In this way the most loving mother soothed the pains of her cruel exile.

Even so, this could not be enough to satisfy her heart, which was unable to find perfect rest in this world. So she was continually sending up sighs to her Lord, exclaiming with David: "O that I had wings like a dove! I would fly away and be at rest!" (Ps 55:6). Who will give me wings like a dove, so that I may fly to my God, and there find my rest? "As a deer longs for flowing streams, so longs my soul for you, O God" (Ps 42:1). As the wounded stag pants for the fountain, so does my soul, wounded by your love, my God, desire and sigh for you.

Yes, indeed, her sighs penetrate deeply the heart of her God, who indeed so tenderly loves her. Being unwilling, then, to defer any longer the deeply desired consolation of his beloved, God graciously hears her desire, and calls her to his kingdom.

—St. Alphonsus Liguori, *The Glories of Mary*

IN GOD'S PRESENCE, CONSIDER . . .

Do I long for Jesus' presence in my life as Mary did? Do I reflect on the events of his life as she must have done?

CLOSING PRAYER

Blessed Mother, make my heart like your heart; help me make my own your longing for your precious Son. My hope is to be with you both in heaven forever.

Mary prepares for death

St. Alphonsus summarizes the account of some ancient writers of the events leading up to her death.

Some ancient historians report that, some days before Mary's death, our Lord sent to her the archangel Gabriel, the same angel who had announced to her that she was that blessed woman chosen to be the Mother of God: "My Lady and Queen," said the angel, "God has already graciously heard your holy desires. He has sent me to tell you to prepare yourself to leave the earth, for he wants you in heaven. Come, then, to take possession of your kingdom. For I and all its holy inhabitants await and desire you."

At this happy announcement, our most humble and most holy Virgin could only reply, with the most profound humility, with the same words she had spoken to St. Gabriel when he announced to her that she was to become the Mother of God: "Behold, I am the handmaid of the Lord" (Lk 1:38). Behold, she answered again, the slave of the Lord. He in his pure goodness chose me and made me his mother; he now calls me to paradise. I didn't deserve that honor, nor do I deserve this. But since he's pleased to show in my person his infinite generosity, I'm ready to go where he pleases. "Behold, I am the handmaid of the Lord." May the will of my God and Lord be always accomplished in me! After receiving this welcome information, she passed it on to St. John.

We may well imagine with what grief and tender feelings he heard the news. It was he who for so many years had cared for her as a son, and had enjoyed the heavenly conversation of this most holy mother. Mary then once more visited the holy places of Jerusalem, tenderly taking her leave of them, and especially of Mount Calvary, where her beloved Son had died. At last she retired into her poor cottage, there to prepare for death. During this time the angels didn't cease their visits to their beloved queen, consoling themselves with the thought that they would soon see her crowned in heaven.

—St. Alphonsus Liguori, *The Glories of Mary*

IN GOD'S PRESENCE, CONSIDER . . .

Why would Mary have welcomed death, instead of fearing it as most people do? How can I imitate her faith in this regard?

CLOSING PRAYER

From a prayer of Blessed Raymond Jordano: *Mary, you assist the dying, protecting them against the snares of the Devil; and you help them also after death, receiving their souls and conducting them to the kingdom of the blessed.*

The Immaculate Conception implies the Assumption

The bodies of Adam and Eve, Blessed John Henry Neman notes, were subject to decay after death because of their sin. So if Mary never sinned, he reasons, why should her body have been subject to that penalty?

One consideration which has led devout minds to believe in the assumption of Our Lady into heaven, without waiting for the general resurrection at the last day, is furnished by the doctrine of her immaculate conception. By her immaculate conception is meant, not only that she never committed any sin whatever, even venial, in thought, word, or deed. More than this, the guilt of Adam, or what is called original sin, never was her guilt, as it is the guilt attaching to all other descendants of Adam. By her assumption is meant that not only her soul, but her body also, was taken up to heaven upon her death, so that there was no long period of her sleeping in the grave, as is the case with others, even great saints, who wait for the last day for the resurrection of their bodies.

One reason for believing in Our Lady's assumption is that her divine Son loved her too much to let her body remain in the grave. A second reason is that she was so transcendently holy, so full, so overflowing with grace. Adam and Eve were created upright and sinless, and had a large measure of God's grace bestowed upon them. In consequence, their bodies would never have crumbled into dust, had they not sinned. If Eve, the beautiful daughter of God, never would have become dust and ashes unless she had sinned, shall we not say that Mary, having never sinned, retained the gift which Eve by sinning lost?

What had Mary done to forfeit the privilege given to our first parents in the beginning? Was her beauty to be turned into corruption, and her fine gold to become dull, without reason assigned? Impossible. Therefore we believe that, though she died for a short hour, as did our Lord himself, yet like him, and by his almighty power, she was raised again from the grave.

—Blessed John Henry Newman, *Meditations and Devotions*

IN GOD'S PRESENCE, CONSIDER . . .

To ponder the reality of our bodies' decay after death can be sobering and even unsettling. Can I be at peace with that reality, knowing that the penalty is due to me as a sinner—and with a confident hope in the resurrection to come?

CLOSING PRAYER

Blessed Virgin, I am dust, and to dust I will return. But your glorious assumption strengthens my hope that "the hour is coming . . . when the dead will hear the voice of the Son of God, and those who hear will live" (Jn 5:25).

If other saints' bodies were raised, so was Mary's

Blessed John Henry Newman reasons that if other saints had their bodies raised, Jesus certainly would not have withheld that grace from his mother.

As soon as we apprehend by faith the great fundamental truth that Mary is the Mother of God, other wonderful truths follow in its train. One of these is that she was exempt from the ordinary lot of mortals, which is not only to die, but to become earth to earth, ashes to ashes, dust to dust. Die she must, and die she did, as her divine Son died, for he was Man. But even though her body was for a while separated from her soul and consigned to the tomb, yet it did not remain there. Instead, it was speedily united to her soul again, and raised by our Lord to a new and eternal life of heavenly glory.

Other servants of God have been raised from the grave by the power of God, and it is not to be supposed that our Lord would have granted any such privilege to anyone else without also granting it to his own mother. We are told that after our Lord's death upon the Cross, "the graves were opened, and many bodies of the saints that had slept"—that is, slept the sleep of death—"arose, and coming out of the tombs after his resurrection, came into the Holy City, and appeared to many" (see Mt 27:52–53). St. Matthew says, "many bodies of the saints"—that is, the holy prophets, priests, and kings of former times—rose again in anticipation of the last day.

Can we suppose that these should have been thus favored, and not God's own mother? Had she no claim on the love of her Son to have what any others had? Wasn't she nearer to him than the greatest of the saints before her? Therefore we confidently say that our Lord, having preserved her from sin and the consequences of sin by his passion, lost no time in pouring out the full merits of that passion upon her body as well as her soul.

—Blessed John Henry Newman, *Meditations and Devotions*

IN GOD'S PRESENCE, CONSIDER . . .

When I consider the decay of the body after death, does it sometimes seem hard to believe that in the end, the souls of the faithful departed will once again be joined to their bodies and transformed in glory? How does Mary's bodily assumption into heaven provide me hope in this regard?

CLOSING PRAYER

From "Thirty Days' Prayer to the Blessed Virgin": *Mother of my Lord and Savior Jesus Christ, grant my petition through the joy beyond words that you felt at your assumption into heaven.*

The death of Mary was precious

St. Alphonsus tells how Mary's death was made sweet and precious in several ways.

How precious was the death of Mary—both because of the special graces that accompanied it, and because of the way in which it took place.

Death is the punishment of sin. So it would seem that the Mother of God—all holy, and exempt as she was from the slightest stain of sin—should also have been exempt from death. She shouldn't have had to encounter the misfortunes to which the children of Adam, infected by the poison of sin, are subject. But God was pleased that Mary should in all things resemble Jesus.

Just as the Son died, it was fitting that the mother should also die. Even more, God wanted to give the righteous an example of the precious death prepared for them. So he willed that even the most Blessed Virgin should die—but by a sweet and happy death.

Let's consider, then, how precious was Mary's death.

Three things render death bitter: attachment to the world, remorse for sins, and the uncertainty of salvation. The death of Mary was entirely free from these causes of bitterness, and it was accompanied by three special graces that rendered it precious and joyful: She died as she had lived, entirely detached from the things of the world; she died in the most perfect peace; and she died in the certainty of eternal glory.

—St. Alphonsus Liguori, *The Glories of Mary*

IN GOD'S PRESENCE, CONSIDER . . .

St. Alphonsus says that "three things render death bitter: attachment to the world, remorse for sins, and the uncertainty of salvation." When my hour of death comes, will my death be bitter, or sweet?

CLOSING PRAYER

From a prayer of St. Alphonsus: *My Queen, don't abandon me at death. You, after Jesus, must be my comfort in that terrible moment.*

Mary's death was unlike any other

St. John of Damascus insists that Mary's death was so different from ours that we can hardly call it a death at all.

How does Mary, the source of the One who is Life, pass through death to life? How can she obey the law of nature who, in conceiving, surpassed the boundaries of nature? How is her spotless body made subject to death? In order to be clothed with immortality, she must first put off mortality, since the Lord of nature himself did not reject the penalty of death. She dies according to the flesh, destroys death by death, and through corruption gains incorruption and makes her death the source of resurrection. Behold how Almighty God receives with his own hands the holy soul of our Lord's mother, separated from her body! He honors her truly—the one who was by nature his servant, yet was made his mother, in his unsearchable abyss of mercy, when he truly became incarnate.

What, then, shall we call this mystery of yours? Death? Your blessed soul is naturally parted from your blessed and undefiled body, and the body is delivered to the grave. Yet it does not remain in death, nor is it subject to decay. The body of the one whose virginity remained unspotted in childbirth was preserved without decay and was taken to a better, more divine place, where there is no death, but eternal life.

The glorious sun may be hidden momentarily by the opaque moon, but even when covered this way, it still shows, and its rays illumine the darkness, since light belongs to its essence. The sun has in itself a perpetual source of light, or rather it is the source of light as God created it. In a similar way, you, Mary, are the perennial source of true light. And if for a time you are hidden by the death of the body, without speaking, even so, you are our light. So I will not call your sacred transformation death, but rather a rest, a going home.

—St. John of Damascus, *First Homily on the Dormition*

IN GOD'S PRESENCE, CONSIDER . . .

Why was Mary's death more like a rest and a homecoming? How can the prospect of my death become more like hers?

CLOSING PRAYER

From a prayer of St. Anselm: *O glorious Virgin, you submitted to death, but you could not be held for long by the bonds of death, because you alone, O Virgin, bore him who was the death of death, and of grave the sting!*

Death cannot claim Mary as its prey

St. John of Damascus explains why death could not hold Mary in the grave.

Long ago the Lord God banished from the Garden of Eden our first parents after their disobedience. They had dulled the eyes of their heart through their sin, and weakened their mind's discernment, and fallen into deathlike apathy. But now, won't paradise receive her who broke the bondage of all passion, sowed the seed of obedience to God and the Father, and was the beginning of life to the whole human race? Won't heaven open its gates to Mary with rejoicing?

Yes, indeed! Eve listened to the serpent, followed his suggestion, and was caught by the lure of false and deceptive pleasure. She was condemned to pain and sorrow, and to bear children in suffering. With Adam, she received the sentence of death and was placed in the recesses of the realm of the dead. But how can death claim as its prey this truly blessed one? Mary listened to God's word in humility and was filled with the Spirit. She conceived the Father's gift through the words of the archangel. Without concupiscence or the cooperation of man, she bore the divine Word, who fills all things, bringing him forth without the pains of childbirth, being wholly united to God.

How could the realm of the dead open its gates to her? How could corruption touch her life-giving body? These are things quite foreign to the soul and body of the Mother of God. Instead, death trembled before her. In approaching her Son, death had learned from experience with his sufferings, and it had grown wiser. The gloomy descent to hell was not for her, but rather a joyous, easy, and sweet passage to heaven.

—St. John of Damascus, *Second Homily on the Dormition*

IN GOD'S PRESENCE, CONSIDER . . .

"In approaching her Son, death had learned from experience with his sufferings, and it had grown wiser." These words call to mind the title of John Donne's poem "Death, Be Not Proud." What is it about Christ's death and resurrection that changed forever the meaning, and the status, of death?

CLOSING PRAYER

Almighty and eternal God, you assumed into heaven, body and soul, the immaculate Virgin Mary, mother of your Son. Grant, through her intercession, that we may always long for you and one day be brought to the glory of the resurrection with her.

In the Assumption, Jesus honored his mother

St. John of Damascus suggests that Mary's assumption was a sign that Jesus continued faithfully to obey the fourth commandment: "Honor your father and your mother" (Ex 20:12).

Realize, beloved in the Lord, the grace of today, the Feast of the Assumption of the Blessed Virgin. Understand its marvelous solemnity. Its mysteries are not terrifying, nor do they inspire overwhelming awe.

Blessed are those who have eyes to see. Blessed are those who see with spiritual eyes.

This night shines like the day. What countless angels acclaim the death of the life-giving mother! Hear how the eloquence of apostles blesses the departure of this body that had received God into its womb. See how the Word of God—who came down in his mercy to become her Son, ministering with his divine hands to this immaculate creature as his mother—receives her holy soul.

O marvelous Lawgiver, fulfilling the law that he himself had laid down, even though he was not bound by it! For it was he who commanded the children to show reverence to their parents: "Honor your father and your mother," he says (Ex 20:12).

The truth of this is apparent to everyone, calling to mind even dimly the words of Sacred Scripture: "The souls of the righteous are in the hands of God" (Wis 3:1). Since that is true, how much more is Mary's soul in the hands of her Son and her God! This is indisputable.

—St. John of Damascus, *First Homily on the Dormition*

IN GOD'S PRESENCE, CONSIDER . . .

If Jesus obeyed the commandment to honor his mother, and Jesus gave Mary to us as our mother, shouldn't we also honor Mary? In what specific ways can I do that today?

CLOSING PRAYER

From a prayer of St. Germanus: *Spouse of God, we celebrate you with faith, we honor you with longing, we venerate you with awe! At every moment we exalt you and reverently proclaim you blessed.*

264   A YEAR WITH THE SAINTS

Mary's assumption into heaven was fitting

Catholics affirm that Mary was assumed into heaven because of the Church's ancient testimony to the event and her eventual definition of that truth as dogma. But Blessed John Henry Newman points to yet another reason for believing: It was a fitting end to her life.

We accept that our Blessed Lady, the Mother of God, was assumed into heaven on the authority of age-old belief. But viewed in the light of reason, it is the fitness of this termination of her earthly course which so persuasively recommends it to our minds. We feel it "ought" to be, that it is "becoming" to her Lord and Son thus to provide for one who was unique and so special, both in herself and her relations to Him.

Mary is the Mother of God. She is not merely the mother of our Lord's manhood, or of our Lord's body, but she is to be considered the Mother of the Word himself, the Word incarnate. He took the substance of his human flesh from her and, clothed in it, he lay within her; and he bore it about with him after birth, as a sort of badge and witness that he, though God, was hers. He was nursed and tended by her; he was suckled by her; he lay in her arms. As time went on, he ministered to her and obeyed her. He lived with her for thirty years, in one house, with an uninterrupted communion, and with only the saintly Joseph to share it with him. She was the witness of his growth, of his joys, of his sorrows, of his prayers; she was blest with his smile, with the touch of his hand, with the whisper of his affection, with the expression of his thoughts and his feelings, for that length of time.

Now, my brethren, what ought she to be, what is it becoming that she should be, who was so favored? It was surely fitting, it was becoming, that she should be taken up into heaven and not lie in the grave till Christ's second coming, who had passed a life of sanctity and of miracle such as hers.

—Blessed John Henry Newman, *On the Fitness of the Glories of Mary*

IN GOD'S PRESENCE, CONSIDER . . .

When some reject the idea that Our Lady was bodily assumed into heaven, might it help them accept that truth if I could lead them to consider how fitting it was that Jesus would honor his mother this way?

CLOSING PRAYER

Blessed Lady, it was fitting that you should not be allowed to remain in the grave. Your assumption confirms for me your Son's promise that if I die in friendship with him, I too will one day live with him in heaven, with my earthly body transformed in glory.

Mary died certain of her salvation

Mary knew that she was full of grace, St. Alphonsus observes, and that she belonged to God. Imagine, then, her joyful confidence that death would take her to heaven!

The certainty of eternal salvation renders death sweet. Death is called a passage, because by death we pass from a short life to an eternal life. Those who die in doubt of their salvation, and who approach the solemn moment with a well-grounded fear of passing into eternal death, have a great dread indeed. But on the other hand, the joy of the saints is indeed great at the close of life, for they hope with some confidence to go and possess God in heaven.

A doctor announced to a nun in St. Teresa's order that her death was approaching. She was so filled with joy that she exclaimed, "How is it, Sir, that you announce to me such welcome news, and demand no fee?" St. Lawrence Justinian was at the point of death and saw his servants weeping round him. He said: "Away, away with your tears! This is no time to mourn." Go elsewhere to weep; if you want to stay here with me, rejoice, as I rejoice, in seeing the gates of heaven open to me, so that I may be united to my God.

In the same way, St. Peter of Alcántara, St. Aloysius Gonzaga, and so many other saints, when they heard that death was at hand, burst forth into exclamations of joy and gladness. Yet even they weren't as certain of possessing divine grace, nor as secure in their own holiness, as Mary was. So imagine what joy the Mother of God must have felt in receiving the news of her approaching death!

She had the fullest certainty of possessing divine grace—especially after the angel Gabriel had assured her that she was full of that grace—and that she already possessed God: "Hail, full of grace, the Lord is with you!"(Lk 1:28).

—St. Alphonsus Liguori, *The Glories of Mary*

IN GOD'S PRESENCE, CONSIDER . . .

I can't presume to know my eternal destiny infallibly. But does my life provide strong evidence that if I continue my present path, I will die in friendship with God?

CLOSING PRAYER

From "The Seven Dolors of Mary at the Death of Jesus": *Mary, in my last hour, when my heart is full of anxiety and pain, strengthen me and console me by your presence, and preserve me from falling into discouragement!*

Jesus comes to embrace Mary as she dies

St. John of Damascus imagines a conversation between Mary and Jesus as she prepares for her assumption.

As Mary was about to die, the King was there to receive with a divine embrace the holy, undefiled, and stainless soul of his mother, now on her way home. We can imagine what she might have said:

"Into your hands, my Son, I commend my spirit. Receive my soul, which is so dear to you, which you kept spotless. I give my body to you, not to the earth. Guard what you were pleased to inhabit and to preserve in virginity. Take me to yourself so that wherever you are, the fruit of my womb, there I too may be. I am drawn to you, who have descended to me. Be the consolation of my most cherished children, whom you promised to call your brethren, when my death leaves them in loneliness. Bless them afresh through my hands."

Stretching out her hands, as we might imagine, she blessed all those present. Then she heard these words:

"Come, my beloved Mother, to your rest. Arise and come, most dear among women; for the winter is past and gone, the harvest time is at hand. You are fair, my beloved, and there is no stain in you. Your fragrance is sweeter than all anointing oils" (see Sg 2:10–12, 4:10).

With these words in her ears, that holy woman gave up her spirit into the hands of her Son.

—St. John of Damascus, *Second Homily on the Dormition*

IN GOD'S PRESENCE, CONSIDER . . .

How do Mary's words, as imagined by St. John, echo the words of Jesus on the Cross? What conversation would I hope to have with Jesus and Mary when the hour comes for me to leave this world behind?

CLOSING PRAYER

From "The Seven Dolors of Mary at the Death of Jesus": *Dearest Mother, when the moment of my death has come, present me as your child to Jesus; say to him on my behalf: "Son, forgive him, for he knew not what he did. Receive him this day into your kingdom."*

Jesus gives Mary his Body one last time on earth

St. Alphonsus, like St. John of Damascus, imagines a conversation between Jesus and Mary when she is about to die. He sees her receiving Holy Communion from the hands of her Son.

The death of Mary was at hand. The angels came in choirs to meet her, as if to be ready for the great triumph with which they were to accompany her to paradise. Mary was indeed consoled at the sight of these holy spirits. But she wasn't fully consoled, because she didn't yet see her beloved Jesus, who was the whole love of her heart. She said: "Holy angels, fair citizens of the heavenly Jerusalem, you come in choirs kindly to console me; and you all do console me with your sweet presence. I thank you. But you don't fully satisfy me, for I don't yet see my Son coming to console me. Go, if you love me; return to paradise, and tell my Beloved to come, and to come quickly, for I am dying with the intensity of my desire to see him." Then behold, Jesus came to take his mother to the kingdom of the blessed. It was revealed to St. Elizabeth that Mary's Son appeared to her before she died, with his cross in his hands, to show the special glory he had obtained by the Redemption. St. John of Damascus tells us that our Lord himself gave her final Communion, saying with tender love, "Receive, my Mother, from my hands that same Body that you gave to me."

Then the mother, having received with the greatest love that last Communion, said, "My Son, into your hands I commend my spirit. I commend to you this soul, which from the beginning you created rich in so many graces, and by a unique privilege preserved from the stain of original sin. I commend to you my body, from which you took your flesh and blood. I also commend to you these my beloved children" (speaking of the holy disciples, who surrounded her); "they are grieved at my departure. You love them even more than I do. Console them, bless them, and give them strength to do great things for your glory."

—St. Alphonsus Liguori, *The Glories of Mary*

IN GOD'S PRESENCE, CONSIDER . . .

What conversation would you imagine between Jesus and Mary as Mary prepared to die and depart for heaven?

CLOSING PRAYER

A prayer for someone at the point of death: *In the name of God the almighty Father who created you, in the name of Jesus Christ, Son of the living God, who suffered for you, in the name of the Holy Spirit, who was poured out upon you, go forth, faithful Christian. May you live in peace this day, may your home be with God.*

The saints vie for Mary's presence

St. John of Damascus imagines how, at the time of Our Lady's departure from this world, the saints in heaven vied with the saints still on earth for her presence with them.

At Mary's death, Adam and Eve, our first parents, opened their lips to exclaim: "You blessed daughter of ours, who removed the penalty of our disobedience! You inherited from us a mortal body, but you have won for us immortality. You received your nature from us, and now you have given us back that nature transformed by grace. You have conquered pain and loosened the chains of death. You have restored us to our former state of innocence before we fell. We had shut the door of paradise, but you gained entrance to the tree of life. Through us, sorrow came out of good; through you, good from sorrow. How can you, who are all beautiful, taste of death? You are the gate of life and the ladder to heaven. Death has become the passage to immortality."

Then all the company of the saints in heaven exclaimed: "You have fulfilled our prophecies. You have purchased this joy for us. Through you we have broken the chains of death. Come, our desire, you who have gained us what we desired!" Then the saints standing by on earth added their words, no less burning: "Remain with us, our comfort, our sole joy in this world! Mother, we have suffered on your Son's account; don't leave us as orphans! Let us have you as a refuge and refreshment in our labors and weariness.

"You can remain if you so desire, just as you can depart from here. If you depart, you dwelling-place of God, let us go, too, if we are truly your children through your Son. You are our sole consolation on earth. As long as you live, we live, and it would be happiness to die with you." When they had all fulfilled their duty of loving reverence and had woven her a rich crown of hymns, they spoke a parting blessing over her, as a God-given treasure, and the last rites.

—St. John of Damascus, *Second Homily on the Dormition*

IN GOD'S PRESENCE, CONSIDER . . .

St. John's imagined scene reflects a poignant reality we may experience at the passing of a loved one who dies in the Lord. Can I recall an occasion when I wanted such a loved one to stay with me a while longer, while still rejoicing that he or she was—I had reason to hope—on the way to an eternal home?

CLOSING PRAYER

Lord Jesus, help me to say to you, as St. Paul once said: I would rather be away from the body and at home with the Lord. But whether I am at home or away, I will make it my aim to please you (see 1 Co 5:8–9).

The Apostles grieve to know Mary will leave them

Who could fully appreciate the sorrow that the Apostles must have felt when they realized that Mary was leaving them? St. Alphonsus imagines the scene.

Many authors assert that, before Mary's death, the Apostles and many disciples who were scattered in different parts of the world were miraculously assembled in her room. When she saw all her dear children in her presence, she addressed them: "My beloved children, through love for you and to help you, my Son left me on this earth. The holy faith has now spread throughout the world. Already the fruit of the divine seed has grown up. My Lord sees that my assistance on earth is no longer necessary. Having compassion on my grief in being separated from him, he has graciously listened to my desire to leave this life and to go see him in heaven. You must remain, then, to labor for his glory. If I leave you, my heart remains with you. The great love I bear you I'll carry with me forever. I go to paradise to pray for you."

Who can imagine the tears and laments of the holy disciples at this sad announcement? Weeping, they exclaimed: "It's true that this world is not a place worthy of you or fit for you. As for us, we're unworthy to enjoy the society of the Mother of God. But, remember, you are our mother. Until now you've enlightened us in our doubts, consoled us in our afflictions. You've been our strength in persecutions. So how can you abandon us, leaving us alone in the midst of so many enemies and conflicts, deprived of your consolation? We've already lost on earth Jesus, our Master and Father, who ascended into heaven. Until now we've found consolation in you, our mother. So how can you leave us orphans without father or mother? Sweet Lady, either remain with us, or take us with you!"

"No, my children," she replied, "this is not according to God's will. Be satisfied to do what he has decreed for me and for you. To you it yet remains to labor on earth for the glory of your Redeemer, and to make up your eternal crown."

—St. Alphonsus Liguori, *The Glories of Mary*

IN GOD'S PRESENCE, CONSIDER . . .

When I lose a loved one, am I able, despite my grief, to entrust that loved one to a loving God, and to continue with the mission I must still complete on earth?

CLOSING PRAYER

Blessed Mother, you know the waves of sorrow that wash over the heart when someone dearly beloved is lost. I ask you, by the grief you felt at the deaths of St. Joseph and Jesus, to be with me and comfort me in my seasons of mourning.

Mary's last words to the Apostles

St. Alphonsus imagines Our Lady's last farewell to the men who would become the foundation of the Church.

The holy Apostles, seeing that Mary was already at the point of leaving this world, renewed their tears. They all threw themselves on their knees around her bed. Some kissed her holy feet, some sought a special blessing from her, some entrusted to her a particular need, and all wept bitterly. Their hearts were pierced with grief at being obliged to separate themselves for the rest of their lives from their beloved lady. As the most loving mother, she had compassion on them all, and consoled each one. To some, she promised her patronage. Others she blessed with particular affection, and still others she encouraged to the work of the conversion of the world.

In particular, she called St. Peter to her. Since he was head of the Church and vicar of her Son, she urged him especially to spread the Faith. She also promised him at the same time her special protection in heaven. In an even more special way, however, she called to herself St. John, who more than any other was grieved at this moment when he had to part with his holy mother. Remembering the affection and attention with which this holy disciple had served her during all the years she had remained on earth since the death of her Son, this most gracious Lady said:

"My own John" (speaking with the greatest tenderness)—"my own John, I thank you for all the assistance you've given me. My son, be assured of it: I won't be ungrateful. Although I'm now leaving you, I go to pray for you. Remain in peace in this life until we meet again in heaven, where I'll wait for you. Never forget me. In all your needs call me to your aid; for I will never forget you, my beloved son. Son, I bless you. I leave you my blessing. Remain in peace. Farewell!"

—St. Alphonsus Liguori, *The Glories of Mary*

IN GOD'S PRESENCE, CONSIDER . . .

Why does St. Alphonsus imagine Our Lady addressing a special farewell to the Apostles, and to St. Peter and St. John in particular? Why would they have needed such words of encouragement about the future as she was leaving?

CLOSING PRAYER

From a prayer of Blessed Pope Paul VI: *O Mary, look upon us who are your children, look upon us who are brothers and sisters, disciples and apostles, a continuation of Jesus. Make us aware of our vocation and our mission.*

Mary breathes forth her soul in love

When Mary died, insists St. Alphonsus, death came not "clothed in mourning and grief . . . but adorned with light and gladness."

The life of Mary being now at its close, the most delicious music, as St. Jerome tells us, was heard in the room where she lay. According to a revelation of St. Bridget, the room was also filled with a brilliant light. This sweet music, and the unusual splendor, warned the holy apostles that Mary was then departing. This caused them to burst forth in tears and prayers again. Raising their hands, with one voice they exclaimed, "Mother, you're already going to heaven! You're leaving us! Give us your final blessing, and never forget us miserable creatures."

Mary, turning her eyes around upon all of them, as if to bid them a last farewell, said: "Goodbye, my children. I bless you. Don't be afraid: I will never forget you." Now death came—not, indeed, clothed in mourning and grief, as it does to others, but adorned with light and gladness. But what shall we say? Why speak of death? Let's say rather that divine love came, and cut the thread of that noble life. Just as a light, before going out, gives a last and brighter flash than ever, so did this beautiful creature, on hearing her Son's invitation to follow him, wrapped in the flames of love, and in the midst of her loving sighs, give a last sigh of still more ardent love. Then, breathing forth her soul, she died.

In this way was that great soul, that beautiful dove of the Lord, loosened from the bands of this life. In this way she entered into the glory of the blessed, where she is now seated, and will be seated, as queen of paradise, for all eternity. Mary, then, has left this world; she's now in heaven. From there, this compassionate mother looks down upon us who are still in this valley of tears. She pities us and, if we desire it, she promises to help us. Let's always beg her, by the merits of her blessed death, to obtain for us a happy death.

—St. Alphonsus Liguori, *The Glories of Mary*

IN GOD'S PRESENCE, CONSIDER . . .

Have I ever been present when the soul of a loved one was "breathed forth" into the arms of God? What lessons did I learn from that poignant experience?

CLOSING PRAYER

From a prayer of St. Germanus: *O sovereign Queen! You are our defense and our joy. Make me worthy to share with you the happiness that you enjoy in heaven.*

Mary died with perfect peace of mind

St. Alphonsus observes yet another way in which Mary's death differed from so many other deaths: She had absolutely no remorse of conscience to torment her.

Peace of mind renders precious the death of the righteous. Sins committed during life are the worms that so cruelly torment and gnaw the hearts of poor dying sinners. As they are about to appear before the divine tribunal, they see themselves at that moment surrounded by their sins, which terrify them, crying out, according to St. Bernard, "We're your works; we won't leave you alone!"

Mary certainly couldn't be tormented at death by any remorse of conscience, for she was always pure and always free from the least shade of actual or original sin. From the moment that she had the use of reason, she began to love God with all her strength. And she continued to do so, always advancing more and more throughout her whole life in love and perfection. All Mary's thoughts, desires, and affections were from God and for God alone. She never uttered a word, made a movement, cast a glance, or breathed, except for God and his glory. She never departed a step or detached herself for a single moment from the love of God.

Imagine how all the lovely virtues she had practiced during life surrounded her blessed bed in the happy hour of her death! That faith so constant; that loving confidence in God; that unconquerable patience in the midst of so many sufferings; that humility in the midst of so many privileges; that modesty; that meekness; that tender compassion for souls; that insatiable zeal for the glory of God; and above all, that most perfect love towards him, with that entire conformity to the divine will. All these virtues surrounded her and consoled her, saying. "We are your works; we will not abandon you. Our Lady and mother, we are all daughters of your beautiful heart. Now that you are leaving this miserable life, we will not leave you. We also will go, and be your eternal attendants and honor in paradise. There, by our means, you will reign as queen of all men and angels."

—St. Alphonsus Liguori, *The Glories of Mary*

IN GOD'S PRESENCE, CONSIDER . . .

If I were to die today, which sins and weaknesses would give me most cause for remorse? Would I be confident that Mary would intercede for me?

CLOSING PRAYER

"Have mercy on me, O God, according to your merciful love; according to your abundant mercy, blot out my transgressions. Wash me thoroughly from my iniquity, and cleanse me from my sin! For I know my transgressions, and my sin is ever before me" (Ps 51:1–3).

Mary died from her love for God

Did Our Lady die of old age? No, says St. Alphonsus; just as her love for God gave her life, so it caused her death.

Well did Mary herself know that her heart was continually burning with divine love. As Bernardine de Bustis says: "Mary, by a unique privilege granted to no other saint, loved God, and was always truly loving God, in every moment of her life, with such fervency, that St. Bernard declares it required a continuous miracle to preserve her life in the midst of such flames."

These words of the Song of Songs have been applied to Mary: "Who is she coming up from the wilderness, like a column of smoke, perfumed with myrrh and frankincense, with all the fragrant powders of the merchant?" (See Sg 3:6.) Her entire self-sacrifice is symbolized by the myrrh, her fervent prayers by the incense. All her holy virtues, united to her perfect love for God, kindled in her a flame so great that her beautiful soul—wholly devoted to and consumed by divine love—arose continually to God like a column of smoke, breathing forth on every side a most sweet fragrance.

"Blessed Mary," says the Abbot Rupert, "just such a column of smoke you have breathed forth as sweet fragrance to the Most High!" Eustachius expresses it in still stronger terms: She is like "a column of smoke, because burning interiorly as a burnt offering with the flame of divine love, she sent forth a most sweet fragrance."

As the loving virgin lived, so did she die. As divine love gave her life, so it caused her death. For the Doctors and holy Fathers of the Church generally agree that she died from no other infirmity than pure love. As St. Ildephonsus says: "Mary ought not to die, but if she does, she should die only from love."

—St. Alphonsus Liguori, *The Glories of Mary*

IN GOD'S PRESENCE, CONSIDER . . .

What does it mean for St. Bernard to say that it took a "continuous miracle" to preserve Mary's life in the midst of her burning love for God? What does it mean for St. Ildephonsus to say that Mary "died from love"?

CLOSING PRAYER

Mary, the Holy Spirit who came down on you and the Apostles in tongues of fire at Pentecost is the same Spirit who had overshadowed you when you conceived Jesus. He is the fiery love of the Father and the Son, and he has dwelt in you in a way unlike his dwelling in any other creature. No wonder your heart is aflame with divine love!

Mary's death was the cause of rejoicing

St. John of Damascus ponders the reasons for the joy surrounding Mary's death.

O wonder surpassing nature! Death, once feared and hated, has here become an occasion of praise and blessing. In days of old it was the forerunner of grief, dejection, tears, and sadness. But now it shines forth as the cause of joy and rejoicing. The death of God's servants is celebrated, because we conclude from their holy end that they have his good pleasure. So we assume that their death is blessed, that they are perfect, blessed, and immoveable in goodness, as the proverb says: "Call no one blessed before his death" (see Sir 11:28).

But we do not apply this proverb to you, Mary. Death was not your blessedness, nor was dying your way to perfection; nor, again, did your departure from here make you secure in salvation. For it is your Son, in his conception and his divine dwelling within you, who has made our sure and true security. So your words were true: From the moment of your Son's conception, not from the moment of your death, all generations would call you blessed. It was you who broke the force of death, paying its penalty, and filling it with grace.

For this reason, when your holy and sinless body was taken to the tomb, the choirs of angels carried it and were all around, leaving nothing undone for the honor of our Lord's mother. Meanwhile, the Apostles carried your body, the true Ark of the Lord God on their shoulders, just as the priests had done with the Ark of the Old Covenant, crossing the River Jordan. They placed your body in the tomb, making the tomb another Jordan, the way to the true land of the gospel, the heavenly Jerusalem, the mother of all the faithful, with God himself as its Lord and architect. But your pure and spotless body was not left in the earth. The abode of the queen, of God's true mother, was prepared in the heavenly kingdom alone.

—St. John of Damascus, *First Homily on the Dormition*

IN GOD'S PRESENCE, CONSIDER . . .

Why can the death of a Christian be a time of joyful hope? Why must we nevertheless avoid presumption about the spiritual state of someone who has died? Why do we pray for the faithful departed?

CLOSING PRAYER

Eternal rest grant to our loved ones, O Lord, and may perpetual light shine upon them. May their souls, and the souls of all the faithful departed, through the mercy of God, rest in peace.

The mother of Life passes through death

Because she was sinless, St. John of Damascus notes, Mary didn't merit death, for death is the wages of sin. But neither did Jesus merit death, yet he willingly took it on for our sakes. And so Mary followed her Son's example.

I don't know whether I can trust my lips to speak of this day! For today Mary, the life-giving treasury and abyss of charity, is hidden in immortal death. But the one who conceived death's destroyer meets it without fear—if we can rightly refer to her holy and life-giving departure from the earth by the name of "death."

For how could she, who brought life to all, be under the dominion of death? Even so, she obeys the law of her own Son, and inherits this chastisement as a daughter of the first Adam, since even her Son, who is Life itself, did not refuse it. As the mother of the living God, she goes through death to him.

Christ, the Life and the Truth, said that where he was to be, there also would be his disciples (see Jn 14:3). How much more certain is it, then, that his mother would be with him!

"Precious in the sight of the LORD is the death of his saints" (Ps 116:15). More than precious, then, is the passing away of his mother. Now let the heavens and the angels rejoice! Let the earth and the people be full of gladness! Let the air resound with song and canticle; let dark night put off its gloom, and imitate, by its twinkling stars, the brightness of day!

—St. John of Damascus, *Second Homily on the Dormition*

IN GOD'S PRESENCE, CONSIDER . . .

Both Jesus and Mary provide us models of redemptive suffering. In my own life, is there any kind of suffering that God is asking me to endure for the sake of someone else? Is there someone who must endure suffering for my sake?

CLOSING PRAYER

From a "Novena to Our Lady of Good Remedy": *Mary, touch the hearts of sinners; bring comfort to the afflicted and the lonely; help the poor and the hopeless; aid the sick and the suffering. May they be healed in body and strengthened in spirit to endure their sufferings with patient resignation and Christian fortitude.*

Mary's body rests in the tomb

Immediately after her death, Mary's body is laid in her tomb. St. John of Damascus imagines that tomb, and venerates the body resting there. But it won't rest there for long.

O sacred and wonderful, holy and venerable body, ministered to now by angels, standing by in lowly reverence! Demons tremble. Men approach with faith, honoring and venerating her, greeting her with their eyes and lips, and in doing so, drawing down upon themselves abundant blessings.

A rich fragrance sprinkled upon clothes or places leaves its scent even after it has been withdrawn. In the same way, now that holy, undefiled body, belonging to God, filled with heavenly fragrance, the rich source of grace, is laid in the tomb so that it may be translated to a higher and better place. Nor did she leave the grave empty: Her body imparted to it a heavenly fragrance, a source of healing and of all good for those who approach it with faith.

We, too, approach you today, O Queen. O Virgin Mother of God, we steady our souls with our trust in you, as with a strong anchor. We lift up mind, soul, and body, and all ourselves to you, rejoicing in psalms and hymns and spiritual songs. And in doing so we reach through you the Lord who is beyond our reach on account of his majesty.

The divine Word made flesh taught us that the honor shown to servants is honor shown to our common Lord. So how can we possibly neglect to show honor to you, his mother? Isn't such honor most desirable? Aren't you honored as the very breath of life? In this way we can best show our service to our Lord himself.

—St. John of Damascus, *First Homily on the Dormition*

IN GOD'S PRESENCE, CONSIDER . . .

What would it have been like to enter Mary's tomb and pay my respects? What would it have been like to visit again, and find that her body was no longer there?

CLOSING PRAYER

From a prayer of St. John of Damascus: *Lord, we recall the memory of your most precious gift, Mary, as the cause of our lasting joy. How she fills us with gladness! The mind that dwells on this holy treasury of your grace enriches itself.*

Mary's body is snatched up to heaven

St. John of Damascus explores the reasons why Mary was taken up to heaven to be united with her Son.

The immaculate body of Mary was laid in the tomb. Then it was assumed after three days to the heavenly mansions. The breast of the earth was no fitting place to receive the Lord's dwelling place, the living source of cleansing water, the grain of heavenly bread, the sacred vine of divine wine, the evergreen and fruitful olive branch of God's mercy. And just as the all-holy body of God's Son, which was taken from her, rose from the dead on the third day, it followed that she should be snatched from the tomb, that the mother should be united to her Son. As he had come down to her, so she was raised up to him, to the more perfect dwelling place—heaven itself.

It was fitting that the one who had sheltered God the Word in her own womb should inhabit the tabernacles of her Son. And as our Lord said he had to be about his Father's business (see Lk 2:49), so his mother had to dwell in the courts of her Son, in the house of the Lord, and in the courts of the house of our God. If all those who rejoice dwell in him, where must the cause itself of joy abide? It was fitting that the body of the one who preserved her virginity intact in her motherhood should be kept from corruption even after death. She who nursed her Creator as an infant at her breast had a right to be in the divine tabernacles. The place of the bride whom the Father had espoused was in the heavenly courts.

It was fitting that she who saw her Son die on the cross, and received in her heart the sword of pain that she had not felt in childbirth, should gaze upon him seated next to the Father. The Mother of God had a right to the possession of her Son, and as handmaid and Mother of God, to the veneration of all creation.

—St. John of Damascus, *Second Homily on the Dormition*

IN GOD'S PRESENCE, CONSIDER . . .

What reasons does St. John offer for the reasonableness of belief in the assumption? Why was it fitting that Mary's body should be taken with her to heaven, rather than left to decay in the grave?

CLOSING PRAYER

From a prayer of Venerable Pope Pius XII: *Immaculate Virgin, we believe with all the fervor of our faith in your triumphal assumption both in body and in soul into heaven, where you are acclaimed as queen by all the choirs of angels and all the legions of saints.*

A riot of praise for Christ and his mother!

St. John of Damascus imagines that at Mary's departure to heaven, a great choir of saints and angels shook both heaven and earth with their praise.

At Mary's departure to heaven, the Apostles—eyewitnesses and ministers of the Word—were there, duly ministering to our Lord's mother, and drawing from her a rich inheritance and a full measure of praise. For how could anyone doubt that she is the source of blessing and the fountain of all good? Their followers and successors also were there, joining in their ministry and in their praise.

A chosen band of spirits from the heavenly Jerusalem were there as well. Not only did the angelic choirs attend. For it was fitting as well that the foremost men and prophets of the Old Testament, who had foretold that she would give birth to the Word of God within time, should be there as an honor guard. Others had obeyed the King heartily under the old law, so that they had stood with honor beside him. Now they had the right to serve as a bodyguard to his mother according to the flesh, the truly blessed and blissful one, surpassing all generations and all creation. All those who are bright and shining in spirit were with her, with spiritual eyes fixed upon her in reverence, and fear, and pure desire.

From all these we hear divine and inspired words, and spiritual canticles appropriate to the parting hour. On this occasion it was fitting to praise the Lord's boundless goodness, his immeasurable greatness, his omnipotence, his generosity surpassing all measure in his dealings with us, the overflowing riches of his mercy, the abyss of his tenderness. They praised him for putting aside his greatness to descend to our littleness, with the cooperation of the Father and the Holy Spirit. Then followed a riot of praise! It was not that each was seeking to outdo the other, for that would have displayed vanity and been far from pleasing to God. Rather, they wanted to leave nothing undone for the glory of God and the honor of the Mother of God.

—St. John of Damascus, *Second Homily on the Dormition*

IN GOD'S PRESENCE, CONSIDER . . .

If saints and angels celebrated Mary's assumption, shouldn't I also celebrate the occasion with great joy, knowing that my mother now reigns in heaven as queen?

CLOSING PRAYER

From the prayer "Hail, O Queen of Heaven": *Rejoice, O glorious Virgin, lovely beyond all others; farewell, most beautiful maiden, and pray for us to Christ!*

The angels welcome Mary into heaven

St. John of Damascus imagines the joyous reception of Our Lady into heaven by the angels awaiting her there. His rich imagery draws from the biblical book called the Song of Songs, in which the bride is welcomed by the bridegroom and his companions.

In your assumption, Mary, angels with archangels bear you up. Unclean spirits tremble at your departure. The air raises a hymn of praise at your passage, and the atmosphere itself is purified. Heaven receives your soul with joy. The heavenly powers greet you with sacred songs and with joyous praise, saying:

"Who is this most pure creature ascending, shining as the dawn, beautiful as the moon, radiant as the sun? How sweet and lovely you are, the lily of the field, the rose among thorns! No wonder the young maidens love you! We are drawn after the fragrance of your anointing oils. The King has brought you into his chamber. There, angelic powers protect you, principalities praise you, thrones proclaim you, cherubim are hushed in joy, and seraphim magnify the true mother, both by nature and by grace, of their true Lord.

"You were not taken into heaven as Elijah was, nor did you penetrate to the third heaven with the Apostle Paul. Rather, you reached all the way to the royal throne of your Son, seeing it with your own eyes, standing by it in joy and a communion beyond words. You are the gladness of angels and of all heavenly powers; sweetness of patriarchs and of the righteous; perpetual exultation of prophets, rejoicing the world and sanctifying all things; refreshment of the weary, comfort of the sorrowful, remission of sins, health of the sick, harbor of the storm-tossed, lasting strength of mourners, and perpetual help of all who invoke you."

—St. John of Damascus, *First Homily on the Dormition*

IN GOD'S PRESENCE, CONSIDER . . .

Why would Mary be the cause of rejoicing for angels? Why would the Old Testament patriarchs and prophets celebrate her entrance into heaven?

CLOSING PRAYER

From a prayer of Venerable Pope Pius XII: *We believe that in the glory where you reign, Mary, clothed with the sun and crowned with stars, you are, after Jesus, the joy and gladness of all the angels and the saints.*

The saints welcome Mary into heaven

The angels weren't the only citizens of heaven to welcome Mary when she arrived there; the saints of all the ages came to honor her as well. St. Alphonsus imagines the scene.

The angels have welcomed Mary at her assumption into heaven. Now all the saints in paradise at that time come to welcome her and salute her as their queen. All the holy virgins come: "The maidens saw her and called her blessed; the queens . . . and they praised her" (see Sg 6:9). "Most Blessed Lady," they say, "we are also queens in this kingdom, but you are our queen. For you were the first to give us the great example of consecrating our virginity to God. We all bless and thank you for it."

Then come the holy confessors to salute her as their mistress; by her holy life, she has taught them so many beautiful virtues. The holy martyrs also come to salute her as their queen. For by her great constancy in the sorrows of her Son's passion, she has taught them, and by her merits she has also obtained for them the strength to lay down their lives for the faith. St. James, the only one of the twelve Apostles who is already in heaven, also comes to thank her in the name of all the other Apostles for all the comfort and help she gave them while she was on earth. The prophets next come to salute her, saying: "Lady, you were the one foreshadowed in our prophecies."

Next come the holy patriarchs of Old Testament times, saying: "Mary, it is you who were our hope. It was for you that we sighed with such longing and for so long a time." Amongst these come our first parents, Adam and Eve, to thank her with still greater affection. "Beloved daughter," they say, "you have repaired the injury that we inflicted on the human race. You have obtained for the world the blessing that we lost by our crime. Through you we are saved. For that, be ever blessed!"

—St. Alphonsus Liguori, *The Glories of Mary*

IN GOD'S PRESENCE, CONSIDER . . .

What other groups of saints can you imagine welcoming Mary when she arrived? What other Old Testament figures might have met her? What might they have said to her?

CLOSING PRAYER

"Sing aloud, O daughter of Zion; shout, O Israel! Result and exult with all your heart, O daughter of Jerusalem! . . . The king of Israel, the Lord, is in your midst!" (Zeph 3:14–15).

Mary's family greets her in heaven

St. Alphonsus imagines the scene when Mary's saintly family members come to greet her upon her arrival in heaven.

When she enters heaven at her assumption, Mary is greeted by her family. St. Zachary and St. Elizabeth come and thank her for her loving visit, with such great humility and charity, in their home. By it they received treasures of grace. St. John the Baptist comes with even greater affection to thank her for having sanctified him by her voice. Imagine how her holy parents, St. Joachim and St. Anne, address her when they come to salute her. With what tenderness they bless her, saying: "Beloved daughter, what a favor it was for us to have such a child! Be now our queen. For you are the mother of our God, and we greet and venerate you."

Who can even imagine the affection with which her dear husband, St. Joseph, comes to salute her? Who can even describe the joy that the holy patriarch feels at seeing his spouse so triumphantly enter heaven and made queen of paradise? With what tenderness he would address her: "My Lady and spouse, how can I ever thank our God as I should, for having made me your husband, you who are his true mother! Through you I merited to assist on earth the childhood of the Eternal Word, to carry him so often in my arms, to receive so many special graces. Ever blessed be those moments that I spent in life in serving Jesus and you, my holy spouse! Behold our Jesus! We rejoice that now he no longer lies on straw in a manger, as we saw him at his birth in Bethlehem. He no longer lives poor and despised, as he once lived with us in Nazareth. He is no longer nailed to a shameful cross, as when he died in Jerusalem for the salvation of the world.

"Instead, he is seated at the right hand of his Father, as King and Lord of heaven and earth. Now, my Queen, we will never again be separated from him. There, we shall bless him and love him for all eternity."

—St. Alphonsus Liguori, *The Glories of Mary*

IN GOD'S PRESENCE, CONSIDER . . .

What conversations would I imagine took place between Mary and her relatives when she arrived in heaven?

CLOSING PRAYER

Blessed Lady, obtain through your Son, I beg you, eternal life for the souls of my family and other loved ones, from the only Giver of every good and perfect gift, the Lord of life.

The Blessed Virgin enters the heavenly temple

St. John of Damascus celebrates Mary's new and fitting home in heaven.

Today the holy Virgin of Virgins is presented in the heavenly temple. Today the sacred and living Ark of the living God, who conceived her Creator himself, takes up her abode in the temple of God not made by hands.

David, her forefather, rejoices. Angels and archangels are in jubilation, angelic powers exult, the angelic choirs of principalities and dominations, virtues and thrones, are in gladness. Cherubim and seraphim magnify God. Nor is it the least of their praise to acclaim the mother of glory.

Today, like Noah's dove, this holy dove—the pure and guileless soul, sanctified by the Holy Spirit—put off the life-giving Ark of her body, which had carried our Lord. She found rest for the soles of her feet, taking her flight to the spiritual world and dwelling securely in the sinless country above.

Today the Eden of the new Adam receives the true paradise, in which sin is forgiven, the tree of life is grown, and our nakedness is covered. For we are no longer naked and uncovered as our first parents were, unable to bear the splendor of bearing the image of God. The serpent, by whose deceitful promise we were made like brute beasts, did not enter into this paradise.

Today the spotless Virgin, untouched by earthly affections, and all heavenly in her thoughts, was not dissolved in earth. Truly entering heaven, she dwells instead in the heavenly dwellings.

—St. John of Damascus, *Second Homily on the Dormition*

IN GOD'S PRESENCE, CONSIDER . . .

Who is "the new Adam," and what is his "Eden"? Who is the "true paradise"? What does it mean to say that we are "no longer naked and uncovered"?

CLOSING PRAYER

From a prayer of Venerable Pope Pius XII: *Mary, your eyes, which wept over the earth crimsoned by the blood of Jesus, are yet turned toward this world racked by wars and persecutions, the oppression of the just and the weak. From the shadows of this vale of tears, we seek your assistance from heaven.*

The mother of the King is a Queen

The universal queenship of Mary, St. Alphonsus reasons, is implied by the universal kingship of her Son.

As the glorious Virgin Mary has been raised to the dignity of mother of the King of kings, it is not without reason that the Church honors her, and wishes her to be honored by all, with the glorious title of Queen. "If the Son is a King," says an ancient writer, "the one who begot him is rightly and truly considered a queen and sovereign."

"No sooner had Mary consented to be mother of the Eternal Word," says St. Bernardine of Siena, "than she merited by this consent to be made Queen of the World and of all creatures."

"Since the flesh of Mary was not different from that of Jesus," remarks the Abbot Arnold of Chartres, "how can the royal dignity of the Son be denied to the mother? . . . Hence we must consider the glory of the Son, not only as being common to, but as one with, that of his mother."

And if Jesus is the King of the universe, Mary is also its queen. "And as queen," says the Abbot Rupert, "she possesses, by right, the whole kingdom of her Son." For this reason, St. Bernardine of Siena concludes that "as many creatures as there are who serve God, so many there are who serve Mary: for as angels and men, and all things that are in heaven and on earth, are subject to the empire of God, so are they also under the dominion of Mary."

—St. Alphonsus Liguori, *The Glories of Mary*

IN GOD'S PRESENCE, CONSIDER . . .

In modern times, we usually think of a queen as the wife of a king. But in ancient Israel, the queen was more like the modern queen mother—that is, the mother of the king. Why do we speak of Mary, then, as Queen of Heaven?

CLOSING PRAYER

From the "Lourdes Hymn": *Immaculate Mary, your praises we sing; you reign now in splendor with Jesus our King! In heaven the blessed your glory proclaim; on earth we, your children, invoke your sweet name. Ave, ave, ave, Maria!*

Let the queen of glory come in!

St. Alphonsus imagines the coronation of Mary as Queen of Heaven.

Let's now imagine how our Savior went forth from heaven to meet his mother on the day of her assumption into heaven. On first meeting her, and to console her, Jesus speaks the words of the Song of Songs: "'Arise, my love, my dove, my fair one, and come away; for behold, winter is past' (Sg 2:10–11). Come, my own dear mother, my pure and beautiful dove. Leave that valley of tears in which, for my love, you have suffered so much. Come in soul and body to enjoy the reward of your holy life. Though your sufferings have been great on earth, far greater is the glory that I have prepared for you in heaven. Enter, then, that kingdom, and take your seat near me. Come to receive the crown that I will bestow upon you as Queen of the Universe."

Behold, Mary is already leaving the earth. She looks at it with affection and compassion: with affection, remembering the many graces she had there received from her Lord; with compassion, because in it she leaves so many poor children surrounded with miseries and dangers. But Jesus offers her his hand, and the Blessed Mother ascends. Already she has passed beyond the clouds, beyond the heavenly spheres. Behold her already at the gates of heaven!

When monarchs make their solemn entry into their kingdoms, they don't pass through the gates of the capital. Instead, the gates are removed to make way for them on that occasion. So when Jesus Christ entered paradise, the angels cried out: "Lift up your heads, O gates! and be lifted up, O ancient doors! that the King of glory may come in" (Ps 24:7). In a similar way, now that Mary goes to take possession of the kingdom of heaven, the angels who accompany her cry out to those within: "Lift up your heads, O gates! and be lifted up, O ancient doors! that the queen of glory may come in."

—St. Alphonsus Liguori, *The Glories of Mary*

IN GOD'S PRESENCE, CONSIDER . . .

Today, I may find myself thrilled to see soldiers coming home from war, or perhaps the inauguration to political office of a favored candidate. If even these events can be occasions of exuberant celebration, how much more should I celebrate the coronation of my heavenly queen, coming home and taking her rightful throne?

CLOSING PRAYER

We rejoice with you, Lord, in welcoming your mother to her heavenly throne; we thrill to know that "at your right hand stands the queen in gold" (Ps 45:9).

The Blessed Trinity welcomes Mary to heaven

Once Mary has been welcomed by the angels, her family, and all the saints, the Most Holy Trinity receives her and places her on her throne. St. Alphonsus imagines the scene.

After having been greeted by the angels and the saints, the humble and holy virgin kneels and adores the divine Majesty. She is totally absorbed in the awareness of her own nothingness. So she thanks him for all the graces bestowed upon her by his pure goodness, and especially for having made her the mother of the Eternal Word.

Then, let him who can, comprehend with what love the Most Holy Trinity blesses her. Let him comprehend the welcome given to his daughter by the Eternal Father, to his mother by the Son, to his spouse by the Holy Spirit. The Father crowns her by imparting his power to her. The Son imparts his wisdom; the Holy Spirit imparts his love.

Then the three Divine Persons, placing her throne at the right of the throne of Jesus, declare her to be the sovereign of heaven and earth. They command the angels and all creatures to acknowledge her as their queen, and so to serve and obey her. Imagine, then, how exalted is the throne to which Mary is raised in heaven!

"The Apostle Paul tells us," says St. Bernard, "that the mind of man can never conceive the immense glory prepared in heaven by God for those who on earth have loved him (see 12 Cor 2:9). Who, then, can ever conceive the glory he prepared for his beloved mother? For she was the one who, more than all others, loved him on earth. In fact, even from the very first moment of her creation, she loved him more than all men and angels united!"

—St. Alphonsus Liguori, *The Glories of Mary*

IN GOD'S PRESENCE, CONSIDER . . .

Though Mary has a unique place as the Queen of Heaven, Sacred Scripture says that all the saints there will reign with Christ, having a share in his glory, authority, and power (see Rom 8:16–17; 2 Cor 3:18; 1 Pt 5:1; 2 Tim 2:12; Rv 2:26-27; 22:5). Is salvation just a kind of eternal fire insurance, or is it much more—a share in God's own nature (see 1 Pt 1:4)?

CLOSING PRAYER

Lord Jesus, I thank you that "the saying is sure": If I have died with you, I will also live with you; if I endure, I shall also reign with you (see 2 Tim 2:11–12).

A great sign appeared in heaven

St. John Eudes explains the symbolism in the Book of Revelation's vision of Mary in heaven.

"A great sign appeared in heaven: A woman clothed with the sun, and the moon under her feet, and on her head a crown of twelve stars" (see Rv 12:1). What is this great sign? Who is this miraculous woman? . . . The woman is Mary, the queen among women, the Sovereign of angels and men. . . .

Mary appears in heaven because she comes from heaven, because she is heaven's masterpiece, the Empress of Heaven, its joy and its glory, in whom everything is heavenly. Even when her body dwelt on earth, her thoughts and affections were all rapt in heaven. She is clothed with the eternal Sun of the Godhead and with all the perfections of the divine Essence, which surround, fill, and penetrate her to such an extent that she has become transformed, as it were, into the power, goodness, and holiness of God. She has the moon under her feet to show that the entire world is beneath her. None is above her, save only God, and she holds absolute sway over all created things. She is crowned with twelve stars that represent the virtues which shine so brightly in her soul. The mysteries of her life are as many stars more luminous by far than the brightest lights of the sky. The privileges and prerogatives God has granted to her, the least of which is greater than anything shining in the firmament of heaven, as well as the glory of the saints of paradise and of earth, are her crown and her glory. . . .

But why does the Holy [Spirit] call Mary "a great sign"? It is simply to tell us that everything in her is wonderful, and that the marvels that fill her being should be proclaimed to the entire world, so that she may become an object of admiration for the inhabitants of heaven as well as for mankind on earth, and so that she may be the sweet delight of angels and men.

—St. John Eudes, *The Admirable Heart of Mary*

IN GOD'S PRESENCE, CONSIDER . . .

This passage from Revelation represents the last reference to Our Lady in the Bible. Many works of art portray her as St. John described her here, with the sun, moon, and stars—and also with the serpent crushed beneath her heel. How does such art tie together the last scriptural reference to Mary with the first, in Genesis?

CLOSING PRAYER

From a prayer of Venerable Pope Pius XII: *O gracious Queen, O resplendent vision of paradise, dispel from our minds the darkness of error by the light of faith!*

The Hail Mary is pleasing to Our Lady

Do you want to say a prayer that pleases our Blessed Mother? St. Alphonsus assures us that she finds no prayer more agreeable than a Hail Mary.

The Hail Mary comes, of course, from the angelic greeting to the ever-blessed Virgin. It's most pleasing to her, because whenever she hears it, she seems to experience anew the joy that she felt when St. Gabriel announced to her that she was the chosen Mother of God. With this purpose in mind, we should often salute her with the Hail Mary. "Greet her," says Thomas à Kempis, "with the angelic greeting; for she indeed hears this sound with pleasure." The Mother of God herself told St. Matilda that she finds no greeting more agreeable than the Hail Mary. Whoever greets Mary will also be greeted by her.

St. Bernard once heard a statue of the Blessed Virgin greet him, saying, "Hail, Bernard." Mary's greeting, says St. Bonaventure, will always bring some grace corresponding to the needs of the one who salutes her: "She willingly salutes us with grace, if we willingly salute her with a Hail Mary."

Richard of Saint Lawrence adds, "If we address the mother of our Lord, saying, 'Hail Mary,' she cannot refuse the grace which we ask." Mary herself promised St. Gertrude that at death she would have as many graces as she had said Hail Marys.

Blessed Alan de la Roche asserts that "as all heaven rejoices when the Hail Mary is said, so also do the demons tremble and flee." This truth Thomas à Kempis affirms from his own experience. He says that once the Devil appeared to him, but then instantly fled on hearing the Hail Mary.

—St. Alphonsus Liguori, *The Glories of Mary*

IN GOD'S PRESENCE, CONSIDER . . .

How often do I pray the Hail Mary? Which of its words or phrases mean the most to me, and why?

CLOSING PRAYER

Our Lady, I join now with the angel Gabriel in saluting you: Hail Mary, full of grace . . .

A meditation on the Hail Mary

St. Alphonsus reflects on the words of this famous prayer, pondering the meaning of each phrase.

Immaculate and holy Virgin! Before you, who are so humble, though endowed with such precious gifts, I'm ashamed to appear—I who am so proud in the midst of so many sins. But miserable as I am, I too will salute you.

"Hail, Mary, full of grace." You are already full of grace; impart a portion of it to me.

"The Lord is with you." The same Lord who was always with you from the first moment of your creation, has now united himself more closely to you by becoming your Son.

"Blessed are you among women." Lady, blessed among all women, obtain God's blessing for us also.

"And blessed is the fruit of your womb." Blessed tree, which has given to the world so noble and holy a fruit!

"Holy Mary, Mother of God!" Mary, I acknowledge that you are the true Mother of God, and in defense of this truth I'm ready to give my life a thousand times.

"Pray for us sinners." But if you are the Mother of God, you are also the mother of our salvation, and of us poor sinners. For God became man to save sinners, and he made you his mother, so that your prayers might have power to save any sinner.

Hurry, then, Mary, to pray for us, "now, and at the hour of our death." Pray always: Pray now, while we live amid so many temptations and dangers of losing God. But still more, pray for us at the hour of our death, when we're on the point of leaving this world to be presented before God's tribunal.

—St. Alphonsus Liguori, *The Glories of Mary*

IN GOD'S PRESENCE, CONSIDER . . .

We may have prayed the Hail Mary since early childhood. But have we ever stopped to reflect carefully on each phrase, as St. Alphonsus has done, and what it means for us personally?

CLOSING PRAYER

From a prayer of St. Alphonsus: *Pray for us, Mary, so that being saved by the merits of Jesus Christ and by your intercession, we may come one day, without further danger of being lost, to salute you and praise you with your Son in heaven for all eternity.*

Some ways to pray the Hail Mary

St. Alphonsus provides some practical advice for praying the simplest and most popular of Marian prayers.

Here are some ways to pray the Hail Mary. First, every morning and evening, when we get up and when we go to bed, we can say three Hail Marys lying down, or at least kneeling. Then we can add to each one this short prayer: "Mary, by your pure and immaculate conception, make my body pure, and my soul holy." We should then, as St. Stanislaus always did, ask Mary's blessing as our mother; place ourselves under the mantle of her protection; and beg her to guard us during the coming day or night from sin. For this purpose it's advisable to have a beautiful image of the Blessed Virgin.

Second, we can say the Angelus, with the usual three Hail Marys, in the morning, at midday, and in the evening. Third, we can greet the Mother of God with a Hail Mary every hour on the hour. Fourth, whenever we go out of the house or return, we can greet the Blessed Virgin with a Hail Mary. That way, whether we are indoors or outdoors, she will guard us from all sin. Fifth, we should honor every image of Mary that we pass with a Hail Mary. For this purpose, those who can would do well to place a beautiful image of the Blessed Virgin on an outside wall of their houses, so that it may be venerated by those who pass by.

Sixth, we would do well to begin and end all our actions with a Hail Mary. They may be spiritual actions—prayer, Confession, Communion, spiritual reading, hearing sermons—or temporal, such as study, giving advice, working, or sitting down for a meal. Happy are those actions that are enclosed between two Hail Marys. Finally, we should say a Hail Mary in every temptation, in every danger, and in every inclination to anger. Do this, and you'll see the immense advantage it brings.

—St. Alphonsus Liguori, *The Glories of Mary*

IN GOD'S PRESENCE, CONSIDER . . .

Do I regularly pray a Hail Mary at any of the times recommended by St. Alphonsus? Are there other times as well when it's my habit to pray this prayer?

CLOSING PRAYER

From the Angelus: *The angel of the Lord declared unto Mary, and she conceived by the Holy Spirit. Hail, Mary . . .*

St. Francis de Sales and the *Memorare*

St. Alphonsus recalls how the Memorare *prayer rescued St. Francis de Sales from despair.*

When St. Francis de Sales was about seventeen, he was pursuing his studies in Paris. At the same time he devoted himself to spiritual exercises and to the holy love of God, in which he found the joys of paradise. Our Lord, in order to try him, and to strengthen the bands that united him to himself, allowed the Devil to persuade him that all he did was in vain, as he was already condemned in the eternal decrees of God. The darkness and spiritual dryness in which God was pleased at the same time to leave him caused the temptation to have greater power over the heart of the holy youth. Indeed, it reached such a pitch that his fears and interior desolation took away his appetite, deprived him of sleep, and made him pale and melancholy.

One evening Francis entered a church and saw a plaque hanging on the wall with the well-known prayer called the *Memorare*: "Remember, O most pious Virgin Mary, that never has it been heard of in any age, that anyone having recourse to your protection was abandoned." Falling on his knees before the altar of the Mother of God, he recited the prayer with tender fervor, renewed his vow of chastity, promised to say the Rosary every day, and then added: "My Mother, if I am so unfortunate as not to be able to love my Lord in the next world, whom I know to be so worthy of love, at least obtain that I may love him in this world as much as possible."

Having thus addressed the Blessed Virgin, he cast himself into the arms of divine mercy, and resigned himself entirely to the will of God. Scarcely had he finished his prayer when in an instant he was delivered from his temptation by his most sweet mother. He immediately regained the peace of his soul, and with it his bodily health.

—St. Alphonsus Liguori, *The Glories of Mary*

IN GOD'S PRESENCE, CONSIDER . . .

What does it say about St. Francis de Sales that he would pray for the grace to love Jesus in this world even if, in his despair, he couldn't hope for heaven? Could I pray such a prayer?

CLOSING PRAYER

From the *Memorare*: *Inspired by this confidence, I fly unto thee, O Virgin of virgins, my Mother; to thee do I come, before thee I stand, sinful and sorrowful. O Mother of the Word incarnate, despise not my petitions, but in thy mercy hear and answer me.*

St. Dominic and the rosary

St. Louis de Montfort was famous for his zeal for the Rosary, called the "angelic psalter" because of the greeting of the angel Gabriel at the Annunciation. Here, St. Louis tells us how Our Lady appeared to St. Dominic, giving him the rosary as we have it today.

St. Dominic, seeing that the gravity of people's sins was hindering the conversion of the Albigensian heretics, withdrew into a forest near Toulouse, where he prayed unceasingly for three days and three nights. During this time he did nothing but weep and do harsh penances in order to appease the anger of almighty God. He used his discipline so much that his body was lacerated.

At this point Our Lady appeared to him, accompanied by three angels, and she said, "Dear Dominic, do you know which weapon the Blessed Trinity wants to use to reform the world?"

"My Lady," answered Dominic, "you know far better than I do, because next to your Son Jesus Christ, you've always been the chief instrument of our salvation."

Then Our Lady replied, "I want you to know that, in this kind of warfare, the battering ram has always been the angelic psalter, which is the foundation stone of the New Testament. So if you want to reach these hardened souls and win them over to God, preach my psalter."

So he arose, comforted, and burning with zeal for the conversion of the people in that district, he made straight for the cathedral. At once, unseen angels rang the bells to gather the people together, and St. Dominic began to preach.

—St. Louis De Montfort, *The Secret of the Rosary*

IN GOD'S PRESENCE, CONSIDER . . .

Have I discovered the power that lies in praying the Rosary? If not, what plan could I make to begin praying it on a regular basis?

CLOSING PRAYER

Hail Mary, full of grace, the Lord is with you; blessed are you among women, and blessed is the fruit of your womb, Jesus. Holy Mary, Mother of God, pray for us sinners, now and at the hour of our death.

St. Dominic confronts demons with the Rosary

St. Alphonsus recalls the story of a demon-possessed man who misled the people by his false religious teaching. When he confronted St. Dominic, he was liberated from the evil spirits by the power of the Rosary.

The Rosary is a powerful weapon against the demons.

St. Dominic was once preaching in the town of Carcassone in France. A heretic there, who had publicly ridiculed the devotion of the Rosary and was possessed by demons, was brought to him. The saint demanded that the evil spirits declare publicly whether the things that Dominic had preached about the most holy Rosary were true.

Howling, they replied, "Listen, Christians! All that this enemy of ours has said about Mary, and about the most holy Rosary, is true." They also said that they had no power against the servants of Mary; and that many, by invoking in death the name of Mary, were saved, despite what they might otherwise have deserved.

The demons concluded: "We are forced to declare that no one is lost who perseveres in devotion to Mary and in devotion to the most holy Rosary. For Mary obtains for those who are sinners true repentance before they die."

St. Dominic then made the people recite the Rosary. And what a miracle took place! At every Hail Mary, many evil spirits left the body of the possessed man, appearing like red-hot coals as they went out. When the Rosary was finished, he was entirely freed. On this occasion, many heretics were converted.

—St. Alphonsus Liguori, *The Glories of Mary*

IN GOD'S PRESENCE, CONSIDER . . .

Have I found that praying the Rosary keeps the Enemy of my soul at bay? Does this incident from St. Dominic's life encourage me to pray the Rosary more fervently?

CLOSING PRAYER

From a "Prayer to the Queen of the Most Holy Rosary": *Queen of the Most Holy Rosary, in these times of such brazen impiety, manifest your power with the signs of your ancient victories, and from your throne, from which you distribute pardon and graces, mercifully regard the Church of your Son.*

The Joyful Mysteries

Blessed Bartolo Longo, a convert from Satanism who became a Third Order lay Dominican, was called the "Apostle of the Rosary." Some of his writings form the basis for the Luminous Mysteries of the Rosary established by Pope St. John Paul II. Here are his prayers for the Joyful Mysteries.

First Joyful Mystery: The Annunciation. O Mary, immaculate lily, through the joy you felt when at the angel's message you became the Mother of God: Obtain for me the virtue of purity and of humility, that I may become your worthy son [daughter] and the brother [sister] of Jesus.

Second Joyful Mystery: The Visitation. O Mary, mother of grace and of charity, through the joy you felt when, upon visiting Elizabeth, you brought joy to the home of Zechariah and the Baptist was sanctified at the sound of your voice: Visit my soul, let it hear your motherly voice, and fill it with love of God and love of neighbor.

Third Joyful Mystery: The Nativity. O Mary, mirror of humility and of poverty, through the joy you felt when, turned away by the inhabitants of Bethlehem and forced to take refuge in a stable from the cold and darkness, you gave birth to the divine Redeemer: Grant that by accepting scorn and poverty I remain faithful to grace and gain the reward of eternal salvation by means of good works.

Fourth Joyful Mystery: The Presentation. O Mary, the perfect model of obedience and of sacrifice, you who offered Jesus to the Eternal Father on our behalf: Place your Child upon my bosom so that, together with you, I may offer him the sacrifice of my passions and of my whole being.

Fifth Joyful Mystery: The Finding of Jesus. O Mary, a shining example of patience, through the joy you felt when, after three days of anxiously searching, you found Jesus in the temple: Grant that I too, seeking Jesus with love in every moment of my life in imitation of you, may find him at last in your arms at the hour of my death, never to lose him again.

—Blessed Bartolo Longo

IN GOD'S PRESENCE, CONSIDER . . .

Which of the petitions in these prayers most deeply resonate with my current spiritual needs and longings? Which of the mysteries bring me the most joy today?

CLOSING PRAYER

From a prayer of Blessed Bartolo: *O blessed Rosary of Mary, sweet chain which unites us to God, bond of love which unites us to the angels, tower of salvation against the assaults of hell, safe port in our universal shipwreck, we will never abandon you.*

The Rosary rescues a wicked nobleman from hell

St. Dominic once prayed for a wicked nobleman to be converted, and God intervened. When the man began praying the Rosary, his heart was transformed. St. Alphonsus tells the story.

In Saragossa, Spain, there was once a nobleman named Peter. He was a relative of St. Dominic, but he was a most wicked man. One day when the saint was preaching he saw Peter enter the church, so he begged our Lord to reveal the state of that miserable sinner to the congregation.

Suddenly, Peter's appearance changed so that he looked like a monster from hell, surrounded and dragged about by many demons. Everyone in the church, even his wife and the servants who accompanied him, fled away.

St. Dominic then sent word to Peter that he should entrust himself to Mary and begin to pray the Rosary. He also sent Peter a rosary with which to pray.

When Peter received the message, he humbled himself and sent someone to thank the saint. Then he himself was given the grace to see the demons who surrounded him. Peter then confessed his sins with many tears to St. Dominic, from whom he received the assurance that they were already forgiven.

Peter persevered in saying the Rosary. He became so holy that one day in church, in the presence of the whole congregation, our Lord allowed them to see him crowned with a triple crown of roses.

—St. Alphonsus Liguori, *The Glories of Mary*

IN GOD'S PRESENCE, CONSIDER . . .

When I pray the Rosary, do I have as one of my intentions my own continuing conversion?

CLOSING PRAYER

From a prayer of St. Thomas Aquinas: *O Mary, my Queen, my hope, and my Mother! I love you; I confide in you. I beg you by the love of Jesus, obtain from God for me a great sorrow for my sins and pardon for them, perseverance in a good life, and a pure love toward God with a perfect conformity to his holy will.*

The benefits of the Rosary

Pope Leo XIII, known as "the Pope of the Rosary," surveys the many ways in which praying the Rosary strengthens our spiritual life.

Now, among the various rites and ways of paying honor to the Blessed Mary, some are to be preferred, inasmuch as we know them to be most powerful and most pleasing to our mother. For this reason, we specially mention by name and recommend the Rosary. The common language has given the name of corona, or crown, to this manner of prayer, which recalls to our minds the great mysteries of Jesus and Mary united in joys, sorrows, and triumphs.

The contemplation of these august mysteries, contemplated in their order, affords to faithful souls a wonderful confirmation of faith, protection against the disease of error, and increase of the strength of the soul. The soul and memory of those who pray this way, enlightened by faith, are drawn towards these mysteries by the sweetest devotion, are absorbed in it, and marvel to see the work of the redemption of mankind, achieved at such a price and by events so great.

The soul is filled with gratitude and love before these proofs of divine love. Its hope becomes enlarged. And its desire is increased for those things that Christ has prepared for all who have united themselves to him through imitation of his example and participation in his sufferings.

The prayer is composed of words proceeding from God himself, from the archangel Gabriel, and from the Church, full of praise and of high desires. And it is renewed and continued in an order at once fixed and varying; its fruits are ever new and sweet.

—Pope Leo XIII, *Octobri Mense*

IN GOD'S PRESENCE, CONSIDER . . .

Pope Leo XIII promises that praying the Rosary will increase our faith, hope, love, gratitude, and understanding. If I pray the Rosary regularly, can I discern an increase in these virtues in myself because of this devotion? If I don't pray the Rosary regularly, does the possibility of such spiritual growth convince me that I should do so more often?

CLOSING PRAYER

From a "Prayer to Our Lady of the Rosary": *Grant, O Virgin Mary, that the study of your mysteries may form in my soul, little by little, a luminous atmosphere, pure, strengthening, and fragrant, which may penetrate my understanding, my will, my heart, my memory, my imagination, my whole being.*

The Rosary makes the creed into a prayer

If you want to ponder and pray the great truths of the Creed, says Blessed John Henry Newman, take up your beads.

It is difficult to know God by your own power, because he is incomprehensible. He is invisible to begin with, and therefore incomprehensible. We can in some way know him, for even among the pagans there were some who had learned many truths about him; but even they found it hard to conform their lives to their knowledge of him. And so in his mercy he has given us a revelation of himself by coming among us, to be one of ourselves, with all the relations and qualities of humanity, to gain us over. He came down from heaven and dwelt among us and died for us. All these things are in the Creed, which contains the chief things that he has revealed to us about himself.

Now the great power of the Rosary lies in this, that it makes the Creed into a prayer. Of course, the Creed is in some sense a prayer and a great act of homage to God; but the Rosary gives us the great truths of his life and death to meditate upon, and brings them nearer to our hearts. And so we contemplate all the great mysteries of his life and his birth in the manger; and so too the mysteries of his suffering and his glorified life.

But even Christians, with all their knowledge of God, have usually more awe than love of him. The special virtue of the Rosary lies in the special way in which it looks at these mysteries; for with all our thoughts of him are mingled thoughts of his mother, and in the relations between mother and Son we have set before us the Holy Family, the home in which God lived. Now the family is, even humanly considered, a sacred thing; how much more the family bound together by supernatural ties and, above all, that in which God dwelt with his Blessed Mother.

—Blessed John Henry Newman,
"Meditation for the Feast of the Holy Rosary"

IN GOD'S PRESENCE, CONSIDER . . .

In Blessed John's day, he insisted, Christians usually had "more awe than love of God." Is the reverse perhaps the case today? Do I tend to have more love than awe toward God? If so, how might praying the Rosary mysteries increase my awe?

CLOSING PRAYER

Mary, teach me both to love God and to fear him, as your blessed Son instructs us (see Mt 22:37; Lk 12:5). Let my fear keep me on the right path, and my love draw me on to him.

The power of the Rosary

There are many ways to approach Mary, Venerable Pope Pius XII notes. But the Rosary holds a special place in Marian devotion, for several important reasons.

We well know the Rosary's powerful efficacy to obtain the maternal aid of the Virgin. By no means is there only one way to pray to obtain this aid. However, we consider the holy Rosary the most convenient and most fruitful means, as is clearly suggested by the very origin of this practice, heavenly rather than human, and by its nature.

What prayers are better adapted and more beautiful than the Lord's Prayer and the angelic salutation, which are the flowers with which this mystical crown is formed? With meditation on the sacred mysteries added to the vocal prayers, there emerges another very great advantage, so that all, even the most simple and least educated, have in this a prompt and easy way to nourish and preserve their own faith.

Truly, from the frequent meditation on the mysteries, the soul little by little and subtly draws and absorbs the virtues they contain, is wondrously enkindled with a longing for things immortal, and becomes strongly and easily impelled to follow the path that Christ himself and his mother have followed. The recitation of identical formulas repeated so many times, rather than rendering the prayer sterile and boring, has on the contrary the admirable quality of infusing confidence in him who prays and brings to bear a gentle compulsion on the motherly heart of Mary.

—Venerable Pope Pius XII, *Ingruentium Malorum*

IN GOD'S PRESENCE, CONSIDER . . .

Do I find myself sometimes feeling that, as Pope Pius says, the recitation of prayers in the Rosary is "sterile and boring"? How might I be able to refresh my appreciation of this devotion, so that instead my soul, "little by little and subtly," absorbs the virtues contained in the mysteries?

CLOSING PRAYER

Pray for us, O holy Mother of God, that we may be made worthy of the promises of Christ!

A sinner is converted through the Rosary

St. Alphonsus relates an incident in the life of St. Dominic that demonstrates the power of the Rosary.

In Rome, during the time of St. Dominic, a woman by the name of "Catherine the Fair" was leading a most disorderly life. She once heard the saint preaching on the devotion of the Rosary, had her name enrolled in the confraternity, and began to recite it. But she didn't change her way of living.

One evening a young man of noble appearance came to visit her. She received him with courtesy. But while they were at supper, as he was cutting bread, drops of blood fell from his hands. Then she saw that there was blood on all the food he took. She asked him what was the meaning of this. The young man replied, "The food of a Christian should be tinged with the blood of Jesus Christ, and seasoned with the remembrance of his passion." Astonished at such an answer, Catherine asked him who he was. "Later," he said, "I will tell you."

As they went into an adjoining room, the young man's appearance changed: He was crowned with thorns, and his flesh was all mangled and torn. He said: "You desire to know who I am? Don't you recognize me? I am your Redeemer. Catherine, when will you cease offending me? See what I have endured for you. You have now tormented me enough; change your life."

Catherine burst into sobs and tears, and Jesus, encouraging her, said: "Love me now as much as you have offended me. And know that I have granted you this grace on account of the Rosary you have recited in honor of my mother." Then he disappeared.

On the next morning Catherine went to St. Dominic to Confession, distributed all she had to the poor, and ever afterwards led so holy a life that she attained a very high degree of perfection.

—St. Alphonsus Liguori, *The Glories of Mary*

IN GOD'S PRESENCE, CONSIDER . . .

If I've been praying the Rosary, can I recall occasions when I saw prayers powerfully answered through my practice of this devotion?

CLOSING PRAYER

From a "Prayer to Our Lady of the Rosary": *O Virgin Mary, grant that the recitation of your Rosary may be for me each day, in the midst of my manifold duties, a bond of unity in my actions, a tribute of filial piety, a sweet refreshment, and an encouragement to walk joyfully along the path of duty.*

Approach Mary confidently through the Rosary

Pope Leo XIII invites us to pray the Rosary with a childlike confidence in the Blessed Mother's assistance.

Nature itself made the name of mother the sweetest of all names and has made motherhood the very model of tender and solicitous love. Yet no tongue is eloquent enough to put in words what every devout soul feels, namely, how intense is the flame of affectionate and active charity which glows in Mary, in her who is truly our mother—not in a human way, but through Christ.

Nobody knows and comprehends so well as she does everything that concerns us: what helps we need in life; what dangers, public or private, threaten our welfare; what difficulties and evils surround us; above all, how fierce is the fight we wage with ruthless enemies of our salvation. In these and in all other troubles of life, her power is most far-reaching. Her desire to use it is most ardent to bring consolation, strength, and help of every kind to children who are dear to her.

Accordingly, let's approach Mary confidently, wholeheartedly begging her by the bonds of her motherhood that unite her so closely to Jesus and at the same time to us. Let's with deepest devotion invoke her constant aid in the Rosary, the prayer that she herself has indicated and which is most acceptable to her. Then with good reason shall we rest with an easy and joyous mind under the protection of the best of mothers.

—Pope Leo XIII, *Magnae Dei Matris*

IN GOD'S PRESENCE, CONSIDER . . .

Do I ever grow weary repeating the prayers in the Rosary? Little children delight in repeating words and phrases, relishing them each time. How might approaching the Rosary like a little child change my experience of this devotion?

CLOSING PRAYER

From a prayer of St. Bernard of Clairvaux: *To you we cry, Queen of Mercy! Turn to us, so that we may behold you distributing graces, bestowing remedies, giving strength. Show us your compassionate face, and we shall be saved.*

Mary speaks to us in the Rosary

Pope Leo XIII suggests that if we meditate carefully on the mysteries of the Rosary, Mary herself will seem to be speaking to us through them.

To ward off the extremely great dangers of ignorance from her children, the Church, which never relaxes her vigilant and diligent care, has been in the habit of looking for the most firm support of faith in the Rosary of Mary. And indeed in the Rosary, along with the most beautiful and effective prayer arranged in an orderly pattern, the chief mysteries of our religion follow one another, as they are brought before our mind for contemplation.

First of all are the mysteries in which the Word was made flesh, and Mary, the inviolate virgin and mother, performed her maternal duties for him with a holy joy. There come then the sorrows, the agony, and the death of the suffering Christ, the price at which the salvation of our race was accomplished. Then follow the mysteries full of his glory: his triumph over death, his ascension into heaven, the sending of the Holy Spirit, the resplendent brightness of Mary received among the stars, and finally the everlasting glory of all the saints in heaven united with the glory of the mother and her Son.

This uninterrupted sequence of wonderful events the Rosary frequently and perseveringly recalls and presents to the minds of the faithful, almost as though they were unfolding before our eyes. This flooding of the souls of those who devoutly recite it, with a sweetness of piety that never grows weary, impresses and stirs them as though they were listening to the very voice of the Blessed Mother explaining the mysteries and conversing with them at length about their salvation. It will not, then, seem too much to say that in places, families, and nations in which the Rosary of Mary retains its ancient honor, the loss of faith through ignorance and vicious error need not be feared.

—Pope Leo XIII, *Magnae Dei Matris*

IN GOD'S PRESENCE, CONSIDER . . .

When I ponder deeply the scenes in Mary's life depicted in the mysteries of the Rosary, do they come alive to me? Do I find myself discovering new insights into the hearts of Jesus and Mary?

CLOSING PRAYER

Grant, we beseech thee, that while meditating on these mysteries of the most holy Rosary of the Blessed Virgin Mary, we may imitate what they contain and obtain what they promise, through Christ our Lord.

Pray the Rosary for peace

In 1969, when multiple wars were raging around the globe, Blessed Pope Paul VI issued the apostolic exhortation Recurrens Mensis October *to encourage Catholics to pray the Rosary. His stated prayer intention was peace—an intention that must be perennial in our fallen world.*

We invite the entire Christian people once more to the practice of a form of prayer which is rightly dear to Catholic piety, and which has lost none of its importance amid the difficulties of the present day. We are speaking of the Rosary of the Blessed Virgin Mary. The intention which we would propose this year to all our sons and daughters, since it seems to us more serious and urgent than ever, is that of peace among men and among peoples. . . .

Prayer, by which we ask for the gift of peace, is . . . an irreplaceable contribution to the establishment of peace. It is through Christ, in whom all grace is given us, that we dispose ourselves to welcome the gift of peace. And in that undertaking, how can we do otherwise than to depend lovingly upon the incomparable intercession of Mary, his mother, of whom the Gospel tell us that she "found favor with God" (Lk 1:30)?

It is the humble virgin of Nazareth who became mother of the Prince of Peace, of him who was born under the sign of peace, and who proclaimed to the whole world: "Blessed are the peacemakers, for they shall be called sons of God" (Mt 5:9). The Gospel teaches us that Mary is sensitive to the needs of men. At Cana, she did not hesitate to intervene, to the joy of the villagers invited to a wedding feast (see Jn 2:1–11). How, then, would she not intervene in favor of peace, that precious possession, if we only pray to her with a sincere heart?

—Blessed Pope Paul VI, *Recurrens Mensis October*

IN GOD'S PRESENCE, CONSIDER . . .

Have I ever prayed the Rosary specifically for peace in the world? Given so many conflicts around the world, could I invite others to join me in that prayer?

CLOSING PRAYER

From a prayer of Pope St. John Paul II: *Mother of Mercy and of hope, obtain for the men and women of the third millennium the precious gift of peace: peace in hearts and families, in communities and among peoples; peace above all for those nations where people fight and die every day. . . . O Mary, Queen of peace, give us Christ, the world's true peace!*

The graces of the family Rosary

Praying the Rosary as a family remains a popular household devotion, full of graces. But Venerable Pope Pius XII knows that busy families sometimes need encouragement to lay aside other concerns and turn to Our Lady together.

We affirm that the custom of the family recitation of the holy Rosary is a most effective means. What a sweet sight, most pleasing to God, when in the evening the Christian home resounds with the frequent repetition of praises in honor of the august Queen of Heaven! Then the Rosary, recited in common, assembles before the image of the Virgin, in an admirable union of hearts, the parents and their children, who come back from their daily work. It unites them piously with those absent and those dead. It links all more tightly in a sweet bond of love, with the most holy Virgin who, like a loving mother, in the circle of her children, will be there bestowing upon them an abundance of the gifts of harmony and family peace.

Then the home of the Christian family, like that of Nazareth, will become an earthly dwelling place of sanctity and, so to speak, a sacred temple. There, the holy Rosary will not only be the particular prayer that every day rises to heaven in an aroma of sweetness, but will also form the most effective school of Christian discipline and Christian virtue. This meditation on the divine mysteries of the Redemption will teach the adults to admire daily the shining examples of Jesus and Mary, and to draw from these examples comfort in adversity, striving towards those heavenly treasures "where no thief approaches nor moth destroys" (Lk 12:33).

This meditation will bring to the knowledge of the little ones the main truths of the Christian faith, making love for the Redeemer blossom almost spontaneously in their innocent hearts. While seeing their parents kneeling before the majesty of God, they will learn from their very early years how great before the throne of God is the value of prayers said in common.

—Venerable Pope Pius XII, *Ingruentium Malorum*

IN GOD'S PRESENCE, CONSIDER . . .

Do I pray the Rosary regularly with my family? If I live alone, do I encourage families I know to pray the Rosary together?

CLOSING PRAYER

From a prayer of Francis Cardinal Spellman: *O Queen of Homes, by the power of the Rosary we beseech you to embrace all the members of our family in the love of your immaculate heart. May you abide with us, and we with you, praying to you while you pray for us.*

A young man is freed of immoral habits

St. Alphonsus tells a story that illustrates how even a small daily habit of devotion to Mary, faithfully practiced, bears wonderful and lasting fruit.

An event recorded by Fr. Paul Segneri, in the work entitled Christian Instructed, is rightly well known. A young man of immoral habits, and laden with sins, went to Confession to Fr. Nicholas Zucchi in Rome. The confessor received him with charity.

Filled with compassion for the young man's unfortunate state, the priest assured him that devotion to our Blessed Lady could deliver him from the accursed vice to which he was addicted. So he gave him as his penance the instruction to say a Hail Mary to the Blessed Virgin every morning and evening, when getting up and when going to bed, until his next Confession. At the same time, he was to offer her his eyes, his hands, and his whole body, begging her to preserve them as something belonging to herself. He was also to kiss the ground three times.

The young man performed the penance, but at first there was only a slight change in his habits. Fr. Zucchi, however, continued to impress on him to maintain the new devotional practice, urging him never to abandon it. At the same time, he encouraged him to trust in the assistance of Mary.

In the meantime, the penitent left Rome with other companions, and for the next few years travelled in various parts of the world. When he returned, he once again sought out his confessor. Fr. Zucchi, to his great joy and admiration, found that the young man was entirely changed, and free from his former evil habits.

"My son," the priest asked, "how have you obtained from God so wonderful a change?"

The young man replied: "Father, our Blessed Lady obtained this grace for me through that little devotion that you taught me."

—St. Alphonsus Liguori, *The Glories of Mary*

IN GOD'S PRESENCE, CONSIDER . . .

Are there vices in my life I need to conquer? Might this simple daily devotion help me to overcome it?

CLOSING PRAYER

"How can a young man keep his way pure? By guarding it according to your word. Turn my eyes away from looking at vanities, and give me life in your ways" (Ps 119:9:10).

A salutation to Mary

This prayer was composed by St. John Eudes, a French missionary and priest who founded the Congregation of Jesus and Mary. A copy of it was found in a book belonging to St. Margaret Mary after her death.

Hail Mary, daughter of God the Father! Hail Mary, mother of God the Son!

Hail Mary, spouse of God the Holy Spirit!

Hail Mary, temple of the Most Blessed Trinity!

Hail Mary, pure lily of the radiant Trinity!

Hail Mary, celestial rose of the ineffable love of God!

Hail Mary, virgin pure and humble, of whom the King of heaven willed to be born, and with your milk to be nourished!

Hail Mary, virgin of virgins! Hail Mary, Queen of Martyrs, whose soul a sword pierced through!

Hail Mary, Lady most blessed, to whom all power in heaven and earth is given!

Hail Mary, my Queen and my Mother, my life, my sweetness, and my hope!

Hail Mary, mother most lovable! Hail Mary, mother most admirable!

Hail Mary, mother of divine Love! Hail Mary, immaculate, conceived without sin!

Hail Mary, full of grace, the Lord is with you! Blessed are you among women, and blessed is the fruit of your womb, Jesus!

—St. John Eudes

IN GOD'S PRESENCE, CONSIDER . . .

St. John has taken the first words of the angel and elaborated richly on Mary's attributes. If you were to write a similar salutation, how would you address her? Which of her titles and attributes would you be sure to include?

CLOSING PRAYER

From a prayer of St. John Eudes: *O glorious Virgin Mary, may all men love and praise you. Holy Mary, Mother of God, pray for us and bless us, now, and at death, in the name of Jesus, your divine Son!*

An aqueduct flowing with grace

St. Alphonsus reminds us that Jesus is the Source of grace, while Mary is its channel.

St. Anselm says, "There is no one who does not partake of the grace of Mary. Who was ever found to whom the Blessed Virgin wasn't kind? Who is there whom her mercy doesn't reach?"

We must understand, of course, that Jesus is the One from whom we receive grace as the Author of grace; grace comes through Mary as a mediatrix. Grace comes from Jesus as a Savior, but through Mary as an advocate. It comes from Jesus as its Source, but through Mary as a channel.

For this reason, St. Bernard says that God established Mary as the channel of the mercies that he wished to distribute to men. He filled her with grace, so that that each one's share might be communicated to him from her fullness, as a full aqueduct. Miserable is the soul that closes this channel of grace against itself, by neglecting to entrust itself to Mary!

When the Devil wishes to become master of a soul, he causes her to give up devotion to the most Blessed Virgin Mary. Once this channel is closed, she easily loses supernatural light, the fear of God, and finally eternal salvation.

—St. Alphonsus Liguori, *The Glories of Mary*

IN GOD'S PRESENCE, CONSIDER . . .

What does it mean for me that God has filled Mary with grace? If I am seeking God's grace for my life, do I turn to her as a channel of that grace?

CLOSING PRAYER

From a prayer of St. Athanasius: *Mary, the archangel saluted you, and called you full of grace. We also address you, saying: Hail, full of grace, our Lord is with you; pray for us, O holy Mother of God, Our Lady and our Queen.*

Now and at the hour of our death

St. Alphonsus illuminates the last phrase of the Hail Mary.

"A friend loves at all times, and a brother is born for adversity," says the Book of Proverbs (17:17). We can never know our friends and relations in the time of prosperity; it is only in the time of adversity that we see them in their true colors. People of the world never abandon a friend as long as he is in prosperity; but should misfortunes overtake him, and more particularly should he be at the point of death, they immediately forsake him.

But Mary doesn't act that way with those who turn to her. In their afflictions, and more particularly in the sorrows of death, the greatest that can be endured in this world, this good Lady and mother doesn't abandon her faithful servants. Instead, just as during our exile she is our life, so also is she at our last hour our sweetness, by obtaining for us a calm and happy death.

From the day on which Mary had the privilege and sorrow of being present at the death of Jesus her Son, who was the Head of all those who are predestined, it became her privilege to assist at their deaths as well. And for this reason the holy Church teaches us to beg this most Blessed Virgin to assist us, especially at the moment of death: "Pray for us sinners, now and at the hour of our death!"

—St. Alphonsus Liguori, *The Glories of Mary*

IN GOD'S PRESENCE, CONSIDER . . .

What would it mean to have a "happy death"? How can I be preparing myself for such a death?

CLOSING PRAYER

From a prayer of St. Thomas Aquinas: *Mary, receive me as your servant, and as your servant protect me always, and especially at the time of my death. You with your powerful intercession must save me; this is my hope, thus may it be!*

Call on Jesus and Mary at death

St. Alphonsus encourages us to turn with confidence to Jesus and Mary in the hour of our death.

Richard of Saint Lawrence affirms that "the devout invocation of the sweet and holy name of Mary leads to the reception of superabundant graces in this life, and a very high degree of glory in the next." "If then, brothers," concludes Thomas à Kempis, "you desire consolation in every labor, turn to Mary. Invoke the name of Mary, honor Mary, entrust yourselves to Mary, rejoice with Mary, weep with Mary, pray with Mary, walk with Mary, seek Jesus with Mary. In short, desire to live and die with Jesus and Mary. By acting this way you'll always advance in the ways of God, for Mary will most willingly pray for you, and the Son will most certainly grant all that his mother asks."

So we see that the most holy name of Mary is sweet indeed to her devotees during life, because of the very great graces she obtains for them. But sweeter still will it be to them in death, because of the tranquil and holy end that it will ensure them. For this name of life and hope, when repeated at the hour of death, is enough to put the demons to flight, and to comfort such persons in their sufferings.

St. Camillus also urged his religious brothers, in the strongest terms, to remind the dying to invoke the names of Jesus and Mary frequently. This was his own custom when caring for others, and how sweetly he practiced it himself on his deathbed. For then he pronounced the beloved names of Jesus and Mary with such tenderness that he enflamed even those who heard him with love. In the end, with his eyes fixed on their venerated images, and his arms in the form of a cross, the saint breathed forth his soul with an air of holiness and in the midst of heavenly peace.

—St. Alphonsus Liguori, *The Glories of Mary*

IN GOD'S PRESENCE, CONSIDER . . .

Have I given much thought to my last moments on earth, and how I hope to spend them? Am I sending prayers ahead to that final hour, even now, by praying the Rosary?

CLOSING PRAYER

From a prayer of St. Alphonsus: *O my sweet Lady and mother, I love you so much, and because I love you, I also love your holy name. I intend and hope, with your help, always to invoke it during life and at death.*

A tender mother in the hour of death

St. Alphonsus recalls the story of a woman to whom Mary herself attended on her death bed.

How great is the tenderness of this good mother, Mary, toward her children at death!

The parish priest of a country place was assisting a certain rich man who was dying, in a magnificent house, and attended by servants, relatives, and friends. But the good priest saw also demons, in the shape of dogs, waiting to carry off his soul, as they in fact did. For he died in sin.

In the meantime, a poor woman was also ill. Desiring to receive the holy sacraments, she sent for the parish priest. But he, being unable to leave the rich man whose soul stood in such need of assistance, sent her another priest. That priest immediately went, carrying the pix that contained the Most Blessed Sacrament.

On his arrival, he saw neither servants, nor attendants, nor fine furniture; for the sick woman was poor, and perhaps lying only on a little straw. But he saw a great light in the room, and near the bed of the dying woman was the Mother of God. Mary was consoling her, and with a cloth in her hand, wiping off the sweat of death.

The priest, seeing Mary, feared to enter. But the Blessed Virgin gestured to him to come in. The priest entered, and Mary showed him a stool, so that he might be seated to hear the Confession of her servant. This he did, and after the woman had received Holy Communion with great devotion, she happily breathed forth her soul in the arms of Mary.

—St. Alphonsus Liguori, *The Glories of Mary*

IN GOD'S PRESENCE, CONSIDER . . .

If my soul were to leave this world today, would I be more like the poor woman in this story, or the rich man?

CLOSING PRAYER

From "Prayer to Our Mother of Sorrows for a Happy Death": *O Mother of Sorrows, obtain for me the grace to receive Holy Communion with most perfect love and contrition before my death, and to breathe forth my soul in the presence of Jesus.*

Mary defends the soul at death

St. Alphonsus reports that demon tempters sometimes assail Christians in their dying moments. But Mary is faithful to dispatch angels for their defense.

How quickly do the rebellious spirits fly from the presence of this queen! If at the hour of death we have only the protection of Mary, what need we fear from the whole of our infernal enemies? When Fr. Emmanuel Padial, of the Society of Jesus, was at the point of death, Mary appeared to him. To console him, she said: "See, at last the hour is come when the angels congratulate you and exclaim: 'O happy labors, O mortifications well rewarded!'" And in the same moment, an army of demons was seen taking its flight, and crying out in despair: "Alas! We can do nothing, for she who is without stain defends him!"

In a similar way, Father Gaspar Haywood was assaulted by demons at his death, and greatly tempted to lose his faith. He immediately entrusted himself to the most Blessed Virgin, and he was heard to exclaim, "I thank you, Mary; for you have come to my aid!" Mary not only assists her beloved servants at death and encourages them, but she herself accompanies them to the tribunal seat of God. As St. Jerome says, writing to the Virgin Eustochia, "What a day of joy will that be for you, when Mary, the mother of our Lord, accompanied by choirs of Virgins, will go to meet you!"

St. Bonaventure tells us that Mary sends without delay the prince of the heavenly court, St. Michael, with all the angels, to defend her dying servants against the temptations of the demons, and to receive the souls of all who in a special way and with perseverance have entrusted themselves to her. The Blessed Virgin assured St. Bridget of this. Speaking of her devoted servants at the point of death, she said, "Then will I, their dear Lady and mother, fly to them, that they may have consolation and refreshment."

—St. Alphonsus Liguori, *The Glories of Mary*

IN GOD'S PRESENCE, CONSIDER . . .

Am I aware that the angels have been sent to defend me, not only when I die, but throughout my life? Do I thank my guardian angel and St. Michael for their assistance?

CLOSING PRAYER

From a prayer of St. Bonaventure: *Michael, the leader and prince of the heavenly army, with all the administering spirits, obeys your commands, O Virgin, and defends and receives the souls of the faithful who have specifically entrusted themselves to you, O Lady, day and night.*

Prayer for a happy death

St. Alphonsus asks Our Lady to remember that when she left this world, she promised not to forget us. He asks for a happy death so that he can be united with her and her Son in heaven.

Most sweet Lady and our mother, you've already left the earth and reached your kingdom. There, as queen, you're enthroned above all the choirs of angels, as the Church sings in her liturgy: "She is exalted above the choirs of angels in the celestial kingdom."

We well know that we sinners aren't worthy to possess you in this valley of darkness. But we also know that you, in your greatness, have never forgotten us miserable creatures. Though you have been exalted to such great glory, yet you have never lost compassion for us poor children of Adam. Instead, it has even increased in you.

Mary, from the high throne, then, to which you are exalted, turn your compassionate eyes upon us, and pity us. Remember too that in leaving this world, you promised not to forget us. Look at us and help us.

See what storms and dangers constantly surround us, and will surround us until the end of our lives. By the merits of your happy death, obtain for us a holy perseverance in our friendship with God, so that we may finally leave this life in God's grace. In this way, we too will one day come to kiss your feet in paradise, and join the blessed spirits in praising you and singing your glories as you deserve.

—St. Alphonsus Liguori, *The Glories of Mary*

IN GOD'S PRESENCE, CONSIDER . . .

Talk about death is strenuously avoided in our culture, but the reality of death remains. Am I willing to risk having an uncomfortable conversation by encouraging my loved ones to pray for a happy death?

CLOSING PRAYER

From "The Seven Dolors of Mary at the Death of Jesus": *O holy Virgin, I beg you that, at my departure from this world, you would turn your merciful eyes toward me, so that in my last agony I may be consoled and strengthened by the light of your face.*

Mary doesn't abandon her devotees at death

We can learn an important lesson, St. Alphonsus tells us, from the story of how St. John of God spent his last moments.

How quickly do the rebellious spirits fly from the presence of this queen! If at the hour of death we have only the protection of Mary, what do we need to fear from all our hellish enemies? O God, what a consolation it will be at that last moment of our lives, when our eternal destiny is so soon to be decided, to see the Queen of Heaven assisting and consoling us with the assurance of her protection.

St. John of God, who was tenderly devoted to Mary, fully expected that she would visit him on his deathbed. So when he didn't see her come to him as he lay dying, he was distressed, and perhaps even complained. But when his last hour had come, the Mother of God appeared and gently reproved him for his lack of confidence.

She addressed him in these tender words, which should encourage all servants of Mary: "John, it is not in me to forsake my devotees at such a moment." It was as though she had said: "John, what were you thinking? Did you imagine that I had abandoned you? And don't you know that I never abandon my devotees at the hour of death?

"If I didn't come sooner, it was because your time had not yet come. But now that it has come, see that I'm here to take you. Let's go to heaven." Shortly afterward, the saint breathed his last and fled to that blessed kingdom, there to thank his most loving queen for all eternity. So let's be of good heart, even though we're sinners, and feel confident that Mary will come and assist us at death, and comfort and console us with her presence—provided only that we serve her with love during the remainder of the time we have in this world.

—St. Alphonsus Liguori, *The Glories of Mary*

IN GOD'S PRESENCE, CONSIDER . . .

Do I serve Mary in such a way now that I can be confident she will come and assist me at death?

CLOSING PRAYER

From a prayer of St. Alphonsus: *Mary, sweet refuge of miserable sinners, when my soul is on the point of leaving this world, drive the Enemy from hell far from me, and come and take my soul to yourself, and present it to the eternal Judge.*

Mary, the last word on our lips

St. Alphonsus recalls the words and experiences of several holy men who witnessed to the power of Mary's name when invoked at death.

"The invocation of the sacred names of Jesus and Mary," says Thomas à Kempis, "is a short prayer, which is as sweet to the mind, and as powerful to protect those who use it against the enemies of their salvation, as it is easy to remember."

"Blessed is the one who loves your name, Mary!" exclaims St. Bonaventure. "Yes, truly blessed is the one who loves your sweet name, Mother of God! For your name is so glorious and admirable, that no one who remembers it has any fears at the hour of death." Such is its power, that none of those who invoke it at the hour of death fear the assaults of their enemies.

Oh, that we may end our lives as did the Capuchin father, Fulgentius of Ascoli, who died singing, "Mary, Mary, the most beautiful of creatures! Let's depart together!" Or to die as blessed Henry the Cistercian died, who passed away in the very moment that he was pronouncing the most sweet name of Mary.

We must beg God to grant us, then, that at death the name of Mary may be the last word on our lips. This was the prayer of St. Germanus: "May the last movement of my tongue be to pronounce the name of the Mother of God." Sweet and safe is the death that's accompanied and protected by that saving name.

—St. Alphonsus Liguori, *The Glories of Mary*

IN GOD'S PRESENCE, CONSIDER . . .

Am I worried that when I am dying, the Enemy of my soul may come to tempt or harass me? In that hour I need only call out the name of Our Lady, which sends demons fleeing.

CLOSING PRAYER

From a prayer of St. Bonaventure: *Mary, come and meet my soul when it is departing from this world, and take it in your arms. Come then and comfort me with your presence. Be my soul's ladder and way to heaven. Obtain for it the grace of forgiveness and eternal rest.*

A monk calls on Mary at death

St. Alphonsus recalls how Mary helped a canon regular in his final battle with the Devil.

In the Austrian town of Reichersberg there was a canon regular named Arnold, surnamed "the Pious" because of the sanctity of his life. He had the most tender devotion to our Blessed Lady. At the point of death, he received the last sacraments, then summoned his religious brothers. He begged them not to abandon him in his last journey. Scarcely had he uttered these words, when, in the presence of all, he began to tremble and roll his eyes. Bathed in a cold sweat, with a faltering voice, he said: "Oh, don't you see the demons who are trying to drag me to hell? Brothers, implore the aid of Mary for me! In her I place my trust. She will give me the victory."

On hearing this, his brothers recited the Litany of our Blessed Lady, and as they were saying, "Holy Mary, pray for him," the dying man exclaimed, "Repeat, repeat the name of Mary! For I am already before God's tribunal." He was silent for a moment, and then said, "It is true that I did it, but I have done penance for it." Then turning to our Blessed Lady, he said, "O Mary, I will be delivered if you help me."

Again the demons attacked him. But he defended himself with his crucifix and the name of Mary. In this way was the night spent. No sooner, however, than the morning dawned, Arnold exclaimed with the greatest calmness, and full of holy joy: "Mary, my sovereign Lady, my refuge, has obtained me pardon and salvation!" Then casting his eyes on that Blessed Virgin who was inviting him to follow her, he said, "I come, O Lady, I come!" And making an effort to go with her even with his body, his soul fled after her to the realms of eternal bliss, as we trust, for he sweetly breathed his last.

—St. Alphonsus Liguori, *The Glories of Mary*

IN GOD'S PRESENCE, CONSIDER . . .

Am I aware of the spiritual battle that is ongoing for the eternal destiny of my soul? Do I recognize that Mary can be for me a great champion in this battle?

CLOSING PRAYER

From "Prayer to Our Lady of Sorrows for a Happy Death": *Dearest Mother, when the moment of my death has come, present me as your child to Jesus; say to him on my behalf: "Son, forgive him, for he knew not what he did. Receive him this day into your kingdom."*

Mercy in the hour of death

St. Alphonsus relates the deathbed conversion of a notorious sinner through the help of Our Lady.

We read in the life of Sr. Catherine of St. Augustine about a woman she knew named Mary. In her youth Mary was a sinner, and in her old age she remained so obstinate in wickedness that she was driven out of the city and lived in a secluded cave. There she died, half consumed by disease, without the sacraments.

Sr. Catherine always prayed to God with great fervor for the souls of the departed. But having heard about the unfortunate end of this poor old woman, she never thought of praying for her. She concluded (as did everyone else) that the woman was irrevocably lost. One day a suffering soul from purgatory appeared and exclaimed: "How unfortunate is my situation, Sr. Catherine! You pray for the souls of all who have died, but on my soul alone you have no compassion."

"Who are you?" asked Catherine.

"I am that poor Mary," she replied, "who died in the cave."

"Are you saved?' said Catherine.

"Yes," she answered, "by the mercy of the Blessed Virgin Mary. When I saw myself at the point of death, loaded with sins, and abandoned by all, I turned to the Mother of God. The Blessed Virgin obtained for me the grace to make an act of contrition. I died, and I am saved. I now lack only a few Masses to be entirely delivered. I beg you to have them said for me. And on my part, I promise always to pray for you." Sr. Catherine immediately had the Masses said. A few days later that soul again appeared to her, shining like the sun, and said: "Thank you, Catherine! Look! I'm going to paradise to sing the mercies of my God and to pray for you."

—St. Alphonsus Liguori, *The Glories of Mary*

IN GOD'S PRESENCE, CONSIDER . . .

Have I given up hope for the salvation of someone who seems far from God? Have I entrusted that person to Mary's intercession?

CLOSING PRAYER

Lord, we believe you when you say that you take no pleasure in the death of the wicked; you rather he would turn from his way and live (see Ez 18:23). We join our desires to yours and to those of Our Lady, who wills perfectly what you will, and seeks those who are lost so that they might return.

A prayer for favor in the hour of death

St. Alphonsus offers a powerful, beautiful prayer to Our Lady, asking for her presence when in his final struggle.

Mary, comforter of the afflicted, console a poor creature who entrusts himself to you. The remorse of a conscience overburdened with sins fills me with distress. I'm in doubt about whether I've sufficiently grieved for them. I see that all my actions are soiled and defective. Hell awaits my death in order to accuse me; the outraged justice of God demands satisfaction. My Mother, what will become of me? If you don't help me, I'm lost. What do you say: Will you assist me?

Compassionate Virgin, console me. Through your prayers, obtain for me true sorrow for my sins. Obtain for me strength to change and to be faithful to God for the rest of my life. Finally, when I'm in the last agonies of death, Mary, my hope, don't abandon me. Then, more than ever, help and encourage me, so that I won't despair at the sight of my sins, which the Evil One will then place before me.

My Lady, forgive my audacity. Come yourself to comfort me with your presence in that last struggle. This favor you have granted to many; grant it also to me. My boldness is great, but your goodness is greater, for it goes in search of those who are most miserable to console them. On this I rely.

For your eternal glory, let it be said that you've snatched a wretched creature from hell, to which he was condemned, and that you've led him to your kingdom. Yes, sweet mother, I hope to have the consolation of remaining always at your feet in heaven, thanking and blessing and loving you eternally.

—St. Alphonsus Liguori, *The Glories of Mary*

IN GOD'S PRESENCE, CONSIDER . . .

Perhaps I may have considered before which of my loved ones I hope will be present when I depart this life. Have I asked Mary to be present as well, and to intercede for me at that difficult time?

CLOSING PRAYER

From a prayer of St. Alphonsus: *Mary, entreat your beloved Son, in his goodness, to grant me the grace to die clinging to your feet, and to breathe forth my soul in his wounds, saying, "Jesus and Mary, I give you my heart and my soul."*

The most lamentable event in world history

Which of the greatest tragedies in recorded history deserves most our pity? Most certainly, St. Alphonsus declares, the passion of Christ and the sorrow it caused his mother.

Who can ever have a heart so hard that it won't melt on hearing the most lamentable event that ever occurred in world history? There was a noble and holy mother who had an only Son. This Son was the most lovable that can be imagined: innocent, virtuous, and beautiful. He loved his mother most tenderly, so much that he had never caused her the least displeasure, but had always shown her all respect, obedience, and affection. So this mother had placed all her affections on earth in this Son.

Hear, then, what happened. This Son, through envy, was falsely accused by his enemies. The judge knew, and himself confessed, that her Son was innocent. Yet in order to avoid offending his enemies, he condemned him to the shameful death they had demanded. This poor mother had to suffer the grief of seeing that amiable and beloved Son unjustly snatched from her in the flower of his age by a barbarous death. Inflicted with torments and drained of all his blood, he was made to die on an infamous cross in a public place of execution. And all this took place as she watched.

Devout souls, what do you say? Isn't this event, isn't this unhappy mother, worthy of compassion? You already understand who it is I'm talking about. This Son, so cruelly executed, was our loving redeemer, Jesus; and this mother was the Blessed Virgin Mary, who for the love she bore us was willing to see him sacrificed to divine justice by the barbarity of men. This great torment, then, that Mary endured for us—a torment that was worse than a thousand deaths—deserves both our compassion and our gratitude. If we can make no other return for so much love, at least we should give a few moments this day to consider the greatness of the sufferings by which Mary became the queen of martyrs.

—St. Alphonsus Liguori, *The Glories of Mary*

IN GOD'S PRESENCE, CONSIDER . . .

Will I give a few moments this day, as St. Alphonsus urges me, to ponder the greatness of Mary's sufferings?

CLOSING PRAYER

From a prayer of St. Paul of the Cross: *O tender Mother, unutterable was your grief in finding yourself deprived of your dear Son, and then in beholding him dead in your arms!*

Mary, Our Lady of Sorrows

St. Bridget of Sweden was a visionary who spoke often with the Blessed Virgin and had a deep love for her. Here she focuses on the role of Mary's sorrows in our redemption.

O Blessed Virgin Mary, immaculate Mother of God,
who endured a martyrdom of love and grief
beholding the sufferings and sorrows of Jesus!
You cooperated in the benefit of my redemption
by your countless afflictions
and by offering to the Eternal Father his only-begotten Son
as a holocaust and victim of propitiation for my sins.
I thank you for the unspeakable love
that led you to deprive yourself
of the Fruit of your womb,
Jesus, true God and true Man,
to save me, a sinner.
Make use of the unfailing intercession of your sorrows
with the Father and the Son,
so that I may steadfastly correct my life
and never again crucify my loving Redeemer by new sins;
and so that, persevering till death in his grace,
I may obtain eternal life
through the merits of his cross and passion.
Mother of love, of sorrow, and of mercy,
Pray for us.

—St. Bridget of Sweden

IN GOD'S PRESENCE, CONSIDER . . .

A lively sense of gratitude deepens our love for those to whom we're indebted. What has God done for me? What am I willing to offer him in return?

CLOSING PRAYER

Giver of all good gifts, how can I even begin to thank you? In return, I offer you all I have and all I am, in this moment and forever.

Gratitude for Mary's sufferings

St. Alphonsus reminds us that even though Jesus' sufferings were "more than enough to save an infinity of worlds," Mary wished to join in his work of redemption through her own sufferings.

St. Ildephonsus didn't hesitate to assert: "To say that Mary's sorrows were greater than all the torments of all the martyrs together, was to say too little." And St. Anselm adds: "The cruelest tortures inflicted on the holy martyrs were trifling, or even as nothing, in comparison to the martyrdom of Mary." St. Basil of Seleucia writes: "As the sun surpasses all the other heavenly bodies in splendor, so did Mary's sufferings surpass those of all the other martyrs."

But here St. Bonaventure, addressing this Blessed Virgin, says: "And why, O Lady, did you also go to sacrifice yourself on Calvary? Wasn't a crucified God sufficient to redeem us? Why would you, his mother, also go to be crucified with him?" Indeed, the death of Jesus was more than enough to save the world, and an infinity of worlds. But this good mother, for the love she bore us, wished also to help the cause of our salvation with the merits of her sufferings, which she offered for us on Calvary. For this reason, as St. Albert the Great says, "Just as we are under great obligations to Jesus for his passion endured for our love, so also are we under great obligations to Mary for the martyrdom she voluntarily suffered for our salvation in the death of her Son."

St. Agnes revealed to St. Bridget, "Our compassionate and gracious mother was satisfied to endure any torment rather than that our souls should not be redeemed, and be left in their former state of damnation." Mary's only relief in the midst of her great sorrow in the passion of her Son was to see the lost world redeemed by his death, and men who were his enemies reconciled with God. So great a love on the part of Mary deserves our gratitude, and that gratitude should be shown by at least meditating upon and pitying her in her sorrows.

—St. Alphonsus Liguori, *The Glories of Mary*

IN GOD'S PRESENCE, CONSIDER . . .

Why are we "under great obligations to Mary" for her suffering? How might I fulfill those obligations? Does it encourage me to know that my reconciliation to God contributed to her relief?

CLOSING PRAYER

From "The Seven Dolors of Mary at the Death of Jesus": *Through these most bitter pangs that lacerated your maternal heart, I beg you, Mary, when I am called before the severe Judge to give an account of my life, unite your great merits to my scant record of good works, so that I may receive a favorable judgment.*

We are the children of Mary's sorrows

St. Alphonsus reminds us that Our Lady's cooperation in our redemption, as she suffered at the Cross, allowed her to bring us forth as her children.

Blessed Simon of Cascia writes: "All who saw this mother silent at the cross, and not uttering a complaint in the midst of such great suffering, were filled with astonishment." But if Mary's lips were silent, her heart was not so, for she unceasingly offered the life of her Son to the divine Justice for our salvation. So we know that by the merits of her sorrows, she cooperated in our birth into the life of grace, and we are the children of her sorrows. "Christ was pleased," says Lanspergius, "that Mary, the one cooperating in our redemption, whom he had determined to give us for our mother, should be present there. For it was at the foot of the Cross that she was to bring forth us, her children."

If any consolation entered the sea of pain that was the heart of Mary, the only one was this: She knew that by her sorrows she was leading us to eternal salvation, as Jesus himself revealed to St. Bridget: "My mother, Mary, because of her compassion and love, was made the mother of all in heaven and on earth." And indeed, these were the last words with which Jesus bid her farewell before his death—this was his last act of entrustment, in the person of St. John, leaving us to her to be her children: "Woman, behold your son" (Jn 19:26).

From that time forward, Mary began to perform this benevolent role of a mother for us. St. Peter Damian attests, "By the prayers of Mary, who stood between the cross of the good thief and that of her Son, the thief was converted and saved, and in this way she repaid a service he had done for her before." For according to an old tradition, this thief had been kind to Jesus and Mary on their journey to Egypt. The Blessed Virgin has ever since continued to perform this same intercessory role for others.

—St. Alphonsus Liguori, *The Glories of Mary*

IN GOD'S PRESENCE, CONSIDER . . .

Is perhaps the cross of the "good thief" my cross, where I suffer for my sins and look to Jesus crucified for forgiveness? If so, do I see Mary standing there, praying for my salvation?

CLOSING PRAYER

From a prayer of St. Alphonsus: *Sweet mother, let your sorrows obtain for me pardon, perseverance, and heaven, where I hope to rejoice with you, and to sing the infinite mercies of my God for all eternity.*

My sins are swords in Mary's heart

St. Alphonsus tells a story that reminds us how our sins are part of Our Lady's suffering.

Fr. Roviglione, of the Society of Jesus, tells how a young man had the devotion of every day visiting a statue of Our Lady of Sorrows. In it, she was represented with seven swords piercing her heart.

The unfortunate youth one night committed a mortal sin. The next morning, going as usual to visit the image, he saw that there were no longer only seven swords, but now eight in the heart of Mary. Wondering at this change, he heard a voice telling him that his crime had added the eighth sword.

This realization moved his heart. Penetrated with sorrow, he immediately went to the Sacrament of Confession. By the intercession of his advocate, he recovered divine grace.

My Blessed Mother, it's not one sword only with which I have pierced your heart! I have pierced your heart as many times as I have committed sins. My Lady, it's not to you, who are innocent, that sufferings are due. Sufferings are due to me—I who am guilty of so many crimes.

But since you have been pleased to suffer so much for me, then by your merits, obtain for me great sorrow for my sins. Help me to develop patience in the trials of this life, for they will always be light in comparison with my demerits, and I have often deserved hell.

—St. Alphonsus Liguori, *The Glories of Mary*

IN GOD'S PRESENCE, CONSIDER . . .

What swords might I be plunging into Mary's heart, even now, because of what I have done or failed to do? How do I plan to relieve her of the suffering I have caused her?

CLOSING PRAYER

From a prayer of St. Alphonsus: *Mother of Mercies, I know that your compassionate heart finds its consolation in assisting the miserable when you can do so, because you don't find them obstinate. Console, then, your compassionate heart, and console me as well, this day.*

A sign that will be contradicted

St. Alphonsus imagines, beyond the few words recorded in Scripture, what St. Simeon may have said to Our Lady when Jesus was presented in the temple.

Watch now as Mary walks to Jerusalem to offer her Son. She hurries toward the place of sacrifice, and she herself carries the beloved Victim in her arms. She enters the temple and approaches the altar. There, beaming with modesty, devotion, and humility, she presents her Son to the Most High. Then holy Simeon takes the divine Child from the hands of the Blessed Virgin. Enlightened by the Holy Spirit, he announces to her how much the sacrifice which she then made of her Son would cost her. With him, her own blessed soul would also be sacrificed. In this moment, St. Thomas of Villanova imagines the holy old man becoming troubled and silent at the thought of having to speak a prophecy so fatal to this poor mother. The saint then looks at Mary, who asks him, "Why, Simeon, are you so troubled in the midst of such great consolations?"

"Royal Virgin," he replies, "I don't want to announce to you such bitter news. But since God wills it this way for your greater merit, listen to what I have to say. This Child, who is now such a source of joy to you—and, O God, for such good reason!—this Child, I say, will one day be a source of such bitter grief to you that no creature in the world has ever experienced the like. This will happen when you see him persecuted by men of every class, and made a butt upon earth for their scoffs and outrages. They will even go so far as to put him to death as a villain before your own eyes.

"You greatly rejoice in this Infant. But see, he is placed as a sign that will be contradicted. Know that after his death there will be many martyrs, who for the love of this Son of yours will be tormented and put to death. Their martyrdom will be endured in their bodies; but yours, Mother of God, will be endured in your heart."

—St. Alphonsus Liguori, *The Glories of Mary*

IN GOD'S PRESENCE, CONSIDER . . .

What words would you imagine St. Simeon saying to Mary at the Presentation? What must Mary have thought and felt to hear such words?

CLOSING PRAYER

Blessed Mother, Our Lady of Sorrows, no grief was ever like your grief. Thank you for enduring the sword that pierced your heart, and for comforting us in our sorrows.

Mary endured a sorrow more cruel than death

St. Alphonsus reports how Our Lady told St. Bridget that "the sorrow announced to her by the holy Simeon never left her heart until her assumption into heaven."

From the day of Jesus' presentation in the temple forward, how sad a scene must love have continually placed before the eyes of Mary—a scene representing all the outrages and mockeries that her poor Son was to endure. See how love would have already pictured him to her: agonized with sorrow in the garden, mangled with scourges, crowned with thorns in the praetorium, and finally hanging on the shameful cross on Calvary!

"Behold, Mother," love says, "what a loveable and innocent Son you offer to so many torments and to so horrible a death! Why should you have saved him from the hands of Herod by fleeing to Egypt, since it is only to reserve him for a far more sorrowful end?" Thus Mary not only offered her Son to death in the temple, but she renewed that offering every moment of her life. She revealed to St. Bridget that "the sorrow announced to her by the holy Simeon never left her heart until her assumption into heaven." For this reason, St. Anselm addresses her this way: "O compassionate Lady, I cannot believe that you could have endured for a moment so excruciating a torment without dying from it, if God himself, the Spirit of Life, had not sustained you."

But St. Bernard affirms, speaking of the great sorrow that Mary experienced that day in the temple, that from that time forward "she died while living, enduring a sorrow more cruel than death." In every moment, she lived dying; for in every moment she was assailed by the sorrow of the death of her beloved Jesus, which was a torment more cruel than any death.

—St. Alphonsus Liguori, *The Glories of Mary*

IN GOD'S PRESENCE, CONSIDER . . .

Do I have any abiding sorrows that I expect to carry until the day I leave this world? Have I brought these sorrows to Mary to ask her to help me bear them?

CLOSING PRAYER

From a prayer of Venerable Pope Pius XII: *From the depths of this vale of tears where sorrowing humanity makes weary progress—through the surges of this sea of ours endlessly buffeted by the winds of passion—we raise our eyes to you, O most beloved mother Mary, to be comforted by the contemplation of your glory.*

Mary's sorrow when Jesus was lost

St. Alphonsus points out that when Mary couldn't find Jesus for three days, she was deprived not only of her Child, but of her Lord.

The Apostle St. James says that our perfection consists in the virtue of patience. "Patience has a perfect work, so that you may be perfect and entire, failing in nothing" (see Jas 1:4). Since our Lord had given us the Blessed Virgin Mary as a model of perfection, it was necessary that she should be burdened with sorrows, so that in her we might admire heroic patience and endeavor to imitate it.

One of the greatest sorrows Mary had to endure in her life was the loss of her Son in the temple. Those who are born blind and have never seen the light of day have little sense of what they are missing. But those who have enjoyed the light, then lost it by becoming blind, suffer considerably.

It's the same with those unhappy souls who, blinded by the mire of this world, have only a little knowledge of God. They suffer only a little at not finding him. On the other hand, consider those who, illumined by heavenly light, have become worthy to find by love the sweet presence of the supreme Good. O God, how bitterly do they grieve when they find themselves deprived of it!

In this light, just consider how much Mary must have suffered from this sword of sorrow that pierced her heart: Having lost her Jesus in Jerusalem for three days, she was deprived of his most sweet presence, accustomed as she was to enjoy it constantly.

—St. Alphonsus Liguori, *The Glories of Mary*

IN GOD'S PRESENCE, CONSIDER . . .

Do I sometimes seem to lose sight of God, or feel as if he is no longer with me? In those times, do I ask Mary to help me recover what I've lost, just as she recovered her Son?

CLOSING PRAYER

Blessed Mother, help me to go looking for God's presence in every moment, in every place, and in every encounter, and help me find him there, even where I least expect him.

The greatest of Mary's sorrows

Which of Mary's sorrows was the greatest? Some have suggested, St. Alphonsus reports, that it was her loss of her young Son in Jerusalem for three days.

The third of Mary's traditional seven sorrows was not knowing what had happened to Jesus when she returned from the Passover in Jerusalem. Some have reasonably asserted that this wasn't just among the greatest of her sorrows, but was in fact the greatest and most painful of all. Why is this?

First, Mary, had Jesus with her in her other sorrows. She suffered when St. Simeon prophesied to her in the temple; she suffered in the flight into Egypt. But in both these sorrows, she was still in company with Jesus. In this third sorrow, however, she suffered far from Jesus, not knowing where he was. Too long indeed were those three days for Mary. They seemed like three ages. They were all bitterness, for there was no one to comfort her. And who can ever comfort me, she said with Jeremiah, who can console me, since the One who alone could do so is far from me? So my eyes can never weep enough: "For these things I weep; my eyes flow with tears; for a comforter is far from me" (Lam 1:16).

Second, Mary, in all her other sorrows, understood well their cause: the redemption of the world according to God's will. But in this sorrow she didn't know the cause of the absence of her Son. Lanspergius observes: "The sorrowful mother was grieved at the absence of Jesus because, in her humility, she considered herself unworthy to remain longer with him or to care for him on earth, and to have the charge of so great a treasure. . . . And who knows?" he wondered; perhaps she thought within herself: "Maybe I haven't served him as I should have; perhaps I've been guilty of some negligence that caused him to leave me." "They sought him," says Origen, "fearing that he might have entirely left them."

—St. Alphonsus Liguori, *The Glories of Mary*

IN GOD'S PRESENCE, CONSIDER . . .

Do I sometimes wrestle with fears that somehow, a loss I've suffered is God's chastisement for my failure to serve him as I should? How might a careful meditation on this episode in Mary's life help me understand God's loving will for me more clearly?

CLOSING PRAYER

Father, teach me the meaning of your promise: "For I know the plans I have for you, says the LORD, plans for welfare and not for evil, to give you a future and a hope" (Jer 29:11).

The only sorrow in which Mary complained

When the Blessed Mother found her young Son at last in the temple, her words were not a rebuke, St. Alphonsus insists. But they were a loving complaint.

The only sorrow in which Mary complained was her search for the boy Jesus in Jerusalem. She lovingly and earnestly asked of Jesus, after she had found him in the temple: "Son, why have you treated us so? Behold, your father and I have been looking for you anxiously" (Lk 2:48).

By these words she had no idea of reproving Jesus, as some heretics have blasphemously asserted. Instead, she meant only to express how great was the grief she had experienced during his absence, because of the great love she bore him. "It was not a rebuke," says St. Dionysius the Carthusian, "but a loving complaint."

This sword so cruelly pierced the heart of the most holy Virgin that the Blessed Benvenuta Bojani desired one day to share the holy mother's pain in this sorrow. When she entreated her for this favor, Mary appeared to her with the infant Jesus in her arms.

But while Benvenuta was enjoying the sight of this most beautiful Child, in a moment she was deprived of it. So great was her grief that she turned to Mary, begging her to lessen it, so that she might not die from grief. In three days the holy Virgin again appeared, and said: "Know, my daughter, that your sorrow is only a small part of the sorrow that I endured when I lost my Son."

—St. Alphonsus Liguori, *The Glories of Mary*

IN GOD'S PRESENCE, CONSIDER . . .

What would you say is the difference between a rebuke and a "loving complaint"? Do I sometimes make "loving complaints" to Jesus in prayer? How does he usually respond?

CLOSING PRAYER

Jesus, sometimes I find myself saying with your disciples in the ship battered by the storm, "Lord, save me, I'm perishing! Don't you care?" (See Mt 8:25; Lk 4:38.) But then you tell me, as you told the sea, "Peace, be still" (Mk 4:39), and my soul is quieted.

Mary's sufferings grew as Jesus grew

When we speak of Mary's sorrows, we typically focus on seven occasions in her life that brought her untold suffering. But St. Alphonsus points out that Mary's suffering grew throughout her life as she became increasingly devoted to her Son, knowing what lay ahead for him.

The sufferings of Our Lady as she offered the infant Jesus to God in the temple didn't end there. No, they only began; for from that time forward, during the whole life of her Son, Mary had constantly before her eyes the death and all the torments that he was to endure. For this reason, the more this Son showed himself beautiful, gracious, and loveable, the more the anguish of her heart increased.

Most sorrowful Mother, had you loved your Son less, or had he been less loveable, or had he loved you less, your sufferings as you offered him to death would certainly have been diminished. But there never was, and never will be, a mother who loved her son more than you loved yours. For there never was, and never will be, a son more loveable, or one who loved his mother more than your Jesus loved you.

O God, had we beheld the beauty, the majesty, of the face of that divine Child, could we have ever found the courage to sacrifice his life for our salvation? Yet you, Mary, who were his mother, and a mother loving him with so tender a love—you were able to offer your innocent Son for the salvation of men, to a death more painful and cruel than ever was endured by the greatest villain on earth!

The angel said to St. Bridget: "As the rose grows up among thorns, so the Mother of God advanced in years in the midst of sufferings. And as the thorns increase with the growth of the rose, so also did the thorns of her sorrows increase in Mary, the chosen rose of the Lord, as she advanced in age; and so much the more deeply did they pierce her heart."

—St. Alphonsus Liguori, *The Glories of Mary*

IN GOD'S PRESENCE, CONSIDER . . .

Have I ever considered how Mary's sorrow would have deepened over the years in light of what St. Simeon had told her in the temple? How do I seek her consolation in my sorrows regarding my loved ones?

CLOSING PRAYER

"The Sorrowful Hail Mary," approved by Pope Pius IX: *Hail, Mary, full of sorrows, the Crucified is with thee; thou art pitiable among women, and pitiable is the Fruit of thy womb, Jesus. Holy Mary, mother of the Crucified, implore for us, the crucifiers of thy Son, tears of contrition, now and at the hour of our death.*

Mary cared for her Child with sorrow

Like a mother whose child has been born with a terminal illness, Mary could never escape for long thoughts about her Son's death. St. Alphonsus considers how these thoughts would have served as a continual stream of sorrow for her.

King David, in the midst of all his pleasures and regal grandeur, heard from the prophet Nathan that his son would die: "The child that is born to you shall die" (2 Sam 12:14). The king could find no peace, but wept, fasted, and slept on the ground. Yet Mary, with the greatest calmness, received the announcement that her Son would die, and she always peacefully submitted to it. But what grief must she continually have suffered, seeing this lovable Son always near her, hearing from him words of eternal life, and witnessing his holy demeanor!

Abraham suffered much during the three days he spent with his beloved Isaac, after learning that he was to lose him. But Mary had to endure a similar sorrow, not for three days, but for thirty-three years! But did I say a similar sorrow? No—her suffering was as much greater than Abraham's as her Son was lovelier than his.

The Blessed Virgin herself revealed to St. Bridget that, while she was on earth, there was not an hour in which this grief did not pierce her soul. Already knowing what her Son was to suffer, the afflicted mother "when nursing him, thought of the gall and vinegar; when swaddling him, of the cords that would bind him; when carrying him in her arms, of the cross to which he would be nailed; when sleeping, of his death." As often as she dressed him, she considered how his clothes would one day be torn from him, so that he might be crucified. And when she saw his sacred hands and feet, she thought of the nails that would one day pierce them. Mary told St. Bridget, "Then my eyes filled with tears, and my heart was tortured with grief."

—St. Alphonsus Liguori, *The Glories of Mary*

IN GOD'S PRESENCE, CONSIDER . . .

What scenes and events in my life have the greatest power to provoke sadness in me? How might I bring those moments to Mary, knowing that she understands them well?

CLOSING PRAYER

Blessed Mother, a cold wind must have blown through your soul when you saw the shadow of the Cross fall across the crib. Thank you for enduring such grief for my sake, and pray for me when shadows lengthen all around me.

A thousand flames of love turned to grief

St. Alphonsus talks about the intensity of Mary's love for her Son—and how devastated she would have been to meet him as he carried his cross to Calvary.

St. Bernardine says that to form an idea of the greatness of Mary's grief in losing her Jesus by death, we must consider the love that this mother bore to her Son. All mothers feel the sufferings of their children as their own. But what mother ever loved her son as Mary loved Jesus? He was her only Son, reared amid so many troubles; a most loveable Son, and tenderly loving his mother; a Son who, at the same time that he was her Son, was also her God, who had come on earth to enkindle in the hearts of all the fire of divine love, as he himself declared: "I have come to cast fire on the earth; and would that it were already kindled!" (Lk 12:49).

We need only imagine what a flame he must have enkindled in that pure heart of his holy mother, empty as it was of every earthly affection. The Blessed Virgin herself told St. Bridget that love had rendered her heart and that of her Son as one. That blending together of Servant and mother with Son and God created in the heart of Mary a fire composed of a thousand flames. But the whole of this flame of love was eventually, at the time of the Passion, changed into a sea of grief. St. Bernardine says of that time: "If all the sorrows of the world were united, they would not equal the sorrow of the glorious Virgin Mary."

Yes! Because, as Richard of Saint Lawrence writes, "the more tenderly this mother loved, the more deeply she was wounded." The greater was her love for him, the greater was her grief at the sight of his sufferings—especially when she met her Son, already condemned to death, and bearing his cross to the place of punishment. This was yet another sword of sorrow.

—St. Alphonsus Liguori, *The Glories of Mary*

IN GOD'S PRESENCE, CONSIDER . . .

How has my experience proven that the more tender the love, the more deep the wound when the beloved is suffering? Do I ask Mary to pray for those I love when they suffer, and to pray for me as well?

CLOSING PRAYER

From a prayer of St. Bonaventure: *Most suffering of all mothers, no more bitter grief than yours can be found; for no son more dear than yours can be found.*

Mary meets Jesus on the way to Calvary

St. Alphonsus imagines the scene when Jesus meets Mary as he carried the Cross to his execution.

Mary goes with St. John to see Jesus on the way to Calvary. She later reveals to St. Bridget: "By the footsteps of my Son, I knew where he had passed; for along the way the ground was marked with blood." St. Bonaventure imagines the afflicted mother taking a shorter way, and placing herself at a street corner, to meet her afflicted Son as he is passing by. While Mary is waiting in that place, how much she must hear spoken against her beloved Son by the crowd! They soon recognize her, and perhaps even mock Mary herself. What a scene of sorrows then presents itself before her: the nails, the hammers, the cords, the fatal instruments of the death of her Son, all of which are carried ahead of him. And what a sword to her heart must be the sound of that trumpet that proclaims the sentence pronounced against her Jesus!

She raises her eyes and sees—O God!—a young Man covered with blood and wounds from head to foot, a wreath of thorns on his head, and two heavy beams on his shoulders. She looks at him, and hardly recognizes him. Yes, because of the wounds, the bruises, and the clotted blood, he can no longer be identified. But at last love reveals him to her, and as soon as she knows that it is indeed Jesus, what love and fear must then fill her heart!

On the one hand, she desires to behold him. On the other, she dreads so heart-rending a sight. At last they look at each other. The Son wipes from his eyes the clotted blood that prevents him from seeing and looks at his mother, as the mother looks at her Son: looks of bitter grief that, like so many arrows, pierce through and through those two beautiful and loving souls.

—St. Alphonsus Liguori, *The Glories of Mary*

IN GOD'S PRESENCE, CONSIDER . . .

Of all the traditional sorrows of the Blessed Mother, some would say this is the most poignant. If I imagine myself present at the scene that day, what do I imagine myself saying and doing—or wishing I could say and do?

CLOSING PRAYER

From a prayer of St. Alphonsus: *My most loving Jesus, by the sorrow you experienced in this meeting, grant me the grace of a truly devoted love for your most holy mother. And you, my Queen, who were overwhelmed with sorrow, obtain for me by your intercession a continual and tender remembrance of the passion of your Son.*

Mary suffered in her Son's suffering

St. Alphonsus observes that, just as it would be for any anguished mother seeing her child tortured and killed, Mary suffered in her soul what her Son suffered in his body.

While other martyrs suffered by sacrificing their own lives, the Blessed Virgin suffered by sacrificing her Son's life—a life that she loved far more than her own. So she not only suffered in her soul all that her Son endured in his body. In addition, the sight of her Son's torments brought more grief to her heart than if she had endured them all in her own person. No one can doubt that Mary suffered in her heart all the outrages that she saw inflicted on her beloved Jesus. Anyone can understand that the sufferings of children are also those of their mothers who witness them.

St. Augustine, considering the anguish endured by the mother of the Maccabees in witnessing the tortures of her sons, says: "Seeing their sufferings, she suffered in each one. Because she loved them all, she endured in her soul what they endured in their flesh." In the same way, Mary suffered all those torments, scourges, thorns, nails, and the cross that tortured the innocent flesh of Jesus. They all entered at the same time into the heart of this Blessed Virgin to complete her martyrdom. "He suffered in the flesh, and she in her heart," writes the Blessed Amadeus. "So much so," says St. Lawrence Justinian, "that the heart of Mary became a mirror of the passion of the Son, in which might be seen, faithfully reflected, the spitting, the blows and wounds, and all that Jesus suffered."

St. Bonaventure remarks: "Those wounds that were scattered over the body of our Lord were all united in the single heart of Mary." In this way, then, through the compassion of her loving heart for her Son, our Blessed Lady was scourged, crowned with thorns, insulted, and nailed to the cross.

—St. Alphonsus Liguori, *The Glories of Mary*

IN GOD'S PRESENCE, CONSIDER . . .

How does Mary's experience of suffering make her an advocate for those who experience bereavement and other loss?

CLOSING PRAYER

From a prayer of St. Bonaventure: *Lady, tell me where you stood. Was it only at the foot of the Cross? No, much more than this, you were on the Cross itself, crucified with your Son.*

Our Lady's sorrow at the Cross

Can we even begin to imagine the depth of sorrow that Our Lady felt as she watched her dear Son die on the cross? Blessed Henry Suso imagines her telling what she experienced on that dreadful day.

All the sorrow that ever could afflict a heart would be like only a drop in the ocean compared to the unfathomable sorrow that my maternal heart at that time endured. Keep in mind that the dearer, the sweeter, the more precious the beloved one is, the more insupportable is his loss and death. Now where on the whole earth was there ever a more tender one born, a lovelier one seen, than my own best beloved one, Jesus Christ, by whom and in whom I had entire possession of all that the world could bestow? I was already dead to myself, and lived only in him. So when at last my own fair Love was slain, then only did I utterly die. And as my only love was but one and, even more, dear to me above all other loves, so my only sorrow was but one, and a sorrow above all sorrows that ever were expressed.

His fair and gentle humanity was, to me, a delightful spectacle. His dignified divinity was, to my eyes, a sweet contemplation. To think of him was my heart's delight; to speak of him was my pastime; to hear his sweet words was music to my soul. He was my heart's mirror, my soul's comfort. Heaven and earth, and all that is within them, I possessed in his sweet presence. When I saw my Love suspended in mortal agony before me, what a terrible sight! What a moment was that! How my heart died within me! How my courage was extinguished! How my strength failed me! How all my senses forsook me!

I looked up, but I could not help my Child. I looked down and saw only those who so cruelly abused him. How narrow then to me was all this world! I had lost all heart; my voice had fled from me; and I had lost all strength.

—Blessed Henry Suso, *The Parable of the Pilgrim*, I, 17

IN GOD'S PRESENCE, CONSIDER . . .

Have I ever meditated for long on the depths of grief and pain suffered by Mary as she watched Jesus die? How might such a meditation increase my love for her, and my gratitude for what she endured in union with her Son for the sake of a sinful world?

CLOSING PRAYER

From a prayer of Blessed Henry Suso: *Pure Lady and noble Queen of Heaven and Earth, touch my stony heart with one of your scalding tears, one of those you shed in bitter distress for your tender Child under the wretched cross, so that my heart of stone may be softened.*

Only a miracle spared Mary's life at Calvary

St. Alphonsus insists that when Jesus sacrificed his body on Calvary, Mary sacrificed her soul through suffering.

Mary was the Queen of Martyrs not only because her martyrdom was longer than that of all others, but also because it was the greatest of all martyrdoms. But who could ever measure its greatness? Jeremiah seems unable to find anyone to whom he can compare this Mother of Sorrows, when he considers her great sufferings at the death of her Son. "To what can I compare you, O daughter of Jerusalem? What can I liken you to, that I may comfort you, O virgin daughter of Zion?" (Lam 2:13).

St. Anselm asserts, "If God had not by a special miracle preserved the life of Mary in each moment of her life, her grief was so great that it would have caused her death." St. Bernardine of Siena goes as far as to say that "the grief of Mary was so great that, were it divided among all men, it would suffice to cause their immediate death."

But let's consider the reasons why Mary's martyrdom was greater than that of all martyrs. First, we must remember that the martyrs endured their torments, caused by fire and other material agencies, in their bodies. But Mary suffered hers in her soul, as St. Simeon foretold: "A sword will pierce through your own soul" (Lk 2:35).

It's as if the holy old man had said: "Most sacred Virgin, the bodies of other martyrs will be torn with iron. But you will be pierced through and martyred in your soul by the passion of your own Son." Now, as the soul is more noble than the body, so much greater were Mary's sufferings than those of all the martyrs.

—St. Alphonsus Liguori, *The Glories of Mary*

IN GOD'S PRESENCE, CONSIDER . . .

Why is the extreme suffering of the soul so much greater than that of the body? What suffering of soul must I endure that I can offer to God?

CLOSING PRAYER

Our Lady of Sorrows, what your Son said of himself in Gethsemane, you could say of yourself at Calvary: "My soul is very sorrowful, even to death; remain here, and watch with me" (Mt 26:38).

Mary's soul was crucified

In a sense, St. Alphonsus concludes, two crucifixions took place on Calvary: that of Jesus' body, and that of Mary's soul.

O God, what a cruel sight it was to behold this Son in agony on the cross, and at its foot this mother in agony, suffering all the torments endured by her Son! Listen to the words in which Mary revealed to St. Bridget the sorrowful state in which she saw her dying Son on the Cross: "My dear Jesus was breathless, exhausted, and in his last agony on the Cross. His eyes were sunken, half-closed, and lifeless. His lips were hanging, and his mouth was open. His cheeks were hollow and drawn in. His face was elongated, his nose sharp, his countenance sad. His head had fallen down against his breast. His hair was black with blood; his stomach collapsed; his arms and legs were stiff; and his whole body was covered with wounds and blood."

All these sufferings of Jesus were also those of Mary. "Every torture inflicted on the body of Jesus," says St. Jerome, "was a wound in the heart of the mother." "Whoever then was present on the Mount of Calvary," says St. John Chrysostom, "could see two altars, on which two great sacrifices were consummated: the one in the body of Jesus, the other in the heart of Mary."

Better still, we might say with St. Bonaventure: There was only one altar—that of the cross of the Son. On it, together with this victim, the divine Lamb, the mother was also sacrificed." So the saint asks this mother, "O Lady, where are you? Near the Cross? No, rather, you are on the Cross, crucified, sacrificing yourself with your Son." St. Augustine assures us of the same truth: "The cross and nails of the Son were also those of his mother; with Christ crucified, the mother was also crucified." As St. Bernardine writes: "At the same time that the Son sacrificed his body, the mother sacrificed her soul."

—St. Alphonsus Liguori, *The Glories of Mary*

IN GOD'S PRESENCE, CONSIDER . . .

What does it mean to say that on Calvary "there were two great altars"? Have I brought my offerings of gratitude to both of those altars?

CLOSING PRAYER

From the *Stabat Mater Dolorosa: Holy Mother, pierce me through! In my heart each wound renew of my Savior crucified. Let me share with thee his pain, who for all my sins was slain, who for me in torments died.*

The soldier's lance pierced Mary's heart

The lance that opened Christ's side passed through the soul of the Blessed Virgin, St. Alphonsus tells us, because her soul could never leave her Son's heart.

So that the joy of the following Passover Sabbath wouldn't be disturbed, the Jewish leaders wanted the body of Jesus to be taken down from the Cross. This couldn't be done unless the criminals were dead. So men came with iron bars to break our Lord's legs, as they had already broken the legs of the two thieves who were crucified with him. Mary was still weeping over the death of her Son when she saw these armed men approaching her Jesus. At this sight she first trembled with fear, then she exclaimed: "My Son is already dead! Don't commit any more outrages against him. I am his poor mother; don't torment me anymore."

She begged them, writes St. Bonaventure, not to break his legs. But as she said this—O God!—she saw a soldier brandish a lance and pierce the side of Jesus: "One of the soldiers pierced his side with a spear, and at once there came out blood and water" (Jn 19:34). At the stroke of the spear the Cross shook and, as it was afterwards revealed to St. Bridget, the heart of Jesus was divided in two. "There came out blood and water"; for only a few drops of blood remained, and even those last few our Savior was pleased to shed, so we might understand that he had no more blood to give us.

The injury of that stroke was inflicted on Jesus, but Mary suffered its pain. "Christ," says the devout Lanspergius, "shared this wound with his mother. He received the insult, but his mother endured its agony." The holy Fathers of the Church insist that this was literally the sword foretold to the Blessed Virgin by St. Simeon: not a material sword, but a sword of grief, which pierced through her blessed soul in the heart of Jesus, where her soul always dwelled. As St. Bernard and others say: "The lance that opened Christ's side passed through the soul of the Blessed Virgin, which could never leave her Son's heart."

—St. Alphonsus Liguori, *The Glories of Mary*

IN GOD'S PRESENCE, CONSIDER . . .

Jesus is the second "Adam" (see 1 Cor 15:45), the Head of the new, redeemed creation, just as the first Adam was the head of the old, fallen creation. Eve, the wife of the first Adam, was created from his side. So why does the Church see in the blood and water flowing from Jesus' pierced side a symbol of the Church?

CLOSING PRAYER

Mary, pray for me, so that the suffering of your Son, through the cleansing water of my Baptism and his precious Blood in the Eucharist, may bathe my heart and purify it.

Mary's martyrdom lasted a lifetime

St. Alphonsus explains why the name "Mary," one of whose meanings is "bitter sea," is fitting for our Lord's mother.

"The passion of Jesus," St. Bernard says, "began with his birth." Mary was in all things like her Son, so in a similar way, she endured her martyrdom throughout her life.

"A bitter sea" is one of the meanings of the name of Mary, as St. Albert the Great asserts. So the words of Jeremiah can be applied to her: "Vast as the sea is your ruin" (Lam 2:13). For just as the sea is all bitter and salt, so also was the life of Mary always full of bitterness at the sight of the passion of the Redeemer, which was ever present to her mind.

The angel revealed to St. Bridget: "There can be no doubt that Mary was enlightened by the Holy Spirit to a far higher degree than all the prophets. So she, far better than they, understood the predictions concerning the Messiah recorded by them in the Sacred Scriptures." He added: "Even before she became Jesus' mother, the Blessed Virgin knew how much the incarnate Word was to suffer for the salvation of men, and had compassion on this innocent Savior, who was to be so cruelly put to death for crimes not his own. So even then, Mary began her great martyrdom."

Her grief was immeasurably increased when she became the mother of this Savior. At the sad sight of the many torments that were to be endured by her poor Son, she indeed suffered a long martyrdom, a martyrdom that lasted her whole life.

—St. Alphonsus Liguori, *The Glories of Mary*

IN GOD'S PRESENCE, CONSIDER . . .

Though the saints may speak of Mary's "bitterness," the intended meaning of the word is her severe distress, not the more common meaning today of a long-term resentment that comes from failing to forgive. Even so, the first sort of bitterness in life can lead to the second sort. Do I have any resentments that I need to relinquish through forgiveness?

CLOSING PRAYER

Blessed Mother, help me strive for peace with everyone through God's grace, so that no "root of bitterness" may "spring up and cause trouble" within me (Heb 12:14–15).

Mary suffered martyrdom without relief

St. Alphonsus observes that Marys' martyrdom was more severe than that of the other martyrs, not just because it was longer and more intense, but because she suffered it without relief.

Here we must reflect on another circumstance that rendered the martyrdom of Mary beyond all comparison greater than the torments of all the martyrs: In the passion of Jesus she not only suffered much; she suffered without the least relief. The martyrs suffered under the torments inflicted on them by tyrants. But the love of Jesus rendered their pains sweet and agreeable. St. Vincent was tortured on a rack, torn with pincers, burned with red-hot iron plates. But Vincent addressed the tyrant with such energy and contempt for his torments, that it seemed as if one Vincent suffered and another spoke—so greatly did God strengthen him with the sweetness of his love in the midst of all he endured. A St. Boniface had his body torn with iron hooks; sharp-pointed reeds were thrust between his nails and flesh; melted lead was poured into his mouth; and in the midst of all this he couldn't tire of saying, "I give you thanks, Lord Jesus Christ."

The more the holy martyrs loved Jesus, then, the less they felt their torments and death. The sight alone of the sufferings of a crucified God was sufficient to console them. But was our suffering mother also consoled by love for her Son, and the sight of his torments? No! For this very Son who suffered was the whole cause of them, and the love she bore him was her only and most cruel executioner.

Mary's whole martyrdom consisted in beholding and pitying her innocent and beloved Son, who suffered so much. So the greater her love for him, the more bitter and inconsolable was her grief. Other martyrs are all represented with the instruments of their sufferings: St. Paul with a sword, St. Andrew with a cross, St. Lawrence with a gridiron. But Mary is represented with her dead Son in her arms. For Jesus himself, and he alone, was the instrument of her martyrdom, because of the love she bore him.

—St. Alphonsus Liguori, *The Glories of Mary*

IN GOD'S PRESENCE, CONSIDER . . .

What does it mean to say that "Jesus himself, and he alone, was the instrument" of Mary's martyrdom"?

CLOSING PRAYER

From the *Stabat Mater Dolorosa*: *Mother, make me feel as thou hast felt; make my soul to glow and melt with the love of Christ, my Lord.*

Grieving with Mary in her first five sorrows

Pope Pius VII approved for the use of the faithful a series of "Seven Prayers in Honor of the Seven Sorrows of the Blessed Virgin Mary." In this first portion of the devotion, we grieve with Mary in her first five sorrows.

I grieve for you, O Mary most sorrowful, in the affliction of your tender heart at the prophecy of the holy and aged Simeon. Dear Mother, by your heart so afflicted, obtain for me the virtue of humility and the gift of the holy fear of God.

I grieve for you, O Mary most sorrowful, in the anguish of your most affectionate heart during the flight into Egypt and your sojourn there. Dear Mother, by your heart so troubled, obtain for me the virtue of generosity, especially toward the poor, and the gift of piety.

I grieve for you, O Mary most sorrowful, in those anxieties that tried your troubled heart at the loss of your dear Jesus. Dear Mother, by your heart so full of anguish, obtain for me the virtue of chastity and the gift of knowledge.

I grieve for you, O Mary most sorrowful, in the consternation of your heart at meeting Jesus as he carried his cross. Dear Mother, by your heart so troubled, obtain for me the virtue of patience and the gift of fortitude.

I grieve for you, O Mary most sorrowful, in the martyrdom that your generous heart endured in standing near Jesus in his agony. Dear Mother, by your afflicted heart, obtain for me the virtue of temperance and the gift of counsel.

—From "Seven Prayers in Honor of the Seven Sorrows of the Blessed Virgin Mary"

IN GOD'S PRESENCE, CONSIDER . . .

For each of these first five sorrows, prayer is offered to obtain a specific virtue and gift of the Holy Spirit. Which of these virtues and gifts do I need most to cultivate?

CLOSING PRAYER

Mary, help me to be humble and generous, chaste, patient, and temperate. Ask the Holy Spirit to give me the gifts of fear of God, piety, knowledge, fortitude, and counsel.

Grieving with Mary in her final two sorrows

Pope Pius VII approved for the use of the faithful a series of "Seven Prayers in Honor of the Seven Sorrows of the Blessed Virgin Mary." In this final portion of the devotion, we grieve with Mary in her final two sorrows.

I grieve for you, O Mary most sorrowful, in the wounding of your compassionate heart when the side of Jesus was struck by the lance and his heart was pierced before his body was removed from the cross. Dear Mother, by your heart thus pierced through, obtain for me the virtue of fraternal charity and the gift of understanding.

I grieve for you, O Mary most sorrowful, for the pangs that wrenched your most loving heart at the burial of Jesus. Dear Mother, by your heart sunk in the bitterness of desolation, obtain for me the virtue of diligence and the gift of wisdom.

Let intercession be made for us, we beg you, O Lord Jesus Christ, now and at the hour of our death, before the throne of your mercy, by the Blessed Virgin Mary, your mother, whose most holy soul was pierced by a sword of sorrow in the hour of your bitter passion. Through you, O Jesus Christ, Savior of the world, who with the Father and the Holy Spirit live and reign, world without end. Amen.

O Mary, Mother of Sorrows, I beg you, by the unspeakable tortures you endured at the death of your Son, offer to the Eternal Father, in my stead, your beloved Son all covered with blood and wounds, for the special grace that I now ask.

—From "Seven Prayers in Honor of the
Seven Sorrows of the Blessed Virgin Mary"

IN GOD'S PRESENCE, CONSIDER . . .

For each of these last two sorrows, prayer is offered to obtain a specific virtue and gift of the Holy Spirit. Which of these virtues and gifts do I need most to cultivate?

CLOSING PRAYER

Mary, help me to be charitable and diligent. Ask the Holy Spirit to give me the gifts of understanding and wisdom.

Mary adores Jesus' wounds

St. Alphonsus imagines Mary's grief as she holds her Son's lifeless body.

Devout souls, listen to what the sorrowful Mary says on the day of her Son's death: "My beloved children, I don't want you to try to console me. No, for my soul is no longer capable of consolation in this world after the death of my dear Jesus." My sovereign Lady, since you won't be consoled, and you have so great a thirst for sufferings, I must tell you: Even with the death of your Son, your sorrows haven't ended. On this day you will be wounded by another sword of sorrow: A cruel lance will pierce the side of your Son already dead, and you must receive him in your arms after he's taken down from the Cross.

And now we must consider the sixth sorrow that afflicted this poor mother. Listen and weep! Until now the sorrows of Mary tortured her one by one. On this day they are all united to assail her. A devout author says that when our beloved Redeemer was dead, the first care of the great mother was to accompany in spirit the most holy soul of her Son, and present it to the Eternal Father.

"I present you, my God," Mary must then have said, "the immaculate soul of your Son and mine. He has now obeyed you to the point of death. Receive him, then, in your arms. Your justice is now satisfied, your will is accomplished. Look! The great sacrifice to your eternal glory is consummated." Then, turning toward the lifeless limbs of her Jesus: "Wounds of love, I adore you, and in you I rejoice. For through you, salvation is given to the world. You will remain open in the body of my Son, and be the refuge of those who turn to you. How many, through you, will receive the pardon of their sins, and by you be enflamed with love for God!"

—St. Alphonsus Liguori, *The Glories of Mary*

IN GOD'S PRESENCE, CONSIDER . . .

If I had held the lifeless body of Jesus, what would I have said to him? What would I have said to his heavenly Father?

CLOSING PRAYER

From the "The Seven Dolors of Mary at the Death of Jesus": *O grief-stricken mother, what did you experience when, after the dead body of your Son had been taken down from the Cross, it was laid in your virginal arms and bathed with your tears? You were spared no suffering as you beheld the large wounds in his hands and feet!*

All sinners have crucified Mary's son

St. Alphonsus reflects on Mary's grief as she holds her Son's lifeless body. She laments the cruelty of sinners of all the ages who have crucified him.

It was revealed to St. Bridget that three ladders were placed against the cross of Jesus to take down his sacred body. According to a compiler of stories about the saints, the holy disciples first drew out the nails from the hands and feet and gave them to Mary. Then one supported the upper part of the body of Jesus, and the other the lower, as they took it down from the Cross. The spiritual writer Bernardine de Bustis depicts the afflicted mother as standing with arms extended to meet her dear Son. She embraced him, then sat down at the foot of the Cross. His mouth was open; his eyes were dim. Next she examined his mangled flesh and exposed bones. She took off the crown of thorns and saw the sad injuries that it had inflicted on that sacred head. She saw the holes in his hands and feet, and she spoke to him in these words:

"Son, to what has your love for men brought you? And what evil had you done to them, that they would have tormented you so cruelly? You were my father, you were my brother, my spouse, my delight, my glory. You were my all." My Son, see my affliction, look at me, console me! But no, you no longer look at me. Speak, say but a word, and console me! But you speak no more, for you are dead. Then, turning to those barbarous instruments of torture, she said, "Cruel thorns, cruel nails, merciless spear! How, how could you torture your Creator this way? But why do I speak of thorns or nails? Sinners, you are the ones who have so cruelly treated my Son.

In this way did Mary speak and complain of us. But what would she now say, were she still capable of suffering? What would be her grief in seeing how men, even though her Son has died for them, still continue to torment and crucify him by their sins?

—St. Alphonsus Liguori, *The Glories of Mary*

IN GOD'S PRESENCE, CONSIDER . . .

Since I'm a sinner, I'm one of those Mary complained about; by my sin, I still continue to torment and crucify her Son. Have I asked Jesus to forgive me for this continuing torment? Have I asked Mary to help me end it?

CLOSING PRAYER

From a hymn by Johann Heerman: *Who was the guilty? Who brought this upon thee? Alas, my treason, Jesus, hath undone thee. 'Twas I, Lord Jesus, I it was denied thee. I crucified thee.*

Mary goes to Jesus' tomb

St. Alphonsus recalls the speculations of several saints about what Mary did as her Son was buried, and as she returned home.

The disciples raised the stone and closed up the holy sepulcher, and in it the body of Jesus, that great treasure—a treasure so great that neither earth nor heaven had a greater one. Mary's heart was buried with Jesus, because Jesus was all her treasure: "Where your treasure is, there will your heart be also" (Lk 12:34).

Before leaving the sepulcher, according to St. Bonaventure, Mary blessed the sacred stone that closed it, saying, "Happy stone, that now encloses the sacred body that for nine months was contained in my womb! I bless you and envy you. I leave you as the guardian of my Son, of that Son who is all my treasure and all my love." Then raising her heart to the Eternal Father, she said, "Father, to you I entrust him—the One who is your Son at the same time that he is mine." In this way, saying her last goodbye to her beloved Jesus and to the sepulcher, she left it and returned to her own house.

"This mother," says St. Bernard, "went away so afflicted and sad that she moved many to tears in spite of themselves. And wherever she passed, all who met her wept" and could not restrain their tears. He adds that the holy disciples and women who accompanied her "mourned even more for her than for their Lord." St. Bonaventure remarks: "The sisters of Our Lady veiled her as a widow, almost covering her whole face." He also says that on her return, passing before the Cross still wet with the blood of her Jesus, she was the first to adore it. "Holy cross," she then said, "I kiss you, I adore you! For you are no longer a shameful gibbet, but a throne of love and an altar of mercy, consecrated by the blood of the divine Lamb, which on you has been sacrificed for the salvation of the world."

—St. Alphonsus Liguori, *The Glories of Mary*

IN GOD'S PRESENCE, CONSIDER . . .

When I attend a funeral, or visit the grave of a loved one, am I able to let the hope of eternal life lighten my grief, with gratitude to Jesus and his mother for opening the door to heaven?

CLOSING PRAYER

From a prayer of St. Alphonsus: *Ah, my buried Jesus, I kiss the stone that encloses you. But you rose again the third day. I beg you, by your resurrection, make me rise glorious with you on the last day, to be always united with you in heaven, to praise you and love you forever.*

Mary returns home to weep for Jesus

St. Alphonsus imagines the first hours Mary spends at home after returning from Jesus' burial.

After accompanying Jesus' body to the tomb, and adoring the Cross as she passed by it, Mary returned home. Once she arrived, the afflicted mother cast her eyes around, and no longer saw her Jesus. Instead of the sweet presence of her dear Son, the memory of his beautiful life and cruel death presented itself before her eyes.

She remembered how she had pressed that Son to her breast in the crib of Bethlehem, and the conversations she had held with him during the many years they had lived in the house of Nazareth. She remembered their mutual affection, their loving looks, the words of eternal life that fell from those divine lips. And then the sad scene she had witnessed that day again presented itself before her. The nails, the thorns, the lacerated flesh of her Son, those deep wounds, those exposed bones, that open mouth, those dimmed eyes, all presented themselves before her. What a night of sorrow was that night for Mary!

The afflicted mother, turning to St. John, mournfully said: "John, tell me where is your Master?" Then she asked Mary Magdalene: "Daughter, tell me, where is your beloved? O God, who has taken him from us?" Mary wept, and all who were present wept with her. Yet you, my soul, fail to weep! So turn to Mary, and speak to her with St. Bonaventure, saying: "My own sweet Lady, let me weep; you are innocent; I am guilty." Beg her at least to let you weep with her. While she weeps for love, you must weep because of sorrow for your sins.

—St. Alphonsus Liguori, *The Glories of Mary*

IN GOD'S PRESENCE, CONSIDER . . .

Am I ever so grieved by my sins that I weep in sorrow because of them? Have I asked Mary to obtain for me the grace of a contrite heart?

CLOSING PRAYER

From a prayer of St. Alphonsus: *My afflicted Mother, I will not leave you alone to weep. No, I will accompany you with my tears. This grace I now ask of you: Obtain for me that I may always bear in mind and always have a tender devotion toward the passion of Jesus and your sorrows.*

Mary's long passion after Calvary

The English poet Francis Thompson acknowledges the terrible pain that Mary must have suffered as she stood by the Cross. But he proposes that she endured "a longer Calvary" in the following years, as she waited for death to reunite her at last with her Son.

O Lady Mary, thy bright crown is no mere crown of majesty;
for with the reflex of his own resplendent thorns Christ circled thee.
The red rose of this passion-tide doth take a deeper hue from thee,
in the five wounds of Jesus dyed, and in thy bleeding thoughts, Mary!

The soldier struck a triple stroke, that smote thy Jesus on the tree.
He broke the Heart of Hearts, and broke the saint's and mother's hearts
   in thee.
Thy Son went up the angels' ways, his passion ended; but, ah me!
Thou found'st the road of further days a longer way of Calvary:

On the hard cross of hope deferred thou hung'st in loving agony,
until the mortal-dreaded word which chills our mirth, spake mirth to thee.
The angel Death from this cold tomb of life did roll the stone away;
and he thou barest in thy womb caught thee at last into the day,
before the living throne of whom the lights of heaven burning pray.

—Francis Thompson, "The Passion of Mary: Verses in Passion Tide"

IN GOD'S PRESENCE, CONSIDER . . .

Have I ever experienced a "hard cross of hope deferred"? How might Mary's experience of that cross make it easier for me to bear?

CLOSING PRAYER

Blessed Virgin, through the consolation of your presence and prayers, help us to bear the burden of hope deferred, looking to your Son, who is our hope of final, eternal joy.

Mary, mountain of shade

St. Germanus gathers together a great heap of common Marian images in this hymn of love to the Blessed Mother. But he adds as well some that are uniquely his, giving us reason to pause and consider their meaning.

Hail, Mary, full of grace!
You are more holy than the saints,
   higher than the heavens,
   more glorious than the angels,
   more venerable than every creature.
Hail, heavenly paradise of fragrance,
   lily giving off the sweetest scent,
   perfumed rose opening to heal men.
Hail, immaculate temple of the Lord,
   built in a holy fashion,
   ornament of divine splendor, open to everyone,
   oasis of mystical sweetness.
Hail, mountain of shade, grazing ground for the holy Lamb
   who takes upon himself the miseries and sins of the world.
Hail, sacred throne of God, blessed dwelling,
   lofty ornaments, costly jewel, magnificent heavens.
Hail, urn of purest gold, who contained Christ the Bread from heaven,
   the gentle sweetness of our souls.
Hail, most pure Virgin Mother, worthy of praise and honor,
   fountain of streams of water, treasure of innocence, splendor of holiness.

—St. Germanus

IN GOD'S PRESENCE, CONSIDER . . .

   What do I think St. Germanus means when he refers to Mary as "oasis of mystical sweetness," "mountain of shade," and "grazing ground for the holy Lamb"? What kind of spiritual landscape is he painting for us to help us understand Mary more deeply?

CLOSING PRAYER

   From a prayer of St. Germanus: *Mary, lead us to the harbor of peace and salvation, to the glory of Christ, who lives forever with the Father and with the Holy Spirit.*

Mary, guide me in the way of salvation

St. Thomas Aquinas is widely known for his carefully reasoned analysis of theological matters. But in this prayer, we hear his heart rise up in sweet devotion to Our Lady, passionate in his praise and gratitude.

Most blessed and sweet Virgin Mary, Mother of God, filled with all tenderness, daughter of the most high King, Lady of the angels, mother of all the faithful: On this day and all the days of my life, I entrust to your merciful heart my body and my soul, all my actions, thoughts, decisions, desires, words, deeds, my entire life and death, so that, with your assistance, everything may be ordered to the good according to the will of your beloved Son, our Lord Jesus Christ. From your beloved Son, beg for me the grace firmly to resist the temptations of the world, the flesh, and the Devil.

My most holy Lady, I also beg you to obtain for me true obedience and humility of heart so that I may see myself truly as a sinner, miserable and weak and powerless, without the grace and assistance of my Creator and without your holy prayers. Obtain for me as well, most sweet Lady, true charity, so that from the depths of my heart I may love your most holy Son, our Lord Jesus Christ and, after him, love you above all others. Grant, Queen of Heaven, that always in my heart I may both fear and love your most sweet Son.

I pray also that, at the end of my life, Mother beyond compare, gate of heaven and advocate of sinners, you will protect me with your great piety and mercy, and obtain for me, through the blessed and glorious passion of your Son, and through your own intercession, the forgiveness of all my sins, which I hope to receive. When I die in your love and his love, guide me in the way of salvation and blessedness.

—St. Thomas Aquinas

IN GOD'S PRESENCE, CONSIDER . . .

Why must I, as St. Thomas prays, "see myself truly as a sinner, miserable and weak and powerless"? If I don't recognize that reality, will I seek "the grace and assistance of my Creator" and Mary's "holy prayers"?

CLOSING PRAYER

From a prayer of St. Mary Magdalen de Pazzi: *Mary, I give myself to you without reservation. Accept me and preserve me!*

Mary, who can repay you?

St. Augustine of Hippo begins his prayer to Our Lady with words of gratitude, trusting that what seems to him like a meager offering of praise will nevertheless be rewarded by her intercession.

Blessed Virgin Mary, who can worthily repay you with praise and thanks for rescuing a fallen world by your generous consent? What songs of praise can our weak human nature offer in your honor, since it was through you that we have found the way to salvation? Accept, then, the poor thanks that we have to offer, even though it may be less than what you deserve. Receive our gratitude and obtain by your prayers the forgiveness of our sins. Take our prayers into the sanctuary of heaven and enable them to make our peace with God.

Let the sins we bring before Almighty God in repentance be forgiven through you. Let what we beg with confidence be granted through you. Accept our offering and grant our request. Obtain forgiveness for what we fear, for you are the only hope of sinners. We hope to obtain the forgiveness of our sins through you. Blessed Lady, our hope of reward is in you.

Holy Mary, help those who are miserable, strengthen those who are discouraged, comfort those who are sorrowful. Pray for your people, plead for the clergy, intercede for all women consecrated to God. Let all who honor you know your assistance and protection. Be ready to assist us when we pray, and bring back to us the answers to our prayers. Make it your concern always to pray for the people of God, for you were blessed by God and were made worthy to bear the Redeemer of the world, who lives and reigns forever.

—St. Augustine of Hippo

IN GOD'S PRESENCE, CONSIDER . . .

What prayers have I recently prayed that haven't been answered as I was hoping for? What other priorities for my spiritual growth might God have in mind for me?

CLOSING PRAYER

From a prayer of St. Alphonsus Liguori: *The Eternal Word came from heaven on earth to seek for lost sheep, and to save them he became your Son, Mary. When one of them goes to you to find Jesus, surely you will not turn him away.*

In Mary, heaven embraced earth

The Marian prayers of St. Bernard of Clairvaux abound with lovely and powerful images to be relished and pondered. Here, he speaks of heaven's embrace of earth when God became Man in Mary's womb.

Mary, our Mother,
the whole world reveres you
as the holiest shrine of the living God,
for in you, the salvation of the world dawned.
The Son of God was pleased to take human flesh from you.
You have broken down the wall of hatred,
the barrier between heaven and earth that had been raised
by Adam and Eve's disobedience.
In you, heaven embraced earth when divinity and humanity
were united in one Person, the God-Man.
Mother of God, we sing your praises,
but we must praise you even more.
Our speech is too feeble to honor you as we should,
for no tongue is eloquent enough
to tell your excellence.
Mary, most powerful, most holy, and worthy of all love:
Your name brings new life,
and the thought of you calls forth love
in the hearts of all who are devoted to you.

—St. Bernard of Clairvaux

IN GOD'S PRESENCE, CONSIDER . . .

What does it mean to me to realize that "heaven embraced earth" in Mary? Do I have a personal sense of God's embrace in Christ—that he himself has come down from heaven to join himself to me in love?

CLOSING PRAYER

From the *Tota Pulchra Es*: *You are all beauty, Mary, and there is no blemish of original sin in you. Your garments are as white as snow, and your face is as the sun. You are the glory of Jerusalem, the joy of Israel, the source of honor to our people.*

God could not make a creature more holy than Mary

St. Leonard of Port Maurice concludes that in making Mary his mother, he gave her the best of everything.

God could create
an infinity of suns,
one more brilliant than the other;
an infinity of worlds,
one more marvelous than the other;
an infinity of angels,
one more holy than the other.

But a creature more holy,
more ravishing,
more gracious than his mother
he could not make.

For in making her his mother,
he gave her at once, so to say,
all that he could give
of beauty and goodness
and holiness and sanctity
in the treasury of his omnipotence.

—St. Leonard of Port Maurice

IN GOD'S PRESENCE, CONSIDER . . .

Why would Mary's status as the Mother of God imply perfections of beauty, goodness, holiness, and sanctity in her creation? Would God create his own mother to be anything less?

CLOSING PRAYER

From a prayer of St. Germanus: *Your name is Our Lady. You alone are Mother of God and raised high over all the earth.*

Fair as the moon, bright as the sun

St. Bernard compares Mary to the moon, radiantly reflecting the light of Jesus, the Sun of Justice, whom the Old Testament prophet Malachi said would one day "rise with healing in its wings" (Mal 4:2).

Of you, Mary, was the question asked, "Who is this that looks forth like the dawn, fair as the moon, bright as the sun?" (Sg 6:10). You came into the world, then, Mary, as a resplendent dawn, preceding with the light of your sanctity the coming of the Sun of Justice. The day on which you came into the world can indeed be called a day of salvation, a day of grace.

You are fair as the moon; for just as among all planets the moon is most like the sun, so among all creatures you are the nearest in resemblance to God. The moon illumines the night with the light it receives from the sun, and you enlighten our darkness with the splendor of your virtues. But you are fairer than the moon, for in you there is neither spot nor shadow.

You are bright as the sun; I mean as that Sun who created the sun. He was chosen among all men, and you were chosen among all women. Sweet, great, all-loveable Mary, no heart can pronounce your name without your enflaming it with your love. Nor can those who love you think of you without feeling themselves strengthened to love you more.

Holy Lady, help our weakness. And who is more fit to address our Lord Jesus Christ than you, who enjoy in such closeness his most sweet conversation? Speak then, speak, Lady; for your Son listens to you, and you will obtain all that you ask of him.

—St. Bernard of Clairvaux

IN GOD'S PRESENCE, CONSIDER . . .

In what other ways can Mary be compared to the dawn and the moon? How do these attributes make her beautiful to her children?

CLOSING PRAYER

From a prayer of St. Bernard: *Lady, you ravish the hearts of your servants by the love and favor you show them. Ravish also my miserable heart, which desires passionately to love you.*

Blessed are you, Mary

The ancient poet Jacob of Sarug, known as "the flute of the Holy Spirit,"
focuses on the intimacy of mother and Son, and the fruits of that intimacy
in our lives.

Blessed are you, Mary, and blessed is your holy soul,
for your blessedness is beyond that of all the blessed.
Blessed are you who have borne, held in your arms, and kissed as
    an Infant
the One who upholds the ages in secret with his word.
Blessed are you, from whom the Savior has appeared on this earth
    of exile,
overcoming the tempter and bringing peace to the world.
Blessed are you, whose pure mouth touched the lips
of the One whom the seraphim dare not look upon in his radiance.
Blessed are you, who have fed with your pure milk
the Source of light and life for all the living.
Blessed are you, because the whole universe rings on the day of
    your memorial,
and angels and men celebrate your festival.
Daughter of the poor, you became the mother of the King of kings.
You gave to this poor world the riches that can make it alive.
You are the ship that is filled with the goodness and the treasures of
    the Father,
who sent his riches once more into our empty home.

—Jabob of Sarug

IN GOD'S PRESENCE, CONSIDER . . .

What spiritual riches in my life have come to me through Mary? What "treasures of the Father" has she brought in to the "empty home" of my soul?

CLOSING PRAYER

From a prayer of St. Bernard of Clairvaux: *You are that chosen Lady in whom our Lord found repose, and in whom he has deposited all his treasures without measure. So the whole world, my most holy Lady, honors your chaste womb as the temple of God, in which the salvation of the world began.*

Could my sin be greater than Mary's mercy?

My sins may be great, St. William of Paris admits, but could they possibly greater than Mary's mercy? Never let it be said!

O Mother of God, I turn to you, and I call upon you not to reject me. For the whole congregation of the faithful calls you and proclaims you the Mother of Mercy.

You are the one who is so dear to God that you are always graciously heard by him. Your mercy was never lacking to anyone. Your most kind graciousness never despised any sinner who turned to you, however enormous his crimes might be.

Could the Church be speaking falsely or in vain when she calls you her advocate, and the Refuge of Sinners? Of course not! Never let it be said that my sins could prevent you from fulfilling the great ministry of mercy that is uniquely your own, by which you are the advocate and mediatrix of peace, the only hope and most secure refuge of the miserable.

Never shall it be said that the Mother of God, who for the benefit of the world brought forth Jesus, the Fountain of mercy, denied her mercy to any sinner who turned to her. Your appointed role is that of peacemaker between God and men. So let the greatness of your compassion, which far exceeds my sins, move you to help me.

—St. William of Paris

IN GOD'S PRESENCE, CONSIDER . . .

Do I ever fear that my sins are too great for God to forgive? That would mean that Christ's sacrifice was insufficient. Do I ever fear that my sins are so great that even Mary can't help me? What would that say about her grace and mercy?

CLOSING PRAYER

"Have mercy on me, O God, according to your merciful love; according to your abundant mercy blot out my transgressions. Wash me thoroughly from my iniquity, and cleanse me from my sin" (Ps 51:1–2).

Mary, be warmth to the world

Caryll Houselander was an English Catholic spiritual writer, poet, and artist. In the concluding verses of a poem about Mary, whom she calls "The Reed" into which God breathed to make "infinite music," she asks Our Lady to soothe our troubled world with her lullaby.

Mary, Mother of God,
we are the poor soil
and the dry dust;
we are hard with a cold frost.

Be warmth to the world;
be the thaw,
warm on the cold frost;
be the thaw that melts,
that the tender shoot of Christ,
piercing the hard heart,
flower to a spring in us.

Be hands that are rocking the world
to a kind rhythm of love;
that the incoherence of war
and the chaos of our unrest
be soothed to a lullaby;
and the round and sorrowful world,
in your hands,
the cradle of God.

—From Caryll Houselander, "The Reed"

IN GOD'S PRESENCE, CONSIDER . . .

For whom is the poet seeking Mary's maternal care? What might it mean to view the world as "the cradle of God"?

CLOSING PRAYER

From a prayer of St. Joachima Vedruna de Mas: *Most holy Virgin, you were constituted mother of sinners at the foot of the Cross. Give us your holy blessing so that, sheltered under your holy mantle, we may follow in your footsteps, and be truly meek and humble of heart.*

Mary, my greatest consolation

St. Germanus recites the difficulties that may afflict us in this life, and turns to the Blessed Virgin as the remedy for each one.

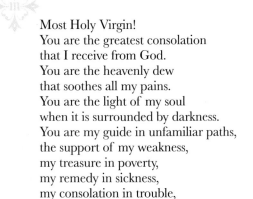

Most Holy Virgin!
You are the greatest consolation
that I receive from God.
You are the heavenly dew
that soothes all my pains.
You are the light of my soul
when it is surrounded by darkness.
You are my guide in unfamiliar paths,
the support of my weakness,
my treasure in poverty,
my remedy in sickness,
my consolation in trouble,
my refuge in misery,
and the hope of my salvation.
Hear my petitions,
have pity on me, as is fitting
for the mother of so good a God,
and obtain for me a favorable reception
of all my petitions at the throne of mercy.

—St. Germanus

IN GOD'S PRESENCE, CONSIDER . . .

How is Mary able to be our consolation in darkness and uncertainty, pain and sickness, weakness and poverty, trouble and misery?

CLOSING PRAYER

From a prayer of St. Alphonsus Liguori: *I now place myself entirely in your hands. Tell me what I must do in order to please God, and I will be ready for all, and hope to do all with your help, Mary—my mother, my light, my consolation, my refuge, my hope.*

Mary will accept our meager praise

St. John of Damascus recalls a story to illustrate that we should tell Mary our gratitude, even if we can't adequately express it.

Neither human tongue nor angelic mind can worthily praise her through whom it is given to us to look clearly upon the Lord's glory. What then? Shall we be silent through fear of our insufficiency? Certainly not. Mingling fear with desire, and weaving them into one crown with reverent hand and longing soul, let's show forth the poor first fruits of our intelligence in gratitude to our queen and mother, the benefactor of all creation, as a repayment of our debt to her.

One day some peasants were ploughing up the soil when a king happened to pass by, in the splendor of his royal robes and crown and surrounded by countless gift bearers. As there was no gift to offer at that moment, one of the peasants was collecting water in his hands, as there happened to be a plentiful stream nearby. From this he prepared a gift for the king, who said, "What is this, my boy?"

The boy answered boldly: "I made the best of what I had, thinking it was better to show my willingness than to offer nothing. You don't need our gifts, nor do you want anything from us except our good will. The need is on our side, and the reward is in the doing. I know that glory often comes to the grateful."

Marveling, the king praised the boy's cleverness, graciously acknowledged his willingness, and made him many rich gifts in return. Now, if that proud monarch so generously rewarded good intentions, won't Our Lady, the Mother of God, accept our good will, not judging us by what we accomplish in praising her?

—St. John of Damascus, *First Homily on the Dormition*

IN GOD'S PRESENCE, CONSIDER . . .

Do I ever worry that my lack of eloquence makes my prayers to Mary unworthy? Should a little child hesitate to tell his mother his gratitude because the only words he knows are "thank you"?

CLOSING PRAYER
Sweet heart of Mary, be my salvation.

Son of God, help me to praise your mother!

If we feel inadequate to praise our Blessed Mother, says St. John of Damascus, then we should ask her Son to help us.

Our Lady is the Mother of God, who alone is good and infinite in his condescension, who preferred to many splendid gifts the two copper coins of the widow in the temple. She will indeed receive us, who are paying off our debt through praise, and make us a return out of all proportion to what we offer.

What shall we say, O Queen? What words shall we use? What praise shall we pour upon your sacred and glorified head, you giver of good gifts and of riches, the pride of the human race, the glory of all creation, through whom it is truly blessed?

The One whom nature did not contain in the beginning was born of you. The invisible One was contemplated by you face to face. Word of God, open my slow lips, and give their speech your richest blessing! Enflame us with the grace of your Spirit, through whom fishermen became orators, and ignorant men spoke supernatural wisdom!

Only then can our feeble voices contribute to your beloved mother's praises, even if it means that her greatness will be extolled by our misery. She is the one chosen from an ancient race, by a predetermined counsel and the good pleasure of God the Father. He had begotten you, Son of God, in eternity within himself; she brought you forth in the latter times—you who are our atoning sacrifice and salvation, our justice and redemption, life of life, light of light, and true God of true God!

—St. John of Damascus, *First Homily on the Dormition*

IN GOD'S PRESENCE, CONSIDER . . .

What does it mean to "pay off our debt through praise"? What is the "return" we receive for praising Our Lady?

CLOSING PRAYER

Mary, I will praise you in the words of my Lord, which foreshadowed your fullness of grace: "Many women have done excellently, but you surpass them all!" (Prv 31:29).

Prayer of total consecration to the Immaculata

Several saints have urged us to make an act of total consecration to Mary. Here is the prayer of consecration to the Immaculata, "the Immaculate One," composed by St. Maximillian Kolbe.

O Immaculata, Queen of Heaven and Earth, Refuge of Sinners and our most loving mother: God has willed to entrust the entire order of mercy to you. I, a repentant sinner, cast myself at your feet, humbly imploring you to take me with all that I am and have, wholly to yourself as your possession and property. Please make of me, of all my powers of soul and body, of my whole life, death and eternity, whatever most pleases you. If it pleases you, use all that I am and have without reserve, wholly to accomplish what was said of you: "She will crush your head" (see Gn 3:15) and "You alone have destroyed all heresies in the whole world."

Let me be a fit instrument in your immaculate and merciful hands for introducing and increasing your glory to the maximum in all the many strayed and indifferent souls, and thus help extend as far as possible the blessed kingdom of the most Sacred Heart of Jesus. For wherever you enter, you obtain the grace of conversion and growth in holiness, since it is through your hands that all graces come to us from the most Sacred Heart of Jesus.

V. Allow me to praise you, O Sacred Virgin

R. Give me strength against your enemies. Amen.

—St. Maximilian Kolbe,
"Prayer of Total Consecration to the Immaculata"

IN GOD'S PRESENCE, CONSIDER . . .

What would it mean for me to give Mary all that I am and have, to become wholly her "possession and property"? Is there at least one aspect of my life that I can give to her wholly today?

CLOSING PRAYER

From a prayer of St. Thomas Aquinas: *Most blessed and most sweet Virgin Mary, full of mercy, to your compassion I entrust my soul and body, my thoughts and actions, my life and death.*

A papal prayer of consecration to Mary

Venerable Pope Pius XII urged Catholics everywhere to consecrate themselves to Mary, so they could fulfill the desires of the Sacred Heart of Jesus.

Most holy Virgin Mary, tender mother of all, to fulfill the desires of the Sacred Heart and the request of the vicar of your Son on earth, we consecrate ourselves and our families to your sorrowful and immaculate heart, O Queen of the Most Holy Rosary, and we entrust to you all the people of our country and all the world.

Please accept our consecration, dearest mother, and use us as you wish to accomplish your designs upon the world.

O sorrowful and immaculate heart of Mary, Queen of the Most Holy Rosary, and Queen of the World, rule over us, together with the sacred heart of Jesus Christ, our King. Save us from the spreading flood of modern paganism; kindle in our hearts and homes the love of purity, the practice of a virtuous life, an ardent zeal for souls, and a desire to pray the Rosary more faithfully.

We come with confidence to you, O throne of grace and mother of fair love. Enflame us with the same divine Fire that has enflamed your own sorrowful and immaculate heart. Make our hearts and homes your shrine, and through us, make the heart of Jesus, together with your rule, triumphant in every heart and home.

—Venerable Pope Pius XII

IN GOD'S PRESENCE, CONSIDER . . .

The demands and influences of a secular world press in around me, indifferent to eternal concerns, corrosive of moral values, preoccupied with wealth, pleasure, power, and celebrity. If I don't intentionally consecrate myself to Jesus and Mary, what hope do I have of resisting the world and challenging its vanities?

CLOSING PRAYER

From a prayer of St. Bonaventure: *Rule over me, my Queen, and don't leave me to myself.*

Prayer to Mary, Mother of Divine Love

In this prayer, Venerable Pope Pius XII widens the focus of our prayers to Mary beyond purely private matters to the concerns of nations, the poor, the oppressed, and the persecuted.

To you, O Mary, are known all the needs of your people and of the whole Church. Mother of Truth and Seat of Wisdom, dissipate the clouds of error that darken our minds. Correct the strayings of our hearts, and inspire in us love for truth and the desire to do good.

Obtain for all people a holy fear of God so that society may know happiness. Give us lively faith that we may trust in those things that are imperishable. Give us that love which is sealed forever in God.

Obtain for families fidelity, harmony, and peace. Stir up and confirm in the hearts of those who govern nations a clear notion of their responsibility, and of their duty to foster religion, morality, and the common good.

And just as your mercy is showered upon souls, O Mary, may it likewise flow over all those ills that afflict this people, and indeed the whole Christian family. Have pity on the poor, on captives, on all who bear persecution for the sake of justice or are stricken by misfortune.

Hail, O Mary, mother of those who wander here below. You are our life, our sweetness, and our hope.

O Mother of Divine Love, send down your motherly blessing on all who pray to you; send it abundantly and consolingly.

—Venerable Pope Pius XII

IN GOD'S PRESENCE, CONSIDER . . .

What concerns of the world beyond my door should I be bringing to Mary in prayer? Might I make it a habit to pray for those I learn about from the daily news who so desperately need heaven's intervention?

CLOSING PRAYER

From a prayer of Pope St. John Paul II: *Mother of all men and women, and of all peoples, you who know all their sufferings and their hopes, you who have a mother's awareness of all the struggles between good and evil, between light and darkness, which afflict the modern world, accept the cry which we, moved by the Holy Spirit, address directly to your heart.*

Perseverance in devotion to Mary

Devotion to Mary can lose its reward, St. Alphonsus warns, if it proves to be short-lived.

We must have perseverance in devotion to Mary. "Perseverance alone," says St. Bernard, "will merit a crown." When Thomas à Kempis was a young man, he used to turn to the Blessed Virgin every day with certain prayers. But one day he left them off. Then he left them off for several weeks, and in the end he gave them up altogether.

One night Thomas saw Mary in a dream. She embraced all his companions, but when his turn came, she said, "What do you expect—you who have given up your devotions? Go away; you're unworthy of my embrace." On hearing this, Thomas awoke in alarm and went back to saying the prayers he had once prayed faithfully.

Richard of Saint Lawrence says with good reason that "he who perseveres in his devotion to Mary will be blessed in his confidence, and will obtain all he desires." But just as no one can be certain of this perseverance, no one before death can be certain of salvation.

The advice given by St. John Berchmans, of the Society of Jesus, deserves our particular attention. When this holy young man was dying, his companions begged him, before he left this world, to tell them what devotion they could perform that would be most agreeable to our Blessed Lady. He replied in the following remarkable words: "Any devotion, however small—provided it is constant."

—St. Alphonsus Liguori, *The Glories of Mary*

IN GOD'S PRESENCE, CONSIDER . . .

Perseverance is an aspect of the virtue of fortitude. Am I persevering in my devotion to Jesus and Mary, or is my devotion feeble and fragile?

CLOSING PRAYER

Mary, pray for me that I will "never flag in zeal, be aglow with Spirit, serve the Lord, rejoice in hope, be patient in tribulation, be constant in prayer" (see Rom 12:11–12).

Place yourself entirely in Mary's hands

St. Alphonsus advises us that Mary knows how to grant us an even greater grace than we could possibly ask.

Blessed Raymond Jordano affirms: "Whoever finds Mary finds every good." He adds: "Her kindness is so great that no one need fear to approach her. And her mercy is so great, that no one is turned away." Thomas à Kempis has her say: "I invite everyone to turn to me; I expect everyone, I desire everyone, and I never despise any sinner, however unworthy he may be, who comes to seek my aid." She's always ready and inclined to help us, and to obtain for us every grace of eternal salvation by her powerful prayers.

When we turn to Mary, it's advisable to entreat her to ask and obtain for us the graces that she knows to be the most expedient for our salvation. This is precisely what the Dominican Brother Reginald did, as it's related in the chronicles of that religious order. This servant of Mary was ill, and he asked her to obtain for him the recovery of his health. His sovereign Lady appeared to him, accompanied by St. Cecilia and St. Catherine, and said with the greatest sweetness, "My son, what do you desire of me?"

The brother was confused at so gracious an offer on Mary's part, and he didn't know what to answer. Then one of the saints gave him this advice: "Reginald, I'll tell you what to do: Ask for nothing. Instead, place yourself entirely in her hands, for Mary will know how to grant you a greater grace than you can possibly ask." The sick man followed this advice, and the Mother of God obtained for him the restoration of his health. If we also desire the happiness of receiving a visit from this Queen of Heaven, we should often visit her by going before her image, or praying to her in churches dedicated in her honor.

—St. Alphonsus Liguori, *The Glories of Mary*

IN GOD'S PRESENCE, CONSIDER . . .

Am I uncertain sometimes what I should be asking God to do for me? Have I prayed that Mary will simply ask him for what's best, knowing that she's better able to discern what's best than I am?

CLOSING PRAYER

From a prayer of St. Germanus: *O my sovereign Lady, guide of my poor judgment, strength of my weakness, covering of my nakedness, treasure of my poverty, remedy for incurable wounds, wiper away of tears, end of sighs, reverser of misfortunes, lightener of grief, loosener of my bonds, my hope of salvation: Listen to my prayers and have mercy on my sighs.*

The Holy Spirit is revealing more of Mary

St. Louis explains why so little was said of Mary in the Gospels, and why the Holy Spirit has increased our understanding of her over the centuries in a way that will culminate when her Son returns in glory.

It is by Mary that the salvation of the world has begun, and it is by Mary that it must be consummated. Mary has hardly appeared at all in the first coming of Jesus Christ, in order that men, as yet but little instructed and enlightened on the Person of her Son, would not remove themselves from him, in attaching themselves too strongly and too grossly to her.

This would have apparently taken place if she had been known, because of the admirable charms which the Most High had bestowed even upon her exterior. This is so true that the ancient writer Dionysius the Areopagite has informed us in his writings that when he saw our Blessed Lady, he would have taken her for a divinity, in consequence of her secret charms and incomparable beauty, had not the faith in which he was well established taught him the contrary.

But in the second coming of Jesus Christ, Mary has to be made known and revealed by the Holy Spirit, in order that by her Jesus Christ may be known, loved, and served. The reasons which moved the Holy Spirit to hide his spouse during her life, and to reveal her only a very little since the preaching of the gospel, continue no longer. God wishes that his holy mother should be at present more known, more loved, more honored than she has ever been.

—St. Louis de Montfort, *True Devotion to Mary*

IN GOD'S PRESENCE, CONSIDER . . .

Am I doing my part to cooperate with the Holy Spirit to make Mary better known, so that through her, Jesus Christ may be known, loved, and served?

CLOSING PRAYER

From a prayer of St. Alphonsus: *Mary, if in times past I have failed to serve you well, and lost so many occasions to honor you, for the future I will be one of your most loving and faithful servants. I am determined that from this day forward no one will surpass me in honoring and loving you, my most lovable Queen.*

The growing science of Mary

Fr. Frederick Faber compares the grand truth about Mary to the great truths of science: In both cases, a truth so grand and complex has endless applications and lessons to teach us.

Mary is like one of those great scientific truths whose full import we never master except by long meditation, and by studying its bearings on a system. Then at last the fertility and grandeur of the truth seem endless. So it is with the Mother of God. She teaches us God as we never could otherwise have learned him. She mirrors more of him in her single self than all the rest of the intelligent and material creation. In her the prodigies of his love toward ourselves became credible.

She is the hilltop from which we gain distant views into his perfections, and see fair regions of him of which we otherwise would not have dreamed. Our thoughts of him grow worthier by means of her. The full dignity of creation shines bright in her. Standing on her, the perfect mere creature, we look over into the depths of the union of the divine and human natures in Christ, which otherwise would have been a gulf whose edges we could never have reached.

The amount of knowledge in the present age is overwhelming. Yet the deepest thinkers deem science to be only in its infancy. Many things indicate this truth. Just as science is yearly growing, yearly outgrowing the old systems that held it within too narrow limits, so is the science of Mary growing in each loving and studious heart all through life, within the spacious domains of vast theology. And in heaven it will outgrow all that earth's theologies have laid down as limits—limits made necessary more by the narrowness of our own capacities than by the real magnitude of the one they define. Yet we would ill use Mary's magnificence, or rather we would show that we had altogether misunderstood it, if we did not use it as a revelation of God, and an approach to him.

—Fr. Frederick William Faber, *Bethlehem*

IN GOD'S PRESENCE, CONSIDER . . .

In what ways has my own understanding of "the science of Mary" increased as I've read these meditations throughout the past year? In which matters do I seek a fuller, clearer understanding of her?

CLOSING PRAYER

From a prayer of St. Gregory Thaumaturgus: *You, Mary, are the vessel and chamber containing all mysteries. You know what the patriarchs never knew; you have experienced what was never revealed to the angels; you have heard what the prophets never heard.*

A prayer for final perseverance

We have no guarantee that if we set out on the journey to heaven, we will arrive in the end. St. Alphonsus fears that he might stumble and fall, so he begs Our Lady to help him to persevere.

Behold at your feet, O Mary, my hope, a poor sinner, who has so many times been by his own fault the slave of hell. I know that by neglecting to turn to you, my refuge, I allowed myself to be overcome by the Devil. Had I always turned to you, had I always called you, I certainly would not have fallen. I trust, O Lady most worthy of all our love, that through you I have already escaped from the hands of the Devil, and that God has pardoned me. But I tremble at the thought that at some time in the future I may again fall into the same bondage. I know that my enemies have not lost the hope of again overcoming me, and already they prepare new assaults and temptations for me.

My Queen and Refuge, assist me! Place me under your mantle; don't allow me to become their slave again. I know that you will help me and give me the victory, provided I call on you. But I dread the thought that in my temptations I may forget you, and neglect to do so. The favor, then, that I seek from you, and which you must grant me, O most holy Virgin, is that I may never forget you, and especially in time of temptation. Grant that I may then repeatedly call on you, saying, "O Mary, help me; O Mary, help me!" And when my last struggle with hell comes, at the moment of death, then, my Queen, help me more than ever.

May you yourself remind me to call on you more frequently either with my lips or in my heart. In this way, being filled with confidence, I can die with your sweet name and that of your Son, Jesus, on my lips. I will be able to bless you and praise you, and never depart from your feet in paradise, for all eternity.

—St. Alphonsus Liguori, *The Glories of Mary*

IN GOD'S PRESENCE, CONSIDER . . .

What do I see as the greatest obstacles in my life to my final perseverance in God's grace? Am I asking Mary's help to overcome those obstacles?

CLOSING PRAYER

From "Thirty Days' Prayer to the Blessed Virgin": *Obtain for me, O sacred Mother of God, perseverance in good works, performance of good resolutions, mortification of self-will, a pious conversation through life, and at my last moments, strong and sincere repentance.*

Hymn to the Mother of God

The Akathist Hymn to the Mother of God dates to the seventh century and comes from the Eastern liturgical tradition. Many consider it to be the queen of all hymns to Our Lady. Here is a short portion that overflows in rich imagery calling for careful reflection.

In honoring your maternity, Mother of God,
we exalt you as the living temple.
For the Almighty Lord
who holds all things in his hands,
the One who has dwelt within your womb,
sanctified and glorified you
and taught all people to sing to you:

Hail, O tabernacle of God, the Word;
Hail, O holiest of all the saints.

Hail, O Ark gilded by the Spirit;
Hail, O limitless treasury of life.

Hail, O precious crown of reverent kings;
Hail, O true honor of zealous priests.

Hail, O unshakable tower of the Church;
Hail, O unbreachable wall of the kingdom.

Hail, O you through whom the flags of victory are raised;
Hail, O you through whom the enemy is routed.

Hail, O healing of my body;
Hail, O salvation of my soul.

Hail, O Virgin and Bride ever pure!

—"Akathist Hymn to the Theotokos," Twenty-Third Chant

IN GOD'S PRESENCE, CONSIDER . . .

Which of these images used to describe Our Lady have the most meaning for me? How do they apply to her?

CLOSING PRAYER

From a prayer of St. Athanasius: *Hail, O full of grace, our Lord is with you. Pray for us, O holy Mother of God, Our Lady and our Queen.*

More about the people quoted and noted in this book

The brief biographical statements below provide a glimpse of the saints and other spiritual writers who have been quoted or noted in this book. You'll want to go even further in reading about them by consulting various print and online resources that provide more complete portraits of their lives.

First, however, a word about Our Lady. The Catholic Church recognizes three levels of honor due to those in heaven. Adoration (*latria*) is the supreme honor due to God. As our Creator, our beginning and our end, he alone is worthy of such worship. Even so, the saints and angels are also deserving of their own veneration (*dulia*), which is different from adoration not only in degree but in kind, since it's given to creatures rather than to the Creator. Nevertheless, it's still a high form of honor, due to them because of their supernatural excellence and union with God.

Above this veneration due to the saints, yet not the kind of adoration due to God alone, is the unique honor (*hyperdulia*) due to the Blessed Virgin Mary because of her unique privilege and supreme dignity as the Mother of God. It recognizes that she's a creature, but one who is more holy and noble than the other saints and even the angels.

For this reason, we'll begin with her biographical sketch. The rest of the saints are alphabetical by first name, since many of them in times past had no last names. Spiritual writers who were not saints are alphabetized in the usual order.

The Blessed Virgin Mary, Queen of All Saints: According to ancient tradition, Mary was the daughter of Sts. Anne and Joachim. She was immaculately conceived, without the stain of original sin. Mary always remained a virgin, taken by St. Joseph as his wife even though their union was never physically consummated.

When the fullness of time had come, the angel Gabriel announced to Mary in Nazareth that she was to give birth to the Savior of the world. Mary gave her fiat, which was her total submission to the will of God. Then, by the Holy Spirit, the Son of God became Man.

This is the mystery of the Incarnation: that God descended into the womb of the Virgin, took from her a human nature that he made his own, and became true Man while remaining true God: one divine Person with two natures, fully human and fully divine, our Lord Jesus Christ. Because Jesus is God, and Mary is his Mother, she's rightly called the Mother of God.

Mary gave birth to Jesus and was intimately involved in his sacred life. She united herself to him and shared in all he did, especially in his sufferings during his passion and death. After our Lord's resurrection and ascension, Our Lady remained on earth for a time to help the early Church in its infancy.

Mary is called the Mother of the Church, because by becoming the mother of the Head (Christ) she also became the mother of the whole Mystical Body. At the end of her earthly life Mary was assumed body and soul into heaven and crowned as Queen of Heaven and Earth. For this reason we call her the Queen of Saints.

Blessed Alan de la Roche: Dominican theologian and preacher, promoter of the Rosary; died 1475.

St. Albert the Great (Albertus Magnus): German Dominican, bishop, theologian, philosopher, scientist, Doctor of the Church; died 1280.

St. Aloysius Gonzaga: Jesuit novice who died caring for plague victims; patron of Christian youth, plague victims, and AIDS sufferers; died 1591.

St. Alphonsus Liguori: Italian bishop, theologian, Doctor of the Church, founder of the Redemptorists; died 1787.

St. Alphonsus Rodriguez: Spanish Jesuit lay brother; died 1617.

Blessed Amadeus of Portugal: Portuguese Franciscan priest and reformer; died 1482.

St. Ambrose of Milan: bishop, Doctor of the Church, one of the four Great Fathers of the West; died 397.

St. Andrew of Candia: See St. Andrew of Crete.

St. Andrew of Crete: Syrian monk and archbishop of Gortyna, Crete; hymnist; died c. 740.

St. Andrew Avellino: Theatine priest and founder of monasteries; died 1608.

St. Anselm of Canterbury: archbishop of Canterbury, Benedictine monk, theologian, philosopher, Doctor of the Church; the "Founder of Scholasticism"; died 1109.

St. Anthony of Padua: Portuguese Franciscan friar, priest, theologian, preacher, mystic, reformer, miracle worker, Doctor of the Church; died 1231.

St. Antoninus: Italian Dominican friar, archbishop of Florence; died 1459.

Arnold of Chartres: French Benedictine abbot and spiritual writer; died after 1156.

St. Athanasius of Alexandria: Egyptian archbishop of Alexandria, Doctor of the Church, defender of the Faith against Arianism; died 373.

St. Augustine of Hippo: North African bishop, theologian, Doctor of the Church, one of the four Great Fathers of the West; among the most influential figures in history; died 430.

Baptista Varani of Camerino: Italian abbess, Order of St. Clare; spiritual writer; died 1527.

Baronius: See Venerable Caesar Baronius.

St. Basil of Seleucia: bishop of Seleucia and poet; died c. 460.

Venerable Bede: English monk, historian, scholar, Doctor of the Church; died 735.

Pope Benedict XVI: German pope, theologian; b. 1927.

Blessed Benvenuta Bojani: Italian Dominican tertiary and mystic; died 1292.

St. Bernard of Clairvaux: French Cistercian abbot, mystic, theologian, Doctor of the Church, preacher of the Crusade, advocate for devotion to Mary; died 1153.

Bernardine de Bustis: Italian Franciscan friar; died 1515.

St. Bernardine of Siena: Italian Franciscan priest, reformer, missionary, preacher, and advocate for devotion to the Holy Name of Jesus; died 1444.

St. Bonaventure: Italian Franciscan cardinal-bishop, Doctor of the Church, Minister General of the Friars Minor and considered the second founder of that order; theologian, philosopher, spiritual writer, advisor to St. Louis, King of France; died 1274.

St. Bridget of Sweden: Swedish mystic, visionary, wife, mother; after the death of her husband founded the Order of the Most Holy Savior; patron of Sweden; died 1373.

Venerable Caesar Baronius: Italian cardinal, Church historian; died 1607.

St. Camillus of Lellis: Italian priest and founder of the Ministers of the Sick; died 1614.

St. Catherine of Genoa: Italian lay mystic and spiritual writer; died 1510.

St. Catherine of Siena: Italian Third Order Dominican mystic and spiritual writer, Doctor of the Church; died 1380.

Chesterton, G. K.: English journalist, essayist, poet, dramatist, Catholic apologist; died 1936.

St. Cosmas of Jerusalem: Syrian bishop of Jerusalem, hymnist; died 773 or 794.

St. Cyril of Alexandria: patriarch of Alexandria, Egypt; Father of the Church, Doctor of the Church; died 444.

St. Cyprian of Carthage: bishop, martyr, and theologian; died 258.

da Casale, Ubertino: Italian Franciscan spiritual writer; died c. 1329.

St. Denis: the ancient text cited by St. Alphonsus under this name was originally attributed to St. Dionysius the Areopagite, but is now believed to be written by a different, sixth-century author termed "Pseudo-Dionysius"; St. Dionysius has sometimes been confused with St. Denis, the martyred first bishop of Paris, France (died c. 250).

Denis the Carthusian: Belgian Carthusian monk, theologian, and mystic; died 1471.

St. Dominic: Spanish priest, founder of the Order of Preachers (the Dominicans); died 1221.

St. Ephraem the Syrian: Syrian deacon, Doctor of the Church, poet, hymnist, biblical commentator; called "the Harp of the Spirit"; died 521.

St. Epiphanius of Salamis: Palestinian priest, abbot, theologian, bishop of Salamis; died 404.

Faber, Fr. Frederick: English convert from Anglicanism; priest, hymnist, spiritual writer, founder of the Brompton Oratory; died 1863.

St. Faustina Kowalska: Polish nun, mystic, visionary, "Apostle of Divine Mercy"; died 1938.

St. Francis Borgia: Spanish Jesuit priest and father general; "second founder of the Jesuits"; died 1572.

St. Francis of Assisi: Italian founder of the Order of Friars Minor (Franciscans), deacon, mystic, stigmatist, reformer; died 1226.

St. Francis de Sales: bishop, Doctor of the Church, theologian, missionary, spiritual writer, spiritual director, Catholic apologist, cofounder of the Order of the Visitation of Holy Mary (the Visitandines) with St. Jane de Chantal; died 1622.

St. Francis Xavier: Spanish Jesuit priest, missionary; died 1552.

St. Fulgentius: Roman Carthaginian abbot, bishop of Ruspe; died 533.

St. Germanus: patriarch of Constantinople, poet, hymnist, spiritual writer; died c. 740.

St. Gertrude the Great: German Cistercian, mystic, visionary, theologian, spiritual writer; died c. 1302.

St. George of Nicomedia: metropolitan of Nicomedia, hymnist, spiritual writer; died after 880.

Pope St. Gregory the Great: Roman Benedictine pope, liturgical reformer, Father of the Church, Doctor of the Church; died 604.

St. Gregory Nazianzen: Cappadocian patriarch of Constantinople, Father of the Church, Doctor of the Church; died 390.

St. Gregory of Nyssa: Cappadocian bishop of Nyssa, Father of the Church; died c. 395.

St. Gregory Thaumaturgus: bishop of Neocaesaria, missionary, miracle worker; died 268.

Blessed Guerric of Igny: French Cistercian abbot; died 1157.

Blessed Henry Suso: Swiss Dominican friar, preacher, reformer, mystic; died 1365.

St. Hilary of Poitiers: Gallic bishop of Poitiers, Doctor of the Church; died 368.

Houselander, Caryll: English Catholic spiritual writer, poet, and artist; died 1954.

Hugh of Saint Victor: Saxon Canon Regular, scholar, theologian, philosopher, biblical commentator; died 1141.

Hugh of Saint-Cher: French Dominican friar, cardinal, biblical commentator; died 1263.

St. Ignatius of Loyola: Basque priest, spiritual writer, reformer, founder of the Society of Jesus (Jesuits); died 1556.

St. Ildephonsus: Spanish bishop, scholar, theologian, spiritual writer; died 667.

Pope St. Innocent III: Italian pope, reformer; died 1216.

St. Irenaeus: bishop of Lyon, theologian, Father of the Church; died c. 202.

Jacob of Sarug: Mesopotamian chorepiscopus, poet, theologian; called "the Flute of the Spirit"; died 521.

St. Jerome: Illyrian priest, confessor, theologian, historian, biblical scholar, Father of the Church, Doctor of the Church, "father of biblical scholarship"; died 420.

St. Jerome Emiliani: Italian priest, cofounder of the Clerks Regular of Somascha; died 1537.

St. Joachima Vedruna de Mas: Spanish founder of the Congregation of Carmelite Sisters of Charity; died 1854.

St. John of Damascus: Syrian monk, theologian, Father of the Church, Doctor of the Church; died between 754 and 787.

St. John Berchmans: Belgian Jesuit scholastic; died 1621.

St. John Chrysostom: Syrian patriarch of Constantinople, Father of the Church, Doctor of the Church; died 407.

St. John Eudes: French priest, seminary founder, founder of the Congregation of Jesus and Mary (the Eudists) and the Sisters of Our Lady of Charity of the Refuge, who spread devotion to the Sacred Heart of Jesus and the Immaculate Heart of Mary; died 1680.

St. John of God: Portuguese layman who served the sick poor and whose efforts led to the founding of the Order of Brothers Hospitalers; died 1550.

St. John Neumann: Bohemian Redemptorist bishop of Philadelphia; died 1860.

Blessed John Henry Newman: Anglican convert, priest, cardinal, educator, spiritual writer, Catholic apologist; died 1890.

Pope St. John Paul II: Polish pope, theologian, spiritual writer; died 2005.

Venerable Juvenal Ancina: Italian bishop of Saluzzo, member of the Congregation of the Oratory, scholar, musical composer; died 1604.

Landolph (Ludolph) of Saxony: German Carthusian prior, theologian; died 1378.

Lanspergius, Johannes: Bavarian Carthusian monk and spiritual writer; died 1539.

à Lapide, Cornelius: French Jesuit priest and biblical scholar; died 1537.

St. Lawrence of Brindisi: Neapolitan Capuchin vicar general, priest, theologian, spiritual writer, Doctor of the Church; died 1619.

St. Lawrence Justinian: bishop and first patriarch of Venice, general of the Congregation of the Canons Regular of St. Augustine, spiritual writer; died 1456.

Pope St. Leo the Great: Italian pope, theologian, Doctor of the Church; died 461.

Pope Leo XIII: Italian pope, theologian, "the Rosary Pope"; died 1903.

St. Leonard of Port Maurice: Italian Franciscan priest, missionary preacher, and spiritual writer; died 1751.

Longo, Blessed Bartolo: Italian convert from Satanism, Third Order lay Dominican; called "Apostle of the Rosary" for his lifelong efforts to promote that devotion; died 1926.

Blessed Louis de Blois (Blosius): Flemish Benedictine abbot and spiritual writer; died 1566.

St. Louis de Monfort (Louis Mary Grignion): French missionary, founder of the Sisters of Wisdom and the Company of Mary; preached devotion to the Blessed Virgin Mary and the Rosary; died 1716.

St. Mary Magdalen de Pazzi: Italian Carmelite mystic; died 1607.

St. Margaret Mary Alacoque: French Visitation nun and mystic; promoted devotion to the Sacred Heart of Jesus; died 1690.

St. Matilda: Saxon queen whose husband became the Holy Roman Emperor; known for her charitable works; died 968.

St. Maximillian Kolbe: Polish Conventual Franciscan priest, martyr of charity, "Apostle of Consecration to Mary"; died 1941.

St. Methodius: bishop of Olympos, spiritual writer, martyr; died 311.

Nicholas of Cusa: German Cardinal, bishop of Brixen, philosopher, theologian, jurist, astronomer; died 1464.

Novarini, Luigi: Italian Theatine priest, spiritual writer; died 1656.

Origen: Egyptian theologian, philosopher, biblical commentator, catechist; died c. 253.

Padial, Fr. Emmanuel: Spanish Jesuit priest, theologian; died 1725.

Blessed Pope Paul VI: Italian pope, reformer; continued the Second Vatican Council begun by Pope St. John XXIII; died 1978.

St. Paul of the Cross: Italian priest, mystic, founder of the Passionists; 1775.

St. Peter Canisius: Dutch Jesuit priest, Doctor of the Church; died 1597.

St. Peter Celestine (Pope Celestine V): pope, monk, founder of the Celestines; died 1296.

St. Peter Chrysologus: Italian bishop of Ravenna, Doctor of the Church; died c. 450.

Peter of Celles: French Benedictine abbot and bishop of Chartres; died 1183.

St. Peter Damian: Italian Benedictine monk, cardinal, reformer, "Monitor of the Popes"; died c. 1073.

St. Peter Eymard: French priest, founder of the Congregation of the Blessed Sacrament and the Servants of the Blessed Sacrament; "Apostle of the Eucharist"; died 1868.

St. Philip Neri: Italian priest, founder of the Congregation of the Oratory; "Apostle of Rome"; died 1595.

Venerable Pope Pius XII: Italian pope, reformer; defined the dogma of the Assumption of Mary; died 1958.

de Ponte, Fr. Louis (Luis de la Puente): Spanish Jesuit theologian and spiritual writer; died 1624.

St. Proclus: patriarch of Constantinople; died c. 446.

Richard of Saint Lawrence: French theologian, canon; died 1250.

Richard of Saint Victor: Augustinian prior, mystical theologian; died 1173.

Rupert of Deutz: Benedictine abbot, theologian, biblical scholar, liturgist; died c. 1129.

Segneri, Fr. Paul: Italian Jesuit priest, preacher, missionary, spiritual writer; died 1694.

Sheen, Archbishop Fulton: American archbishop, theologian, television and radio evangelist; died 1979.

Blessed Simon of Cascia: Italian Augustinian Hermit and preacher; died 1348.

St. Sophronius: Arab monk, theologian, poet, and patriarch of Jerusalem; died 638.

St. Stanislaus Kostka: Polish Jesuit novice; died 1568.

Suárez, Francisco: Spanish Jesuit priest, philosopher, theologian; died 1617.

St. Tarasius: patriarch of Constantinople; died 806.

Tauler, Johannes: German Dominican preacher, theologian, and mystic; died 1361.

St. Teresa of Ávila: Spanish Carmelite nun, mystic, theologian, Doctor of the Church; died 1582.

Tertullian: North African theologian, apologist, biblical exegete, "Father of Latin Christianity"; died c. 225.

St. Theophilus of Alexandria: Egyptian patriarch of Alexandria; died 412.

St. Thérèse of Lisieux: French Carmelite, Doctor of the Church, known as "The Little Flower"; died 1897.

St. Thomas Aquinas: Italian Dominican priest, Doctor of the Church, known as "The Angelic Doctor"; died 1274.

Thomas à Kempis: German Canon Regular, priest, spiritual writer; died 1471.

St. Thomas of Villanova: Spanish Augustinian friar, preacher, spiritual writer; died 1555.

Thompson, Francis: English poet and spiritual writer; died 1907.

Venantius Fortunatus: Italian bishop of Poitiers, poet, hymnist; died 609.

St. Vincent Ferrer: Valencian Dominican friar, missionary, theologian, logician; died 1419.

St. Vincent Pallotti: Italian priest, founder of the Pallotines; died 1850.

St. (Abbot) William: French abbot, missionary; died 1203.

William of Paris: French bishop of Paris, theologian; died 1249.

Acknowledgments

"The World's First Love" (p. 15) is from Archbishop Fulton Sheen, *The World's First Love* (New York: McGraw-Hill, 1952), pp. 4–5.

"Mary was the first to adore her Son" (p. 49) is from St. Peter Julian Eymard, *Our Lady of the Most Blessed Sacrament: Readings for the Month of May* (New York: Sentinel Press, 1947), pp. 11–12.

"Mary follows in our footsteps" (p. 83) is from Pope Benedict XVI, "Mary, the Exemplar," General Audience, August 16, 2006, from *L'Osservatore Romano*, Weekly Edition in English, 23 August 2006, p. 11.

"Mary, Our Lady of Victory" (p. 148) is from Paul Thigpen, *Manual for Spiritual Warfare* (Charlotte, N.C.: TAN Books, 2014), pp. 233–34.

"*O Stella Maris!*" (p. 160) is copyright © 2007 Paul Thigpen. Used with permission.

"On Christmas Eve, Before the Blessed Sacrament" (p. 216) is from Paul Thigpen, *Jesus, We Adore You: Prayers Before the Blessed Sacrament* (Ann Arbor, Mich.: Servant Publications, 2001), pp. 117–18.

"A great sign appeared in heaven" (p. 287) is from St. John Eudes, *The Admirable Heart of Mary*, Charles D. Targiani and Ruth Hauser, trans. (Fitzwilliam, N.H.: Loreto Publications, 1945), p. 4.

"Mary, be warmth to the world" (p. 353) is from Caryll Houselander, "The Reed" in *The Flowering Tree* (New York: Sheed & Ward, 1945), p. 67.

About the Author

Paul Thigpen, Ph.D, is the Editor of TAN Books, an imprint of Saint Benedict Press. An internationally known speaker, best-selling author, and award-winning journalist, Paul has published forty-four books in a wide variety of genres and subjects. His most popular titles include *The Rapture Trap: A Catholic Response to "End Times" Fever* (2001); *The Burden: A Warning of Things to Come* (2013); and *Manual for Spiritual Warfare* (2014).

In addition, Paul has published more than five hundred journal and magazine articles in more than forty religious and secular periodicals. His work has been circulated worldwide and translated into twelve languages. He is also past editor of *The Catholic Answer*, a national bimonthly magazine that answers questions about the Catholic faith.

Paul holds a Ph.D. (1995) in Historical Theology from Emory University and has served on the faculty of several universities and colleges. In 2008 he was appointed by the United States Conference of Catholic Bishops to their National Advisory Council for a four-year term. He has served the Church as a theologian, historian, apologist, evangelist, and catechist in a number of settings, speaking frequently in Catholic and secular media broadcasts and at conferences, seminars, parish missions, and scholarly gatherings.